M000020596

Short Story Theory at a Crossroads

Short Story
Theory at a
CROSSROADS

Edited by
SUSAN LOHAFER and
JO ELLYN CLAREY

Louisiana State University Press
Baton Rouge and London

Copyright © 1989 by Louisiana State University Press
All rights reserved
Manufactured in the United States of America
First printing

98 97 96 95 94 93 92 91 90 89   5 4 3 2 1

Designer: Laura Roubique Gleason
Typeface: Palatino
Typesetter: G&S Typesetters, Inc.
Printer and Binder: Thomson-Shore, Inc.

Library of Congress Cataloging-in-Publication Data
Short story theory at a crossroads / edited by Susan Lohafer and Jo
    Ellyn Clarey.
        p.   cm.
    Includes index.
    ISBN 0-8071-1546-0 (alk. paper)
    1. Short story.   I. Lohafer, Susan.   II. Clarey, Jo Ellyn, 1947–   .
PN3373.S395   1989
801'.953—dc19   89-30723
                                                            CIP

The paper in this book meets the guidelines for permanence and durability of the
Committee on Production Guidelines for Book Longevity of the Council on Library
Resources. ∞

Contents

Preface

Short story critics have traveled alone, their critical paths often crossing but rarely converging. No more than a decade ago, referring to a "field" of short story criticism would have seemed odd—even though various critics, pursuing various agenda, wrote about short stories. Here and there, however, someone devoted a career to the study of short fiction. Doing so meant seeking out and affirming the work of others in the past as well as looking for, indeed *creating,* arenas for current discussion of short story theory. In 1985 we organized a gathering of critics practicing in the field. On that occasion, we met for the first time people whose work was essential to our own and to the syllabus of any course in short story theory.

After the meeting, we determined to belie Frank O'Connor and draw our "lonely voices" together in this collection of essays. Our aim has been to mark the "state of the art" in short fiction theory, to strike a balance between a timely collection and a telling one. In our eyes, this volume is a prototype, not so much a blueprint as a working model of a field of study. Nothing would please us more than to turn our readers into future designers of better models.

The selections are organized so as to map out the field conceptually. Introductions to the five sections help clarify our arrangement and tie it in with the history and nature of short story criticism. Admittedly, these introductions have a point of view from which our contributors must be clearly excused, but we believe the editorial framework provides a certain background and coherence. Finally, of course, the essays can and do stand forth individually, to speak for themselves.

Our foremost debt is to the voices behind the essays, our contributors. They are the reason for this book, and they are its content and value. We are grateful to them for their inspiration, and also for their diligence and patience throughout the editorial process. Thomas E. Lewis, 1985 executive secretary of the Midwest Modern Language Association, made possible the forums which generated so many of the essays included here. Both the University of Iowa and Iowa State University funded the computer preparation of the manuscript and provided experts to solve our technical problems. We are also grateful to Professor William Kupersmith, a colleague at Iowa, who helped us with the new language of the computer and the old language of Latin. We deeply appreciate this help. Finally, we want to add our thanks to Ann Charters and William Peden, whose thoughtful readings of our text—and our intentions—helped bring these pages to light, and to Catherine Landry, whose editorial hand has passed over them with great care and intelligence. As always in a project involving so many people, the personal obligations and tolerances and kindnesses are past counting. Still, they are the fabric of the experience, and we will remember them long and fondly.

I

The State of the Art

SUSAN LOHAFER

Introduction to Part I

About a third of the contributors to this volume are people who write (that is to say, have published) samples of the genre this book is about: the short story. Whether such experience is a help or a hindrance we cannot say; yet it is unlikely a collection of new essays on, for example, the theory of the novel, chosen *by* critics *for* critics, would include so many practitioners (however occasional) of the genre itself.

Why? The answer is in part historical. Until not so long ago, the ones who theorized about stories were the ones who wrote them: Poe, Chekhov, Henry James, H. E. Bates, Frank O'Connor, Eudora Welty. Spottily in the sixties, but afterwards more often, study of the short story as a genre attracted "pure" critics, narrative theorists, people whose lifework is the construction of meaning from literary culture. It is their presence—in growing numbers—that lets us say "field" of short story criticism. Stories can now be career investments.

Stories have always been "there"—in the hunters' camp, the ladies' quarterly, the children's bedroom, the freshman classroom. As listeners, readers, teachers, and critics, we have needed, used, revered them—but taken them for granted till forced to do otherwise. And, of course, those who've done the forcing have had something at stake. Think of Poe. In giving us a prescription for the short story—a thing of power and unity—he was doctoring a psyche that was fragile, unstable. And Frank O'Connor. If we quote, still, his tribute to Gogol, to the "lonely voice" in "submerged populations," it may be because he had a nation at heart. Both of these men made famous critical pronouncements; yet they were only saying what had to be true for the sake of their art. Were they biased? Self-serving? Of course,

3

but they were also intuitive. Failing to be objective, they found the essential.

So, however, did Vladimir Propp, a "pure" critic who had a stake in the objective.[1] Studies of oral folktales, and especially Propp's work with recurrent, serially ordered functions in fairy tales, did give the story a far-reaching phylogeny. Indeed, the earlier work of the Formalists (Shklovsky, Tomashevsky, and especially Boris Eikhenbaum) was a striking development in the twenties. They and structuralists like Propp—all of whom had something to say about kernels of narrative—would later become a rich resource for short story critics. But if we look at what was being written in English about the short story in the twenties, we find little academic criticism. We do find Sherwood Anderson and Ring Lardner making light of the "rules." The thirties and forties give us William Saroyan and Elizabeth Bowen, Katherine Anne Porter and H. E. Bates—artists, proponents, and brilliant describers of the short story form as urgent, exquisite, visceral, impressionistic, and sacredly immune to critical dissection.

By the start of the forties, the "new" aesthetic was firmly established. And it was modernism, rather than the short story per se, that "arrived" in academia. Hindsight, helped by people I'll be mentioning soon, points to Joseph Frank as seminal, and A. L. Bader as representative.[2] Writing in 1945, they viewed narrative as an elliptical, spatially designed network of references, and all but prescribed a certain kind of reader for the modern text—or any text that mattered. Moreover, this reader had to be trained, had to be sensitive to the internal resonances, the patterned imagery, the multiple tensions of syntax and diction. These concerns, now so familiar, were, of course, the litany of New Criticism. And they proved to be the charter of professional short story criticism.

It is hard, if not impossible, to overestimate the importance of a school of critics who put their noses to the page. Once again, the short, artful prose narrative became, as it had been for Poe, second only to the lyric poem in its promise of reward for the "sensitive"

1. Vladimir Propp, *Morphology of the Folk Tale* (Bloomington, 1958).

2. Joseph Frank, "Spatial Form in Modern Literature," *Sewanee Review*, LIII (1945), 221–40, 433–56, 643–53, rpr. in Frank, *The Widening Gyre: Crisis and Mastery in Modern Literature* (New Brunswick, N.J., 1963), 3–63, copyright © 1963 by Rutgers, The State University; A. L. Bader, "The Structure of the Modern Short Story," *College English*, VII (1945), 86–92, rpr. in Charles E. May (ed.), *Short Story Theories* (Athens, Ohio, 1976), 107–15.

reader. More accessible than poetry, more manageable than novels, it was just the right size for a demonstration. All that was needed was a way of getting the critical mission into the classroom. It happened in many ways, but none is more important than the publication, in 1943, of Brooks and Warren's classic anthology, *Understanding Fiction*.[3]

A veritable bible for the teacher of short fiction, this many-times-revised book has had an enduring influence on the way short fiction has been analyzed, taught, and generally perceived. In "Letter to the Teacher," substantially reprinted in the 1959 edition, Brooks and Warren offer a view of fiction that implicitly foregrounds the short story form. They tell us that students need to be carried past their "threshold interests" (in a particular subject matter, in simply "what happens") into an appreciation based upon "the total structure, upon a set of organic relationships, upon the logic of the whole." The features of compression, economy, irony, and tension—thought to be the very means by which "the more broadly human values implicit in fiction" reveal themselves—just happen to be the definitive characteristics of the literary short story.[4] Although the editors warn against the tyranny of critical viewpoints, and see interpretation as a highly individual activity, nevertheless the passion and coherence of their approach has guided and inspired generations of "close readers."

Understanding Fiction is a seminal book, and it spawned in the marketplace. Hundreds of anthologies are now available. New ones arrive, it seems, every month. Old ones return—updated. Many of these textbooks are valuable, for they refresh the canon, redo the categories. But few, if any, remake our thinking. Few are the vehicles of new concepts or insights we would honor as "theory." Underneath the slick new covers is, all too often, the same old catechism of theme and tone, character and setting. There are, of course, exceptions. Some anthologies invite the reader to place the stories in relation to ideas about stories—even, in the case of Ann Charters' *The Story and Its Writer* (1988), in the context of short story criticism. Still, it may be that the greatest obstacle to the development of short story criticism has been the simple ubiquity, the serviceability, of the short story textbook. For the majority of doctoral students, staffing undergraduate courses, these texts—even the best loved of them—are utilitarian.

3. Cleanth Brooks and Robert Penn Warren, *Understanding Fiction* (New York, 1943).

4. *Ibid.*, xii–xiii.

And it may be that the story, already in the shadow of the novel, is again demeaned. Ph.D. in hand, how many of us project a career in short fiction studies? Where is the excitement, the timely challenge, the gain in prestige? For whom is there a stake here?

To answer that question, we have to look back to the sixties. Let us imagine that decade, so crowded in every other way, as an empty stage for short story criticism. The curtain in the rear is a flickering of faces: Joyce, Woolf, Hemingway, Faulkner. . . . In the center hangs a life-size portrait of Edgar Allan Poe holding a volume of Hawthorne's stories.

Onto that stage, in 1961, walk three people. The first two, Eugene Current-Garcia and Walton R. Patrick, are the editors of an anthology—but a very different kind from the many before and after its time. Entitled *What Is the Short Story?—Case Studies in the Development of a Literary Genre*, this book is not about understanding fiction but about studying one genre of fiction: the short story.[5] Interestingly enough, the 1959 edition of *Understanding Fiction* had a new section in which four authors wrote about their own stories. Although these essays are in the old tradition of practitioner commentary, their very presence is the beginning of a critical perspective beyond the close-reading exercise. In 1961, Current-Garcia and Patrick go a step further; they devote a full half of their book to things that have been said about the short story form. The editors, themselves, have no "theory." Their effort is one of retrieval, survey, and education. They offer not only famous dicta by famous authors—Poe on Hawthorne, Joyce on epiphanies, Anderson on (or rather, against) plot—but also clippings from the short story's "press." Most of us have heard of Brander Matthews' *Philosophy of the Short-Story*, but how many of us know it was savaged in England? Here we can read that anonymous review from the London *Academy*. In collecting these snippets of historical editorializing, Current-Garcia and Patrick are building a frame for the second half of their volume. There we find sample stories by Poe, Hawthorne, James, and so on. Once again, we have a classroom anthology of stories for discussion. Its editors are heralds on the stage of criticism. The first main character has yet to arrive.

He is Austin M. Wright, and he, too, enters in 1961. Although not yet the author of the novels for which he will later be honored, he

5. Eugene Current-Garcia and Walton R. Patrick (eds.), *What Is the Short Story?* (Rev. ed.; Glenview, Ill., 1974).

seems very much the inheritor of the writer-critic as well as the modernist tradition. His book, *The American Short Story in the Twenties*, is a writer's tribute to his heritage, a loving analysis of the ways in which short fiction changed in that brilliant decade.[6] He is concerned to a great extent with themes and ideas, and how they differ on either side of that great divide—World War I. He knows, and easily, informally cross-references, hundreds of stories. They are his "canon" of representative works, chosen mainly for their familiarity, but also for their power to reveal what is "new" in the twenties. In a section on form, Wright classifies stories loosely according to the genres of tragedy and comedy, and on the relations between kind of action and kind of effect. Aristotle and Poe are surely in the background, and in the foreground are Anderson and Porter. As we will see in Section III, Wright moves to much more particular and original notions of form in his later work. His achievement in 1961 is a matter of initiative in dealing with the genre in the first place; it is a matter of using stories as the premise and vehicle of literary history.

Let us imagine 1963 as an interlude on our stage, a bountiful moment that is both an interruption of and an impetus to our parade of critics. In that year, Frank O'Connor publishes *The Lonely Voice: A Study of the Short Story*. In many ways, it is a personal commentary, a practitioner's notebook—as was Sean O'Faolain's *The Short Story* in the previous decade. But it is more; it is a think piece on the relation between storytelling and society. The conclusion: stories prosper in times of social upheaval, and in places where individuals are alienated. Stories are the cry of "the lonely voice." They are also the highest form of narrative art. Not since Poe has anyone spoken with such authority and passion in behalf of the "slight" form. Enduringly quotable, this book is, at last, a *genius loci*, a rallying point.

We should not therefore be surprised by the appearance, in 1964, of an academic journal for articles about stories: *Studies in Short Fiction*. All of us owe a debt to its editors for publishing the comments of, for example, Eileen Baldeshwiler—though the journal was never intended to be a forum solely and specifically for genre theory. The short story had another friend in William H. Peden, whose 1964 book, *The American Short Story*, captured the variety and vitality of the national voice in its characteristic medium of literary expression. In the sixties, too, Russian Formalist essays came to us anew in a collec-

---

6. Austin M. Wright, *The American Short Story in the Twenties* (Chicago, 1961).

tion edited by Lee T. Lemon and Marion J. Reis. And even though few took notice at the time, the University of Michigan's Department of Slavic Languages and Literatures published a translation of Eikhenbaum's *O. Henry and the Theory of the Short Story*.[7]

For a new phase of awareness, we must look to 1966. Someone is entering our stage on the left, near the portrait of Poe holding a volume of Hawthorne. It is Mary Rohrberger, author of *Hawthorne and the Modern Short Story*.[8] From any point of view, her position on the stage is commanding. Her book is tied to the great tradition of attention to imagery (Rohrberger's mentor, after all, was Richard H. Fogle). It is also a study of modernist aesthetics linked to Romantic symbolism. Rhetorically and logically it has a dominant aim: to define the short story as distinct from novels and from "simple" short narratives. At the very least, we might say she is underwriting, theoretically, the class of stories that require "close reading." But her scope is more ambitious; she is relating the short story to major topics and concerns of American criticism. Rohrberger is writing for the benefit of those who must classify texts in order to do their job properly. She has an extraordinarily clear notion of service to a specialized field of literary scholarship. By implication, that field must exist. In a sense, she calls it into being by assuming its presence and giving it guidelines. Still, short story theory did not begin, or even flower, in the sixties; what happened was that the conditions for an academic specialty were finally visible and operative. The curtain comes down on a crowded stage.

In many ways, the seventies was a decade of consolidation. It was time to complete the work of Current-Garcia and Patrick, whose anthology *What Is the Short Story?* (revised and reissued in 1974) had paired criticism and stories. In 1976, Charles May eliminated the stories. He wanted an anthology of criticism, not of short story texts for the apprentice reader. From the point of view of strategy, he may have made the first, if not the biggest, move toward a forum for theory. He, too, went searching for scattered essays and articles. Naturally he included some of the same ones that appear in *What Is the Short Story?* (Poe, Matthews), but he could also draw heavily on the journal *Studies in Short Fiction*.

7. Lee T. Lemon and Marion J. Reis (eds. and trans.), *Russian Formalist Criticism: Four Essays* (Lincoln, Nebr., 1965); B. M. Eikhenbaum, *O. Henry and the Theory of the Short Story*, trans. I. R. Titunik (Ann Arbor, 1968).

8. Mary Rohrberger, *Hawthorne and the Modern Short Story: A Study in Genre* (The Hague, 1966).

One of May's discoveries was a 1958 essay from *Modern Fiction Studies*, called "What Makes a Short Story Short?"[9] This remarkable piece was written by Norman Friedman, and later found its way into his 1975 book, *Form and Meaning in Fiction*. Using a detailed schema derived from Aristotle's "causes," and borrowing from Elder Olson's list of narrative units (speech, episode, and so on), Friedman explains, systematically, the meaning of size in fiction. In its coolness and rigor, this essay is a constant adversary to subjective commentaries, as well as to any form of short story chauvinism—especially the claims for intrinsic differences between short and long narratives. Controversial as its message may be, this essay transcends its own terms. It does something vital for the future of short story criticism. It asks a purely theoretical question about generic form, regardless of period or literary "movement," and answers in truly theoretical terms. By retrieving this essay and others, by drawing them together, May focused their power as genre criticism. He turned his collection into a resource for academic critics, students of narrative theory, specialists in short fiction studies. Had there been no *Short Story Theories*, the present volume would never have appeared.

Another kind of foundation was laid in 1977. The Barnes and Noble Critical Idiom Series (later taken over by Methuen) added a monograph on the short story form. For many readers, Ian Reid's little book of history and definition draws the lines for future study of the genre per se. It even acknowledges some of the relevant work in fields outside traditional literary studies. Chiefly important here is Gerald Prince's *A Grammar of Stories: An Introduction*, published in 1973.[10] Coming out of linguistics and heading into discourse analysis, this book can lead us into a whole new arena for genre studies.

And so we come to the eighties. In addition to the Twayne critical histories of the short story, under the general editorship of William H. Peden, two collections of essays appeared in 1982: *The Teller and the Tale: Aspects of the Short Story* (proceedings of the Comparative Literature Symposium in Lubbock) and a special issue of *Modern Fiction Studies*.[11] In the next few years, several single-author books of theory

9. Norman Friedman, "What Makes a Short Story Short?" *Modern Fiction Studies*, IV (1958), 103–17, rpr. in Friedman, *Form and Meaning in Fiction* (Athens, Ga., 1975), copyright © 1975 by the University of Georgia Press.

10. Ian Reid, *The Short Story* (1977; rpr. New York, 1979); Gerald Prince, *A Grammar of Stories: An Introduction* (The Hague, 1973).

11. Wendell M. Aycock (ed.), *The Teller and the Tale: Aspects of the Short Story* (Lubbock, Tex., 1982); *Modern Fiction Studies*, XVIII (Spring, 1982).

arrived. It is now possible to identify a scattered but committed group of people who are known, professionally, as short story theorists. The trends, problems, contributions, and future of their work are discussed from many points of view in the pages that follow. We hope this collection will be both a companion and a sequel to previous efforts to establish a forum for short story theory. Indeed, the three opening essays refine, evaluate, and even reformulate the sketchy history outlined above.

These three essays are by Friedman, Rohrberger, and Wright—critics whose work I have already emphasized. Here they contemplate the "state of the art" of short story criticism, insofar as it offers a theory of the genre. As we have seen, these people have helped to make the very history they now discuss. Each has had a pioneering, career "stake" in the field and now has, therefore, a special view of it. If there should seem to be a dash of polemic, a flair of personality, that is only to be expected in this come-as-you-are field. Here, then, are the proclivities, the defenses, the enthusiasms, the blind spots, the incomparable insights of three different artisans of short story theory.

We begin with Norman Friedman. And *he* begins, not at the start of things historically, but at the root of things logically. His essay, "Recent Short Story Theories: Problems in Definition," asks how the field of short story theory can prosper if it fails to be rigorous—that is to say, if it doesn't have ways of testing the validity of critical arguments. His aim, of course, is not to make us better logicians but to keep our thinking from collapsing, to guard against flawed, and therefore often monistic, views of short story art. In the course of his discussion, Friedman gives an organized review of major critics, including Rohrberger, May, and several others in this book; however, the subject of his essay is really the conduct of research, the ways in which it may add to our body of knowledge. He wants us to do justice to the variety of this genre. The methodology of definition, the strategies of induction and deduction, the rules of argumentation—these are means to that end. Along the way, he takes his own stand on the key issue: what makes the short story different? In effect, this essay is an updated, broadly informed sequel to his late-fifties' essay on the shortness of short stories. Even more, though, it is a jeremiad, a call-to-attention. We had better know what we are talking about, agree on fundamentals, and build coherently on one another's work. Friedman opens the volume with a challenge to his colleagues.

It is countered in the very next essay. We asked Mary Rohrberger, one of the critics targeted by Friedman, not only to respond to him, but to set forth her own views of the "state of the art." Her essay, "Between Shadow and Act: Where Do We Go from Here?" is, as its title suggests, more ruminative than polemic. Standing back from these two opening essays, we might square them off. We might see each as militating for a different notion of what knowledge is and how it is "found." Is it a structure we build from the ground up, or is it a maze we lay and often retrace? In calling for rigor and consistency and additive coherence, Friedman seems to be drawing from a model of knowledge familiar to the sciences—although he is well aware that the goals and substance of the humanities are different. On the other hand, Rohrberger assumes that in matters literary, progress is made in a literary way. Enacting its premise, her essay moves as her mind does—in personal, recursive paths of connection and speculation. According to her, knowledge about short stories comes by way of, and is often expressed in, metaphor—and that is as it should be. Knowledge is not quantitative but qualitative; in multiple reseeings lie unique variations that neither add to a sum nor cancel one another out; they enrich and complicate the circuits of thought—as do stories themselves. What this essay offers is, finally, not an answer to any challenge, but a meditation on the theme of short story theory. It is a literary essay about a literary activity.

To oversimplify, we might say that Friedman is looking for home plate, a known perimeter, and a few well-anchored bases to touch; Rohrberger thinks we will catch more flies if we find our own spot where the grass is greenest. Cumulative, objective progress; compounded yet unique insights. For his part, Austin Wright avoids this dichotomy. His offering is called "On Defining the Short Story: The Genre Question." In his chaste, inquiring prose, he reminds us of the fundamental issues of the last thirty years: the privileging of some classes of stories (short story versus story or simple narrative; lyrical versus epical; epiphanic versus action-based), differences in the working notion of genre itself (historically derived or logically prescribed), and the oldest problems of methodology (inductive or deductive).[12]

12. These distinctions have been used, sometimes with slight variations in wording, by so many critics that it is hard to make attributions. However, one may look specifically at Rohrberger's *Hawthorne and the Modern Short Story*, Eileen Baldeshwiler's "The Lyric Short Story: The Sketch of a History" (*Studies in Short Fiction*, VI [1969], 443–53, rpr. in May [ed.], *Short Story Theories*, 202–13), and Thomas M. Leitch's work in this volume.

Wright begins, as he did in 1961, with the idea of a canon; however, he proposes that it be as inclusive as possible. Indeed, he is outlining a project for multiple researchers, pooling their instincts and knowledge. In this way, he responds to the call for objectivity while recognizing that each mind has its quirks and inspirations. Beginning with Friedman's minimalist definition of the short story, Wright builds up a series of boundary conditions within which we are likely to find most of the texts we know as short stories. He argues for a notion of genre based on a cluster of characteristics rather than a checklist of works. Additions, omissions, and variations in the cluster help us identify interesting subgenres. In one sense, Wright's essay is the blueprint for a real experiment, a cooperative effort needing people and dollars; in a more philosophical way, it is a parable for the times in short story criticism: be organized but fluid, rigorous but open.

Since this is the introduction to the three opening essays in this volume, any attempt to resolve issues or draw conclusions would be premature—and preemptive. So, too, would be any discussion of theory itself as a critical activity. Friedman, Rohrberger, Wright, and all the other critics represented herein have their own points of view, implicit or explicit, on these "larger" questions. As editors, we have a desire, not for synthesis, but rather for a sense of community that thrives on debate. Let us begin.

NORMAN FRIEDMAN

Recent Short Story Theories: Problems in Definition

In discussing short story theory, we have a tendency to talk at
cross-purposes. I do not mean simply a tendency to disagree; I
mean, rather, an apparent difficulty in agreeing on what it is
we are disagreeing about. There is even more of this difficulty, I suspect, among literary critics than among those in other disciplines. We
seem to lack the two essential things needed for any intellectual en-
deavor: an accepted set of procedures for conducting our investigations and attempting to come to conclusions, and—what is a conse-
quence of the first—an ability to build in concert upon one another's
findings in some sort of cumulative fashion.

Literature presents many facets for inspection, and thus there are
many sorts of questions we can ask about it. Different answers to different questions are not in themselves competitive. We have the possibility of genuine debate only when we are looking at the same facet
and asking the same question about it. And we have the possibility of
genuine knowledge building only when we can look at that facet in
the same way, can bring our assumptions out in the open and put
them to the test, and can agree on what constitutes a plausible reasoning process for validating conclusions. If, after all this, we still disagree—and I am not claiming we should or even can find the same
kinds of agreement people in the sciences should and can look for—at
least we will know how and why we disagree. That too is a useful
kind of knowledge.

I am well aware that the nature of our subject matter militates
against the search for hard data and conclusive proof. I am also aware
that such things are difficult to find even in the sciences—not only in
the social sciences but in the physical sciences as well. And I am

aware, finally, that there has been recently a pervasive trend in all these fields toward a skepticism and a nominalism which doubts not only the possibility of language ever describing reality but also the possibility of knowledge of reality itself.

I do not believe, however, that this trend aims at the destruction of all intellectual discipline. Its proponents, after all, are still busy giving talks and writing books and articles. I believe, on the contrary, that this trend aims at a thorough-going questioning of all our assumptions and procedures, with a view to finding some more accurate way of building knowledge. And that way will result in a firmer grasp of what we cannot do as well as of what we can. It aims, in other words, to make us more careful about our claims—and more modest. And that is all to the good.

Modern criticism has proposed correctly that we cannot simply take a literary work as having a one-to-one correspondence with reality, and deconstructionism, far from being the radical departure from the old New Criticism it sometimes presents itself as, is simply a logical continuation of it. If we cannot take a literary work as a one-to-one presentation of reality, neither can we take criticism itself as a one-to-one presentation of that work. Whereas a literary work is an interpretation of reality, criticism is an interpretation of that interpretation—and is therefore tentative and in constant need of correction.

Practical criticism, which is more concerned with understanding a given text than with these matters of theory, can go a certain distance without a specific concern for definitions, provided that it works within the general context of an awareness that a literary work is an interpretation of reality rather than reality itself. Understanding a given text, that is, depends as a basic step upon our taking what happens within it as a formal set of verbal and imagined relationships rather than as something that has happened in real life. However, we need to make a distinction between this kind of informed reading and the special activity of genre definition.

As we narrow down the inquiry, we must become more concerned with logical consistency. The concept of literature as an art is easier to deal with than the concepts involved in its subdivisions. We can set literature off from life, as well as from the other arts, more clearly than we can set off its branches from one another. Indeed, this is precisely the problem many short story critics have in trying to define the genre. How can we talk about something before we know what we are talking about? Don't we have to mark off our field of inquiry before studying it? Isn't it better to interpret and evaluate any given work relative to its kind rather than applying a single universal standard to all kinds? The answers depend upon how we go about making our definitions.

The standard textbook procedure is *per genus et differentiam:* we must locate the class in which the item to be defined belongs, and then we have to subdivide that class into at least two subclasses in order to distinguish the item to be defined from the adjoining or related items. I am belaboring here what may appear to be the obvious because, of the many works on short story theory I have consulted for this essay, only a very few show any real appreciation of the problems involved in making a definition, and even fewer manage to avoid the errors which may be entailed in making it.

If looked at in these terms, the oft-ridiculed formula "A short story is a story that is short" is not so circular as it at first appears. Story is the genus, or class, in which the item to be defined belongs, by which is meant, in the present context, "narrative fiction in prose." The term *story* can mean other things in other contexts. While narrative is the true classifying trait for story, stories need not be fictional (as in news stories) or in prose (as in verse narratives). Nevertheless, it is clear that "narrative fiction in prose" will be sufficient for the purpose at hand. It follows that shortness is the differentiating trait which allows us to subdivide the class into at least two subclasses, according to length—short and long. Also, since the facts seem to warrant it, we can add medium (for the novella).

It does not matter in the least that we have not yet defined more precisely what we mean by *short, medium,* and *long* because these are relative terms, and all we need to know at this point is that *long* means "more than short," and so on. The system makes logical sense as it is, and more precise definitions can only be established pragmatically— an issue to which we shall return in a moment. Nor does it matter in the least that our definition is, so far, simply mechanical, quantitative, and external: that it says nothing about the genre in question—its subjects, its themes, its structures, and so on—that is intrinsic and qualitative. It is best *not* to say anything about such important issues at this point, for rushing ahead can—and does—result in some of those errors alluded to above.

The question now is, what *can* we do with this definition? First, we can mark off our field of inquiry: it includes all "narrative fiction in prose which is short." Next, we may proceed either inductively or deductively. If we assume that an a priori definition is needed to call the field of study into view, then we are proceeding deductively. If we assume, on the other hand, that we already have a working knowledge of what is included in the field of study, and that all we need is a way of conceptualizing it, then we are proceeding inductively. The first approach fits the evidence to the definition, whereas the second fits the definition to the evidence. To make an inductive definition, in other words, we assume that the thing to be defined already exists as a given beforehand and that the problem is to formulate a definition which will fit it. Otherwise, we will never be able to test it, for there will be nothing against which to test it. A deductive definition is, in the present context, like a self-fulfilling prophecy: assuming there is *something* in the field of study that it points to, it can never be wrong— nor, by the same token, can it ever be right either, for that which is not falsifiable cannot be verified.

Let us follow the inductive procedure a bit further. Assuming we will have little trouble deciding what goes into the class of "narrative fiction in prose," we may resolve the problem of shortness pragmatically by including in the subclass short story all those works of "narrative fiction in prose" that are considered to be short by writers, the reading public, publishers, critics, and scholars. This is our given, and this allows us to talk about something before we have defined it. We can then align this subclass side by side with the subclasses of novella and novel according to the same pragmatic distinctions and see if we can emerge with general specifications of length. And we can certainly do this—it certainly has been done—so long as we remember that we can only come up with central tendencies rather than absolutes, and that there always is and must be a certain amount of overlap at the edges in such cases.

The next step in the inductive process is to assemble a fair sample of what are generally considered to be short stories and to examine their traits simply as they appear in the sample, and then to compare these traits with those similarly derived from a fair sample of novellas and novels. Of course, the inductive method does not let us make this examination without implying or stating controlling assumptions about and definitions of the traits we are looking for. To be inductive in the true sense is not merely a matter of observing and collecting evidence, even if such were possible. We always need not only controlling assumptions and definitions but also a guiding hypothesis. Through the inductive approach we are trying to let the evidence correct the assumptions, definitions, and hypotheses. Even though the evidence itself is examined by means of a process that is necessarily partly deductive, then, what we make of it can be corrected by submitting it to inductive tests.

The tests require that the sample be a fair and representative portion of the whole group being investigated; that the definition be neither so narrow as to exclude what common sense tells us belongs in the definition nor so broad as to include things which common sense tells us do not belong; and that the hypothesis should be complete, coherent, and economical. Ian Reid, for example, provides not so much a definition of the short story as a cogent study of the problems of defining it—in terms of its history, of its cross-cultural labels, and of its relation to similar forms.[1] With a clear sense of the evolution and proliferation of genres and of the differing and shifting meanings of similar terms, Reid balances delicately between definitions which are too narrow and those which are too broad, between characteristics which are essential to the genre and those which are simply found frequently—or found at a given time.

There is further the requirement that we may not assume that there is only one correct way of defining something: a definition is always relative to the context and purpose of the inquiry, which in turn will determine which traits we select for the initial two steps of the definition. Mary Louise Pratt's article ("The Short Story: The Long and Short of It") contains much good sense concerning the logical problems of defining literary genres, especially the short story, and she shows that genres are not essences but rather based variously on subject matter, narrative situation, surface linguistic form, end effect, mode of execution of the text, and so on.[2]

This initial definition contains only a single *differentia* and is therefore merely a preliminary step at a high level of generality. It marks off our field of study, but it does not actually complete the job of defining the genre. Trying to particularize the definition of a genre on the basis of a single and general *differentia,* which is all too common, is doomed to failure from the start. What is needed instead is a set of multiple *differentiae*—a scheme of further possible subdivisions—to be applied in various combinations so as to do justice to the variety of poten-

1. Ian Reid, *The Short Story* (1977; rpr. New York, 1979).
2. Mary Louise Pratt, "The Short Story: The Long and the Short of It," *Poetics,* X (1981), 175–94.

tialities involved. Short stories, common sense tells us, are short in various ways and for various reasons.

And there is finally the fact that it is less feasible to deduce thematic traits from formal traits or formal traits from thematic traits than to deduce formal traits from a formal definition, for it is necessary to keep one's categories consistent at each level of differentiation. The significance of these tests will emerge more fully as we proceed.

The most completely inductive study of the short story I have seen is Helmut Bonheim's, which is based on an analysis of six hundred short stories and three hundred novels as a way of testing out short story theories. I need not go into the details of his elaborate—and necessarily tedious—study, but I can report on his conclusions. These he presents as tendencies rather than absolutes. With regard to the manner of opening a story, Bonheim finds that techniques of anteriority and the use of pronouns without referents occur more frequently in the short story than in the novel, which simply means, as others have noted, that the short story tends to begin close to the end. With regard to endings, he finds that stories tend to end more frequently with quoted speech, have more ironic conclusions, and finish more often with a question. These factors mean overall that story endings tend to be somewhat more open and tentative. He concludes, however, that no single ingredient of the many proposed short story definitions, other than shortness, cannot be found in novels as well. The work of A. Leslie Willson on the German short story also concludes that no single definition can cover the multitude of examples considered.[3]

We seem to be left, then, in something of a quandary. Perhaps there *is* no inherent difference, other than the external factor of length, between the short story, the novella, and the novel. Or perhaps, more fruitfully, the differences have to be seen as a matter of degree rather than of kind. Nevertheless, such negative findings do not prevent certain other critics—Mary Rohrberger, Valerie Shaw, and Charles May— from using a single-trait approach in postulating differences of kind rather than merely of degree. And their approach is necessarily deductive, beginning with a concept of what the short story is about and

3. Helmut Bonheim, *The Narrative Modes: Techniques of the Short Story* (Cambridge, Eng., 1982); A. Leslie Willson, "Constancy and Variation: The Short Story in Germany," in Wendell M. Aycock (ed.), *The Teller and the Tale: Aspects of the Short Story* (Lubbock, Tex., 1982), 87–102.

then deducing what consequences this context must have with regard to the story's shortness. A sign of the slippery ground which underlies this approach is that the line of reasoning is reversible, and the cause of shortness can be deduced from conceptions of what the short story is about. That is to say, these critics assume that the short story has a characteristic subject matter which in turn calls forth a characteristic structure, or that it has a characteristic structure which in turn calls forth a certain subject matter. The problem with this procedure is that it mixes the categories.

By "deductive" I do not mean that these critics have not read many short stories and are not prepared to support their theories by citing and analyzing appropriate examples. Nor do I mean that the richness, interest, and value of their work on other levels are therefore nullified. I mean simply that citing and analyzing examples are not enough to insure that the logic coheres; the relation between theory and example must be subjected to inductive tests. Let us see how this difference looks in practice.

These scholars derive their approach, as many do—with various modifications—from Poe's theories of the short story being read in one sitting and the lyric being the only true form of poetry, and from Frank O'Connor's concept of loneliness in the short story. They are also indebted to the traditional distinction between romance and realism.[4] Mary Rohrberger's theory is representative.[5] For her, the short story belongs to the tradition of romance, which in turn leads to the modernist tradition of symbolism. Thus the plot of the short story, however realistic on the surface—and, of course, it need not be— contains emotional depths relating it to myth and dream and thereby to the lyric. Realizing that this definition is logically too narrow to include all of the things which common sense calls short stories, and especially all those stories which are in the tradition of realism per se, she coins an additional category for them called the simple narrative, thereby keeping her definition of the short story pure. Logically also, if she can limit her definition of the novel to the tradition of realism— and here critics of this sort often call upon the work of Ian Watt—she can keep the category of the long romance pure also, relying on the

4. *Cf.* William Peden, "Realism and Anti-Realism in the Modern Short Story," in Aycock (ed.), *Teller and the Tale*, 47–62.

5. Mary Rohrberger, *Hawthorne and the Modern Short Story: A Study in Genre* (The Hague, 1966); Mary Rohrberger and Dan E. Burns, "Short Fiction and the Numinous Realm: Another Attempt at Definition," *Modern Fiction Studies*, XXVIII (1982), 5–12.

work of Richard Chase on the American novel to substantiate this point.[6]

But these categories land Rohrberger—and others as well—in a curious dilemma: not only must the category of romance exclude the novel, but the short story also must be seen as closer to romance than to either the simple narrative or the novel. We have lost, then, the criterion of shortness altogether, which loss shows up also in the way Rohrberger and others deal with the question of modernism. They can show that the modern short story has certain period characteristics, such as the reliance upon images and symbols in addition to or instead of a traditional plot, and they can show how it both resembles and differs from the traditional short story, but they cannot show how these traits separate the modern short story from the modern novel or the modern poem. For such traits are, of course, period traits and not genre traits. And there are other difficulties as well, such as whether the modern short story is more traditional or more modern than the modern novel, or whether the modern story is basically similar to or different from the traditional story.[7]

Valerie Shaw is another who postulates a deductive, single-term, and mixed-category definition. Following O'Connor's theory that story typically presents lonely people on the fringes of society, and despite the fact that she argues that it is too narrow, she develops an approach of her own which sees story as dealing characteristically with the borderline between permanence and change, actual and strange, mundane and extraordinary, reality and dream, and which deduces from this supposed borderline feature the structural characteristics of story as embodying the tension between surface brevity and deep intensity, spontaneity and artifice, richness and concision, involvement and detachment, suggestiveness and hard outline.[8]

Once again, however, one cannot help but think that these same

6. Ian Watt, *The Rise of the Novel* (Berkeley, 1957); Richard Chase, *The American Novel and Its Tradition* (Garden City, N.J., 1957).

7. *Cf.* Joseph M. Flora, "The Device of Conspicuous Silence in the Modern Short Story," in Aycock (ed.), *Teller and the Tale*, 27–46; János Szávai, "Towards a Theory of the Short Story," *Acta Litteraria Academiae Scientiarum Hungaricae*, XXIV (1982), 203–24; Warren S. Walker, "From Raconteur to Writer: Oral Roots and Printed Leaves of Short Fiction," in Aycock (ed.), *Teller and the Tale*, 13–26; and Gordon Weaver, "One Writer's Perception of the Short Fiction Tradition: How Would Edgar Allan Poe Make a Duck?" in Aycock (ed.), *Teller and the Tale*, 119–32.

8. Valerie Shaw, *The Short Story: A Critical Introduction* (London, 1983); Frank O'Connor, *The Lonely Voice: A Study of the Short Story* (Cleveland, 1963).

traits could be used to define the lyric, for example. Further, Shaw relates this theory, as does Suzanne Ferguson, to that form of modernism which has come to be called impressionism—that is, the form which represents how an object appears to an observer rather than how it ostensibly is in itself. Thus art is seen as an attempt to objectify the subjective, which ties in with those other theories of story, such as Rohrberger's, which view it as dealing with inner and emotional experience rather than outer and intellectual experience. And this is offered as a rationale for explaining why story deals with epiphanic moments—instants of crisis or change or realization—rather than the unfolding process of change. Unlike Ferguson, however, Shaw forgets that there is such a thing as the impressionist novel as well, for this is a period rather than a genre distinction, and the category is too broad.

So Shaw herself is forced to conclude that, although the novel can use the same materials as the short story, the two forms differ with regard to patterning, pacing, and ending. But this concession weakens the connections she has been forging between theme and form, and calls into question her opening assertion that the short story is a distinct form with its own methods. Although hers is a rich and insightful book, crowded with authors and analyses and period distinctions, it nevertheless does reflect a confusion of logic in her genre definitions as well as in the relations between the traditional and modern story.

Ferguson, however, encounters a couple of problems of her own.[9] First, in acknowledging that the modern story is similar to the modern novel, she must then deal somehow with the fact that the differences will therefore necessarily be merely of degree rather than of kind. Her way of handling this problem is to argue that since modernism is in part a matter of leaving things out, and since the short story has fewer parts to begin with, modernism affects the story more sharply than it does the novel. To make things scarce, in other words, in an already limited field is to make things scarcer still. But it could just as easily be argued that dismembering a larger and more complex entity would leave it more deprived than a smaller entity, since the larger and more complex a thing is, the more dependent it is on each of its parts and the easier it will disintegrate if any of its parts are miss-

9. Suzanne Ferguson, "Defining the Short Story: Impressionism and Form," *Modern Fiction Studies*, XXVIII (1982), 13–24.

ing. A worm, after all, survives amputation much more successfully than a human. However this may be, the fact remains that it is difficult to distinguish modern story from modern novel as far as their modernism is concerned.

Ferguson's second problem is related to the first: she argues that while modern story can dispense with plot, the modern novel cannot. As we begin thinking of the many exceptions—*Finnegans Wake*, for example—she covers herself by saying she means to refer only to the impressionist novel and not to the post-impressionist novel. In this way she narrows the definition so that the argument will apply.

Charles May has been the clearest and most consistent proponent of the deductive, single-term, and mixed-category approach, insisting on an inherent relationship between a characteristic structure and a characteristic theme.[10] For over ten years he has been developing a carefully thought out and increasingly more-elaborate defense of the basic proposition that the short story is short because it deals with a special, brief sort of experience and that this experience is most suited to the short story. He is referring to the fleeting moment of mythic perception when the mystery of life breaks through our mundane perception of reality—in short, the epiphany. It follows from this that the novel—that is, the Ian Watt novel—deals with our mundane perception of reality.

May does not acknowledge that there are other kinds of novels than the realistic and that some of them *do* deal with fleeting moments of mythic perception—as do a number of Virginia Woolf's novels, for example, and, I would argue, Joyce's *Ulysses*. Interestingly enough, Anthony Burgess is even more deductive in claiming that the difference between story and novel does not have to do with length at all but rather with structure: revelation is characteristic of story, whereas resolution is characteristic of novel. If a novel is based on the former rather than the latter, then it is in reality a short story—and his example is, of course, *Ulysses*. Harry Levin has argued in like manner that *For Whom the Bell Tolls* is in reality an expanded short story.[11]

---

10. Charles E. May (ed.), *Short Story Theories* (Athens, Ohio, 1976)—see especially May's introduction, originally published in 1973; May, "The Unique Effect of the Short Story: A Reconsideration and an Example," *Studies in Short Fiction*, XIII (1976), 289–97; May, "The Nature of Knowledge in Short Fiction," *Studies in Short Fiction*, XXI (1984), 327–38.

11. Anthony Burgess, "On the Short Story," *Journal of the Short Story in English*, II (1984), 31–47; Harry Levin, "Observations on the Style of Ernest Hemingway," *Contexts of Criticism* (1951; rpr. Cambridge, Mass., 1957).

Similarly, John Gerlach has claimed that certain stories of Henry James and H. G. Wells are in fact condensed novels. Each of these conclusions seems to be based on the assumption that there is something inherent in short fiction other than its shortness; this is what I have been calling an a priori assumption in that it causes us to rule out (or rule in) examples which common sense tells us belong (or do not belong).

I do not deny that authors can make mistakes and publish stories that are too short or novels that are too long, but I do not think we can make such judgments on the basis of genre principles; I think, rather, that we must make them on the basis of analyses of particular cases. I can think of no empirical or logical reason why an action of smaller size cannot be successfully expanded into a work of novel length, so long as there seems to be some formal and artistic reason for doing so, or why an action of larger magnitude cannot be condensed down to the length of a short story, so long as it seems to serve some formal and artistic purpose.

Returning to May, we note that he does not acknowledge as well that many short stories themselves do not deal with epiphanic moments—unless he would go along with Rohrberger's claim that these stories belong to a different genre. Indeed, Barry Menikoff comments on how both of these critics narrow down the definition of the short story to the epiphanic form. May explicitly criticizes Thomas Gullason for arguing that the short story can encompass a change process as well as a brief moment, and he does so on the grounds that the former is a feature characteristic of the novel. Gullason, it seems, has been urging that we recognize a variety of story forms.[12] Finally, there is the dilemma which many of these romance-epiphanic theories have in common—their acknowledgment that the short story does share this feature with the lyric. What happens, then, to the short story as a separate genre?

We have here, again, a period rather than a genre distinction: all modernist forms, including the novel as well as the verse epic, have moved toward the subjective moment. If it is the case that the lyric has traditionally focused on the subjective moment—or at least cer-

12. Barry Menikoff, "The Problematics of Form: History and the Short Story," *Journal of the Short Story in English*, II (1984), 129–46; Thomas A. Gullason, "The Short Story: An Underrated Art," *Studies in Short Fiction*, II (1964), 13–31, rpr. in May (ed.), *Short Story Theories*, 13–31; Gullason, "Revelation and Evolution: A Neglected Dimension of the Short Story," *Studies in Short Fiction*, X (1973), 347–56; Gullason, "The Short Story: Revision and Renewal," *Studies in Short Fiction*, XIX (1982), 221–30.

tain kinds of lyric—then it can be said that modernism has lyricized the other forms. But all modernist forms have also moved toward the principle of objectivity, which could present us with something of a paradox. But despite the fact that Joyce, Pound, and Eliot—and the New Critics after them (and Coleridge, Hazlitt, Shelley, and Keats before them)—all proposed theories of impersonality, what they meant was not that literature should exclude the subjective but rather that it should embody the subjective in objective forms: the objective correlative. Thus, while *A Portrait of the Artist* is just as much about Stephen's inner growth and epiphanic moments as *Stephen Hero*, it is presented more objectively. That is to say, there is more distance between the author and his protagonist in the revised version. And the same goes for the modern lyric itself.

However this may be, the issue of modernism is not the same as that of defining any of its genres, for it cuts across distinctions of genre. We cannot derive particular forms from a general principle; such distinctions must be looked for elsewhere. One promising direction is in the study of endings, in that it attempts to derive structural distinctions from structural principles. Susan Lohafer and John Gerlach are the chief exemplars here. Gerlach lists nine precursors in the study of endings in his bibliography, which includes such well-known studies as those by Robert Adams, Frank Kermode, David Richter, and Barbara Herrnstein Smith.[13] And they all hark back, of course, once again to Poe. Additionally, Bonheim and Shaw also deal with this issue, although not as centrally.

Such studies are more inductive than deductive, at least potentially, for they begin with the only observable commonality which all short stories share and which does indeed separate them from novellas and novels—their shortness—and they attempt to deduce the short story's structural features from that observation. In avoiding the mixed-category approach they are on much more operable grounds.

These approaches follow two of Poe's principles. The first is that the desired singleness of effect can only be achieved by a work which is short enough to be read at a single sitting—say, a few hours, or fifty to seventy-five pages. And the second is that if everything is so constructed to answer to the end, then the end controls the beginning and the middle. Denying that Poe's formula necessarily results in me-

---

13. John Gerlach, *Toward the End: Closure and Structure in the American Short Story* (University, Ala., 1985).

chanical tales and surprise endings, these new approaches recast the story in present-day reader-response terms and ask what the imminence of the end in a short story does to the readers' experience of the work as they move through it.

Before going on, even though I think these approaches are promising, I would like to question the meaning of the principles on which they are based. It has never seemed to me that a novel lacks singleness of effect simply because it cannot be read at one sitting. What we do when we put down a novel and pick it up at some other time to resume reading is see where we left off, briefly recall what came before, and then go ahead as if nothing had interrupted us. We keep building the whole piecemeal in our heads as we go along, and when we finish we have the completed whole for contemplation. Curiously, Poe's principle works the other way when it comes to what the author experiences during the process of writing a short story, for it normally takes much longer to write anything than it does to read it. How, then, does the writer manage to hold onto singleness of effect if the process of composition takes more than a single sitting?

The only thing on a common-sense level that distinguishes novel reading from short story reading is that the reader is bound to recall more of the details in the short story than in the novel, mainly because of the way memory works in relation to quantity and duration.[14] And all that we can logically deduce from this fact is that each detail will therefore carry more weight in the short story. Suzanne Hunter Brown's essay on "Tess" experiments with this deduction. She takes an ostensibly detachable portion of the novel *Tess of the d'Urbervilles* and compares the reading of it as if it were an independent short story with the reading of it in its novelistic context. Her conclusion is that the reader sees the same text differently in these two instances.[15] My response to this sort of reader-oriented criticism is, yes, it may very well be that we read things differently according to our different expectations regarding longer and shorter works, and then again, no, it may not. I am not sure that when I begin reading a shorter novel, I have different expectations than when I begin a longer story. Nor am I sure, when I am writing what may turn out to be either, that my writing can predict which it shall be. In either case, we exercise a certain

14. *Cf.* John Wain, "Remarks on the Short Story," *Journal of the Short Story in English,* II (1984), 49–66.

15. Suzanne Hunter Brown, "'Tess' and *Tess:* An Experiment in Genre," *Modern Fiction Studies,* XXVIII (1982), 25–44.

kind of negative capability and are simply waiting to see what happens. And even if I am dealing with a shorter story in contrast to a longer novel, I am not sure that the difference will be what this sort of approach claims.

I am prepared to concede, however, that both reader and writer may typically experience a difference between works on the shorter side and those on the longer. My experience of reading a shorter lyric is indeed different from that of a longer novel, as is the experience of the writing. I am aware, for instance, that I am going to be able to read the poem in less time, and this in turn will enable me—probably induce me—to pay more attention to each word, phrase, line, and so on. Similarly, when I am writing a poem, I feel the same sort of concentrated attentiveness.

Some longer novels, however, require exactly the same sort of attentiveness—*Ulysses*, for example—and what we are left with is the phenomenon I referred to before, that in reading longer works we naturally break them up into smaller units and then at the end try to reconstitute them into the whole which they suggest. The main difference, then, would be a matter of difference in recall of details. But Joyce was only partly joking when he said that he expected the reader to devote as much time to reading *Ulysses* as he had spent in writing it—or was it *Finnegans Wake?*

Lohafer and Gerlach do touch upon these points of memory and detail, but they claim more for the effects of brevity. And they do not consider the converse: that because a short story takes less time to read, even though we may remember its details for a while, it may make *less* of an impression on us in the long run than a novel, simply because we spend less time with it.

Poe's other point, that the end controls the beginning and middle, is merely to say, as Rohrberger quite rightly points out, that a short story is an art form. It is the *imminence* of the end, however—its relative closeness to the beginning—which creates effects differentiating it from longer and shorter works.

If knowing the end affects how a writer composes his story, so too will its imminence affect how the reader experiences it. This means for Lohafer that the story interrupts, displaces, and becomes part of our other life rhythms during the reading process.[16] The structure of a

16. Susan Lohafer, *Coming to Terms with the Short Story* (1983; rpr. Baton Rouge, 1985).

narrative, like the structure of a sentence, both resists and forwards our impetus toward closure. Because we can complete it at one sitting, the experience of closure in a story relates differently to our other life rhythms than reading a novel or a poem. It creates a rhythm of its own which is definite enough to displace our life rhythm until it is over. We can enter, move through, and leave story without interruption, and thus we build the story world as we read, apart from the other claims on our attention. So a story binds us more closely to the sentence than a novel and less closely to the word than a poem. Since the end is pushed closer to the beginning, each sentence carries a special urgency and calls for a higher level of attention.

Lohafer then goes on to analyze the two special features of sentences that complicate closure: density, which is an aspect of syntax, and intensity, which is an aspect of diction. Interestingly, an apparently simple syntax and diction, as in Hemingway, can complicate closure just as much as a complex syntax and diction, as in Henry James, for the impetus to closure can be slowed down as much by suggestiveness as by fullness.

I have called this approach inductive because it avoids mixing the categories and does not rest on a priori assumptions about the genre. Also, since it sees no sharp break between traditional and modern story as such, it avoids mixing period and genre distinctions. To be more fully inductive, however, Lohafer would have had to demonstrate that a novel does not fit into our other life cycles and does not displace our living time, and that a poem does so but in a different way. As I have suggested, though, there is no real difference between our experience of longer and shorter works except as regards how much we can remember of the whole when we are finished. Our life rhythms are just as displaced while reading a novel as while reading a shorter work, even admitting that we have to postpone closure. Indeed, in oral cultures the recitation of a longer work, such as an epic poem, before an audience can run on continuously for many hours without interruption. Perhaps technology, as it "advances," shortens the human attention span, and what we really ought to be talking about, *pace* Marshall McLuhan, is the effect of the medium upon the message. But it is true that the function of detail will be different in a shorter work. Thus far we can agree with this approach.

But then Lohafer does hazard a move into correlating structure and theme, and therefore crosses over into a priori assumptions. As the reader enters, moves through, and gets out of a story, so too does its protagonist, and therefore the theme of most stories is either coming home or leaving home. While the novel is measured by the rhythm of a life space, the story is measured by the rhythm of a day. The notion that a story represents a moment of change or insight and/or an experience or transition at a boundary is apparently well-nigh irresistible.

Gerlach, on the other hand, while developing his own scheme of the signals of closure, admits that these are the same in all genres. The difference is more of degree than of kind: the novel advances and develops its theme, while the story just shows it. Then he makes a useful distinction between two different forms of narrative, direct and indirect. The first foregrounds the movement toward closure; the second foregrounds the movement away from closure. Both movements are present in any narrative; the difference is a matter of which predominates. He also sees that although the modern short story depends more on the indirect form, it nevertheless depends on our experience of direct forms for its success. In the modern story, in other words, we are asked to supply what the author omits. It seems to me, however, that these distinctions, valid though they may be, can apply just as well to the novel and that his argument that the short story shows rather than develops its theme is undermined by them.

Furthermore, Gerlach goes on to say that each form correlates with a certain sort of subject matter: the indirect form is more suited to stories of wish fulfillment, as well as to those which embody the inconclusiveness of reality, an awareness of our limits; while the direct form is more suited to stories of heightened psychological experiences. Not only do these correlations seem somewhat inconsistent within themselves, but also the notion that form should be appropriate to content can never really be demonstrated in general. The suitability of form to content can only be demonstrated in individual works, and the fact that certain structures and devices embody certain potential powers and limitations cannot be used a priori to predict how they can be used in any particular case.

Thus, for example, Gerlach claims, as others have done, that a condensed novel, such as James or Wells wrote, cannot properly be called a short story. A condensed novel is simply a plot of novel length which has been abstracted down to story size. It has all the parts of a novel, but they are represented on a reduced scale. It is as if such writers had more novels to write than they had time for, and so they dashed off some in abbreviated form in order to get them off their chests. Since the short story, on the other hand, according to these theories, is that genre in which the anticipation of the end is always present and in which, therefore, the beginning and middle are constructed and represented differently than they are in the novel, a condensed novel cannot be called a short story. It does not utilize the supposed special powers and limitations defining the genre.

Once again, as with Rohrberger and May, an item which does not fit the definition is excluded solely on the basis of the definition. The evidence is made to fit the definition rather than the definition the evidence. It would make more sense, however, to expand the definition and give the condensed novel the benefit of the doubt; perhaps it is a legitimate form of the short story, having is own perfectly valid aesthetic principles. I do not think we can argue from the structural fact of shortness to any other structural fact except the recall of detail, and least of all can we argue from a structural to a thematic fact or vice versa. We must remain content, if we persist in trying to attack the problem of the short story from a single vantage point—whether from that of the epiphanic moment, of closure, or of some other trait—with relative differences of degree rather than logical differences of kind. As Gerlach himself concludes, "I prefer to think that the short story embodies the same laws as longer narrative modes, but more obviously, and in that sense is unique." Except for the last clause, which is once again contradictory, this is where we are left.

For my own part, I do not really believe there is any such thing as *the* short story more specific than "a short fictional narrative in prose." Within that definition we cannot logically or empirically rule out actions of any kind or size, any techniques, or any end effects. We can only begin with the fact of brevity and explore its possible causes.

In my own work on fiction theory, I started with Aristotle's method of defining tragedy in the *Poetics,* for it seems to me a useful way of defining other kinds of literature as well. In terms of this schema, we account for the whole of a literary work when we have examined its four causes: material (the means, or language), efficient (the manner, or techniques), formal (the object of imitation, or structure), and final (the end, or intended effect). Using Elder Olson's distinctions among speech, scene, episode, and plot, we can begin to talk about the size of the action (an issue of magnitude, an aspect of structure)—a particularly useful concept in discussing the short story.[17] A story may be short either because it embodies a small action, primarily scene or epi-

17. Norman Friedman, *Form and Meaning in Fiction* (Athens, Ga., 1975), Chap. IX; Elder Olson, "An Outline of Poetic Theory," in R. S. Crane (ed.), *Critics and Criticism* (Chicago, 1952), 546–66.

sode, or because, having a large action, it portrays that action on a condensed scale and/or with a significant omission of parts (aspects of technique). Perhaps it can also be distinguished in terms of its special effect and/or the special quality of its language, but these are much more tenuous than the others and much harder to distinguish in relation to shorter and longer forms.

The point is, then, that within our fixed definition of the short story as a short fictional narrative in prose, we find a range of possibilities regarding the size of the action, the manner or representation, and the nature of the end effect. Many different kinds of stories are, therefore, feasible, and we come to our relative judgments in kind by holding the fixed definition constant and seeing what variables and combinations of variables appear as we look at actual stories. In this way we will be able to assess the powers and limits of the genre.

But we cannot either logically or empirically specify that the short story, *because* of its shortness, deals with epiphanic sorts of actions, or with human experience at the boundary, or with arrivals and/or departures, or with romance more than realism. Nor can we specify that it deals with certain sorts of themes or that it embodies a certain kind of life vision. We cannot even specify, as our reader-response critics are attempting to do, that it has a certain effect upon the reader because of its shortness, for it does, after all, share this trait with other forms as well—the longer lyric poem, for example, and the essay. We must be prepared to recognize the wide variety of possibilities that can fall under the heading of short fictional narrative in prose, and we must be careful to distinguish among features which are exclusive to the form, features which are independent of the form, and those which are accidental and historically conditioned.

Thus, we can talk about the characteristics of biblical short narrative, for example, or of the modern short story as opposed to the premodern story, or about the epiphanic story, or of the differences that the imminence of the end makes, and so on, but we cannot logically and empirically use such characteristics as defining traits of the short story as a genre. They must be seen, rather, as extrageneric characteristics, features which they share with certain other genres, whether because of period traits or because of the fact of shortness, but which nevertheless have assumed a particular importance in this genre as well. A study of the epiphanic story, for instance, might profitably begin by showing in what ways and for what reasons it differs from other sorts of stories. It might then go on to show how the treatment of the epiphanic moment both resembles and differs from that in the novel and novella, then in the lyric. And it might very well conclude with some sort of useful definition—not of the short story— but of the epiphanic short story. We need a more inductive approach, then, based upon multiple distinctions, keeping the categories consistent, and observing the fundamental principle of suiting a definition to the facts rather than trying to suit the facts to the definition.

MARY ROHRBERGER

Between Shadow and Act: Where Do We Go from Here?

Some charges would be difficult to support if they were brought against literary academicians. One is that we understate our theses, whatever they may be. As graduate students we learned well the effect of forceful statements, and our mentors taught us in one seminar paper after another how to use evidence in ways most advantageous to our arguments. In the press of the competition for grades or tenure or in the excitement of the literary chase, how many of us have actually stopped to listen to the nagging voice suggesting that there just may be exceptions to what we are propounding?

Another charge against us that would be difficult to sustain is that we are anything less than a most articulate group. Happily, we do not find it difficult to invent a plethora of designations for conditions already perhaps reasonably named. Although one would think that students of literature (of all things) would be least likely to insist on absolutes, we, apparently more than our colleagues in the sciences, find it hard in our literary theories and genre definitions to accept the kinds of shadings and ambiguities that our interpretations suggest we value highly in literary artifacts.

Lately, some of us have been looking to the sciences to provide models for differentiation among genres. William O'Rourke, in "Morphological Metaphors for the Short Story," in this volume, uses zoology and modern physics to say, "A short story is a micro-form, space-time, exoskeletal phenomenon and can be explained most completely by the intertwining of these metaphors; as in quantum theory, each metaphor needs to be laid atop the others." I like the definition. It conforms to my view of the short story and the views of many others; as O'Rourke says, the short story is "whole, discrete, intact, three-dimensional," as opposed to the novel, which is "vertebrate, endo-skeletal, two-dimensional; it expands toward all points of a compass, limited only by the size of the frame."

By casting the definition into different descriptive terms, O'Rourke provides a more contemporary nomenclature and sends my thoughts flying in several directions, ultimately to come to rest at the same point. I think of Thomas M. Disch's wonderful story about the pogono-phore, which through all of its life can only climb up and down its shell to read and reread a pogonophore's preprinted circuit.[1]

The Text

I

Up. Uppity, up, up. The Top.

II

Down. Downy, down, down. Thump. The Bottom.

III

Pogonophores resemble slender worms. They can reach a length of fourteen inches with a diameter of less than a twenty-fifth of an inch. Long tentacles, Disch says, wave from their top ends. I cannot help but relate the pogonophores that Disch describes with "superstrings" currently being hailed by larger and larger numbers of theoretical physicists. Superstrings are tiny, one-dimensional elongations of en-ergy. They can wiggle and curl. They can spin, rotate, or vibrate. Many scientists think that matter, at its most fundamental level, is composed of superstrings and their shadows. Superstrings and anti-superstrings. Poetry in action. Just like the pogonophore going up and down its translucent white shell writing and reading its text.

The concept of superstrings reminds me of Einstein and his search for an organizing principle of the universe, which calls to my mind a statement attributed to him regarding modern quantum physics: the-ory decides what we can observe. I think also of a book by Jeremy Campbell called *Grammatical Man,* in which he links together knowl-edge obtained from disciplines as seemingly disparate as biology, physics, linguistics, mythology, psychoanalysis, mathematics, philos-ophy, and information theory. Campbell refers to the famous mathe-matician Kurt Goedel, who published in 1931 a paper so startling in its implications that it took forty years to reach even some of the many areas of knowledge where it had relevance. Goedel, though working

---

1. Thomas M. Disch, "The Squirrel Cage," in Philip Stevick (ed.), *Anti-Story: An Anthology of Experimental Fiction* (New York, 1971), 207.

specifically in mathematics, actually dealt with the much broader question of what the human mind can know. He posited that given a complex and consistent system, limitations of knowledge of that system are an intrinsic part of the system. Campbell explains, "There will always be true statements which can neither be shown to be true nor proved to be false within the confines of the system."[2] In other words, systems can never be completely defined.

What we need to do as theorists of the short story is to avoid throwing out theories because we see exceptions or because boundaries between categories are fuzzy. A table is a flat surface with legs. When we have a table that comes out of a wall and is held in position by wall and brace, like an ironing board, do we call it something other than "table"? Is it within the realm of possibility that we could have a hovering table similar to the lawn mowers recently advertised in sales catalogs? We would probably call the hovering object "table," too, on the basis of ghost legs and not worry that our genre classification is absurd or wrongheaded. In a book called *Animal Species and Evolution*, Ernst Mayr makes a similar point:

> Taxonomy is not alone in encountering difficulties when trying to assign concrete phenomena to categories. Most of the universally accepted concepts of our daily life encounter similar difficulties. The transition in category from subspecies to species is paralleled by the transition from child to adult, from spring to summer, from day to night. Do we abandon these categories because they are borderline cases and transitions? Do we abandon the concept tree because there are dwarf willows, giant cactuses, and strangler figs? Such conflicts are encountered whenever one is confronted with the task of assigning phenomena to categories.[3]

The point that I wish to make is that every aspect of the short story that is described more fully or named differently can lead us to increasingly more fruitful investigations. We are not in a terminological bog or a critical thicket.

Of course, we will agree and disagree for many reasons, not the least of which is that many of our theories and definitions depend on our interpretations. When I say that short story theorists have been circling around what Poe said about the nature of the short story for over one hundred years, my conclusion is based not only on my understanding of Poe's criticism but also on my understanding of his

2. Jeremy Campbell, *Grammatical Man* (New York, 1982), 109.

3. Ernst Mayr, *Animal Species and Evolution* (Cambridge, Mass., 1963), 22.

stories, which reflect *his* understanding of the genre.[4] And, of course, there is my understanding of Hawthorne's stories which occasioned Poe's review; and there is my experience with and degree of understanding of all the stories that I have read and heard about both before Poe's time and between his time and mine.

When Poe talks about a predetermined effect, is he talking about the way he said he constructed "The Raven," or is his understanding more closely aligned with that single effect of unity that characterizes his and Hawthorne's stories? "Tales" Poe called these stories, which he then distinguished from the essays in *Twice-Told Tales*. It is of the essays that Poe speaks about a strong "undercurrent of suggestion" running continuously beneath the upper stream of the "tranquil thesis." Later, when discussing "The Minister's Black Veil," Poe surely suggests multivalence as he describes an *"obvious"* meaning that "would be found to smother" the "insinuated one."[5]

When we ask ourselves how short is short or why short is short, we often forget that Poe talked about those issues too; one must admit, however, that his discussion was in the context of how a poem may be too brief to produce "an intense or enduring impression." Still, in context, Poe does seem to be comparing the tale to the poem. Surely, then, we may interpret Poe to say about the tale: "Without a certain continuity of effort—without a certain duration or repetition of purpose—the soul is never deeply moved. There must be the dropping of the water upon the rock."[6]

We, Poe, all of us use metaphors. What has dropping water upon a rock have to do with it? Would the rock have been better dropped into water so that concentric circles could result? But, then, water dropped on rock creates an insistent presence marking time as well as tension. If I interpret correctly, Poe is saying we need a sense of duration, repetition, and tension in short stories, and as he states in the most famous of all his paragraphs, we need design. For the emphasis is on the artifact, on a product made by an artist. The artist, however,

---

4. See, for example, my *Story to Anti-Story* (Boston, 1979), 1–9, and "Fiction Writers on Writing Short Fiction: The State of the Definition," in Frank N. Magill (ed.), *Critical Survey of Short Fiction* (Englewood Cliffs, N.J., 1981), II, 811–17.

5. On multivalence, see Mary Rohrberger and Dan E. Burns, "Short Fiction and the Numinous Realm: Another Attempt at Definition," *Modern Fiction Studies*, XXVIII (1982), 5–12.

6. Edgar Allan Poe, "Review of *Twice-Told Tales*," in Charles E. May (ed.), *Short Story Theories* (Athens, Ohio, 1976), 45–51.

needs a kind of cocreator, a reader, who participates in the story with an art kindred to that of the author to accomplish the desired sense of "the fullest satisfaction."

Based on my interpretations, I give to Poe what I consider to be his just due. But another critic of the short story, a colleague whose work I respect, Thomas Gullason, makes the point that Poe's review has been for much too long the basic source of our stereotyped views of the short story. Gullason refers to "Poe's prescriptions" and suggests that countless numbers of professional and academic critics take a similar inflexible and predictable theoretical view of the short story. What Gullason apparently objects to is a "dictionary" description of the short story as the art form most suited to a limited view, a form that by definition cannot provide full characterization and can reflect only a single mood. Gullason insists that "in the hands of a first-rate talent, a story is not only dynamic and expanding, it is multiple in its effect, or layerings, as it mirrors and transforms a scene or episodes (cycles) from 'life.'"[7] Who would object to this definition? Not I; nor do I believe that Poe would, since Gullason's definition so clearly reflects the kind of stories written by Poe himself and by Hawthorne.

Of course, the definition that Gullason gives us does not distinguish short story from novel, though perhaps Gullason deliberately avoids the issue, since some critics do not want us to talk about the short story with reference to the novel at all. Often these critics believe that novel theory is far more advanced than short story theory and that inherent in a comparison of the forms is a denigration of the shorter one. Mary Louise Pratt insists that it is hardly surprising that the short story should be defined in terms of the novel, since the novel is the dominant, normative genre of prose fiction. Pratt offers four propositions, each based on the assumption that bigger is better: 1) "the novel tells life, the short story tells a fragment of a life"; 2) "the short story deals with a single thing, the novel with many things"; 3) "the short story is a sample, the novel is the whole hog"; 4) "the novel is a whole text. The short story is not."[8]

Pratt's kind of statement, besides being based on what I consider faulty assumptions, seems to suggest that theorists of the novel have their house in order to such an extent that agreement is the rule,

7. Thomas Gullason, "The Short Story: Revision and Renewal," *Studies in Short Fiction*, XIX (1982), 221, 230.

8. Mary Louise Pratt, "The Short Story: The Long and the Short of It," *Poetics*, X (1981), 182, 184, 185, 186, with the permission of North-Holland Publishing Company, Amsterdam.

rather than the exception. Although it is true that people have been theorizing concerning the structure of the novel for a longer period of time than people have been concerned with the definition of the short story, it is not necessarily true that novel theory is much farther along. If "we" do not know how short is short, neither do "they" know how long is long. A novel, Malcolm Bradbury tells us, is "a fictional prose discourse that is, in the Aristotelian formulation, 'necessarily of a certain magnitude.'"[9]

One thing that we can say about theorists of the novel is that when they seek to distinguish the novel from other genres they do not often compare long and short prose fiction. Rather, they usually compare novels with other genres, such as poetry. Bradbury contends that the novel is not a traditional literary genre, "like tragedy or comedy, but a general form like poetry or drama; a form recognizable, moreover, to writers when they write one and to readers when they read one, but subject to broad and narrow uses and not to be defined even as clearly as poetry and drama."[10]

Bradbury's comment suggests that theorists of poetry have an easier time with definition, a conclusion that may be accepted by prose fiction scholars but hardly by academicians trying to define poetry, especially those forms not described by Aristotle. Barbara Herrnstein Smith, in her book *Poetic Closure: A Study of How Poems End*, makes what seems an obvious point. "Closure occurs," Smith declares, "when the concluding portion of a poem creates in the reader a sense of appropriate cessation. It announces and justifies the absence of further development; it reinforces the feeling of finality, completion, and composure which we value in all works of art; and it gives ultimate unity and coherence to the reader's experience of the poem by providing a point from which all preceding elements may be viewed comprehensively and their relations grasped as part of a significant design."[11] Of course, the same is true for all works of art.

But though Smith seems to have a relatively easy time working with poetic conventions announcing closure in metered poetry, she has a difficult time speaking about elements of closure when she examines free verse. She states:

9. Malcolm Bradbury, "An Approach Through Structure," in Mark Spilka (ed.), *Towards A Poetics of Fiction* (Bloomington, 1977), with the permission of Indiana University Press.

10. *Ibid.*

11. Barbara Herrnstein Smith, *Poetic Closure: A Study of How Poems End* (Chicago, 1968), 36.

If, as I have been suggesting, the formal resources of closure decrease as the form of the poem is increasingly undetermined, it is clear that the closure resources of free verse are minimal. This is not to say, however, that the formal structure of free verse is negligible or that it offers no such resources. Generalization is particularly hazardous here because it is difficult to produce or discover a definition of "free verse" that embraces all its acknowledged varieties, that can be stated in positive terms which do not amount merely to a celebration of artistic liberation, and that allows us to distinguish it from, rather than simply oppose it to, other more conventional forms.

And problems with genre definition are immediately apparent in the writings of critics concerned with a full range of genres. I approximate in the chart below a diagram from an article on genre theory written by Thomas G. Winner.[12] If we were to find a place on the diagram for prose fiction, we would have to locate it somewhere near the lyric, the

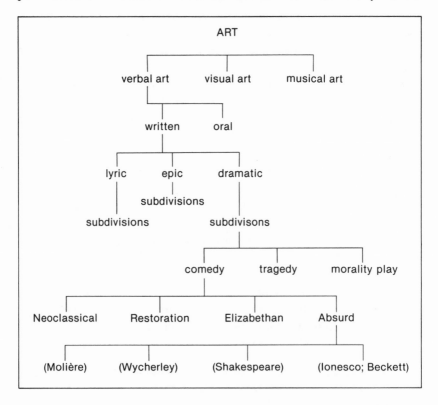

12. *Ibid.*, 84; Thomas G. Winner, "Structural and Semiotic Genre Theory," in Joseph P. Stelka (ed.), *Theories of Literary Genre* (University Park, Pa., 1978), 264.

epic, and the dramatic, or we could oversimplify and place prose fiction securely under epic, then subdivide again into long and short prose fiction.

If we wanted to illustrate greater complexity, we could try a diagram similar to what Robert Scholes provides in his article "An Approach Through Genre."

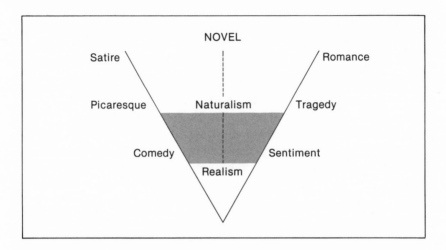

I am not sure, however, where the short story would fit on an approximation of Scholes's grid, since the lyric has no place, and since a link with lyric (also deriving from Poe) has been emphasized by one modern critic after another: Brander Matthews, Nadine Gordimer, Gullason, and Elizabeth Bowen, to mention only a few, as Susan Lohafer does in her book *Coming to Terms with the Short Story.* Eileen Baldeshwiler, for example, makes the point that poetic elements characterize a number of examples of short fiction. She points to two basic, recurring kinds of stories, which she terms mimetic and lyric. The mimetic she distinguishes as the larger group of narratives marked by "external action developed 'syllogistically' through characters fabricated mainly to forward plot, culminating in a decisive ending that sometimes affords a universal insight, and expressed in the serviceably inconspicuous language of prose realism." The other kind of story, Baldeshwiler says, concentrates on internal "changes, moods, and feelings, utilizing a variety of structural patterns depending on the shape of the emotion itself, relies for the most part on the open ending, and is expressed in the condensed, evocative, often figured language of the poem."[13] In a series of articles, Baldeshwiler has been adding to her list of lyric short story writers: Turgenev, Chekhov, Katherine Mansfield, D. H. Lawrence, Sherwood Anderson, Katherine Anne Porter, Eudora Welty, John Updike. I can hardly quarrel with Baldeshwiler's arrangement of categories since it so closely parallels my own—I subdivide the short story genre into what I call the simple narrative and the short story proper.

Our differences seem to me to result, in part, from our particular interpretations of stories. For example, "The Legend of Sleepy Hollow," like other Irving stories, seems to me lacking in clear focus and, moreover, extremely redundant; thus I conjecture that Hawthorne wrote the first short story, at least as Poe defined it. And, in my view, if Poe's stories and Hawthorne's and Melville's aren't lyric, then I don't know what a lyric story is. My canon of lyric stories would encompass every major writer of short fiction whose stories are characterized by symbolic substructures, where patterning is defined by a principle of organization and where degrees of tensions or expectations and gratifications involve us in a steady rhythmic process toward a particular ending necessitated by the pattern involved. The existence in a fiction of a linear plot line does not exclude that fiction from partaking of the qualities of lyricism. Plot is simply one of many elements of narrative. The decisive point is how meaning is derived—whether from plot or from patterning, which includes plot.

Other critics and writers of short stories seem to agree, though many use other terms and some focus on stories in the modern mode. Thomas M. Leitch, in "The Debunking Rhythm of the American Short Story," in this volume, distinguishes between two types of structure: the anecdotal and the epiphanic. He comments: "All short stories, we might say, proceed to a revelation that establishes a teleology, a retrospective sense of design, informing the whole story. . . . [A] story's teleology is felt as prospective and imminent, however uncertain we are of its precise form." Leitch goes on to say that if the climactic revelation in the story comes to one of the characters as a result of his or another character's actions, then the story is anecdotal; and if the story ends with a revelation whereby patterns make the story's events intelligible, then the story is epiphanic. What Leitch

13. Robert Scholes, "An Approach Through Genre," in Spilka (ed.), *Towards A Poetics of Fiction*, 48; Susan Lohafer, *Coming to Terms with the Short Story* (1983; rpr. Baton Rouge, 1985); Eileen Baldeshwiler, "The Lyric Short Story: The Sketch of a History," *Studies in Short Fiction*, VI (1969), 443, rpr. in May (ed.), *Short Story Theories*, 202.

says is true about all short stories, not simply those in the twentieth-century modernist mode. Hawthorne's "Dr. Heidegger's Experiment" is anecdotal; his "Wives of the Dead" is epiphanic.

In "Recalcitrance in the Short Story," also in this volume, Austin M. Wright makes a point similar to Leitch's and mine with regard to two basic structures for short fiction. Wright argues that readers' understanding and appreciation of a work depend upon their being able to recognize its potential form, perhaps in a moment of revelation. What Wright seems to be suggesting is that the greater the recalcitrance in a story, the more the story is epiphanic; the lesser the recalcitrance, the more the story is mimetic. Wright himself relates his thesis to features of the short story discussed by others: "What Eudora Welty calls 'mystery' in the short story is a sign of recalcitrance at the level of the fictional world. . . . The lyric short story is recalcitrant in its rejection of overt action. The open-ended story . . . is recalcitrant in its rejection of conventional beginnings and ends. . . . The concept of recalcitrance gives another dimension to the impact of epiphanies and discovery stories, and it offers an aesthetic explanation for stories of episode, disclosure plots, and static plots, as well as the flourish of metafictional stories."

In addition, Wright labels as recalcitrance Susan Lohafer's forces of anticlosure at the level of the sentence, Joseph Flora's "device of conspicuous silence," and the historical shift described by Dan Burns and me: "As the form [of the short story] evolves from Hawthorne through Barthelme, the reader is increasingly called upon to supply the temporal, causal, and overt thematic links formerly supplied by the author. Thus the contemporary reader is required to participate in a kinship relationship with the author that is even more active than the one Poe suggests."[14]

In her introduction to *The Faber Book of Modern Short Stories*, Elizabeth Bowen makes a similar distinction. She distinguishes between the kind of stories written by Maupassant and the kind written by Chekhov. "Tchehov stands . . . for an emancipation of faculties, for a romantic distension of the form of the story to let in what might appear inchoate or nebulous. Maupassant stands for astringency, iron relevance."[15]

Ignoring the kinds of stories that are more prosaic than lyric, Eu-

14. Rohrberger and Burns, "Short Fiction and the Numinous Realm," 6.
15. Elizabeth Bowen, Introduction to *The Faber Book of Modern Short Stories*, in May (ed.), *Short Story Theories*, 153.

dora Welty speaks of the short story as being "bathed" in an atmosphere of its own, which "is what makes it shine." She remarks: "The first thing we see about a story is its mystery. And in the best stories we return at the last to see mystery again." Nadine Gordimer compares the short story with "the flash of fireflies" and says that the present moment seen by the light of that flash is the only reality of which we can be sure. This is why, she contends, the novel is a dying form and the short story lives on. Alberto Moravia observes that the short story is "unquestionably purer, more essential, more lyrical, more concentrated and more absolute" than the novel.[16]

Suzanne Ferguson refuses to distinguish at all between the novel and the short story. She prefers to differentiate between nineteenth-century realism and twentieth-century impressionism, which she defines as the basic modernist practice in both long and short fiction. She does make the point that in the realm of plot the modern short story seems to be most different from the modern novel. She says the "deletion of expected elements of the plot" is the "hallmark of the modern story." Here she points to two basic methods of deletion which result in elliptical and metaphoric plots. In elliptical plots elements are omitted; in metaphoric plots the "unexpected" or the "dissonant" substitutes for that which is omitted.[17]

In her book, *The Short Story: A Critical Introduction,* Valerie Shaw also appears to refuse to define short stories while, at the same time, she makes important distinctions between them and novels. But though at the beginning of her book she remarks, "It seems reasonable to say that a firm definition of the short story is impossible," at the end of her study, she seems to be making reasonably firm statements, basically in terms of the brevity of the form.

> It is the degree and nature of the reticence conveyed by the short story at its best that give the genre its own decorum, a tactfulness consisting of respect for silences or unstated feelings, and displaying itself formally in the "artful compromise" by which, Henry James proposed, the "space-hunger and space-cunning" of a writer's material can be "kept down." The surface of a story, James explained, was made "iridescent, even in the short piece, or what is beneath it and what probes and gleams through," and it is this that produces "the only compactness that has a charm . . . the

16. Eudora Welty, "The Reading and Writing of Short Stories," 163; Nadine Gordimer, "The Flash of Fireflies," 180; and Alberto Moravia, "The Short Story and the Novel," 151, all in May (ed.), *Short Story Theories.*

17. Suzanne Ferguson, "Defining the Short Story: Impressionism and Form," *Modern Fiction Studies,* XXVIII (1982), 16, 17.

only spareness that has a force . . . the only simplicity that has a grace—those, in each order, that produce the *rich* effect." In many of the stories presented in this study as attaining a "rich effect," silence is of paramount significance.

Shaw concludes, "The short story's success often lies in conveying a sense of unwritten, or even unwritable things: the story teller accepts the limitations of his art, and makes his freedom an aspect of those same restrictions."[18] The silence of which Shaw writes is at the very base of the short story and the lyric: the that that is unsaid but somehow manages to be said.

My own distinction between the simple narrative (I don't like the term, but have difficulties with all the others, too) and the short story proper is founded mainly on the presence or absence of symbolic substructures. Both categories partake of the qualities of unity and coherence; but in the simple narrative interest lies primarily on surface level. There are no mysteries to be solved, no depths to be plumbed. Meaning is apparent, easily articulated and accomplished by simple ironic reversals. This kind of "plot" story, "character" story, or "setting" story is mainly representational and linear. Readers experience an immediate feeling of satisfaction in completion of the form. The short story, on the other hand, leaves readers with a set of emotions that cannot be easily sorted; readers are often confused as to meanings and find it almost impossible to state them. In this kind of story, reader satisfaction must be postponed until questions presented by the symbolic substructures are answered. In this way the short story makes of readers cocreators, active participants in the revelation of meaning, and it is in this interaction that satisfaction ultimately rests.[19]

I find it difficult, as Norman Friedman rightly points out, to distinguish short stories with symbolic substructures from novels with a similar construction.[20] The only real difference I see is the amount of detail used and the density of the symbolic structure, both of which have an impact on brevity and, consequently, effect. It is in this area that I am personally most interested in the continuing efforts of my colleagues.

I would be interested to learn the ways in which language is "pres-

18. Valerie Shaw, *The Short Story: A Critical Introduction* (London, 1983), 21, 263–64, with the permission of Longman.

19. See my *Hawthorne and the Modern Short Story: A Study in Genre* (The Hague, 1966).

20. Friedman also points out rightly the similarities between Charles May's thinking and my own. About what I call the short story proper, I find myself agreeing with May in almost every particular.

surized" in fiction that is short. One of the great Latin American writers of short fiction, Julio Cortázar, makes the point that if short story and novel were compared to boxers in a boxing match, "the novel would win by points and the short story by a knockout." Suzanne Hunter Brown directs her attention to the effect of brevity on the perception of short stories. Brown concludes that brevity reinforces close attention to detail, a heightening of aesthetic intensity, and the ordering of textual elements in nonsequential patterns. Her demonstration with a reading of a segment of *Tess of the d'Urbervilles* as a short story, however, seems to me to be weakened by the fact that a segment cannot actually be separated from a whole, by the fact that *Tess* is highly metaphoric as a whole, and by the fact that the novel itself proceeds in terms of symbolic substructuring. I find Dan Burns's approach more reasonable, since he uses an actual short story and a separate novel (Nabokov's "Tyrants Destroyed" and *Bend Sinister*) to make his point that the major difference between short story and novel "is merely the degree to which the 'world' of the work is particularized."[21] If Burns is correct and the only difference between short story and novel is the amount of detail used, then what we are really talking about is the relative density of each piece. Our concern, then, should be not only with brevity but also, and perhaps more importantly, with density.

Susan Lohafer works with the imminence of end in short fiction. She concludes that a story binds us more closely to a sentence than does a novel and less closely to the word than does a poem. "It has always been clear that a short story's chief difference from longer fiction has to do with the aesthetics of brevity, but no one has gone very far toward explaining Poe's original conception of the 'unity of expression.' I'd simply point to the function of closure in defining a rhythm. Periodicity, in biology, history, and aesthetics, is engendered by the notion of closure—not the other way around. Short fiction, it has been said, is the most 'end-conscious' of forms. Readers of short fiction are the most 'end-conscious' of readers."[22]

With regard to spatially rather than temporally structured stories, Lohafer makes the point that closure is "a function of converging ref-

21. Julio Cortázar, "Algunos aspectos del cuento," trans. Kenneth Fleak, in "Latin American Short Fiction," *Studies in Short Fiction*, XX (1983), 301; Suzanne Hunter Brown, "'Tess' and *Tess*: An Experiment in Genre," *Modern Fiction Studies*, XXVIII (1982), 38; Dan E. Burns, "*Bend Sinister* and 'Tyrants Destroyed': Short Story into Novel," *Modern Fiction Studies*, XXV (1979), 510.
22. Lohafer, *Coming to Terms*, 94.

erences. The overall design becomes clear as separate strands of imagery either intersect or reveal their parallelism."[23] Lohafer's grammar of fiction is surprisingly similar to Barbara Herrnstein Smith's grammar of poetry, especially with reference to free verse.

So, where are we? Perhaps, as I observed at the beginning of this essay, we are still circling around what Poe said. I do not, however, find this possibility at all bothersome when I consider how long we have been circling around Aristotle. The circuits of the human mind are infinitely more complex than those of Disch's pogonophore. There is a great deal more to play and replay.

But why bother? I can answer for myself. I believe with Robert Scholes that "generic study . . . [is] the central element in a poetics of fiction." He continues: "If writing is bound by generic tradition, so is reading. Even a little child must come to learn what stories are before he likes listening to them. He has, in fact, to develop a rudimentary poetics of fiction before he learns to respond, just as he develops a grammatical sense in order to speak. In the adult world, most serious misreadings of literary texts and most instances of bad critical judgment are referable to generic misunderstandings on the part of reader or critic."[24] That is one answer. Another is that as long as we articulate and exchange information, we live, continuing to define ourselves and our creations in the only ways we can. We have no options. We simply go on from where we are, somewhere between shadow and act.

23. *Ibid.*, 101.
24. Scholes, "An Approach Through Genre," 41, 43.

AUSTIN M. WRIGHT

On Defining the Short Story: The Genre Question

Many of our difficulties in defining the short story can be traced to two problems. One is historical, arising from the attempt of early critics to distinguish the short story from any mere story that was short. Brander Matthews in particular built on Poe's famous insistence on a "unified effect"; the famous passage describes, or rather prescribes, a quality, which became the first conceptual wedge to split off the genre by something other than shortness. Matthews made the split explicit by putting a hyphen between *short* and *story* and ruling out the sketch, the still life.

Unity of effect is nebulous; it is hard to use as a measuring stick. And Matthews' insistence that the "Short-story" have a plot did not stand up well in the early twentieth century, when everybody—the short story writer especially—was trying to get rid of plot.[1] The hyphen has disappeared along with the definition, but the concept of short story as something special has remained, without agreement as to what it is. Nowadays, despite the recent flourish of short story criticism, we dispute not only the definition but the canon itself, the question of what works are or are not short stories. Hence the difference between those who trace the genre back to Boccaccio, *The Arabian Nights*, and the Bible, and those who would have it begin with Irving or Poe, or, still more narrowly, Chekhov or Joyce. Some distinguish between the short story and the modern short story; for others the only kind of short story is the modern.

The other problem is theoretical: there is ambiguity in the concept of genre itself. Most attempts to define genre (except for such precise

1. Brander Matthews, *The Philosophy of the Short-Story* (New York, 1901), 35, 32.

and conventional forms as the sonnet) confront similar obstacles. Most of the theoretical difficulties in recent definitions are examined carefully in Norman Friedman's summary of recent efforts, which opens this volume. I would like, however, to call attention to two especially important questions concerning the relationship between the definition and the canon. We'll begin with the question of which comes first. Efforts to define the short story run into a chicken/egg problem. We must decide: Are we trying to articulate a concept already intuitively clear (trying to find terms to mark off this already understood entity?), or are we trying to establish a new category? Are we trying to rationalize our belief that X is a short story and Y is not, or are we creating terms to give a name to X and Y? Again, would my inclusion of a story by Boccaccio in the ranks of the short story precede my attempt to define the short story, or would it follow my establishment of a definition?

Tzvetan Todorov's distinction between theoretical and historical genres (essentially the same as Friedman's between deductive and inductive genres) is pertinent here.[2] A theoretical genre is determined deductively; it is established by a congruence of characteristics derived from a system. A historical genre is discovered through induction, that is, by the observation of an existing body of works or characteristics which are seen to have recurred together. To define *short story* as a story which is short is to identify a theoretical category (leaving aside the question of how *story* itself is defined). The modern short story, the lyrical short story, the story of unified effect, and most versions of short story discriminated from stories that are merely short, are historical genres. The identification of such categories is usually a valuable contribution to our understanding of the art; it becomes problematic only when a historical genre is mistaken for a theoretical one or a subgenre is made to represent the whole genre.

More important, however, is the question of how the defined genre relates to the individual works in the canon. It makes a difference whether a genre is conceived as a category of works or as a cluster of characteristics. I prefer the latter view. When genre is conceived as a category, as it usually is in casual writing, it tends to become nothing more than a pigeonhole, and it gives rise to fruitless questions, such as whether this or that work belongs to it. Such questions, which are

2. Tzvetan Todorov, *The Fantastic: A Structural Approach to a Literary Genre*, trans. Richard Howard (Ithaca, 1975).

especially hostile to borderline works (like the extremely short stories and quasi essays discussed in Section II) as well as to new and original works in general, would not arise at all if genre were not imagined in this way. The question "Is X a short story or is it not?" always seems a bit unreal. It tends to throw the whole concept of genre into disrepute, since when the answer is a clear yes or no, the question seems pointless, and when the answer is uncertain, the question distracts attention from the real interests of the work.

If a genre is a cluster of characteristics, however, borderline and original works can be handled easily and naturally. We can speak of ways in which a work *partakes* of the short story and ways in which it does not, and the discrimination will enhance a fine description of what the work actually does. The genre is an "ingredient" in the work. We can say Text A possesses all the conventions belonging to our definition of the short story, and Text B possesses only some. We can distinguish between stories fully in the tradition of the genre as we have defined it and those which deviate in various ways.

There are other advantages as well. We can discriminate more easily between subgenres if a genre does not have wall-like boundaries. We can multiply genres and subgenres and use this multiplication to enrich our descriptions of individual works, as we see the forces of a number of finely defined genres (clusters of conventions) operating in them. The metaphors themselves ("cluster" and "ingredient" rather than "box") emphasize connections between one work and others; they point out both the work's dependence on the genre and its independence; they reflect the relationship of the genre to its larger context—useful things to remember when we are reading or studying a work. And they will help protect us from the danger of generic criticism, namely, its tendency to quit once it has classified the work.

How does one establish a definition of this sort? If I were to try, my procedure would be as follows. I would begin by recalling the widest possible variety of works called short stories by respectable critics, readers, and writers of all kinds. I would not confine myself to the kinds of stories that began with Irving and Poe, and I would be prepared for one or more subgenres of the modern short story. Therefore my initial list would indeed go back to Boccaccio as well as the Bible and *The Arabian Nights*; it would include Irving and Poe, Maupassant and Chekhov, Joyce and Anderson, and now forgotten figures of the turn of the century like Katherine Fullerton Gerould and Wilbur

Daniel Steele. It would include O. Henry as well as Joyce, the short tales of James, which some critics reject as condensed novels (by what can only be an a priori definition), and in the contemporary scene Jorge Luis Borges, Donald Barthelme, and Robert Coover. I would also allow works generally recognized as borderline, like Anderson's prose poems or Faulkner's "Carcassonne"—though I would perhaps star them or tag my memory not to forget that most critics do indeed consider them borderline.

Ideally, this canon would consist of all such works I know—as well as those I ought to but do not. Ideally, in the collective critical enterprise it would include all works all critics know—which is to say simply that the process of definition operates on the whole field. It would be circumscribed in practice, of course, by our enormous limitations, which is why the process of definition will continue to be a collective and evolving enterprise. In practice my canon would be a sample, chosen to be as representative of the whole as I could make it but always subject to change.

With this sample, I would undertake two operations. First, I would try to identify characteristics applicable to all the works in question, including the borderline cases. This would give me minimal criteria that would constitute necessary outer limits: criteria without which a work could not be considered a short story at all. This first step is admittedly a categorizing rather than clustering move in that it has the power to exclude a work absolutely from the field. It is, however, inductive in that it is based on our experience of what critics have and have not called short stories ("Heart of Darkness" has been responsibly called a short story, but I am not aware of any so-called short story longer than that work). As a preliminary step, it indicates merely that certain items in the cluster of generic traits are generally regarded as essential or indispensable.

Second, and more important, I would search, in as systematic a way as possible consistent with an inductive approach, for common conventions generally at work through the canon. I would not expect all characteristics to be found in all works, but I would look for those that tend to recur, those that constitute what we expect to encounter when we sit down to read what we have been told is a short story.

The operative phrase in such a definition might be "tends to": the short story "tends to" be or do this or that. The properties in such a definition may be numerous. One particular story might display more of these properties than another, and two stories from different traditions might share relatively few. A subgenre would be a more specific cluster, composed of some of the properties of the short story as a whole but not others, and with some peculiar to itself.

Such a definition would be flexible. In combination with definitions of other genres, it would permit easy discussion of hybrid relationships and the respects in which short stories resemble or partake of those other genres. It would help us to recognize the characteristics of particular groups of stories—overlapping and merging subgenres of infinite possibilities. It would be easy to revise, to enlarge and refine, so as to accommodate not only new critical insights into the art but actual changes in it. If developed carefully and thoughtfully, it could incorporate the best observations of all those critics past and present who have been looking for central or diagnostic attributes of the short story.

I am not in a position here to attempt such a definition myself (though this book as a whole might be the beginning of one). But I can suggest roughly its outlines. For outer limits (first of the two steps discussed above), probably we will find no traits more specific than those in Friedman's definition of the short story, "a short fictional narrative in prose," which I will restate here as a prose narrative dealing with a fictional world, never much longer than "Heart of Darkness." Narrative (not drama), fictional world (making no claim to historical or factual truth), and a maximum length do seem, in this superficial view, to be absolute minima that, if ignored, would exclude a work from the genre. I include no lower limit to length since extremely short pieces have been called short stories often enough to suggest that any specific lower limit is a tendency rather than an absolute. The length of "Heart of Darkness" for the upper limit appears arbitrary; I would like to say "not more than a certain length," but what is "certain"? Maybe the upper limit should also be a tendency rather than an absolute; however, we might then lose the length test altogether. We might find ourselves without any criterion at all to exclude a story as long as *War and Peace* (or, if that seems ridiculous, *The Sound and the Fury*), if perchance we should find such a work with most of the other properties of the short story. "Heart of Darkness" approaches the upper limit of any work I have ever heard called a short story and will do until a better measure of maximum length can be found.

As for an orderly, inductive determination of the primary general characteristics of the genre as a whole (second of the steps mentioned above), obviously I can make no attempt to work it out here. As a collective enterprise it is bound to be eclectic, for (as the essays in this book demonstrate) each critic's premises and methods lead to different distinctions, different names for things, different emphases. There is no solution to this as long as critical languages remain diverse. My own sense of the genre—based on what I know, organized by critical distinctions that I find useful, but not tested by any systematic survey of the field—includes such tendencies as the following: 1) The short story tends to be between five hundred words long and the length of Joyce's "The Dead" (we have here a difference between the normal upper limit and an absolute one: "Heart of Darkness" is exceptional). 2) It tends to deal with character and action in its fictional world (this is more specific than my outer-limit designation of, simply, a fictional world). 3) This action tends to be externally simple, with few developed episodes and no subplots or secondary lines of action. Is this too vague? I am trying to avoid the classic "single action," which suggests a false precision. "Externally simple" is a relative term, referring here to the jointedness of the action; comparing the jointedness of James's "The Real Thing" with that of *The Spoils of Poynton* illustrates what I mean here. Obviously it is a loose distinction, but if a joint is a link (or gap) between disparate, fully developed episodes introducing significant new circumstances into the plot structure, any novel tends to have more joints than even a fairly complicated short story like "The Real Thing." I call this simplicity "external" to avoid ruling out internal complexity, which is subtlety, for subtlety is one of the great tendencies of the modern short story.

As I seek further specification, I find myself beginning to make a distinction hitherto avoided between what I want to call the short story and other short prose narrative forms. Differences are appearing between works in the "center" of the canon—by which I mean works whose status as short stories is almost universally accepted—and the controversial cases I mentioned earlier. Accordingly, referring now to prominent but less definitive attributes, I would note that 4) the short story in this sense tends to be more strongly unified than other short prose narrative forms. *Unified* here is a relative term; I mean that the parts tend to function in multiple and economical ways, that there is a minimum of waste and arbitrariness. If one objects to the notion of unity, one could call this quality intensity. It is reflected in the great contemporary interest in closure, and our definition could well incorporate the various methods of closure that John Gerlach finds. This definition could also borrow from Susan Lohafer and find another aspect of this intensity in the effect of sentences in the short story.[3] Intensity is also manifest in 5) the preference in short stories for plots of small magnitude, plots of discovery, static or disclosure plots, Joycean epiphanies, and the like, as well as in 6) the tendency, especially in modern stories, to leave significant things to inference. Intensity is also evident in the affiliation that critics have noted between the short story and the lyric, as well as the emphasis on metaphor and symbolism.

Probably a definition of the short story cannot say much more about the manner of its telling (its narrative principles or point of view) than that it is essentially narrative and does leave things to inference: Hemingway's "The Killers" and "Hills like White Elephants" stretch the boundary to the dramatic as far as it can go. Short stories may be in first person or virtually omniscient; they may be internal or external; they may divide into scenes or be entirely monologue. Nor do I think a general definition can specify a kind of subject matter (neither loneliness nor inner life nor realism nor mystery) or any particular effect. More specialized definitions, however, including definitions by subject matter, by effect, by techniques, and other observable features, can easily be developed for any number of subgenres the critic may wish to distinguish.

We need conscious definitions for critical terms like *short story*, for if we do not have them, we will be groping around with whatever unconscious definitions are in our heads. The latter may not only interfere with our communications with one another but also be full of unnoticed contradictions. Of course, a definition satisfactory to all, agreeable to formalists, structuralists, poststructuralists, feminists, individualists, and all the various critical splinter groups, is impossible. But some definitions are more broadly useful than others. A definition of the genre as a category of works is likely to be a straitjacket or a prison wall. It offers little incentive to extend understanding of the genre beyond whatever understanding produced the definition in the first place. It lacks the flexibility to relate to other definitions, and it stymies critical exchange. A definition of the genre as

3. John Gerlach, *Toward the End: Closure and Structure in the American Short Story* (University, Ala., 1985); Susan Lohafer, *Coming to Terms with the Short Story* (1983; rpr. Baton Rouge, 1985).

a cluster of conventions, however, may facilitate not only discourse among critics but continuing insight into the art itself.

Even the contributors to this book will not agree on a final definition. But we can perhaps agree that certain questions will help clarify our differences. The meaning of "genre" may be one such question.

II

What Is a Short Story?

SUSAN LOHAFER

Introduction to Part II

The question "How do we define the short story?" is as old as
the practice of short story criticism. Nobody seems to have answered it satisfactorily. That much we agree on. Faced with the
problems of definition, we, like researchers in most other fields, have
changed our idea of what knowledge is, and hence our model of
knowledge seeking. The scholars whose essays appear in the previous section debate the means and criteria of knowing what we are
talking about. In the present section, we see how three different short
story critics have solved the problem for themselves.

Charles May is an old hand in the field. Most of us have used his
collection *Short Story Theories* to orient ourselves, to refresh our memories of "what Poe said," to review some of the few articles on theory
published over the years, and to meet a range of authors commenting
on the craft (Frank O'Connor and Eudora Welty, for example). Were
that volume to be updated, it would surely have to include May's own
1984 article "The Nature of Knowledge in Short Fiction." That piece
has become a bull's-eye for both attackers and defenders of the theory
that short stories have an epistemology of their own. May's newest
work, in this section, draws the target in basically the same shape but
brings it closer to contemporary theory.

According to May, the short story is that literary discourse which is
closest to prediscourse story, or, in the words of Ernst Cassirer and
Mircea Eliade, the "mythico-religious Urphenomenon." At a crucial
time and place in literary history—nineteenth-century America—a
development occurred in relations between story and discourse, and
the short story was born. To explain, May draws upon the Russian
Formalists, aligning their meanings for *motivation* and *metaphor* (lin-

guistically based) with and against a broader set of meanings (psychologically based). He then coordinates what can be described in these terms with what can be described in more traditional terms of literary history—Romanticism and realism. Turning to the classic stories of Irving, Poe, Hawthorne, and Melville, May shows us characters caught between "as if" realism and primal story. Author and/or narrator can deal with mythic configurations of meaning only through the figures of discourse itself, through rhetorical structure, metonymy, and metaphor.

Tensions between story and discourse are resolved as discourse. That line of argument is familiar to students of narratology; however, for May, the myth-stuff is never fully acculturated in the discourse, but remains as the problematic, the mysterious. Once again, then, May finds the origin, development, and generic characteristics of the short story centrally, explicitly, and uniquely tied to the hierophanic. This time, however, he demonstrates his thesis in terms of *literariness*, as the Formalists defined it.

Some readers question May's recurrent premise that, by definition, the novel is bound by realistic conventions, the short story by aesthetic ones. Now, reading this current essay, some may object to his elaborate terminology. Does it build new connections or decorate old ones? Must the argument depend on Formalist terms? These are interesting questions, though more likely to occur to critics at large than to short story theorists. For May is *not* a narratologist, exhaustively mapping the features of discourse; instead, he is a voice reminding us that story is primal, at odds with system. Writers like Eudora Welty and Flannery O'Connor have always spoken of the mystery at the center of story. Most critics set it off in brackets. May embraces it. Young scholars in the field must all confront him, one way or another. We are quite sure the debates will continue among readers of this essay.

For John Gerlach, the question "When do we have short story?" is also alluring. For him, though, essential "storyness" is not a matter of origins, of relations to an "Ur" form of story in myth; instead, it is a matter of relations between text and reader—how, or in what terms, the text makes us think. To test the boundary conditions of "storyness," Gerlach looks at samples of narrative in borderline cases: the lyrical essay, the prose poem, the "minimal" story. Reflecting the work of story grammarians like Gerald Prince, Gerlach focuses on event as a sine qua non of story. But story is not short story. For the latter to exist, we must be made to see the significance of the event or events. We must be made to speculate about character in space and time.

In his essay, Gerlach pays attention to the way readers construct what they read—if necessary, building on very slight hints—on the basis of genre expectations. We want meaningful conflict; we have to be able to sense the completed narrative discourse as a "closed" short story. It is in this distinction that Gerlach reminds us of his critical book, *Toward the End: Closure and Structure in the American Short Story*, which appeared in 1985. But Gerlach is also a short story writer. Perhaps that is why he does not say "the *reader* 'writes' the story" (which usually means the reader is not at all like a writer, but very much like a critic). What Gerlach offers us, instead, is a pragmatics of reading modeled on the traditional concerns and questions of the story maker—how to move a character, through fictional space-time, toward significant closure.

To those who are looking for checklists or intricate theory, Gerlach's essay may be too tentative, his examples too limited. Others may believe the argument—that the reader, by deploying conventions of "short-storyness," tests for its presence—yields a foregone conclusion, or a circular one. To some, the alignment of metaphor with the meditative or essayistic, the distinction between lyric and story, may seem to ignore the antinarrative features of some postmodern fiction. Supposing that these objections need countering, readers may need to change their idea of argument itself, for this is an essay in the sense of exercise and exploration. It demonstrates what is meant by "reading-for-short-storyness." In doing so, it confirms what has always been prominent in short story theory—a preference for enactment over abstraction, for relativity over neatness. Throwing the definition of "storyness" back upon real-life experiences of story finding, Gerlach corrects for the artificiality of much reader-response criticism.

Genre study, a field for system builders, can use a little undermining. Who, after all, says what genre is: does the text tell the reader—or is it the other way around? For Douglas Hesse, flip-siding is not a problem in the study of genre. It is a method. Rather than testing the limits of story, he posits a boundary zone in which a class of short stories may be read as personal essays—and vice versa. While he draws on the "grammar" of story (the three-event syntax), he finds it embedded in both stories and essays. Indeed, he has written elsewhere about the story in essays. Is genre, then, simply a matter of proportions, or maybe just of labeling, of editorial fiat and reader compliance?

In his experiments, Hesse identifies a freestanding discourse and reads it twice, once as story, once as essay. The result is not a pragmatics of reading but a pragmatic skepticism about reading conventions and modes of discourse. Perhaps what we are seeing here is a flip side of expertise; Hesse is a specialist not only in genre studies but in the theory and pedagogy of expository writing. He is used to looking at test cases, at writing in which genre is indeterminate. As an expositor himself, he knows how to give himself "assignments," to use strategies (like the inversion of labels) for changing perspectives and finding ideas. That is what Hesse does for other short story critics. He puts genre in relation to the modes of discourse and our tactics for reading them.

It is sometimes hard to tell the difference between serious play and playing at seriousness. Some readers may be confused by the games Hesse plays. Detecting, or suspecting, a core of assumptions about how texts are read, they may not accept a "let's try it" approach. Perhaps it is a matter of becoming acclimated. The influences on Hesse's work are many and varied: rhetorical studies, philosophy of language, reader psychology, and deconstructive criticism, to name but a few. In effect, he is showing us that narrative theory, in today's world, cannot stay within genres.

None of the contributors to this section wrote with its title in mind. "What is a short story?" is an editorial frame, a grouping device. Yet the question is implied in each of the essays. It is a different kind of question for each author: historical-psychological for May (the "what" implying "when" and "why"); typological-organic for Gerlach (the "what" implying "where" and "how"); and philosophical-functional for Hesse (the "what" implying "if" and "wherefore"). What kind of criticism *is* this?

Obviously, short story theory has caught up with the interest in reception theory that underlies reader-response criticism in narrative studies. Even so, students of narratology may well think that, as usual, short story theory is lagging behind the avant-garde and that, as usual, it remains steadfastly nontechnical. That is to say, we have still to take into account the work of the last decade—for example, work derived from Freud through Jacques Derrida and Jacques Lacan, and from feminism, Marxism, and indeed poststructuralist semiotics; we have still to create a lexicon of our own.

Whence comes the pressure to define the genre, and why does the value of these projects lie in their failure to be definitive? Is it simply that the field is relatively new, or is there something about the genre that defies definition? Let us suggest another possibility. Let us look at who has been attracted to short story theory. Although there have been many exceptions, in the main it is *we* who are resistant to definition—to ideological agreement, to alignment in schools, to system building itself. Eclectic in our methods, intermittent in our practice, and scattered geographically, we thrive on the dubious, the mercurial—as does the genre we study.

An absence of agreement, of broadly shared method, however, does not mean we have nothing in common. All three of the critics in this section are interested in what stories do for the reader: metaphorically encode a primary myth (itself, of course, metaphoric); satisfy a paradigm of narrative closure; balance a "verticalized" meaning (expository mode) with a "horizontalized" event-sequence (narrative mode). We also pay attention, historically, typically, to the *writers* of story and their views of form. And, to varying degrees (May least, Hesse most), we write a criticism that tends to be practical, case oriented, eclectic.

By and large, short story critics are skeptics in the marketplace of contemporary theory. Nevertheless, we often apply, and even more often subsume, much that goes on in the arena of narrative theory. So, for example, there is a case to be made for the prevalence, muted but essential, of frame theory in the three essays discussed here. Only once is the term used; never is a name dropped. Yet the effect of all three of these pieces is simply (and fundamentally) to say story is a frame. It is impossible to define the short story genre; one can, however, describe, deploy, and evaluate a variety of frames that allow us to know, and respond to, "short-storyness" in the world. That is what these articles do. There is nothing definitive about them. There is, however, a great deal that is informing and enabling—amid what is provoking, engaging, artful, contradictory, insightful, heuristic.

CHARLES E. MAY

Metaphoric Motivation in Short Fiction: "In the Beginning Was the Story"

The most common critical remark made about the short story is that it began as a unique genre in America in the early nineteenth century, particularly with the works of Irving, Hawthorne, Poe, and Melville. As is the case with many critical judgments about the short story, this clichéd claim has not been examined as it deserves to be. If the short story tradition did indeed begin in the nineteenth century, an understanding of its origins might not only provide a basis for developing a generic history of the form but also clarify some of the conventions of the short story—such as its highly patterned structure, its lack of character development, and its thematic limitations. These conventions have always characterized the form and have perhaps prevented it from taking a respected place in literary history and criticism.

I take the quoted phrase in my title from Isak Dinesen's story "The Cardinal's First Tale," in which Dinesen's raconteur makes a distinction between story and a new art of narration that, for the sake of realism and individual characters, sacrifices the story. Whereas this "novel" literature, the Cardinal says, is a human product, "the divine art is the story. In the beginning was the story." And within our whole universe, he continues, "the story only has authority to answer that cry of heart of its characters, that one cry of heart of each of them: 'Who am I?'" By *story*, I understand the Cardinal to mean that same linguistic phenomenon which Claude Lévi-Strauss refers to as myth—that "part of language where the formula *traduttore, traditore* reaches its lowest truth value," for its "substance does not lie in its style, its original music, or its syntax, but in the *story* which it tells."[1] Conse-

1. Isak Dinesen, *Last Tales* (New York, 1957), 23–26, with the permission of Random House, Inc.; Claude Lévi-Strauss, "The Structural Study of Myth," in Richard and Fer-

quently, I take *story* also to mean that which the Russian Formalists defined as the sequence of actions existing prior to and independent of any particular discursive presentation of the events, and thus to be distinguished from *plot, sujet,* or *discourse.* Thus, I am purposely using *story* in two different but related ways: historically, to suggest the precedence of story as myth over short story as discourse, and theoretically, to make use of the accepted precedence of story as sequence over discourse as rhetorical representation.

I am also using both *metaphor* and *motivation* in two different ways. First, I use *metaphor* to refer to that primary process phenomenon that Freud says gives rise to the mythological conception of the world, that is, "psychology projected to the outer world"—what Ernst Cassirer and Mircea Eliade call the "mythico-religious Urphenomenon," the hierophanic experience or symbolic act by which one projects subjective meaning onto the external world and then makes the "mistake" of responding to it "as if" it were external. Second, I use *metaphor* in the aesthetic sense, the way William H. Gass defines it, as "a kind of model-making—in terms of system, presentation, and inference"— very much like the form and method of fiction itself. Peter Brooks also uses the term this way to suggest that narrative operates as a metaphor by combining differences through perceived similarities and appropriating them to a common plot. Since plot is the "structure of action in closed and legible wholes," says Brooks, "it thus must *use* metaphor as the trope of its achieved interrelations, and it must *be* metaphoric insofar as it is totalizing."[2] Thus I use *metaphor* to refer both to that psychological process that gives rise to myth or story and to that rhetorical process by which story is transformed into discourse.

By *motivation,* I mean our common-sense notion of what makes a person act or, more specifically, what makes a person act in a particular way. Readers, when they respond to characters in a fiction as if they were real, are often concerned with psychological motivation. I am also, however, using the term in the aesthetic sense of the Russian Formalists to designate the network of literary devices that justify the introduction of individual motifs or groups of motifs in a work. Boris Tomashevsky differentiates, for example, between realistic motivation, which justifies the motifs or themes in a work that create the illu-

---

nande DeGeorge (eds.), *The Structuralists from Marx to Lévi-Strauss* (Garden City, N.J., 1972), 173–74, with the permission of Doubleday & Co., Inc.

2. William H. Gass, *Fiction and the Figures of Life* (New York, 1971), 65; Peter Brooks, *Reading for the Plot: Design and Intention in Narrative* (New York, 1984), 91, with the permission of Random House, Inc.

sion of external reality, and artistic motivation, such as defamiliariza-
tion, which justifies the demands of artistic structure.[3] The very notion
of motifs, that is, those perceived similarities which are appropriated
in a plot, arises from the compromise between the demands of realistic illusion and the demands of artistic structure, says Tomashevsky.
Thus, I am using *motivation* to refer to the psychological cause of so-
called real or story events, as well as to refer to the aesthetic cause of
so-called rhetorical or discourse events.

It is helpful to keep both the relationships and the distinctions between these terms in mind. Otherwise, in discussing the origin and
nature of the short story, we may fail to distinguish between the conventions of mythic story and the conventions of the particular discourse known as the short story. We may fail to make clear whether
we take prediscourse sequences to have the properties of real-life
events or to have the properties of mythic story. We may fail to clarify
the difference between myth as the core of prediscourse *fabula* and
metaphor as the core of narrative discourse. And finally, we may attribute the actions of fictional characters to psychological motivation
when the events are more properly caused by story or discourse
motivation.

I agree with Boris Eikhenbaum that the short story is a fundamental, elementary form. Furthermore, I suggest it is a form which has
remained close to the primal narrative that embodies and recapitu-
lates mythic perception, and whose characteristics are compression
rather than expansion and concentration rather than distribution. It is
also a form whose style of presentation is more apt to be Hebraic than
Homeric, as Erich Auerbach defines the terms. Instead of presenting
details in fully externalized form, completely fixed both spatially and
temporally, it makes use only of those details which are necessary for
the purposes of the story, and its progress seems to be directed toward a single goal. Moreover, it is more closely related to the romance
than to the realistic mode, and consequently its characters are more
apt to be, as Northrop Frye suggests, stylized figures rather than "real
people." The short story is, in my opinion, as Frye argues for the romance form, the structural core of all fiction in its derivation from
folktale and myth.[4]

3. Boris Tomashevsky, "Thematics," in Lee T. Lemon and Marion J. Reis (eds. and
trans.), *Russian Formalist Criticism: Four Essays* (Lincoln, Nebr., 1965), 81–85.

4. B. M. Eikhenbaum, *O. Henry and the Theory of the Short Story*, trans. I. R. Titunik
(Ann Arbor, 1968), 4; Erich Auerbach, *Mimesis*, trans. Willard R. Trask (Princeton,

Even though the short story derives directly from this mythic-story and aesthetic-romance tradition, its appearance in the early nine-teenth century was necessarily conditioned by two assumptions about art's relation to reality—the realistic and the Romantic—which com-bined in the short story in a particular way to create a new mode of discourse. These two terms have theoretical value in distinguishing between the tendency toward what Frye calls the representational and the displaced, on the one hand, and the tendency toward the for-mulaic units of myth and metaphor, on the other (that is, between re-ality and imagination). They also have historical value in reminding us that the nineteenth-century short story, although it derived from primitive myth and medieval romance, had to come to terms with the realism of the eighteenth-century novel and the self-conscious imagi-nation of nineteenth-century poetry.[5]

What I wish to argue is that although Irving, Hawthorne, Poe, and Melville began with the conventions of story/myth/romance, they sub-jected those conventions to the demands of *vraisemblance*, or realistic motivation, not as the novel did by the accumulation of metonymic detail and the development of the self through time but rather as the Romantic poets did, by means of metaphoric projection and hiero-phanic revelation. The early short story writers followed the impulse of the Romantic poets to demythologize the old ballads and folktales and remythologize them by presenting them as basic psychic pro-cesses. The ballad story, the legend, and the romance, which had pre-viously existed as received story, became infused with the subjectivity of the poet or the teller and were given a metaphoric structure. Whereas in Romantic poetry the lyrical element was dominant, in the short story, the lyrical, to use Georg Lukacs' phrase, was subsumed behind the hard outlines of the event.

I wish to consider the four most representative and familiar stories of Irving, Hawthorne, Poe, and Melville—"The Legend of Sleepy Hollow," "Young Goodman Brown," "The Fall of the House of Usher," and "Bartleby the Scrivener"—to show that what makes the stories seem to constitute a "new" genre is their self-conscious combination of the conventions of the realistic and romance forms. Basically, in the short story the demands of realism compel a transition from charac-

---

1953), 6–11; Northrop Frye, *Anatomy of Criticism* (1957; rpr. Princeton, 1973), 395, and *The Secular Scripture* (Cambridge, Mass., 1976), 15.

5. Frye, *Secular Scripture,* 37.

ters being motivated by their function in the story to characters being motivated by metaphoric projection. Moreover, I wish to demonstrate that the interaction of these aesthetic demands becomes thematized within the four stories themselves. The combination of romance and realistic conventions creates fundamental moral implications and thematic issues in the short story that have characterized the tradition up to the present.

Although the folk figures of Irving, the allegorical figures of Hawthorne, the unitary figures of Poe, and the symbolic figures of Melville exist more as functions of the story than as problematical characters in an "as if" existentially real world, nevertheless they differ from characters in the completely function-bound tales that existed before them in that such figures as Ichabod Crane, Young Goodman Brown, Roderick Usher, and Bartleby seem to exist both as real people in a real world and as representative figures manipulated for the purposes of the story. In many contemporary, self-reflexive short stories, this background aesthetic tension is foregrounded so that the conflict between fiction and reality becomes the self-conscious conflict of the characters. Characters become inextricably enmeshed in their own dual fiction-reality status; the two realms entangle to suggest that all existential dilemmas are fictional, just as all fictional dilemmas are existential.

In the short story form, this tension between the demands of the aesthetic and the demands of verisimilitude becomes more crucial than in the novel, both because the story's shortness demands an aesthetic rather than a natural or essential form and because the short story remains closer to its ancestry in mythic story structure than the novel does. In the short story, a fictional character may seem to act according to the conventions of verisimilitude and plausibility; however, since the shortness of the form prohibits the realistic presentation of character by extensive metonymic detail, and since the history of the short tale is one in which a character confronts a crucial event or crisis rather than develops over time, the very form and tradition of short fiction militate strongly against the central conventions of realism.

Characters in short fiction, to use Frye's terms, are both social personae in a realistic fiction and symbolic projections in a romance fiction. The difference between characters in romance and characters in the nineteenth-century short story is that whereas characters in the old romance form act "as if" driven by an obsession, according to

Angus Fletcher's helpful definition, characters in the short story are driven by a realistic, albeit mysteriously motivated, psychological obsession, as they are in "The Fall of the House of Usher" and "Bartleby the Scrivener," or else they seem propelled forward by the demands of the prediscourse story from which they have been displaced, as they are in "The Legend of Sleepy Hollow" and "Young Goodman Brown." By means of *vraisemblance*, as Tzvetan Todorov defines it, the work, however, attempts to make us believe it conforms to reality rather than to its own laws, even as the mythic and aesthetic laws of the story drive the characters relentlessly toward the end.[6]

If, however, a fictional character acts on the principles of story and of discourse—that is, acts as if he were indeed a fictional character rather than an "as if" real character, acts according to the demands of story and of metaphor, but does so within the simultaneous similitude of a real world—the character becomes transformed into metaphor in the process of the story, becomes caught in the discourse of his own obsessive metaphoric making. It is my view that the short story as a genre originates in the nineteenth century in just this way— this is the process whereby both realistic motivation and romantic projection transform the old romance story into the new short story discourse.

A distinction can be made between "The Legend of Sleepy Hollow" and "Young Goodman Brown" on the one hand, and "The Fall of the House of Usher" and "Bartleby the Scrivener" on the other. The structure of the first two results from the self-conscious interrelation between techniques of verisimilitude and the stuff of the old projective or romance legend, whereas the structure of the second two depends on the interaction between a character metaphorically transformed by his obsession and a realistic character who unsuccessfully tries to recuperate the metaphoric figure. What the narrators of these last two fail to do within story, they succeed in doing in discourse. "The Legend of Sleepy Hollow" and "Young Goodman Brown" focus on characters caught within the primary process story realm, whereas in "The Fall of the House of Usher" and "Bartleby the Scrivener," characters have transformed themselves into aesthetic objects by means of metaphoric projection. Although it may be too neat to suggest such a development, it could be said that the shift from the

6. Angus Fletcher, *Allegory* (Ithaca, 1964), 40; Tzvetan Todorov, "Introduction," *Communications*, XI (1968), 2–3.

first two stories to the second two is the shift from story motivation to metaphoric motivation.

"The Legend of Sleepy Hollow" begins with the conventions of realism, but as the narrator takes pains to be "precise and authentic" in giving the events a specific locale, the place of the short story immediately becomes transformed into myth. Although Sleepy Hollow is a "real" place, it is also the place of legend and myth, the place of story itself. Not only does the area abound with tales and superstitions, but a "dreamy influence . . . pervades the very atmosphere," and the people seem under some spell that makes them believe marvelous things.

Ichabod Crane enters this story realm from the practical Yankee world of Connecticut, filled with the everyday ambitions of economic reality. However, the most emphasized aspect of Ichabod's personality is his appetite—an appetite for the physical and, even more important, for the marvelous. No tale is too monstrous for his capacious swallow; and his powers of digesting these stories are equally extraordinary. Because of the influence of Cotton Mather, however, Ichabod differs from the inhabitants of Sleepy Hollow in that, whereas they respond to story as story, he responds to story as reality.

At the end of "The Legend of Sleepy Hollow," although we have a plausible explanation for Ichabod's departure, we also have a story explanation more in keeping with the atmosphere of the area and the ancestry of the tale. And indeed Ichabod has become the stuff of story—the subject of a favorite tale told round the winter evening fire. Moreover, there is one particular and crucial detail in the story suggesting that "The Legend of Sleepy Hollow" is a compromise between realistic and romance form: the fact that there are two different motivations for Ichabod's departure—the confrontation with the headless horseman, which is the emphasized climax of the story, and the tête-à-tête with Katrina, which, in keeping with the realistic convention of a limited point of view, is not described at all. If we consider only the realistic motivation of the story, Katrina's turning Ichabod away would be sufficient to dismiss the interloper Ichabod from Sleepy Hollow and would therefore make the arrival of the headless horseman unnecessary. However, because "The Legend of Sleepy Hollow," although it is realistically motivated to embody a social theme, is really about the triumph of the story world over that of the practical, it must be the metaphoric motivation that drives Ichabod away. Ichabod, because of his ability to swallow and digest story and then project story reality onto the external world, is transformed into the stuff of story by the very process of the discourse itself.

Whereas "The Legend of Sleepy Hollow" derives from the folktale tradition, "Young Goodman Brown" derives from the allegorical tradition. The tale, however, is not pure allegory, for the event that dominates it—Brown's journey into the forest—seems to be both realistically motivated and story motivated at once. The discourse is thus a compromise between these two kinds of motivation. Moreover, Brown himself seems to be both a character typical of allegory, that is, a psychologized archetype, and an "as if" character who has his own psychological makeup.

The compromise is established when Brown says he must go into the forest this one night of all nights in the year. Since there is no realistic motivation for Brown's journey into the forest, no indication that it is a social custom for everyone to make this journey in his turn, the cause of the journey must be ritual or legend; the journey must be motivated by the nature of the underlying allegorical story from which this particular discourse derives. Brown, however, does not act like an allegorical figure, for he "has scruples" about his "present evil purpose" in the forest and even considers turning back. An allegorical figure cannot challenge the code-bound structure of the allegory itself; he can only follow its preestablished demands. Moreover, that the devil resembles Brown and that his words seem to spring from Brown himself suggest the latter is a realistic figure able to create mental projections, not an allegorical projection himself.

The allegory-realism compromise seems to turn primarily on the most emphatic allegorical reference in the story—the name of Faith. Although the narrator tells us that Faith is "aptly named," which might suggest the quality of being faithful rather than an allegorical embodiment of Brown's own faith, each time her name is invoked in the story, it is a crucial turning point in the story's status as either allegory or realism or both. When Brown cries out, "With heaven above and Faith below, I will stand firm against the devil," he hears Faith's voice in the forest; when he cries out "Faith!" and the forest echoes him, the ribbon comes floating down. When he cries, "My Faith is gone. . . . There is no good on earth; and sin is but a name," he begins his mad dash through the forest. Finally, however, when he speaks to Faith directly, telling her to look up to heaven and resist the wicked one, the allegorical realm of the story is terminated, and Brown is once more back in everyday reality—prompting the narrator to ask the self-reflexive question, "Had Goodman Brown fallen asleep in the forest and only dreamed a wild dream of a witch-meeting?" Just as Ichabod Crane enters into a realm of story to become a fictional character, so too does Goodman Brown enter into an allegorical realm, which transforms him into the archetypal Puritan.

By making "The Fall of the House of Usher" and "Bartleby the Scrivener" the recollections of first-person narrators, Poe and Melville make the combination of romance/story conventions and the rules of realism even more explicit. Both Usher and Bartleby seem to be more functions of the story than "as if" real characters. Our basic question about both is, what is the *matter* with them? But indeed they have no matter. One narrator says he cannot connect Usher's expression with any idea of simple humanity; the other says there is nothing ordinarily human about Bartleby. One narrator continually reiterates his puzzlement and his failure to understand Usher; the other narrator continually urges Bartleby to follow the rules of common sense and common usage. Instead of being caught within legend or allegory, as are Ichabod and Brown, both Usher and Bartleby are caught within that primary process phenomenon whereby they cannot distinguish between the map and the territory. They both make the metaphoric mistake of projecting their own subjectivity onto the external world and then responding to it as if it were external.

In "The Fall of the House of Usher," this mistake centers on Usher as the ultimate Romantic artist who desires to cut himself off from external reality and live within the realm of pure imagination, although he fears the loss of self such an ultimate gesture would inevitably entail. His belief that the house has sentience because of the particular organization of its parts is a metaphor for the Romantic aesthetic of organic unity. In a sense, Usher *does* live within the artwork, which is both the house and the obsession he has created. Whereas the *fabula* of "The Fall of the House of Usher" is indeed Usher's aesthetic obsession, the discourse is the teller's account of the transformation of Usher into a figure of imagination who ultimately vanishes into pure subjectivity.

In "Bartleby the Scrivener," instead of a realistic character entering into the aesthetic realm of primary process, as is the case in Poe's tale, the movement is reversed, and an obsessed aesthetic figure invades the realm of secondary process reality, realistically represented as the practical and prudent world of the law office on Wall Street. We can no more ask what is the matter with Bartleby than we can of Usher.

We cannot know what he is thinking, for he is thinking nothing; he is simply the embodiment of his own obsession. For Bartleby, there is no distinction between the wall as signifier and the wall as signified; the wall *is* the reason he "prefers not to." The only answer to the question of what the wall is and what it signifies is, of course, ironically, "nothing." The wall is a dead letter to Bartleby, just as Bartleby himself becomes a dead letter to the narrator. Again, whereas the *fabula* here is Bartleby's obsession, the discourse is the narrator's impossible attempt to recuperate a metaphoric figure into the realm of secondary process thinking.

The recollection of the "story" of Usher and Bartleby by the two narrators makes possible in discourse what was not possible in the story itself. Although the story focuses on the narrators trying to understand primary process figures by secondary process means, the discourse understands the figures in the only possible way to understand them—by rhetorical structure and by metaphor. What is realistic about such early short stories as "The Fall of the House of Usher" and "Bartleby the Scrivener" is what Erich Heller says is new about nineteenth-century realism generally, that is, "the passion for understanding, the desire for rational appropriation, the driving force toward the expropriation of the mystery."[7] These two stories are dramatizations of just that effort at appropriation.

The problem is that the tellers, like Coleridge's Ancient Mariner at the beginning of the nineteenth century and Conrad's Marlow at the end, can only tell the story. They are unable to reduce it to conceptual content; however, they can tell the story in such a way that makes it different from the mere story events—by narrating a story that itself is about a character caught by the demands of discourse. The short story is thus transformed into a tissue of repetitions, parallels, and metaphoric motifs—that is to say, paradigmatic structure emerges out of the mere syntagmatic succession or sequence of events because the world of the story itself is seemingly determined by the obsession of the central, function-bound character.

Mimetic characters, such as the narrators in these two stories, do not make a story realistic if the situations they confront evade their power to incorporate them within the expectations of the familiar, natural world. The realistic impulse creates a realistic work only when

7. Erich Heller, "The Realistic Fallacy," in George J. Becker (ed.), *Documents of Modern Literary Realism* (Princeton, 1963), 596.

the impulse succeeds in convincing the reader that the phenomenon described has been, or can be, naturally, socially, or psychologically incorporated. If the mystery is solved by placing the phenomena within the framework of the natural, the social, or the psychological, then the realistic succeeds. However, if the knowledge arrived at is inchoate, metaphysical, and aesthetic (that is, not satisfactorily solved by the natural, social, or psychological), the only resolution possible is an aesthetic one.

Jonathan Culler has argued generally, as I am arguing particularly here, that although we usually think of story as being prior to discourse, there are times when narratives themselves question or subvert this priority by presenting events, not as givens, but "as the products of discursive forces or requirements." Culler says, for example, that although Oedipus' guilt is determined by a past event not yet revealed, Oedipus acts in response to the demands of the play's signification. Although Culler says these two logics cannot be synthesized since each works to the exclusion of the other, I agree with Peter Brooks that what Culler describes is the mix between the metaphoric and the metonymic that constitutes the very nature of narrative.[8] Because of its self-conscious attempt to combine the metaphoric structure of the old romance with the metonymic structure of the new realism, this "double logic" becomes particularly crucial in the development of the short story.

The thematized interrelationship between metonymic "as if" real characters and metaphoric "mythic" reality has characterized the development of the short story up to the present. To mention only a few examples, in Stephen Crane's "The Blue Hotel" a character becomes so convinced that the world he has entered is the world of pulp westerns that he transforms that world into the very fictional reality he most feared; in Sherwood Anderson's "Death in the Woods," the narrator creates a discourse about a stereotyped figure which transforms her into an archetypal figure; in Bernard Malamud's "The Magic Barrel," a young rabbi creates and confronts a mysterious psychologized projection of his own deepest need; in Raymond Carver's "Why Don't You Dance?" an unnamed character metaphorically externalizes his failed marriage on the front lawn and then silently watches a young couple repeat that failure in "play."

8. Jonathan Culler, *The Pursuit of Signs* (Ithaca, 1981), 175; Brooks, *Reading for the Plot*, 29.

The theme and technique of the short story perhaps have always focused on the power of metaphor and story itself to answer that cry of heart of each of its characters, *"Who am I?"* As opposed to the novel, the short story says one does not find the answer to that question in a similitude of the real world, but rather by being caught up within the role that the story demands and being therefore metaphorically transformed—so that one finds oneself by losing oneself. "The divine art is the story. In the beginning was the story."

JOHN GERLACH

The Margins of Narrative: The Very Short Story, the Prose Poem, and the Lyric

Demarcations between modes of narrative, and between genres themselves, are not firm. We may even take pleasure in fluidity, enjoying the journey through a catalog of epigraphs, an essay on fast fish and loose fish, a sermon on woe and delight, soliloquies with stage directions, inserted reports from passing ships, and a three-day chase after the Big White One. We are willing to call all that narrative, maybe even a novel. At the other end of the scale, though, when we take out the microscope, the challenge is different. When do we finally reach the minimum unit of story, that is, a freestanding, complete, and satisfying prose fiction? Might a story even become something else—a poem, for instance? If that is possible, do such discriminations ultimately matter? Are we likely to look at a work differently if it is, or is not, a story?

Contemporary narrative theory has considered the question of minimum units of narrative. Roland Barthes believes such units are even smaller than a sentence and that they are subsumed within larger patterns. He does not, though, concern himself with the unity of these larger patterns. Another critic, Helmut Bonheim, divides narrative into four modes within a story (description, report, speech, and commentary) and shows how they can be used to compare stories diachronically and to compare novels with short stories. But he apparently requires no minimal arrangement of these modes to create a story.[1]

1. Roland Barthes, "Introduction to the Structural Analysis of Narratives," in *Image—Music—Text*, trans. Stephen Heath (New York, 1977), 91, 115–16; Helmut Bonheim, *The Narrative Modes: Techniques of the Short Story* (Cambridge, U.K., 1982).

Gerald Prince, on the other hand, does identify a minimal unit of narration; it is defined by a time differential within a sequence of events. The sentence "John ate and Mary ate" is a mere statement, but "John ate and Mary ate, then Bill ate," because of the element of separation in time, is in his terms narration.[2] Near the end of *Narratology*, Prince introduces the concept of "narrativity," characterized by such features as concreteness, definite rather than probable location in time, and humanized significance, a concept that proves helpful in making the distinction between mere narrative and story. Examples throughout his book, however, are frequently his own creations; we could more instructively distinguish story from narrative by looking at actual examples and by considering boundaries between related genres.

Conventional wisdom suggests that not every narrated or recounted event is a story proper. Consider as the first piece of evidence an essay of about 850 words by Kristin Knutson. She begins with a description of her father's search for ice to skate on and the way children from her town gather behind him, then focuses on a smaller excursion, just her father, her brother, and herself. They discover a pond where the ice is "so perfectly clearly frozen that it could hardly be seen at all." The three of them watch the fish, then skate and imagine how they must in turn have looked to the fish below. She returns to the pond later but never to ice so clear, and so she searches still: "To see the world like that . . . through that clear suspended vision, nothing hidden, clouded, or malformed in between—that . . . would be heaven enough!"[3]

This is narrative, but it is a story only in the loose sense of being an account of someone's experience, a description that would apply as well to a lyric poem. Indeed, the impulse here seems primarily lyric. Although the account begins with Knutson's father, he is demoted to an adjunct, another looker, and the true focus is on the pond and its symbolic significance. There is conflict: the speaker would like to regain that sense of vision, of oneness and interchange with objects, that is the traditional desire of the Romantic poet but cannot, so she resorts to the poet's strategy, understanding event as metaphor. The conflict is not between characters; characters are defined as viewers,

2. Gerald Prince, *Narratology: The Form and Functioning of Narrative* (Berlin, 1982), 64, with the permission of Mouton de Gruyter, a division of Walter de Gruyter & Co.

3. Kristin Knutson, "In Search of a Clear View," *The Christian Science Monitor*, January 4, 1979, p. 20.

and the conflict, if we can say one exists, is in the speaker. Essays are, of course, not fiction, and on those grounds alone we might disqualify them from consideration, but even if they were fiction, we would still note differences of the kind observed above.

If we are to proceed inductively, we should consider a work that does seem to have the impact of a story. The minimum length is certainly below the 850 words of Knutson's essay. Scott Sanders averages about 400 words for many of the stories in *Wilderness Plots*. Enrique Anderson Imbert, in "Taboo," used just 32, or more precisely in the Spanish, 31. Here is the English version of "Taboo":

> His guardian angel whispered to Fabian, behind his shoulder:
> "Careful, Fabian! It is decreed that you will die the minute you pronounce the word *doyen*."
> "Doyen?" asks Fabian, intrigued.
> And he dies.[4]

We might wish to deny "Taboo" the status of story and call it a joke. Most readers will, after all, laugh before wondering whether it *is* a story. But "Taboo" feels, to some extent, like a story. It has the voltage of a story; a whisper promptly leads to death. It recites an event, a rather striking one. And it is certainly complete. Stories tend to tie things up, to dispose of matters; Fabian is certainly disposed of.

Completion itself does not of course make a story. Essays are complete; poems are complete. And even though "Taboo" describes an event, is the description of an event the only requisite for the sense of story? Isn't looking at fish through ice also an event? Why does recounting that event not create a story proper?

If we do wish to continue considering "Taboo" a story, it seems easier to talk about conventional elements of fiction that are missing from "Taboo" than what is present. We have only the suggestion of spatiality (we know the angel is positioned behind Fabian's shoulder). We know little about Fabian, though he has at least an uncommon name. He is not Carlos or Juan, but Fabian. We know he dies, but do not witness his death throes. We have conflict of a sort, but the true antagonist, God, does not appear. Since Fabian had no chance against his opponent, we might wonder whether this was really a battle, a contest at all. Without an honorable conflict we may begin to doubt if

4. Enrique Anderson Imbert, "Taboo," in *The Other Side of the Mirror*, trans. Isabel Reade (Carbondale, Ill., 1966), 69, with the permission of Southern Illinois University Press.

there really is a story, if there has been time to tie things up, let alone to develop them.

We would best proceed with a less disputable example of a story, one with the elements "Taboo" seems to lack. Scott Sanders' "The Crime of Poverty," from *Wilderness Plots*, will serve well:

Unlike the cells for murderers, the cells for debtors were provided with iron-barred windows. Through his grating Gallipolis Jennings could watch the goings-on of his fellow citizens who were fortunate enough not to have been sullied by the crime of poverty. His own poverty had been honestly arrived at, with the benefit of every calamity you would care to mention, including a mud slide and a bank failure. His family boarded with neighbors while he studied the grain in the timbers in his cell.

Creditors occasionally stopped by to chat with him on the subject of money. But how was a man to conjure silver coins out of thin air? First he borrowed a spinning wheel from the sheriff's wife, thinking he could buy his way out of debt with yarn. But even after his fingers grew deft at the work, he calculated he would still need upwards of nine years of spinning to clear himself. Next he tried candle making, and that cut the time down to seven years. Clearly he would have to find work outside, or he would turn to mold before paying his debts.

He signed his plow, wagon, and horses over to the creditors as security, for which sacrifice he was allowed to spend the daylight hours outside jail. But he was never allowed to wander farther than four hundred and forty yards in any direction from his cell. Even at that he was lucky, the sheriff explained, because back in 1799 the boundary had been set at only two hundred yards. "That's a piece of English law I could live without," Jennings replied. "Just see you obey it," said the sheriff.

Four hundred and ten yards from the jail was a saddlemaker who agreed to hire Jennings—but at a bargain wage, in view of his criminal status. In 1805 the prison bounds were reduced by federal statute to four hundred yards. So Jennings had to hunt a closer job. His wife and children moved back to Rhode Island. His horses aged in the paddocks of his creditors.

He learned blacksmithing, laboring the first six months without pay on account of his inexperience. When the blacksmith moved his shop to a brick building some five hundred yards from the jail, beyond the legal limit, Gallipolis Jennings took advantage of a moonless night to quit Ohio altogether, and go see what Indiana had to offer in the way of employment.[5]

5. Scott R. Sanders, "The Crime of Poverty," in *Wilderness Plots: Tales About the Settlement of the American Land* (New York, 1983), 36–37, copyright © 1983 by Scott Russell Sanders, reprinted by permission of the author and the author's agent, Virginia Kidd.

Conventional fictional elements implicit in "Taboo" are explicit here. Setting is well defined, initially a cell with "iron-barred windows," later the space within four hundred yards of the jail. We know the time, the early nineteenth century; we know the location, Ohio. We know the character's name, first and last, and it is one even more particular than Fabian's. Perhaps Jennings is from Gallipolis, a city in southern Ohio settled mostly by Frenchmen who wished to remember their origins, or perhaps he has actually been named after the city.

The pattern of conflict is much more clearly established than that in "Taboo." Gallipolis is not someone interrupted by a whisper over his shoulder in some undefined time and place but a man who has committed a specific and definable crime, the crime of poverty. Although the real antagonist is economic and social—the differentials of economic productivity among spinning, candle making, and saddle making—that opponent is at least partially personified in the blacksmith. He does not actively defraud Gallipolis, but he has no scruples about taking advantage of the prisoner's situation. Most significantly, Gallipolis, in his search to free himself, alternately succeeds and fails, approaching his goal while at the same time circumstances push him away. We have, in other words, a plot, and the presence of plot we identify with story.

One more element of "The Crime of Poverty" may shed light on the relation of event to story. Let us suppose that after signing over his property, thus being "allowed to spend the daylight hours outside jail," Gallipolis, instead of attempting various jobs, takes "advantage of a moonless night to quit Ohio altogether." Suppose the story ends there. Most readers would concede that this version is much weaker, and might not be a story at all. Gallipolis would have solved his problem in an insignificant way—a criminal had a chance to flee, and he did. That is an event, but not a significant event; we expect as much from a criminal. The significance of the full version is that the alleged criminal has displayed through his effort and patience more honesty and a truer sense of justice than the unincarcerated righteous. Our perception of his criminality has changed; an action becomes a thematic statement. We could also say that this interpretation reduces to the statement "A criminal had a chance to slip away, and he did," but we would understand "criminal" ironically and the action would have significance, which Gerald Prince calls "point."[6] This added ele-

6. Prince, *Narratology*, 159.

ment, the final fullness that converts closure into completeness, is more than a matter of turning a poor story into a good one. Events require thematic magnitude if they are to create story, and such events must change our perception of character. Plot, however, is not required to establish the sense of story, as we may see by returning to the tale of Fabian.

One of the reasons that "Taboo" seems like a story is that we sense point and can speculate sensibly on questions of character and motive. We must construct a good deal on our own, but the story provokes such construction. It does so just as Sanders' story did, through irony—a guardian angel is supposed to guard, and in this case, he does not. He is either a bumbler who exposes Fabian to danger or, by divine foreknowledge, is part of a plan to eliminate Fabian. In either case, with angels such as this, one hardly needs devils. We may also search for clues to Fabian's character, and all we will find is that he was "intrigued," but we can do a great deal with that word. It suggests something about human nature as opposed to divine sanction. Humans are curious, uncertain, given to investigation. God knows, sets up systems, possibly entraps. One can be done in for a good deal less than eating an apple. But if God entraps, we should be wary of snickering. God always has the last word, so our laughter will be tinged with fear. Similarly, we may ponder the significance of the word *doyen*. Why has God chosen this particular word for Fabian? Is the "senior member of any organization" such a reprehensible concept? Does the word suggest God himself, the most senior member of all, he who does not want his name spoken?

Lest I go too far with a translation, I should note that the Spanish for the first word we have focused on, *intrigued*, is *azorado*, which translates more precisely as "frightened" or "terrified." This is quite a different concept, and one that would change our interpretation, but not one that would change our perception of "storyness." In the same way, in the Spanish original the word that tricks Fabian is not *doyen* but *zangolotino*, which means something like "mother's darling." If we reinterpret his disaster in that light, we might wonder whether Fabian was a bit of a mother's darling and was being punished for priding himself on that. Or perhaps the specific forbidden word is utterly meaningless, and the essence is the arbitrariness of the selection. God will decide what words we are to avoid, for his own good reasons.

In English or in Spanish, we do fill in. And that may be the key to something else essential: a story is an invitation to construct explanations, explanations about causality, connections, motives. When we feel we are constructing them significantly (that is, with point, the other essential element), we sense story. "Taboo" does not provide answers to questions it poses, but the futility of asking, and the comic conjunction of God's absolute power and his bureaucratic arbitrariness, present us with an ultimate puzzle: in this case it is impossible to distinguish between absolute power and absolute foolishness. Perhaps that is why we laugh: we are confronted with ultimate impenetrability, with a word game that invites, then frustrates story possibilities and in that very frustration creates a story. It makes us think of people, who they are and what they do, people in time and space. Fabian never had a chance, but most of us think he should have. There is no shifting advance and retreat toward a goal that characterizes a plot in this story, but there is advance and retreat in the reader's resolution of theme. Brief as "Taboo" is, it exhibits point, the significance taken on by an event that has become a theme through paradox. In Prince's words, a narrative with full narrativity would "represent, or illustrate, or explain, something which is unusual and problematic, something which is (made) relevant for and matters to its receiver: the illocutionary force of a narrative should be equivalent to that of a series of exclamatory (and not merely informative) assertions about events in time."[7] Story proper is more accurately defined by speculations it encourages on the part of the reader than by what actually occurs in the reported event. Plot is not necessary, nor is a fleshed-out sense of character and setting, as long as the reader is prodded to think in terms of character and motive.

We ought to turn now to the question of whether stories can ever become poems. Prose poems provide a good starting point, since they present themselves in a form visually indistinguishable from that of a very short story. Even though they resemble stories, they are commonly regarded as the province of the poet. As Stephen Fredman has recently argued, prose poems "evidence a fascination with language (through puns, rhyme, repetition, elision, disjunction, excessive troping, and subtle foregrounding of diction) that interferes with the progression of story or idea, while at the same time inviting and examining the 'prose' realms of fact and reclaiming for poetry the domain of truth."[8] We may test these claims by looking at "The Dachau Shoe," by the poet W. S. Merwin.

7. *Ibid.*

8. Stephen Fredman, *Poet's Prose: The Crisis in American Verse* (New York, 1983), with the permission of Cambridge University Press. See also Michael Benedikt, *The*

My cousin Gene (he's really only a second cousin) has a shoe he picked up in Dachau. It's a pretty worn-out shoe. It wasn't top quality in the first place, he explained. The sole is cracked clear across and has pulled loose from the upper on both sides, and the upper is split at the ball of the foot. There's no lace and there's no heel.

He explained he didn't steal it because it must have belonged to a Jew who was dead. He explained that he wanted some little thing. He explained that the Russians looted everything. They just took anything. He explained that it wasn't top quality to begin with. He explained that the guards or the kapos would have taken it if it had been any good. He explained that he was lucky to have got anything. He explained that everybody was picking up something. A lot of guys wanted flags or daggers or medals or things like that, but that kind of thing didn't appeal to him so much. He kept it on the mantelpiece for a while but he explained that it wasn't a trophy.

He explained that it was no use being vindictive. He explained that he wasn't. Nobody's perfect. Actually we share a German grandfather. But he explained that this was the reason why we had to fight this war. What happened at Dachau was a crime that could not be allowed to pass. But he explained that we could not really do anything to stop it while the war was going on because we had to win the war first. He explained that we couldn't always do just what we would have liked to do. He explained that the Russians killed a lot of Jews too. After a couple of years he put the shoe away in a drawer. He explained that the dust collected in it.

Now he has it down in the cellar in a box. He explains that the central heating makes it crack worse. He'll show it to you, though, any time you ask. He explains how it looks. He explains how it's hard to take it in, even for him. He explains how it was raining, and there weren't many things left when he got there. He explains how there wasn't anything of value and you didn't want to get caught taking anything of that kind, even if there had been. He explains how everything inside smelled. He explains how it was just laying out in the mud, probably right where it had come off. He explains that he ought to keep it. A thing like that.

You really ought to go and see it. He'll show it to you. All you really have to do is ask. It's not that it's really a very interesting shoe when you come right down to it but you learn a lot from his explanations.[9]

Prose Poem: An International Anthology (New York, 1976), 47; and for a bibliography on items about prose poems, see Donald Wesling, *The New Poetries: Poetic Form Since Coleridge and Wordsworth* (Lewisburg, Pa., 1985), 217.

9. W. S. Merwin, "The Dachau Shoe," in *The Miner's Pale Children* (New York, 1970), 243–44, copyright © 1970 by W. S. Merwin, reprinted with the permission of Atheneum Publishers, an imprint of Macmillan Publishing Company, and Harold Ober Associates Incorporated.

If story were merely a matter of establishing character and setting, "The Dachau Shoe" would qualify, for it seems more solidly defined than "Taboo." We know the narrator has been in Gene's house, and that establishes space, though the narrator is of course not speaking from that space. We can sense closure, for Gene returns in the fourth paragraph to the circumstances of finding the shoe. We can sense point in Gene's attitude toward the shoe. Taking the shoe, he maintains, was not stealing, and the shoe is not a trophy—both indications either that Gene suffers from guilt, suspecting he has stolen, has in fact taken a trophy, or that he disputes the tendency of those who come to the house to think of the shoe as a trophy. A more objective justification for his defense could be proposed: "what happened at Dachau was a crime that could not be allowed to pass"; to take nothing at all for remembrance would be to act as if nothing had happened. The act of taking the shoe, and thinking about it, is an act with thematic import, and our effort to interpret that significance intensifies the sense of point.

But it is still difficult to see "The Dachau Shoe" as a story proper, for the shoe seems to become the central object, much as the pond and ice were central to the ice-skating essay. There is an embedded event, the taking of the shoe, and we could even say that talking about the shoe is also an event, but that is only to twist further the meaning of event. An event considered, meditated upon, loses some of its status as pure event. Furthermore, the repetition of "he explained" or "he explains," occurring twenty-four times, mostly in initial position, foregrounds the discourse itself, calling attention to the signifier rather than the signified, a trait we associate with poetry. What this prose poem does not do, and what lyric poetry—I am not speaking of poetry in its clear narrative forms such as the ballad—does not do, is encourage us to extend our imagination along the lines of characters and conflict, space and time.

Lyrics may appear to encourage such extensions but in fact constrain them. Consider three brief examples from Yeats, Keats, and Wordsworth. Yeats in "Lapis Lazuli" gives us two Chinamen in a place filled with imaginary sense details—a bird flies overhead, the Chinamen climb up a slope (which certainly implies a sense of space and depth), and plum or cherry branch will "doubtless" sweeten a hut they might reach—but Yeats set the Chinamen in motion only to leave them sitting and staring with "glittering eyes." These are men carved into lapis lazuli; they are illustrations of an argument, proof against assertions by "hysterical women" that artists have no reason to be gay. We are meant to imagine them in space and to accept them as characters in that sense, but we are not encouraged to imagine them, to use the terms of another poem by Yeats, among those who are begotten, born, and die.

The device of putting characters into works of art is a common poetic means of evoking a character while preventing its extension. Keats in "Ode on a Grecian Urn" depicts a fair youth beneath a tree and a mysterious priest leading a heifer toward a sacrifice. Then we are teased into contemplation of a "little town by river or sea shore," but these details are used only to contrast with a statement about the condition of mortality, about those outside the poem who *are* fated to the round of begetting and death. So, too, in Wordsworth's "Solitary Reaper" the speaker's thoughts may range from Arabia to the Hebrides to find equivalents for what he hears, but the singer, the reaper, sings on, frozen in a timeless moment. However sensually evoked, such figures are not to be taken as people in a narrative, people to whom things happen under the pressure of time.

Robert Browning's "My Last Duchess," a dramatic monologue, presents a more ambiguous case. The former duchess is presented as a portrait, but we may rather easily detach her from it, encouraged as we are to consider her as someone whose "looks went everywhere," who would take boughs broken for her, who would ride a white mule around the terrace. We want to take her out of the portrait and give her continuity. We want, in other words, to put her in a story and create time and space for her. But part of the impact of the poem ultimately derives from our inability to do so. In "final perspective," to use the words of Robert Langbaum, "she takes her place as one of a line of objects in an art collection; her sad story becomes the *cicerone*'s anecdote lending piquancy to the portrait. The duke has taken from her what he wants, her beauty, and thrown the life away; and we watch with awe as he proceeds to take what he wants from the envoy and by implication from the new duchess."[10] "My Last Duchess" is a poem that approaches story specifically to make the reader realize that the duchess's life cannot be articulated sequentially, that her past is irrevocable; and blockage in this instance is part of what makes the poem work as a poem. Many other poems do build stories, and are no less poems for doing so, but then they cease to become lyrics.

In this respect "The Dachau Shoe" has an ambiguous status. If we

10. Robert Langbaum, *The Poetry of Experience: The Dramatic Monologue in Modern Literary Tradition* (Rev. ed.; New York, 1985), 84.

wish to read it as a revelation of Gene's character, as if it were a psychological investigation of a man who had been to Dachau, then we might as well call it a story, for Gene, the character, would be the focus of our interest. I do not think Merwin wants to center our attention on him, and that is why he has added the final paragraph, inviting the reader into the action. The layers of telling—Gene trying to make sense of the shoe, and the narrator trying to make sense of Gene's telling, and then the narrator explicitly inviting the reader to go himself and "learn"—serve to draw attention more to theme than to character. We are not really being asked to look at Gene as a character with a problem but, rather, through the layering are asked what we would do with the problem if we were the narrator or Gene. The line between story and poem is, then, a rather thin one: if we take a character as reflector upon an idea, we have a poem; if we take him as a character who happens to be thinking, we have a story.

The circuit may of course flow the other way—metaphor, so often at the center of lyric, particularly the Romantic lyric, can work its way into prose. Gallipolis fears he might turn to mold before paying his debts, an image central to the story. It represents a fear of loss of self into object, and for the reader can be taken as a fear of loss of status of character in narrative into decoration, idea, metaphor. Gallipolis defies becoming mold and wishes to remain a person, free to choose, act, move. In the presence of narrative, aware of a strong pattern of conflict and extendable space, we do not focus on metaphor as an end in itself. And so when Gallipolis heads off to "see what Indiana has to offer in the way of employment," he heads into an imaginative space quite different from the little town not on the Grecian urn. The difference is not that we know there is a real Indiana. Because we believe we are reading a story, we accept the illusion of a person who has the right to walk beyond our field of vision into a life of his own.

Length and fictionality are not sufficient in themselves to imply story. Hawthorne's "A Rill from the Town Pump," for example, with its emphasis on stringing together observations under the central illusion of a speaking pump, is not a story but rather a sketch, despite its proximity to true stories within *Twice-Told Tales*. Stories depend not on extensive evocation of space and time but on the illusion in the reader that space and time are the ground upon which the figures of character are conceived. Stories, like all complete, satisfying forms such as essays and poems, exhibit point—point enacted not as the stasis of metaphor or reflection but under the illusion of space and time.

DOUGLAS HESSE

A Boundary Zone: First-Person Short Stories and Narrative Essays

> Just as one of the first things a fiction writer learns is that he needn't actually be writing fiction to write a short story—he can tell his own history or anyone else's as exactly as he remembers it and it will still be "fiction" if it remains primarily a story—an essayist soon discovers that he doesn't have to tell the whole truth and nothing but the truth; he can shape or shave his memories as long as the purpose is served of elucidating a truthful point.
> —EDWARD HOAGLUND

> Narrative becomes a *problem* only when we wish to give to *real* events the *form* of story.
> —HAYDEN WHITE

Consider two venerable pieces, "A Hanging," by George Orwell, and "The Use of Force," by William Carlos Williams. Both are told in the first person, consist entirely of past-tense narratives of a single series of events, cover about the same amount of time, are about the same length. Yet Paul H. Connolly's collection *On Essays* includes the former and *The Norton Anthology of Short Fiction* the latter. Suppose, however, that both collections had been produced by the same publisher in identical formats using the same typeface. Suppose, further, that an inept press operator had confused the keylines so that the pieces appeared in the wrong volumes. Suppose that we had never before read these pieces. Would the transposition strike us as odd?

One of the currently most fashionable pronouncements about genre comes as a shrug: few works, finally, are generically pure. Classifying them is more a matter of specifying which emphases count than positing a set of qualities that exclude all other classifications. A generative set of rules for all possible works acknowledged as being of the same genre cannot be written. Paul Hernadi has stated the paradox precisely with his observation, after Karl Popper, that "things

85

may be similar in *different respects.*" Ludwig Wittgenstein's concept of "family resemblance," which he demonstrated with the impossibility of defining explicitly and eternally the essential qualities of games, exactly delineates the nature of the problem.[1]

Part of what I argue, then—that a precise boundary line between essays and short stories does not exist—varies a familiar theme. Even my proposal that a number of essays and short stories flourish in a sort of boundary zone has been anticipated by Gary Saul Morson's description of "boundary works." In these works, as Morson says, "it is uncertain which of two mutually exclusive sets of conventions governs"; however, I disagree with his assertion that the conventions are altogether exclusive.[2] Beyond a demonstration that such works exist lie two provocative questions: what happens to our readings if we subvert genre labels, and do those labels have inherent or assigned status?

Most short story border wars have been fought with the novel over the Sudetenland of length; critics have led similar skirmishes between the essay and longer prose works. (Mary Louise Pratt, for example, has argued the length issue in reference to the short story, Charles Whitmore in reference to the essay.) Although theorists of both genres regularly make comparisons with poetry, there has been a truce between the short story and essay. Only Johannes Hedberg has directly engaged the matter. He states that essays differ from short stories in that they consist of facts sifted through the author's imagination and have unlimited scope in terms of subject and form.[3] But this conclusion ignores stories which seem to meet both criteria and essays that are unabashedly fictional. Perhaps the "all too obvious" difference between fiction and nonfiction accounts for the critical neglect of this issue. But for the stories and essays with which I am concerned, the distinction is largely unassailable. Their basic characteristics are a first-person narrator, the possibility and *seeming* actuality of a one-to-one correspondence between the words on the page and some actual state of affairs in the world, relative brevity, and the dominance of

1. Paul Hernadi, *Beyond Genre: New Directions in Literary Classification* (Ithaca, 1972), 4; Ludwig Wittgenstein, *Philosophical Investigations*, trans. G. E. M. Anscombe (New York, 1953), 66–71.

2. Gary Saul Morson, *The Boundaries of Genre* (Austin, 1981), 48.

3. Mary Louise Pratt, "The Short Story: The Long and the Short of It," *Poetics*, X (1981), 175–94; Charles Whitmore, "The Field of the Essay," *PMLA*, XXXVI (1921), 551–64; Johannes Hedberg, "What Is a 'Short Story'? And What Is an 'Essay'?" *Moderna Sprak*, LXXIV (1980), 113–20.

narration. If a first-person short story were "obviously" fiction, it would have no more place in the present discussion than an essay that contains no narrative.

Both genres have consistently defied The One True Definition to the point that expending further energy toward this end appears fruitless, if success is measured by permanent proof.[4] Earlier champions of both genres have even insisted on the autonomy of individual works. Georg Lukacs' view that the form of essays merges *with* the essay, whereas the forms of other literary works are limits imposed from without, resembles the claim Sherwood Anderson tried to make for the short story. Reviewing the issue more generally, Marie-Laure Ryan attributes current tendencies to substitute "text" for traditional genre labels partially to the failure of definitions and partially to "a desire among both critics and writers to deprogram the reading public by freeing the act of writing from any kind of convention."[5]

Since the early 1970s, the most interesting issues in genre theory have shifted from taxonomy to psychology, from how to label a work to how a given label affects our perceptions of that work. So it is that Heather Dubrow, in her compact book in Methuen's Critical Idiom Series, characterizes genre as a code of behavior between the writer and reader which spells out what can or cannot happen in a given work. Of course, as both Dubrow and Morson point out, a literary work may operate against its genre, but this is possible only if there is some set of conventional expectations to be ignored; Bertolt Brecht's *Verfremdungseffekt* can be only as powerful as the existing expectation that plays create worlds whose characters go about their business oblivious of audiences. Dubrow asserts further that literary responses are

4. For overviews of attempts at definition, see Susan Lohafer, *Coming to Terms with the Short Story* (1983; rpr. Baton Rouge, 1985); Richard Chadbourne, "A Puzzling Genre: Comparative Views of the Essay," *Comparative Literature Studies*, XX (1983), 133–53; and J. C. Guy Cherica, "Literary Perspective of the Essay: A Study of Its Genetic Principles and Their Bearing on Hermeneutic Theory" (Ph.D. dissertation, University of South Carolina, 1982).

5. George Lukacs, "The Nature and Form of the Essay," trans. Anna Bostock, in *Soul and Form* (Cambridge, Mass., 1978), 7; Sherwood Anderson, "Form, Not Plot," in *A Story Teller's Story* (New York, 1924), 351–62, rpr. in Eugene Current-Garcia and Walton R. Patrick (eds.), *What Is the Short Story?* (Rev. ed.; Glenview, Ill., 1974), 70–73; Marie-Laure Ryan, "Introduction: On the Why, What, and How of Generic Taxonomy," *Poetics*, X (1981), 109, with the permission of North-Holland Publishing Co., Amsterdam.

not innate but learned. What we "see" in a work is conditioned by what we've learned to see in other works we judge it to be like. As Mary Louise Pratt observes, "The reader who picks up a work of literature of a given genre already has a predefined idea of what the nature of the communication situation is" and will read accordingly.[6]

We seldom encounter unlabeled texts. When we do, we engage a complexly recursive process of hypothesizing what kind of work it is (or is like) and reading in that light until we need to readjust our hypothesis. An interesting test case is E. B. White's "The Flocks We Watch by Night." Now submerged in *One Man's Meat*, the piece was originally printed in the *New Yorker*. Because in *One Man's Meat* it is surrounded by essays in which White writes about activities on his farm, our first inclination is to read "I" as "White" and the work as essay. Susan Lanser notes, in fact, that until we're clued otherwise, we tend to equate a first-person narrator with the text's author.[7] (Consider how insistently Sylvia Plath's novel *The Bell Jar* collapses into autobiography in lower-level literature classes.) Often the clue comes from outside the text, its being published in a certain type of anthology, for example. The more one reads "The Flocks We Watch by Night," even within the context of *One Man's Meat*, the more *essay* doesn't seem quite to fit it. The action is too elliptical, Charles too much a character, the boy too undifferentiated. If one first encounters the piece in the *New Yorker*, the inclination to read it as story dominates from the start.

Suzanne Hunter Brown recognizes the effects of both framing and labeling in her experimental reading of a section of Hardy's *Tess of the d'Urbervilles* as a short story. She explains that doing so invites us to attend to different features in different ways. I adopt her method below. But exchanging the essay and short story labels is a trickier experiment. What Brown really has studied is the effect of brevity, not the phenomenon of the short story—or perhaps this *is* the short story. If so, we might invoke something parallel to Suzanne Ferguson's argument that the short story is not a distinct genre but a manifestation of impressionism: the genre is really "brevity," not "short story."[8] (The

6. Heather Dubrow, *Genre* (London, 1982), 2, 37; Mary Louise Pratt, *Toward a Speech Act Theory of Literary Discourse* (Bloomington, 1977), 204.

7. E. B. White, "The Flocks We Watch by Night," *New Yorker*, November 11, 1939, and *One Man's Meat* (New York, 1942); Susan Sniader Lanser, *The Narrative Act: Point of View in Prose Fiction* (Princeton, 1981), 151.

8. Suzanne Hunter Brown, "'Tess' and *Tess*: An Experiment in Genre," *Modern Fic-*

challenge, of course, is that not all "short" stories are "short stories.") Reading short stories as essays and essays as short stories confutes assumptions about how the works refer, how narrative stands in relation to point, and what readers should pay attention to while reading.

George Orwell's "A Hanging," Read as a Short Story

"A Hanging," not "Hangings," but then not "The Hanging," either. The story takes place one particular morning. The narrator watches a prisoner led from his cell to the gallows, watches a dog chase after him, reflects on what it means to kill someone, hears the prisoner chant a mantra, hears the execution command, sees the corpse, joins in the joking at the end. We know the location, Burma, shares its name with a place in South Asia, but we don't assume that real Burma is story Burma. Likewise, since we are dealing with a story, the narrative "I" doesn't refer to the author, no matter how likely that may seem to readers familiar with Orwell's background. The incident happens only on the page; it has no historicity, though something like it could have happened, sometime, somewhere, even in real Burma. The dog, the prisoner? Words on paper. Even the paragraph of reflection, normally an essay signal, can easily be assimilated into this story reading, since what a character thinks is part of any story in which he thinks.

Readers perceive narratives in two dimensions, one horizontal or successive, the other vertical or configurational, those perceptions, of course, being complexly intertwined and recursive. In her essay in this volume, Brown aligns the various synonyms used to differentiate these processes: on the one hand, synchronic, paradigmatic, spatial, vertical, configurational, and achronological; on the other hand, diachronic, syntagmatic, linear, horizontal, successive, and chronological. Paul Ricoeur has formulated the most cogent expression of the two principles: "Every narrative combines two dimensions in various proportions, one chronological and the other nonchronological. The first may be called the episodic dimension, which characterizes the story as made out of events. The second is the configurational dimension, according to which the plot construes significant wholes out of scattered events. . . . To tell and to follow a story is already to re-

---

tion Studies, XXVIII (1982), 25–44; Suzanne Ferguson, "Defining the Short Story: Impressionism and Form," *Modern Fiction Studies,* XXVIII (1982), 13–24.

flect upon events in order to encompass them in successive wholes." Ricoeur further identifies the configurational dimension as having its logical culmination in the "thought" of a piece.[9]

Concerned above all with expressing thoughts and ideas, however tentative, the essayist's main formal task is to create a significant horizontal dimension. The short story writer faces a different formal problem, that of investing successively ordered actions that point the reader's expectations toward "end" with a vertical dimension significant enough to forestall "So what?" The distinction between essays and short stories on this count is not as large as it is between essays and novels, precisely because of the same relative length of the two shorter forms. Indeed, Brown concludes that short stories, because of their brevity, invite readers to order the text configuratively rather than successively. Conversely, essays that offer an end-directed series of events invite a reading as short stories.[10]

Reading "A Hanging" as a short story means looking at the unfolding action rather than at the argued point. What constitutes the point of this piece is troublesome anyway. The clearest candidate is the abstractive exposition: "It is curious, but till that moment I had never realised what it means to destroy a healthy, conscious man. When I saw the prisoner step aside to avoid the puddle, I saw the mystery, the unspeakable wrongness, of cutting a life short when it is in full tide."[11] But the rest of the essay testifies less to the wrongness of the action than to the failure of others to recognize that wrongness, or worse, the failure of I to do anything but acquiesce. Adjusting the point to something like "People at executions behave insensitively," or "Executions produce complicated emotional reactions in a thinking witness," trivializes the piece. Because a single point is so hard to define, we may doubt the "essayness" of "A Hanging" and pursue our experiment of reading it as a story.

Reading through the lens of short story conventions, we are interested in following change through a sequence of events. Now a man lives, now he dies. But this sequence is hardly the most significant in

9. Paul Ricoeur, "Narrative Time," *Critical Inquiry*, VII (1980), 178–79.

10. Brown, "'Tess' and *Tess*," 37. One common theoretical practice has been to make a quick initial slice of "literary" essays from "practical" ones, as do Robert Scholes and Carl Klaus in *Elements of the Essay* (New York, 1969). As far as I know, no one has considered the extent to which the increasing rewards for a horizontal reading characterize gradations of the spectrum from practical to literary.

11. George Orwell, "A Hanging," in *Collected Essays* (London, 1961), 11.

the story. Two things make this clear. First, the knowledge that a piece is a short story encourages us to expect a certain syntactic shape, consisting of three events, and there are only two here.[12] Second, ever since Poe and, later, Eikhenbaum characterized short stories as highly concentrated toward their conclusions, theorists have regarded end-directedness as one of their important distinguishing features. The prisoner dies three quarters of the way through "A Hanging"; Orwell's epiphany occurs even earlier, about halfway. Convention prompts us to expect the most significant moment to come later. We find it in the final scene, in which even "I found that I was laughing quite loudly."

The story in "A Hanging" is not of the prisoner but of the witnesses, and particularly the narrator. The puzzle that pulls the short story reader is not so much what will happen to the prisoner as what will happen to I. This opens two possible interpretations of I's final behavior. One is that his earlier abstract realization was only a passing thought. I hasn't learned anything. This reading is tempered by the final juxtaposition of the drinking officials and the dead man one hundred yards away, and by its being preceded immediately by the appearance of the ironically shallow head jailer, Francis. But it becomes more plausible the more one gets away from the work as an essay. The other, more "natural" reading is that I is caught between his terrible understanding of death and his need to affirm his membership in the community of the living. In either case, I is more a character swept along by events than an interpreter of their meaning. Note the difference between these readings of outcome and the essayistic point we looked for earlier.

Another effect of reading "A Hanging" as a short story is the changed significance of "extraneous" events. The dog's performance, in either a story or an essay, has a dramatic effect. But an essay heightens the dog's thematic import, its frivolity contrasting with the guards' solemnity, the handkerchief through its collar inviting a comparison between living dog and destroyed prisoner. In the short story this thematic resonance still sounds, but the dog becomes more visible as

12. This three-part structure has been almost universally cited. For example, see Tzvetan Todorov, *The Poetics of Prose*, trans. Richard Howard (Ithaca, 1977), 111, or Robert Scholes, "Language, Narrative, and Anti-Narrative," In W. J. T. Mitchell (ed.), *On Narrative* (Chicago, 1982), 205: "A story is a narrative with a certain very specific syntactic shape (Beginning-middle-end or situation-transformation-situation) and with a subject matter which allows for or encourages the projection of human values upon this material."

a force retarding the prisoner's steps. Reading "A Hanging" as a short story may not change the text, but it alters how we attend to what's in the text.

William Carlos Williams' "The Use of Force," Read as an Essay

"The Use of Force" announces in its title a general subject—it's not "A Use of Force," after all. Given many possible strategies and organizational methods—the freshman writing texts, of course, have them neatly, perfectly categorized—the author settles on narration as the mode for exploring and explaining. Or maybe the event came first, the understanding later. What is important is that the conventions for reading essays make us expect the narrative to serve a point. (There is a shift in status here from story as genre to story as mode.) The narrator, a doctor, visits a sick girl. Suspecting diphtheria and unable to glean anything from her parents, he tries to examine her throat, but she fights back. The parents ineffectively try to help, which makes him more and more furious. Just before he succeeds he recognizes:

> But the worst of it was that I too had got beyond reason. I could have torn the child apart in my own fury and enjoyed it. It was a pleasure to attack her. My face was burning with it.
>
> The damned little brat must be protected against her own idiocy, one says to one's self at such times. Others must be protected against her. It is a social necessity. And all of those things are true. But a blind fury, a feeling of adult shame, bred of a longing for muscular release, are the operatives. One goes on to the end.[13]

If this is an essay, we regard this passage as the abstractive exposition that relates the point of the piece.

"The Use of Force" rushes toward conclusion. The reader knows early on that diphtheria has spread through the schools and is deprived of any mystery about what he will learn. The essay-reading convention that narrative is subordinate to point merely intensifies an already-evident concentration on the meaning of force. The story question is who exerts force against whom and with what result. The answer is certainly I against the child and the child against I. And also

13. William Carlos Williams, "The Use of Force," in *The Doctor Stories* (New York, 1984), 59–60, copyright © 1938, 1962 by William Carlos Williams, reprinted by permission of New Directions Publishing Corp.

I against the parents, who grow "more and more abject, crushed, exhausted," and the girl against the parents, too. But the essay question concerns less the dynamics of the situation than the nature of force, which expands through frustration, overcoming its wielder's rationality. Curiously, the essay reader's eagerness to find or supply an overarching abstraction arrests the kinds of associations that the short story invites, particularly the rape overtones as I attempts to penetrate this "unusually attractive little thing" and achieve muscular release.[14] Reading a work as key to some more general truth involves a different set of perceptions than reading it as representing some action, however meaning laden. We expect an essay story to show the way things are, a short story the way things happen.

Now I'd like to look at two pieces extremely close to each other in the boundary zone, an essay, "Aces and Eights," by Annie Dillard, and a story, "Able, Baker, Charlie, Dog," by Stephanie Vaughn. Both describe actions that seem possible. Both are narratives comprised of episodes, both alternate exposition and narration, both shuffle chronological order.

Annie Dillard's "Aces and Eights": An Essay in the Boundary Zone

A woman, a child, a cabin, a weekend. Memories. These are the elements of "Aces and Eights." The essay begins with the narrator at the cabin recalling the time immediately before the trip there. The action shifts briefly to the present, cedes to a childhood memory, then returns to the present. The child writes on a blackboard; the narrator thinks back to earlier visits. Finally we are told of their arrival at the cabin. It's Friday afternoon, and the essay ends Sunday. Although time is jumbled both locally in the present and globally between past and present, we sort it out, primarily because we're used to fiction that does this and because we even have the help of such theoretical apparatus as Meir Sternberg's *Expositional Modes and Temporal Ordering in Fiction.*[15]

Among several incidents in the essay, one in particular stands out. It begins, "Once, many years ago, there was a child of nine who loved

14. *Ibid.,* 58, 56.

15. Meir Sternberg, *Expositional Modes and Temporal Ordering in Fiction* (Baltimore, 1978).

Walter Milligan." She's a precocious child who knows the world's fragility and vows, "I will until I die love Walter Milligan and hate my sister and read and walk in the woods." Then follows a precise description of the place where she took this vow. I never identifies the girl, but it's fairly clear from the details of the story that the girl is I at a younger age. So why this fictional distance in the middle of an essay? The incident takes on added significance when the narrator and child one day meet Noah Very, a longtime resident of the area who knew I when she was a child. All three are inside Very's cottage. A double space appears before this exchange:

> "How old are you?" Noah asks the child.
> "Nine."
> "And what grade are you going into?"
> "Fourth." She cannot hide a look of contempt. Her whole class is going into fourth grade.[16]

And then another space appears in the text. Who is "the child" in this segment? The one who joined I at the cabin, of course. But wait, she's nine. Coincidence? Perhaps. But the double space indicates time has passed, a half hour or twenty-seven years, we can't quite be sure. This complex identity question, reminiscent of E. B. White's collapsing of time in "Once More to the Lake," gets murkier.

Hoaglund remarks, "Essays have fewer levels than first-rate fiction—a flatter surface." This is an odd thing to say. Shifting references to time and possibly to character force our attention to the surface of the piece. It's translucent and doesn't disappear immediately in deference to "meaning." Dillard's I insists, "Here a concern for truth forces me to confess that although I am writing in the present tense, actually some years have elapsed since this weekend in the country." How many? We've seen enough of this conceit even in short stories to be cautious about accepting it as proof of truth. Morson describes a special class of boundary works as "threshold literature," texts intentionally invested by their authors with an in-between generic status.[17] Certainly this description pertains to "Aces

---

16. Annie Dillard, "Aces and Eights," in *Teaching a Stone to Talk* (New York, 1982), 164, 172.

17. Edward Hoaglund, "What I Think, What I Am," *New York Times Book Review*, June 27, 1976, copyright © 1976 by The New York Times Company, reprinted by permission, and rpr. in Paul Connolly (ed.), *On Essays* (New York, 1981), 45–47; Dillard, "Aces and Eights," 170; Morson, *Boundaries of Genre*, 50.

and Eights," indeed, to virtually all the pieces in Dillard's collection *Teaching a Stone to Talk.*

Stephanie Vaughn's "Able, Baker, Charlie, Dog": A Story in the Boundary Zone

"Able, Baker, Charlie, Dog" also requires our sorting through events of several years. The story begins with the narrator at twelve, flashes back to when she was four and the family waited out a Manila hurricane, then ahead to six in the States, finally to the year they moved to Fort Niagara. Two incidents later, I returns to the day the story opened, the frame complete. Awakened by her drunken father, she follows him outside and watches him cross the frozen Niagara. The frame explodes. He quits the army. The narrator is in high school, then graduate school. The father dies. This is a wide span of time for a short story, but the important thing is that the narrator justifies all of these events as clarification for an epiphanal moment, as if the story has an expository function. At the end I sorts through the experience:

> Able, Baker, Charlie, Dog. I could remember the beginning of the alphabet, up through Mike and Nan. I could remember the end. X-ray, Yoke, Zebra. I was his only child, and he taught me what he knew. I wept then, but not because he had gone back to Ohio to read about the Eskimos and sell the artifacts of civilized life to homeowners and builders. I wept because when I was twelve years old I had stood on a snowy riverbank as he became a shadow on the ice, and waited to see whether he would slip between the cracking floes into the water.[18]

In the Dillard essay I described above, the twisted chronology helps open a reading of the piece as fiction. It is odd, then, that similar manipulations seem to have just the opposite effect in "Able, Baker, Charlie, Dog." Nelson Goodman argues that although narrative normally survives all sorts of contortion, enough twisting may destroy it. "Some stories," he says, "when reordered in certain ways are no longer stories but studies." Thus the "order of the telling so groups incidents reported as to bring out kinships and contrasts that cut across and obliterate—or at least blur—the story line. Narrative gives

---

18. Stephanie Vaughn, "Able, Baker, Charlie, Dog," in Tobias Wolff (ed.), *Matters of Life and Death: New American Short Stories* (Green Harbor, Mass., 1983), 208.

way to exposition." [19] It's not the altered order of telling but the new alignment of its parts into certain configurations that renders a story a study or essay. This is what happens when a psychologist's report organizes the patient's life into the most meaningful shape for the psychologist's purposes. Vaughn's short story resists the label essay; however, one of the things that help locate it in the boundary zone is the way the story's events are aligned.

What is the effect of the reminder that I in this story is identified as Gemma Jackson, not Stephanie Vaughn? Many would say the work is clearly short story and not essay. But does this detail really change our reading? Do we make the same decision about Mr. Spectator, the Rambler? The important question is, what would happen if the story were told *about* Gemma Jackson, not *by* I? The center of action would still rest with Jackson, but the center of attitude would lie rather with the narrator who tells us all such things. "Point of view, of course." Yet I stress this because the key feature of the personal narrative essay is the conjunction of action, attitude, and I.

One way we foreground stories is by reading them not as "always" stories, which relate some event we assume is typical and therefore representative, but as "once" stories, which are representative of nothing but themselves. "Onceness" in an essay makes it read like a short story. "Alwaysness" in a short story moves it toward essay. The former quality creates the sense of possibly emblematic but unanalyzed incident, the latter the sense of "this is how things are."

The kinds of complexity I described in "Aces and Eights" and "Able, Baker, Charlie, Dog" suggest that both are "once" stories. But short stories may contain elements of "always" that are not in the form of abstractive exposition. Consider the first paragraph of "Able, Baker, Charlie, Dog."

> When I was twelve years old my father was tall and awesome. I can see him walking across the parade ground behind our quarters. The wind blew snow into the folds of his coat and made the hem swoop around his legs. He did not lower his head, he did not jam his hands into the pockets. He was coming home along a diagonal that would cut the parade ground into perfect triangles, and he was not going to be stopped by any snow-

19. Nelson Goodman, "Twisted Tales; or, Story, Study, and Symphony," *Critical Inquiry*, VII (1980), 115, 119, rpr. in Mitchell (ed.), *On Narrative*, 111, 115, and in Goodman, *Of Mind and Other Matters* (1984).

storm. I stood at the kitchen door and watched him through a hole I had rubbed in the steamy glass.

The first sentence refers to a specific time generally: when I was twelve. The second appears to continue to do this as the narrator forms a generalized picture of how her father looked. The key clause is "I can see him," which can either be taken as literal optical sight or invoked memory. The "was coming" of the fifth sentence seems to push toward "onceness," but this walk can be seen as a typical action emblematic for the narrator, as in "He was always coming." Even the last sentence doesn't dispel this view, since we can read "I stood" as "It was customary for me to stand." But the next paragraph shatters the "always" quality: "My grandmother and mother fidgeted with pans of food that had been kept warm too long. It was one o'clock on Saturday and he had been expected home at noon."[20] However, "onceness" doesn't consign the work purely to the story realm, since plenty of essays feature a single "once" story.

"Alwaysness" may also be evident in the nature of action and the verb tense. Consider a passage from Joan Didion's essay "In the Islands" (which isn't in the boundary zone):

> We spend, my husband and I and the baby, a restorative week in paradise. We are each the other's model of consideration, tact, restraint at the very edge of the precipice. He refrains from noticing when I am staring at nothing, and in turn I refrain from dwelling at length upon a newspaper story about a couple who apparently threw their infant and then themselves into the boiling crater of a live volcano on Maui. We also refrain from mentioning any kicked-down doors, hospitalized psychotics, any chronic anxieties or packed suitcases. We lie in the sun, drive out through the cane to Waimea Bay. We breakfast on the terrace, and gray-haired women smile benevolently at us. I smile back. Happy families are all alike on the terrace of the Royal Hawaiian Hotel in Honolulu. My husband comes in from Kalakaua Avenue one morning and tells me that he has seen a six-foot-two drag queen we know in Los Angeles.[21]

The three repetitions of *refrain* suggest each sentence is a static proposition, not the report of one particular event. Five sentences later,

20. Vaughn, "Able, Baker, Charlie, Dog," 196.
21. Excerpt from "In the Islands," from *The White Album* by Joan Didion. Copyright © 1969, 1979, 1989 by Joan Didion. Reprinted by permission of Farrar, Straus and Giroux, Inc., and George Weidenfeld & Nicholson Limited.

"one morning" signals a specific action. But the interesting sentences in the passage are the four beginning with "We lie in the sun." Do they report a succession of events ("Once we lay in the sun, and then, once, we drove out" and so on), or do they function as active exposition ("The customary thing to do was lie in the sun")? It depends on whether one assigns them thematic significance or informational, essay or narrative. The present tense used throughout the passage wrinkles it even further; it is the "So then I say to her" of the past made present.

"Conversation with My Father," by Grace Paley, opens, "My father is eighty-six years old and in bed." He wants his daughter, I, to write a story, "'a simple story just once more,' he says, 'the kind de Maupassant wrote.'" But then comes a shift to past tense: "Finally I thought of a story that had been happening for a couple of years across the street." I said. He said. A "once" story. Father and I go back and forth about how stories should be told, and I offers a second, longer version of the story, which he scorns, and the narrator responds by continuing it. Why? "That woman lives across the street. She's my knowledge and invention. I'm sorry for her."[22] This is addressed to the reader, not the father, and with it Paley returns to the "always" of her concerns as a storyteller.

Steven Berg included "Conversation with My Father" in *In Praise of What Persists*, a collection of authors' statements on what has influenced them. In his acknowledgments Berg says, "Grace Paley's essay is reprinted from *Enormous Changes at the Last Minute*."[23] But Paley herself suggests the piece is a story, not an essay. In a brief prefatory note to her volume, she affirms: "Everyone in this book is imagined into life except the father. No matter what story he has to live in, he's my father, I. Goodside, M.D., artist and storyteller." The father may be real but he lives in a story. Need I be Paley? Let I be a character, and "storyness" predominates. Let "alwaysness" arise, and "essayness" comes forth.

Any "misreadings" I've proposed so far do not depend on selectively using information from outside the text, now denying Orwell's historical presence in Burma in order to make "A Hanging" a short story,

---

22. Grace Paley, "Conversation with My Father," in *Enormous Changes at the Last Minute* (New York, 1974), 161, 162, 167, copyright © 1960, 1962, 1965, 1967, 1968, 1971, 1972, 1974 by Grace Paley, reprinted by permission of Farrar, Straus and Giroux, Inc.
23. Stephen Berg (ed.), *In Praise of What Persists* (New York, 1983).

now insisting that Williams' experience as a pediatrician is enough to equate him with I in "The Use of Force," thereby making it an essay. Rather, I suggest that even if we admit all available information about the authors, it is impossible to tell from the pieces themselves whether they are fact or fiction.

If we could be sure who I is, perhaps the matter would be unproblematic. In personal essays, I is the author, though in the persona in which she portrays herself. A collection of twelve essays may have twelve different I's yet a single referent in the world beyond the page. First-person short stories share this name. In them, however, we assume that I is not some version of the author. But there is a problem with I as a name in a short story, a problem clearest when one considers stories related orally. Imagine listening to a storyteller beginning, "When I was twelve years old, my father was tall and awesome." Try not to equate the I with the teller, that person sweating and breathing, issuing words that demand our acceptance as hers. It's virtually impossible unless she announces beforehand, "I'm going to tell you a story whose narrator is a sixty-year-old black man," and she's a thirty-year-old Swede. Or perhaps the teller uses a trick, an accent we recognize as affectation. Yes, here is the fingerprint of fiction. But such affectation occurs even in essays. Stories do have extra tricks available: "I stood on Ganymede gazing at Jupiter." Yet stories in the boundary zone don't use them.

The fundamental issue is reference. Essays are supposed to refer to a real world beyond the page; short stories are not. William H. Gass declares that fiction doesn't represent but creates, that "there are no descriptions in fiction, only constructions." Yet no text, even a non-fictional one, can establish out of itself its faithfulness to real events in the world, and certainly not by announcing, "This is a true story." In the *Tractatus Logico-Philosophicus,* Wittgenstein views language as comprised of propositions, each of which is a possible picture of reality whose truth can be determined only by a comparison to the world. The impossibility of a proposition containing its own sense helps explain the difficulty of sorting fact from fiction in these story essays. The average reader cannot compare the propositions of "A Hanging" with reality to know if they were actual events in Orwell's life, though they are certainly possible ones. If the essay were set in the Sea of Tranquility, the question would be easier. But what does one do with a sentence like, "I was walking down the street last week"? If we know the writer has spent the past month in traction, we can judge the sentence. But if we don't? The amount of energy it would take to identify a piece as essay or story on the basis of fact versus fiction should tell us that this kind of sentence-by-sentence search is not an especially productive method of deciding whether a work is an essay or a short story. The presence of confusion may help us place it in the boundary zone, but after that can come only bickering. (Those wishing to pursue the issue may find L. B. Cebik's *Fictional Narrative and Truth* a useful point of departure.) [24]

This is neither to trivialize the importance of knowing whether something is factual or fictional nor to dismiss the effect on a reader of that information. The survivors of the Holocaust have crucial reasons for fighting to preserve its events as real and not to allow them to lapse into legend or, as some would reconstruct history, lie. Jerzy Kozinski's *The Painted Bird* pales before one Auschwitz memoir. Precisely this compels producers of sensational television movies to bill them as based on true events. It's the obverse of Martin Steinmann's contention that superordinate genre conventions of fiction invite readers to free writers of the obligations of realism because in doing so readers know they will gain the rewards of artistry. Robert Scholes and Robert Kellogg, writing about autobiography, have noted that readers who are told a character represents a real person expect less symmetry and significance from their stories. [25] The cliché "Truth is stranger than fiction" implies partly, "Isn't it remarkable that real events can display as much order as fiction?"

Story essays gain much of their power from the ability to reveal symmetry and significance where the reader expects little, while short stories gain theirs, paradoxically, from the fact that readers expect much. The writer has every chance to make things fit because everything has been invented to suit the purpose; all details must count.

Perhaps more than anyone else, Hayden White has been troubled by the compulsion to narratize history—to impose on reality the form of a story—since real events don't offer themselves as stories. Historiographers have generally regarded annals (which list events) and chronicles (which aspire to narrative but lack the closure of stories) as

24. William H. Gass, *Fiction and the Figures of Life* (New York, 1971), 17; Ludwig Wittgenstein, *Tractatus Logico-Philosophicus*, trans. D. F. Pears and B. F. McGuiness (London, 1961); L. B. Cebik, *Fictional Narrative and Truth* (Lanham, Md., 1984).

25. Martin Steinmann, "Superordinate Genre Conventions," *Poetics*, X (1981), 243–61; Robert Scholes and Robert Kellogg, *The Nature of Narrative* (New York, 1966), 257.

inferior to "history proper." White disagrees. He explains that the "value attached to narrativity in the representation of real events arises out of a desire to have real events display the coherence, integrity, fullness, and closure of an image of life that is and can only be imaginary." He contends that for events to take the form of story some subject must provide the impulse. Usually that subject is "The State." This leads to his concern that "every historical narrative has as its latent or manifest purpose the desire to moralize the events of which it treats."[26]

White either ignores the fact that any writing, even of lists, necessarily involves "moralizing" insofar as the writer records what she thinks *should be* recorded, or recognizes it but views "storying" as moralizing in a particularly insidious way. In any case, what is striking is that essayists fervently embrace the very qualities that White deplores in historiography. A narrative essay highlights, not hides, its status as one writer's version of the world. Truth in essays comes not from their reporting real things but from the writer's convincing us that she really does see the world this way.

The common quality in the boundary zone I've described is I-centeredness. The pieces here create a world that exists only because I does; not I am, I is. As ever-present reminder that someone wrote and ordered the words, I figures more clearly than any other name the making of meaning in a piece of writing. The words are ordered because I's life is ordered.

The first time I read James Alan McPherson's "Why I Like Country Music," the first piece in *Elbow Room*, I was certain that the reviewer who furnished the blurb about "twelve deeply felt short stories" on the back of the Fawcett-Crest edition must have mistaken the genre. "No one will believe that I like country music." This first sentence implies, though, that by the end of this piece *we* will believe it, despite the narrator's telling us nine sentences later, "I tend to argue the point, but quietly, and mostly to myself." (All this protesting cues a certain irony both about whether he actually does like it and, if so, why.) The piece begins with seemingly autobiographical exposition and, after a page, a story clue: "Dear Gloria: This is the truth of how it

26. Hayden White, "The Value of Narrativity in the Representation of Reality," *Critical Inquiry*, VII (1980), 7–8, 9, 27, 18, rpr. in Mitchell (ed.), *On Narrative*, 3–4, 5, 23, 14.

was." But here begins a second layer of exposition, one stretching some eleven pages, nearly half the story, as the narrator tells us about a childhood heartthrob, about his rival, and about his fourth-grade teacher. Finally, we arrive at a particular event, a day in May, a square dance. And when the dance ends, I takes us through an unknown number of years to the present ruminating self, who says: "And although it is difficult to explain to you, I still maintain that I am no mere arithmetician in the art of the square dance. I am into the calculus of it." [27]

The work's essaylike quality of savored meditation comes mainly from our sense of the narrator as self-describer. I am not referring to the possibility of substituting "McPherson" for "I" but to I's posture as explainer: "Gloria was born and raised in New York; she has come to believe in the stock exchange as the only index of economic health. My perceptions were shaped in South Carolina; and long ago I learned there, as a waiter in private clubs, to gauge economic flux by the tips people gave. We tend to disagree on other matters, too, but the thing that gives me most frustration is trying to make her understand why I like country music." The story bristles with pointed exposition, especially in reference to the issues of North and South, youth and age, meekness and authority. The key figure is Mrs. Esther Clay Boswell, the harsh teacher who addresses her students, I included, as "black buck rabbits and you few cottontails mixed in." [28] I turns the analytic lens on himself, too, preserving the past-through-the-consciousness-of-the-present stance he establishes at the outset. The dance incident occasions the movements of thought, justifying their narration. It shapes experience that is generalized through the past tense of "always," not "once": I would, she would, these people at this time in this place would.

In *The Narrative Act*, Susan Lanser offers some thirty criteria for describing point of view. Each of her spectra (all qualities are expressed as scales of degree) is grouped under one of three general aspects: the narrator's status, mode of contact, and stance. Some of them help characterize the point of view in "Why I Like Country Music" and that of boundary-zone pieces in general. Lanser, of course, presents

27. James Alan McPherson, "Why I Like Country Music," in *Elbow Room* (New York, 1975), 9, 10, 30, copyright © 1974 by James Alan McPherson, by permission of Little, Brown, and Company.

28. *Ibid.*, 9, 15.

these for analyzing individual texts, not identifying a subgenre. And undoubtedly there are boundary-zone works that violate this cluster.

1. On a scale of authorial equivalence (I=author) versus authorial separation, the point of view tends toward the former.
2. On a scale of heterodiegesis (uninvolved third person) versus autodiegesis (narrator as protagonist), the point of view tends toward the latter.
3. On a scale of human limitation of knowledge versus omniscience, it tends toward the former.
4. On a scale of direct versus indirect contact with the narratee, it tends toward the former.
5. On a scale of narrative self-consciousness versus narrative unselfconsciousness, the point of view tends toward the former.
6. On a scale of open survey (panoramic overview) versus fixed concurrence (fixed ordination of a single character), it tends toward the latter.
7. On a scale of fixed focalization versus free focalization, it tends toward the former.
8. On scales of diegesis versus mimesis and explicitly presented ideology versus embedded ideology, the point of view tends to gravitate toward the middle. Note that more essayistic works, if one regards persuasion as the reason for essays, tend toward the former, and more short story-like toward the latter.[29]

A simpler way to characterize point of view in the boundary zone is with Norman Friedman's typology of eight categories. He distinguishes between "I as Witness" and "I as Protagonist." The former Friedman describes as the use of a minor character within a story, which denies the author any direct voice at all. By characterizing witness narrators only in terms of what they can and cannot see, he denies them the dimension of interpretive stance that he assigns exclusively to protagonist narrators, who are "limited almost entirely to [their] own thought[s], feelings, and perceptions." When Friedman does mention a minor intermediate category, he focuses on the mode of transmission: "The protagonist tells his own story . . . to someone of his own acquaintance who thereupon relays it to the reader in his

---

29. Adapted from a table in Lanser, *The Narrative Act*, 224.

own person" à la Marlow and Jim. Far more worth pondering are narrators who are witnesses of their own stories, interpreters of their meaning and reason for their existence, as in "A Hanging," in which I narrates the execution as protagonist in the story of the revelation it engenders. Seymour Chatman's flow chart of Wayne Booth's distinctions between real author, implied author, and narrator reminds us that I's potential for collapsing the distance between real author and narrator has long been noted.[30] Boundary-zone short stories and essays, though, strike a peculiar balance between concealing and foregrounding I's position as interpreter and point maker, teller and world maker.

Interest in the boundary zone requires a willingness to be tentative, to shift ground, to look from two sides. I am offering no rules of definition, but some guidelines in the game of assigning genre labels. Once it is evident that a work is in the zone, we can ask certain questions. What happens when we "try" the conventions of essay, and those of short story? What are the relations between exposition and narrative? What do we observe about "onceness" and "alwaysness"? What are the complications of the reference of I? Pursuing these questions may not help pin down genre. We should, however, become more aware of what it means to assign the labels we use.

There are signs that the boundary zone is growing more crowded. More than forty years ago Harry Shaw noted the collapse of fact and fiction and attributed it to public interest in real events. Twenty years ago Richard Kostelanetz described the absence of omniscient narrators from modern short stories. In 1984 Philip Lopate speculated on the rising popularity of essays "in disguise." Gary Saul Morson proposed "boundary works"; deconstructionists propose "texts."[31]

Perhaps proliferation in the boundary zone has less to do with an increased acceptance of the validity of personal experience than it has to do with the concern for survival in the "tough, real" modern world in which fact, not fancy, gives one a competitive edge; with disen-

30. Norman Friedman, *Form and Meaning in Fiction* (Athens, Ga., 1975), 150, 152, 394; Seymour Chatman, *Story and Discourse: Narrative Structure in Fiction and Film* (Ithaca, 1978), 151.

31. Harry Shaw, "Some Clinical Notes," *Saturday Review of Literature*, November 22, 1941, p. 3ff; Richard Kostelanetz, "Notes on the American Short Story Today," *Minnesota Review*, V (1966), 214–21, rpr. in Charles E. May (ed.), *Short Story Theories* (Athens, Ohio, 1976), 214—25; Philip Lopate, "The Essay Lives—in Disguise," *New York Times Book Review*, November 18, 1984.

chantment with metafiction and the desire for what moral fiction can offer; with the loss of imagination; with a poverty of life that allows even autobiographical accounts to satisfy readers in the way that fiction used to because readers' experiences bear so little resemblance to writers'. Whatever the case, the central issue here is *not* fact versus fiction but the peculiar ways in which the authors of each of these pieces render their narratives neither transparent nor opaque but translucent, holding our attention as meaning-full events, not just as see-through containers of points. For the most part there are obvious differences between essays and short stories; yet, at some point, we rely on authors or editors saying what they are.

III

How Does Story End?

SUSAN LOHAFER

Introduction to Part III

The history of the short story, whether it began with Petronius, Boccaccio, or Poe, changed in the early decades of the twentieth century. Textbooks call it "the rise of the open-ended story." After 1914, to write a story that tied up experience, summed things up, or gave clear answers was to reveal a simplicity, a banality—not to mention an innocence—that just wasn't "modern." A reader, though, might wish for more help at the end of a story. After all, it was the function of art to enclose and interpret some portion of experience; it was the nature of short stories to click at the end. It was their special power—their formal duty.

Or so it seemed to critics who took rather literally what Poe said about the aesthetics of short fiction. Until well past the turn of the century, appreciation of the short story as a genre was founded upon concepts like "totality" and "single effect." For the most part, what emerged was a view of the story as highly contrived and made-to-order, as if reconstructed from the "final" piece in a puzzle. Many writers accepted a formula—O. Henry is the famous example—but others rebelled. Some well-known cases were made for a less tidy, more organic, more suggestive idea of form. Anderson and Porter come to mind, with their diatribes against plot. Of course, no fine story, from whatever period, is a box into which all stray meaning is locked; however, the "open" story foregrounded the ambiguity, self-consciousness, and relativity of meaning.

Critics, many of whom developed their theory from Joyce and their craft from New Criticism, began to see the modern story as an exercise in sensibility and inference, rather than a gift of revelation. Readers had to figure things out for themselves. Critics were there to help them. Flipping through old issues of the *Explicator*, for example, one can see the industry—in both senses—founded on this special relationship between the "difficult" story (normally open to some degree) and the trained critic. That relationship was durable; it still exists, but it did little to help short story criticism as a field.

What did help was new perspectives on the genre as a whole (see Part I). Some critics, having come to respect (if not live by) the story that does not "resolve," now saw closure as the key to story aesthetics. That is one of the ironies of short story criticism, but also one of its fresh developments. In their introductory essays in this volume, Norman Friedman and Mary Rohrberger discuss the interest in closure. Looking for a foothold, a vantage point from which the short story might make a unique and serious claim on theory, critics seized upon its one clear distinction from the novel: its shorter span, its foregrounded "end." Closural studies became one focal point for a number of influences at work in the field: the lingering effects of formalist criticism; the interest in narrative grammars; the work of Barbara Herrnstein Smith on closure in poetry; and the appeal of reader-response criticism, which highlights the brevity of the reading experience and the consequent imminence of the end in this narrative genre.

Two of the contributors to this volume, John Gerlach and I, have in recent years developed theories of closure that may serve as background for this section. My own notion of closure followed from an organic model of periodicity, involving resistance overcome. Gerlach's developed partly out of the work on closural signals in poetry. He identifies five signals in short stories: "solution of the central problem [old-fashioned resolution], natural termination [*e.g.*, end of a visit, a day, a life—similar to my organic periods], completion of antithesis [including return to the beginning], manifestation of a moral [or simply emergence of a theme, in modern fiction], and encapsulation."[1] For me, closure is a function of discourse features that do not depend on plot resolution; for Gerlach, ways of handling closure change and become an index to other historical developments in form—including openness.

In other words, the study of closure, at least as we two define it, can accommodate both traditional form and modern experiment. Closural studies provide the mixed bag of theory and application so

---

1. John Gerlach, *Toward the End: Closure and Structure in the American Short Story* (University, Ala., 1985), 8.

attractive to short story critics. In particular, Gerlach and I share biases that, in some form, date back to Poe: an effort to ground short story aesthetics in fundamental cognitive patterns; a concern with the way endings condition the whole of the text and the experience of reading it; and a definition of *form* that readily moves back from the theoretical toward concrete, descriptive, story-by-story analysis.

All three of the upcoming pieces share this common ground, too, though in varying degrees and ways. Austin Wright's essay "Recalcitrance in the Short Story" grows out of his earlier work on longer fiction (*The Formal Principle in the Novel*, 1982) and the formal innovations of modern short stories (*The American Short Story in the Twenties*, 1961). Yet the connection with closural studies is clear. His essay is about the recalcitrance offered by the endings of stories. The very idea of recalcitrance shares much with my concept of the resistance generated by discourse itself, but Wright defines it specifically in relation to thwarted expectations of form. He is talking about endings that resist our need to assimilate them, to make sense of the whole they create. Although at first it may seem that his five kinds of final recalcitrance overlap in many ways with Gerlach's five kinds of closural signals, the difference is significant. In Wright's work there is a strong phenomenological bias, an emphasis not so much on universal cognitive patterns as on an illusion of sense, or meaning, a semantic congruence between text and mind that we try to realize but never can.

Wright is frank about his effort to combine functional, reader-based criticism with an allegiance to the "formal principle," the shape that art imposes on life. Some readers may wish he had said more about his connection to reader-response criticism; certainly his notion of reading—a process of continually revising (complicating, correcting) the whole that is grasped at each point—suggests Wolfgang Iser's notion of the "horizons" serially perceived by the reader. Others may believe that in illustrating how recalcitrance is overcome, Wright is only reviving New Criticism. And is it true, as he remarks, that certain stories, like Frank O'Connor's "Guests of the Nation," do not display final recalcitrance? Some readers may challenge that claim—if only to display their own ingenuity. Questions such as these may indeed arise, but they are tugs on a fabric that holds its shape. This is an essay that draws upon contemporary theory but relies, finally, on a timeless sensitivity to literary experience.

Moving from Austin Wright to Thomas Leitch, we can see the eye on closure refocusing. In his essay "The Debunking Rhythm of the

American Short Story," Leitch argues that a particular kind of closure is characteristic of a particular field of stories—those in the American grain. In order to define the sort of ending he means, he sets up a larger scheme of story types: within the category of stories that reach an antithesis (Gerlach's antithesis-closure is mentioned), we find stories of ignorance yielding to knowledge, but also stories of supposed knowledge yielding to disillusionment. Leitch studies this second subcategory. He is interested in the story that shows false knowledge removed but not replaced by anything true or more reliable. This is the story with the debunking rhythm, defined by a closure that withholds assurances about identity, meaning, and purposeful action. In making his argument, Leitch is careful to avoid the fallacies described by Norman Friedman in the first essay of this volume. He clarifies the degree to which the debunking rhythm is a national phenomenon (American as opposed to British), a generic phenomenon (characterizing the short story as opposed to the novel), and a period phenomenon (modern as opposed to premodern). In the end, he is able to make some fascinating suggestions about the role of the short story in American literary history.

For some readers, the very air of logical clarity in Leitch's essay will provoke a doubt. Is it indeed true that stories that debunk an assumed knowledge, and offer no substitute, are withholding new knowledge? Isn't disillusionment a newly "knowing" state of mind? This view of the debunking rhythm, which sees it as coordinate with, rather than opposed to, an Aristotelian view of action, is developed in Leitch's book *What Stories Are: Narrative Theory and Interpretation*, published in 1986. In the present essay, however, he takes another tack. That American culture should foreground storytellers, perceptions of discontinuity and instability, and the special devices of short fiction is not hard to believe—but we may want more explanation. The claim that the short story is the "unmarked" narrative form in American fiction (a view not developed in Leitch's 1986 book) is the startling conclusion of this essay and the tantalizing promise of work-to-come. Readers may pick at threads that bind largely and loosely. But there is an exhilarating spaciousness to the ideas expressed here. Bold and central, they stir up new thoughts about American storytelling.

Both Wright and Leitch refine our understanding of closure by showing how it is tested, thwarted, or at least complicated. The end of a story may not end our involvement with it; we may be forced to re-read and rethink. Any good story is going to leave the reader cogitating (a part of reader-response I call "deferred cognitive closure"), and some stories require a great deal of thought even to yield tentative meaning (as Wright illustrates). The end of a story, however, may seem equivocal for yet another, more physical reason. Stories that are read as part of a meaningful sequence make different claims on our attention than isolated stories; their terminal boundaries are more like scrims than final curtains. The meaning of each story is implicated in the meaning of all. This is the phenomenon Robert Luscher explores in "The Short Story Sequence: An Open Book."

Before he can develop a theory of the story sequence, he needs to counter that prejudice, as old as Poe, in favor of the isolated story, the self-sufficient entity, the discrete experience. As Poe himself explained, however, the short story needs an active reader, one who participates in the making of meaning. In the story sequence, the reader is called upon to expand and complicate this enterprise. Each successive story, while complete in itself, is also part of an unfolding design that transcends it. Like Wright, Luscher takes for granted the human need to find form; coherence, wholeness, and integrated sense will always beckon us. Readers of story sequences need to exercise their "pattern-making faculties" very actively, within and across the boundaries of individual story closure. The reward is a perception of a "dynamic sequential unity" far richer than any one story can provide. As context for his argument, Luscher places the story sequence in relation to the mere aggregate of stories on one side, and the single long fiction (or novel) on the other. He, like Leitch, is careful to note the relation of general modernist traits—in this case, fragmentation and spatial organization—to his special case of story aesthetics.

In a way, Luscher may seem to be returning us to the days of explication, with story raised to the "sequence" power. Many of the best-known examples of the genre—*Dubliners, Winesburg, Ohio, The Golden Apples*—are favorites of the New Critics. We are reminded of the emphasis on internal patterns but may wonder, for example, about the special case of the final story in a sequence, the one in which story closure and sequence closure coincide. The questions that arise are likely to be nagging ones—not so much argumentative as just plain curious. In writing about the story sequence, Luscher has joined the current interest in closural (and anticlosural) phenomena with a new sensitivity to this hybrid genre. Scholarship in this area is gaining momentum. Forrest Ingram's 1971 book, *Representative Short Story Cycles*, remains the standard reference, but has now been joined by a special issue of the *Journal of the Short Story in English* (1988), by Susan Garland Mann's *The Short Story Cycle: A Genre Companion and Reference Guide* (1988), and by a number of dissertations. There is evidence in the profession of increasing attention to this very teachable form. Luscher's work is a contribution and a spur to appreciation of the story sequence.

All three of the essays in this section are about formal patterns in short fiction; all acknowledge the importance of endings in shaping these patterns. Still, there are slight differences in the way each scholar is thinking of closure. Wright's five kinds of recalcitrant endings are defined in terms of their inadequacy as explanations; their resistance is overcome when gaps in relevance are filled. Closure arrives when there is semantic completion of a specific interpretation. For Leitch, closure is a matter of logical relations. Kinds of endings follow from plus-or-minus epistemes in a model of human knowledge. Luscher is closer to Wright. Both assume a form-finding, pattern-building activity as fundamentally human. Both are looking toward a satisfying, literary interpretation of the text. Yet, perhaps because he remains longer on an abstract plane, Luscher rests his case more directly on the cognitive operations that drive interpretation.

Although within the scope of this essay Luscher cannot work through a full set of examples, he, like Wright and Leitch, is tempering theory with practice. Each of these critics illustrates what might almost be called a new ethic in genre criticism of the short story: that is, the need to work inductively with large samplings of stories and/ or readers. This is one of the ways in which short story criticism has moved beyond the exegesis of individual stories toward a theory of short fiction.

Nevertheless, we can still see the endemic practicality of short story criticism—whether we call it functional, as Wright does, or simply note how closely theory dogs experience with individual texts. Closural and anticlosural studies, in particular, seem based in living acts of readership. In becoming theoretical, they become, incidentally, pedagogical. It is easy to imagine notions of recalcitrance, debunking, and trans-story dynamics being put to use in the classroom. Each theory offers leverage on hundreds of stories taught every day across the country. There is nothing arcane or difficult about the concepts themselves; on the contrary, they are remarkable for their lucidity and good sense. They are revitalizing. They offer a fresh look at overcriticized stories, a new angle on historical developments, a sure way into that puzzling text we want to teach or write about.

AUSTIN M. WRIGHT

Recalcitrance in the Short Story

In every short story—indeed, in every formed work of fiction—two opposing forces are visible: the force of a shaping form and the resistance of the shaped materials. Let us consider the resisting force. I call it recalcitrance or, as it resists the form, formal recalcitrance. In traditional formal criticism it is usually overlooked. In nonformal or antiformal criticism of the last thirty years, it has been vigorously studied and advertised under a variety of names, but its true relation to the premises of formal criticism has seldom been recognized. Let us consider here that relationship and ask in particular what special role, if any, formal recalcitrance may play in the art and criticism of the short story.

The notion of formal recalcitrance may rescue formal unity from some of its disadvantages. This may be useful to short story criticism. Ever since Poe and Brander Matthews distinguished the short story from stories merely short, a notion of unity has been implicit in the concept of the short story. The tradition of the short story, as articulated by Poe, and reiterated by Joyce and others, has always stressed the vital functioning of parts in a whole ("In the whole composition there should be no word written, of which the tendency . . . is not to the one preestablished design"), and this stress is reflected to this day, when short story critics study such matters as closure or consider how the proximity of the end affects short story sentences.[1] Yet from the point of view of mainstream criticism, unity—organic wholeness, the integrated work—is a backwater, an eddy; it is regressive, reactionary, imprisoning, or downright mystifying.

1. Edgar Allan Poe, "Review of *Twice-Told Tales*," in Charles E. May (ed.), *Short Story Theories* (Athens, Ohio, 1976), 48.

The idea of formal recalcitrance makes formal unity more flexible. One of the remarkable things about it is how it can bring together into a single scheme certain interests valued by formal critics and other interests, seemingly incompatible, valued by antiformalists.

If by *form* here I mean a work's unique principle of wholeness, its organizing, shaping, unifying principle (or the possibility of such a principle, whether or not it can be finally described), then formal recalcitrance is simply the resistance offered by the materials to that form as it tries to shape them. It includes resistance to both the author's creating process and the reader's recreating one. Thus, on the one hand, there is the commonplace that much of the effectiveness of a form depends on the stubbornness of its materials: the statue is the more impressive for being hewn from marble. On the other hand, there is the argument, put forth in my study of the novel a few years ago, that the interest and life of a form for the reader depend strongly on what impedes or delays perception of that form; recalcitrance saves the form from triviality, boredom, banality.

Unfortunately, in traditional formal analyses of fiction recalcitrance has no place. Nor was I able in my own study to develop a practical way to deal with it. The issue may be clarified if we consider how a form looks to us. Our illusion of understanding a novel is essentially a perception of a form. Rather, it is an illusion of form, a conviction that we are in the process of discovering a form, a belief that further contemplation or rereading will enable us to find a comprehensive principle of coherence. Such a principle, we imagine, would be capable of accounting for everything. We are convinced it exists; further reading or reflection will disclose it fully. But this is not to say we actually perceive it. Generally, we do not—not as well as we think we could with a little more contemplation. It is better, therefore, to regard the form of a work not as a fully realized entity but as an emergent hypothesis of reading; then a work of art becomes a composition that "displays a created form in the process of becoming visible."[2]

What is important is the process. From this point of view recalcitrance—seen in whatever slows down or interferes with this process—is of utmost importance. If a form comes into view too easily and ceases to evolve as we reflect on it, we find it banal; if the process is stalled and our quest for a form is too stubbornly frustrated, we

2. Austin M. Wright, *The Formal Principle in the Novel* (Ithaca, 1982), 39, copyright © 1982 by Cornell University Press, used by permission of the publisher.

find the work chaotic. The "life" of a form—its power to interest us actively, to give us that immediacy and involvement which belong to all fiction we enjoy—depends upon our encounter with the resistance of the materials, the recalcitrance that seems constantly to be yielding to the shaping form.

Recalcitrance is amply appreciated by contemporary critics under the name of discontinuity or disruption. The various levels of naturalization described by structuralists are part of the process that I call "resolving" recalcitrance.[3] Unfortunately, such criticism, in elevating recalcitrance, tends to reject the form that is its reason for being. Recalcitrance, they seem to say, is good not because it enhances the form but because it destroys the form, a view that, in my opinion, discards the function of recalcitrance. To me the primary naturalizing force is the pursuit of the unique form. By minimizing this, such theorists deprive the concept of resistance of its explanatory power, since neither the function nor the object of that resistance is acknowledged. On the other hand, when a formal critic treats the form as a fully realized principle, recalcitrance disappears. This always happens in traditional formal analysis. The value of "difficulty" in the composition baffles us; it remains unanalyzable.

Recalcitrance comes into its own when we translate the whole question of formal structure into one of formal behavior. The view of form as a partially perceived hope, a hypothesis of future discovery, makes this possible. The work is no longer an immutable object which we do or do not understand but an active entity in a process of change (that is, our understanding is changing). It engages us in a struggle between the vision of a potential and eventual unity and the obstructions to that vision. It is from this point of view, form seen as behavior (constructive in the writer, perceptual in the reader), that the opposition of the two forces appears: the shaping force versus the resisting force.

In one's first encounter with a new form, everything is recalcitrance. As the form becomes gradually visible, this is replaced by the perceived richness and complexity of the form and its restrictive conventions. If the form becomes totally visible (total banality, perhaps an imaginary condition), recalcitrance disappears altogether. It is this disappearance that makes recalcitrance difficult to fix in analysis,

3. See, for example, Jonathan Culler, *Structuralist Poetics: Structuralism, Linguistics, and the Study of Literature* (Ithaca, 1975), 134–60.

where its residue may remain disguised under such terms as *intensity* and *obscurity*.

Let us consider what kinds of recalcitrance may be distinctive to the short story. First we should briefly examine recalcitrance in the novel, which except for the consequences of its length is the closest genre. At one level the whole material of the novel is resistant: it is the "writerly" text we have to read through before we can see a whole. There is the original resistance of the language itself, which has to be understood, interpreted, before a story can be seen. There is the generic resistance of fiction as such, the implicit conventions (so familiar we scarcely notice the impediment) by which we relegate people, events, world, to the category of the fictitious, the imaginary, the "not necessarily real." Then there is the dense substance of the fictional world itself, the multi-faceted resistances to our efforts to conceive the characters, what they are doing, and how they are to be judged, recalcitrance that increases as they depart from the stereotypes. There is recalcitrance in every restrictive convention, such as a limitation upon the point of view, or narrative manner. Subtlety in general always begins as recalcitrance, as does originality. Resistance has been overcome in every conclusion, every perception, every judgment to which the novel leads us that is not simply explicit. It remains, after all our rereading and reflection is done, still unabsorbed, in every mystery, every failure to hold everything in our memory at once, every ambiguity or obscurity that leads us to regard our perception of the form as hypothetical and incomplete, not definitive.

All this is characteristic of formed fiction in general—novel and short story. The novel also has a special and powerful recalcitrance in its great length. As it extends, as the material adds up, our perception is impeded in almost every aspect, both of the fictional world and of the formal composition. As Percy Lubbock has noted, a novel recedes in our memory even while we read.[4] Its length not only extends opportunities to develop other kinds of fictional recalcitrance but obscures the form of the whole by clouding it in forgetfulness and by compounding its complexity. In the novel, more than most fictional forms, much recalcitrance usually remains unabsorbed; even in the book we know best, we are conscious of unreconciled recalcitrance in what we have forgotten or failed to notice, and we look forward to rereading to recapture our losses.

Criticism of the short story has discovered many features that

4. Percy Lubbock, *The Craft of Fiction* (1926; rpr. New York, 1957), 1–2.

clearly function as resistance. What Eudora Welty calls "mystery" in the short story is a sign of recalcitrance at the level of the fictional world. What functional critics, including me, have called a technique of "leaving things to inference," and justified as giving a more vivid or "dramatic" effect to the mimesis, acquires a more profound aesthetic significance when seen also as recalcitrance. The lyric short story is recalcitrant in its rejection of overt action. The open-ended story, instead of being formless, as the term would suggest, is recalcitrant in its rejection of conventional beginnings and ends, resolved by subtler notions of form. The concept of recalcitrance gives another dimension to the impact of epiphanies and discovery stories, and it offers an aesthetic explanation for stories of episode, disclosure plots, and static plots, as well as the flourish of metafictional stories.

Susan Lohafer's study of the forces of anticlosure provides an excellent analysis of recalcitrance at the level of the sentence: the reader "undergoes a sequential process which is yearning toward a static result: he is experiencing an impetus toward closure, blocked by various kinds of interference which are in one way and another removed, surmounted, absorbed." What she calls "deferred cognitive closure" is also recalcitrance. So is what Joseph Flora calls "the device of conspicuous silence" and the activity described as follows by Mary Rohrberger and Dan Burns: "As the form [of the short story] evolves from Hawthorne through Barthelme, the reader is increasingly called upon to supply the temporal, causal, and overt thematic links formerly supplied by the author. Thus, the contemporary reader is required to participate in a kinship relationship with the author that is even more active than the one Poe suggests."[5] By bringing these variously described phenomena under the single heading of recalcitrance, we can provide a unifying rationale for them at the formal level, to fortify explanations offered at other levels. And we discover thereby a further reason, common to all these aspects, why they are so essential to the strength and attractiveness of the short story genre.

The question to consider here is, if length in a novel is a formal ad-

5. Eudora Welty, "The Reading and Writing of Short Stories," in May (ed.), *Short Story Theories;* Austin M. Wright, *The American Short Story in the Twenties* (Chicago, 1961), 327–62; Susan Lohafer, *Coming to Terms with the Short Story* (1983; rpr. Baton Rouge, 1985), 42; Joseph M. Flora, "The Device of Conspicuous Silence in the Modern Short Story," in Wendell M. Aycock (ed.), *The Teller and the Tale: Aspects of the Short Story* (Lubbock, Tex., 1982), 27–45; Mary Rohrberger and Dan E. Burns, "Short Fiction and the Numinous Realm: Another Attempt at Definition," *Modern Fiction Studies*, XXVIII (1982), 6.

vantage, a source of recalcitrance, does short fiction or the short story provide another formal quality to compensate for it? Is there some kind of recalcitrance peculiar to the short story? Recalcitrance in general may be analyzed according to whatever distinctions one uses in analyzing a form. Thus in the terms I prefer, recalcitrance could be studied as it affects the revelation of the fictional world (characters, action), of the treatment (narrative principles, point of view), of the language and style, and of the formal principle itself. To distinguish recalcitrance peculiar to the short story, however, we must look for whatever kinds are peculiarly associated with or enhanced by shortness.

Of course a story may compensate through nonformal means: the mimetic material itself, the "object of imitation," may possess a natural interest that requires no great development to bring out. The story is relevant to us, psychologically, morally, imaginatively, or educationally, and that is its value. This is the way of not only parables and fables but also many realistic stories of contemporary life. The form is relatively unimportant, and the story may be told in other ways. Again, a story may compensate by presenting an unusually visible and clear form, marked by some interesting abstract pattern or symmetry. This is the way of many surprise stories and anecdotes, if anecdotes are what James called them, stories of something "that has oddly happened to someone." [6] The oddness, whatever other interest it may also have, is often the imposition of some pattern in events, an unexpected appearance of form in the world, as in a surprising coincidence or turn. Too-easy visibility means banality, yet before we reach that point, the perception of a pattern in events can focus our attention and give us pleasure.

That is not specific to the short story, however. Of short story recalcitrance—recalcitrance associated with shortness—there seem to be at least two kinds. There is first a general recalcitrance common to all short works, manifest in the intensity of detail that shortness confers. In general, the shorter the work, the more prominent the details. Words and images, as well as characters and events, stand out more vividly than they would in a larger context. This attention to the parts, found in all short fiction and poetry, implies recalcitrance in the act of attention, the arresting of notice at every significant point. In effect,

6. R. P. Blackmur (ed.), *The Art of the Novel: Critical Prefaces by Henry James* (New York, 1934), 181.

shortness intensifies recalcitrance at the ground level of language, even as it loses recalcitrance at the overall level of formal unification. This—which is the kind Lohafer examines—I call inner recalcitrance.

In the second kind, the effect of shortness is concentrated in the ending. The normal effect of an ending is to reduce recalcitrance, as in most novels and much traditional short fiction. In many of our most significant twentieth-century short stories, however, the ending (temporarily) aggravates it, presenting a new challenge to the reader that can only be resolved by reflection after the reading. This I call final recalcitrance—meaning that it is instituted by the end of the story, not that it cannot be resolved (that would be permanent recalcitrance).

Final recalcitrance is an obstacle to artistic comprehension caused by the seemingly premature placing of the end, an effect of incompleteness requiring the reader to look back, recalculate, and reconsider, so as to satisfy the expectation of wholeness that he has brought to the story. A familiar model for this is the Joycean epiphany. Material is accumulated which tends to raise large expectations. The sudden termination, without any evident forewarned rationale, may bewilder us at first (witness the usual dismay of contemporary students with "Araby"), but it forces us to seek a unifying principle subtle enough to bring the details into a single compass. In Joycean epiphanies, this principle is usually found in either the kind of structure I call a discovery plot, in which the protagonist's discovery is implicit, embodied in images with emotional and moral significance, or a disclosure plot (Norman Friedman's "static plot"), in which the essence of an unchanging situation is imagistically and symbolically conveyed.[7]

Let me illustrate how final recalcitrance works by using the familiar example of Joyce's "The Dead." Imagine reading this story for the first time. It moves leisurely from Gabriel's arrival through the events of the party, with many characters, considerable conversation, a number of inconclusive incidents; the party breaks up, and Gabriel and his wife go to their hotel; his lust is stirred, but she tells him of her youthful lover who died. Gabriel reacts, goes through a sequence of emotions, and finally falls asleep conscious of the snow falling all over Ireland. Although my own first reading of this story occurred long ago, I am fairly sure it was somewhat confused, and even the most intelligent and knowledgeable reader is likely on first reading to wonder about things in the story that seem to be forgotten when it ends in

7. Norman Friedman, *Form and Meaning in Fiction* (Athens, Ga., 1975), 174–79.

Gabriel's hotel room. The final scene and especially the cover-all imagery of snow do give a nice closural effect, and the sympathetic reader may well feel the story has reached an appropriate end, is complete, and conveys a strong and moving experience. This feeling of completeness, this sense that we understand the story (implied in our being moved by it), might be taken as an intuitive recognition of the form of the whole.

This so-called intuitive perception, however, is probably an illusion. If we are comfortable with the story at this point, our feeling arises less from a sense of an already complete perception than from a sense of active and continuing discovery on our part. This appears if we try to formulate an explicit understanding of our intuitively grasped form. If, for example, having read through the snowfall at the end, we ask what this story is about, our answer may be that it is a discovery plot for Gabriel: the line "The time had come for him to set out on his journey westward" implies recognition of something. (His discovery is different, of course, from the discovery we are engaged in.) But if we ask what he has discovered, we run into problems. He has discovered, through his wife's revelation, how unromantic he has always been. But the mere formulation of this response calls our attention to all the elements in the story which it does *not* account for, including the sentence just quoted. Surely most of the party material is irrelevant to such a discovery. So we take another step. Gabriel discovers not merely how unromantic but how fatuous, how smug and self-satisfied, he is, as evidenced by his behavior at the party, his anxieties, his clashes with Lily, Miss Ivors, and Gretta herself, his speech. This is better, but it does not take account of the fact that his various embarrassments, which he takes as signs of his fatuousness, are products of his own judgment of himself. It is he who judges himself as smug, self-centered, emotionally dead, and in the process of so judging to some extent refutes the charge.

If now we ask why the story makes such a point of people like Freddy Malins and Mr. Browne, we may better appreciate Gabriel's strong role as a leader and facilitator in the smooth functioning of this society. All this, plus the strong emphasis on his kindness and generosity, makes him much more complex and sympathetic than our first descriptions had implied. This is better still, but it does not explain the emphasis on the conversations at the party, most notably the discussions of the past and death, or the emphasis on death in Gabriel's thoughts. Nor does it account for the snow throughout the story and at the end. The snow insists on its symbolism in a number of directions—death, sleep, forgetfulness, time, peace, equality, concealment, paralysis—and Gabriel's discovery and his response to it are put in a context of fatality, forcing us to complicate our interpretation still more: not only to see his emotional state as a kind of living death and to bring out his impotence in the face of it, but to place his ego, his love, his cares, indeed the whole world in which he has been so busy and involved, in the shadow of death and ultimate forgetfulness—a perspective of obliteration in which, ultimately, none of it will matter anymore. His goodness as well as his weakness, along with Gretta's romance and the lives of everyone present, are all covered in his final rueful and compassionate vision of mortality, and the discovery turns out to have much greater scope and depth than may have at first appeared.

Each step in the process I have described represents a discovered complication in the form of the story. It also represents a significant point of recalcitrance resolved. Such recalcitrance exists in every perception that one's tentative comprehension of a story is not complete—beginning with the initial confusion I noted at the start. The process could go on; my sketch leaves much recalcitrance untouched still. It has not accounted for details like the anecdote of the horse and King Billy's statue, or Bartell D'Arcy's cold, or obviously major components like the questions of Irish hospitality and Irish patriotism, or the fact that the snow is "general all over Ireland," or, for that matter, the sentence with which we started, referring to "his journey westward"—all of which a further analysis would treat.

Such recalcitrance depends on the convention that "every thing in the story counts," that is, the assumption of a form—a convention implicit in all short stories, even those most deliberately open-ended. Without that assumption there would be no pursuit of a form and no recalcitrance, either. Recalcitrance does not automatically accompany that convention; it depends on the accumulation of details whose significance is not immediately evident.

It is different from novelistic recalcitrance. Many novels do require us to draw significant inferences at the end: *The Portrait of a Lady* compels us to infer that what Isabel chooses is more important than what happens to her. The end of *As I Lay Dying* throws new comic light on Anse and the other Bundrens. Many novels require us to put together at the end what we have read and to formulate a principle not totally obvious. Yet this post-reading reflective process has already been thoroughly prepared for in the long process of the reading. Our view of the form is seldom drastically altered by the end. Although the length of the novel allows the form to escape us, the tendency of almost any novel's end is to mitigate this resistance by seeming to confirm one or another interpretation of form already building in the novel, whereas the ending of a short story aggravates recalcitrance by cutting off our expectations for clarification.

Leaving inner recalcitrance aside, I would now like to distinguish five varieties of final recalcitrance which have become prominent in this century. Space limitations must keep my examples brief. In the first variety the story ends in an unresolved contradiction at the level of character or action. I call this mimetic resistance; formally, if not psychologically, this is the simplest kind. In D. H. Lawrence's "The Horse Dealer's Daughter" the action seems complete, the sequence of events leading to the end is fully explicit, the feelings of the two main characters are described, and yet the reader is left with a sense of contradiction in the feelings of both characters and in their reasons for doing what they do (for example, the nature of Dr. Fergusson's "love," which arises so suddenly and for so little apparent cause). A sense is established that the characters themselves do not understand what motivates them. The contradictions force the reader to look for deeper motives and to seek further understanding in the symbolic imagery which surrounds the characters, and there is some ambiguity of feeling that seems to remain unresolvable. Other stories showing different kinds of mimetic resistance include Lawrence's "The Prussian Officer," Joyce's "Eveline," Anderson's "The Strength of God" and "The Teacher," Porter's "That Tree," Hemingway's "The Short Happy Life of Francis Macomber," and Updike's "A Sense of Shelter," in all of which a complete, decisive action includes an ambiguity or contradiction in motivation that forces us to a more complicated interpretation of the event than may have at first appeared. The ends of these stories stop short of explaining what has happened, and we are forced to explain for ourselves. The ambiguity at the end of some tales by James, such as "The Lesson of the Master," tends to be more explicitly spelled out than in the above examples but belongs in this category too. In a variant, the reader is required to reconstruct not merely motivation but a cause-and-effect chronology, as in the fairly obvious example of Faulkner's "A Rose for Emily."

A more complicated resistance appears in stories whose final moment or event appears to be, abstractly, an explanation of what has gone before—that is, a discovery or judgment or clarification—yet which fails, at the level of explicitness, actually to explain. It does not pull things together as it seems intended to. In stories with this kind of resistance, unexplaining explanation, the reader must draw his own conclusions. This is the type of the epiphany story described above—of "The Dead," or "Araby," and less bold precursors like Stephen Crane's "The Open Boat." Lines at the ends of these stories— "They felt that they could then be interpreters"; "I saw myself as a creature driven and derided by vanity"; "The time had come for him to set out on his journey westward"—seem to indicate discovery, the protagonist making sense of the preceding events, except that the sense is not obvious to the reader. In some *Winesburg, Ohio* stories, like "Hands," "Respectability," and "Loneliness," the story ends shortly after a flashback has been explicitly presented as the cause for the situation previously shown, and yet the offered causation complicates as much as it resolves and leaves us with contradictions we must reconcile on our own. In Flannery O'Connor's "The Artificial Nigger," the cause for the reconciliation of Mr. Head and Nelson is shown, but the manner of its working must be inferred by the reader.

Resolution of recalcitrance in these stories requires us to apply variable assumptions about character and the universe. The Anderson stories depend on a psychology of the unconscious, the Joyce stories on a more inclusive psychology including that of the unconscious. "The Open Boat" requires an idea of the cosmos. Stories like Flannery O'Connor's "Parker's Back" and "Revelation," also in this category, introduce a religious instinct into the psychology. Belief in the power of ritual and social pressure resolves recalcitrance in Faulkner's "Red Leaves."

A typical recent example of a story with an unexplaining explanation is Raymond Carver's "Distance." A divorced father tells his grown daughter an anecdote of his earliest married days. The story seems intended to explain what went wrong in the marriage, yet in the anecdote the couple, after a brief conflict, reconciles. The explanation does not explain. The reader is forced to fill in, to discover perhaps the narrator's regret and mourning for a naïve past when his problems seemed to have solutions.

In the third variety of resistance, the unexplaining explanation is itself suppressed. In stories of unexplained juxtaposition, the reader is confronted with an array of disparate materials and no explanation of what unites them. Hemingway's "In Another Country" looks like a single experience, but what connects the "hunting hawks" to the major and the therapeutic machines and the major's loss? The reader must find a rationale—probably here (again) an implied discovery for the narrator, put in concrete, nonintellectual terms, concerning the vulnerability of all people to loss and death, not just men in war. Another unexplained juxtaposition appears in Faulkner's "Dry September," in which a lynching episode is presented from several points of view and in which the center of the story is found within a compound protagonist. Virginia Woolf's "Kew Gardens" juxtaposes a diversity of fragmentary scenes in a common place. Ann Beattie's "Waiting" juxtaposes external signs of the heroine's unexplained distress (her concerned friend's remarks and the "tears streaming down [her] cheeks") with a sequence of ostensibly casual conversations and limited memories.

A special type within this category, in which one incident provides a pattern to rationalize the juxtaposition of otherwise unrelated incidents, may be represented by Katherine Anne Porter's "Theft." Here the heroine's discovery that she has robbed herself is provoked by an encounter with a thief, which gives meaning to her otherwise haphazard and fragmentary memories of the day. Similarly, in Robert Penn Warren's "Blackberry Winter," the boy's encounter with the menacing stranger provides a key to the other seemingly loosely related incidents of the day.

Still another type of unexplained juxtaposition is seen in stories like Hemingway's "The Killers" and "Hills like White Elephants" and Faulkner's "That Evening Sun," wherein a significant action is begun, a conflict with a range of possible outcomes, but the narrative is terminated before any of these outcomes is reached. Here, too, we are forced to revise our notion of the focus of the story, in these cases to the conclusion that the story has a disclosure (static) rather than a dynamic (change) plot and that the issue is precisely the failure of resolution. Many stories combine the recalcitrance of unexplaining explanation with radical juxtapositions. The boss's wretchedness at the end of Katherine Mansfield's "The Fly" looks like a revelation, but we need to apply a psychology of the unconscious and the screening of feelings in order to understand the juxtaposition of otherwise unrelated moments in this story. On a larger scale, the dream in "Flowering Judas" confronts a juxtaposition of diverse problems, as does on a still larger scale Marlow's articulation of horror in "Heart of Darkness." "The Dead" also works this way.

In a fourth variety, symbolic recalcitrance, the ending leaves unexplained the import of some conspicuous symbolic scheme. Conrad's "The Secret Sharer" does this in a realistic context. Despite the heavy emphasis on Leggatt as a projection of the narrator's "second self," the psychological implications of this doubling—the full nature of the internal drama in the narrator which is thus externalized—are never made explicit. In stories of Kafka, such as "The Hunger Artist" and "The Metamorphosis," as in Shirley Jackson's "The Lottery," a symbolic scheme appears to organize the fictional world. The reader is invited to interpret the symbols but is given little or no explicit guidance as to how. This differs from the effect of novels like *The Trial* and *The Castle*, where the problem has been developed at length and is not notably intensified by the truncation of the ending. Unlike our other varieties, this sort of recalcitrance is not peculiar to the modern short story. It exists in any parable or fable in which the "moral" is not spelled out, though the challenge in most parables is less strong than in our examples.

The fifth variety of resistance, modal discontinuity, challenges the reader at a more fundamental level. In this kind, which has become prominent recently, resistance is produced by a contradiction in what we may call the "fictional mode" in the piece—the primary assumptions on which the coherence of the fictional world depends. This may be a clash or poise or ambiguity between two conflicting conceptions of causation, as, in a not-so-modern example, the ghostly and realistic psychological explanations of "The Turn of the Screw," or, closer to our time, the religious and realistic explanations of violence in such stories as Flannery O'Connor's "A Good Man Is Hard to Find" and "Greenleaf": has grace actually been manifested; has the devil appeared? These stories by O'Connor also show another kind of modal discontinuity in the abrupt switch from comic expectations to serious violence. A contrary switch appears in stories like Donald Barthelme's "The School" and Kurt Vonnegut's "Next Door," where an essentially comic development is disrupted just before the end, not by an emergence of unexpected gravity but by the opposite—a deflection of the potentially serious direction the comedy seems to be taking by a descent into a new level of absurdity. When approaching death in the schoolroom is diverted by the children's demand that the teacher make love to his assistant, and the embarrassment of this is relieved when a new gerbil walks in, the story has moved into a new fictional world, and the reader must find a new kind of formal principle to accommodate the change.

Joyce Carol Oates's "How I Contemplated the World from the Detroit House of Correction and Began My Life Over Again" illustrates a more extreme contradiction in fictional modes. Here, the reality of an action is undermined but not destroyed by an insistence upon the act of creating that action. The girl in the story composes notes for a school essay in which it is impossible to tell to what extent the experiences she describes are "real" and to what extent they are invented. The reader is left facing two balanced possibilities. An adequate resolution probably requires a conception of form in which they continue to coexist—a kind of "creative plot" and "narrator-controlled fictional world" in which ambiguity itself is the first principle. (Sue Simpson Park, however, reads this story literally, reconstructing a chronology of the girl's troubles and seeing the disjointedness of her "notes" as an expression of her state of mind—an ingenious, but in my opinion not a persuasive, resolution.)[8]

This is metafiction; John Barth's "Lost in the Funhouse" and Robert Coover's "The Magic Poker" are other well-known examples. Other Coover stories differ from the latter in that the explicitly creating author is absent—stories such as "The Babysitter," "The Elevator," and "Quenby and Ola, Carl and Swede." These develop a series of contradictory or incompatible narratives involving a certain few characters in a specific place and time. No explanation is offered for the contradictions, no way of resolving them is given, no implied priority helps us determine which are "fantasies" and which are "real": all are equally fantastic and equally real. The primary suspense is the question how the contradictions will be joined. The ending boldly cuts the question off. There is *no* final truth in "The Babysitter," not even the possibility that the evening was routine and all the catastrophes were imaginary. In stories of this kind, recalcitrance is never completely resolved: it is not assimilated into a resolving psychology or symbolism or vision; it remains a contradiction, and whatever we say about its naturalizing form (no doubt another kind of creative plot), we must incorporate the contradiction into its description.

We must not overstate the case for a distinctive short story recalcitrance. The five kinds of final recalcitrance I have described are neither exhaustive nor mutually exclusive. Doubtless there are other

8. Wright, *Formal Principle*, 70–74, 116–17; Sue Simpson Park, "A Study in Counterpoint: Joyce Carol Oates's 'How I Contemplated the World from the Detroit House of Correction and Began My Life Over Again,'" *Modern Fiction Studies*, XXII (1976), 213–24.

kinds, and my distinctions could be replaced by others. (For example, what John Gerlach calls the "indirect mode" of the short story—"An awareness of ending, and the reader's delay in reaching it"—although not equivalent to any of the specific kinds of recalcitrance I have described, is clearly a source of recalcitrance.)[9] And although all short stories probably display inner recalcitrance, not all modern stories display final recalcitrance. A list of stories that do not would be impressive: it would include Graham Greene's "The Basement Room," Paul Bowles's "A Distant Episode," and Frank O'Connor's "Guests of the Nation," as well as many stories by Henry James. Stories with discovery and disclosure (static) plots and metafictional stories are more likely to make use of final recalcitrance than stories with dynamic plots and larger actions.

So I cannot say final recalcitrance defines the modern short story. I am not even sure of a steady progression toward the more radical kinds of recalcitrance, certainly not if there is a tendency now to retreat from the metafictional mode. Better to say only that final recalcitrance is the most extreme of the distinctive kinds of resistance the short story has developed. Along with inner recalcitrance and the kinds associated with modern fiction in general, it provides some measure of the health of the art. An analysis of recalcitrance, when it is recognized *as such*—as a step or interruption on the way to a potentially discoverable form, rather than the destruction or refutation of an inadequate one—can throw yet more light on what makes a good story such an exciting experience for us.

9. John Gerlach, *Toward the End: Closure and Structure in the American Short Story* (University, Ala., 1985), 43.

THOMAS M. LEITCH

The Debunking Rhythm of the American Short Story

Academic study of the short story began, ironically enough, just as writers like Chekhov, Joyce, and Stephen Crane were about to create stories that would render the newly formulated definitions and accounts of the short story inadequate, or at least incomplete. Brander Matthews, whose pioneering study *The Philosophy of the Short-Story* was published in 1901, defines "the Short-story" in contradistinction to "the Sketch" by observing that "while a Sketch may be still-life, in a Short-story something always happens. A Sketch may be an outline of character, or even a picture of a mood of mind, but in a Short-story there must be something done, there must be an action." Later theorists of fiction, though agreeing with Matthews that "the Short-story and the Sketch . . . melt and merge one into the other," have most often used plot as the sine qua non by which to distinguish short stories from other discursive modes of similar length, while acknowledging at the same time that according to this account, a great number of short stories which have appeared since about the turn of the century are not stories at all.[1]

Short story theory has continued to distinguish between two kinds of stories, or two structures for stories, which we might call the anecdotal and the epiphanic. The anecdotal story, typified by Hawthorne's "The Birthmark," Poe's "The Gold-Bug," and the Sherlock Holmes stories of Arthur Conan Doyle, presents an Aristotelian action with a beginning, middle, and end; the epiphanic story, represented by

---

1. Brander Matthews, *The Philosophy of the Short-Story* (New York, 1901), 35, 36. This problem has been widely discussed in essays on the short story's ontology. Ian Reid reviews the principal candidates for the defining qualities of the short story in his monograph *The Short Story* (1977; rpr. New York, 1979), 54–65.

Chekhov's "The Lady with the Dog," Joyce's "Ivy Day in the Committee Room," and Crane's Civil War stories, adumbrates a fictional world not by developing a plot involving purposive agents but by unfolding particular sensations or emotions and proceeding to a climactic revelation that does not necessarily take the form of a complete overt action. The distinction between the two kinds of stories is often made in different terms, but critics have almost universally begun their analysis of short fiction by distinguishing between stories which do have an intelligible plot and stories which do not. Readers who search in vain through their weekly issues of the *New Yorker* for stories that actually tell a story—that is, for those that satisfy the requirements Matthews and others have laid down concerning the plot—are testifying on the most fundamental level to the persisting inadequacy of our terminology, and our critical methodology, for analyzing the short story.

Matthews' analysis of the short story is derived principally from Poe, but Poe himself neither makes the distinction I have been describing nor, more surprisingly, makes such a distinction necessary. According to Poe, every word in a short story should work toward the production of a single unified effect on the reader, but Poe does not assume that the primary vehicle of that effect must be a coherent plot: indeed, the whole idea of an Aristotelian plot, which assumes moral agents acting deliberately to compass rational ends, becomes deeply problematic in stories like "The Fall of the House of Usher," "The Pit and the Pendulum," and "The Tell-Tale Heart," which are presented as stories about what happens to the principals rather than what they actively do. Poe's stories are so full of incident that it is easy to assume that Poe prescribes an eventful plot as a requisite for short fiction, but his emphasis in his review of *Twice-Told Tales* on the "single *effect*" or "preestablished design" of the short story would be as germane to the stories in *Dubliners* as to his own.[2]

Defining the short story in Poe's terms, as a prose discourse short enough to produce a unitary effect on its audience, rather than in terms of an anecdotal plot which it may or may not contain, allows us to see the anecdote as a special case or subset of the epiphanic story. All short stories, we might say, proceed to a revelation that establishes a teleology, a retrospective sense of design, informing the whole story. Events and details whose significance puzzles or eludes us in

2. Edgar Allan Poe, "Review of *Twice-Told Tales*," in Charles E. May (ed.), *Short Story Theories* (Athens, Ohio, 1976), 47, 48.

the course of our reading become clear in their import only at the story's conclusion. Since readers familiar with the conventions of short fiction naturally anticipate this sense of a revelatory ending which will resolve their questions, a story's teleology is felt as prospective and imminent, however uncertain we are of its precise form. The most puzzling stories, we assume, will eventually make sense; if they do not, we feel let down. If the climactic revelation is made available to one of the characters as a result of his actions, the story has the force of anecdote; if the story ends with a revelation detached from any particular course of action, or if the audience alone perceives the pattern which makes the story's events intelligible, the story's wholeness is epiphanic. The events of an action or plot are simply one vehicle for the revelation that makes the story a unitary whole capable of producing a single effect on its audience.

Another way to make the same point would be to say that the short story is the narrative mode that foregrounds closure. As John Gerlach has pointed out, however, short stories do not so much foreground closure as the audience's anticipation of closure.[3] Short stories are everywhere shaped by our expectation of an imminent teleology, but it does not follow that they will display such a teleology. Indeed the development of the short story since Gogol and Poe, the so-called modern short story, is marked by a movement toward endings of greater openness or indeterminacy. Particularly in the American short story, the reader's movement from bewilderment to authoritative revelation, from ignorance to knowledge, is complemented by what we might call the debunking rhythm of the short story, a rhythm that depends on a special use of antithesis. Gerlach, following Roland Barthes, describes antithesis, the movement from one belief or situation to its opposite, as a "particularly stable" narrative trope because it suggests an exhaustive demarcation of boundaries and so the conclusion of the story's investigation or survey of the world.[4] The exposition of a short story like Hemingway's "Big Two-Hearted River" or "Madame de Mauves" does not simply bewilder the audience but rather provides a false or illusory order of events: Nick Adams is just going on a fishing trip; Longmore is quite capable of understanding

3. See John Gerlach, *Toward the End: Closure and Structure in the American Short Story* (University, Ala., 1985), 160: "The short story is that genre in which anticipation of the ending is always present."

4. *Ibid.*, 10.

the nature of Madame de Mauves' position. The revelation with which short stories end can simultaneously provide a stable sense of closure and adumbrate a new order that displaces the assumptions of the exposition. Often, however, this displacement does not correspond to a movement from ignorance to knowledge but simply indicates a debunking or unknowing of the illusions that the story began by encouraging. Paco in "The Capital of the World" and the older waiter in "A Clean, Well-Lighted Place" undergo experiences which do not so much enlighten audiences by means of authoritative revelations as disabuse them of their illusions about the world the story presents and represents without substituting any positive or more comprehensive wisdom. In Henry James's "The Figure in the Carpet" and "In the Cage," the audience moves again not so much from ignorance to knowledge as from a false sense of certainty to a more authentic sense of uncertainty about the revelations James persistently withholds.

It is clearly impossible for a story to chart a progression from ignorance to knowledge—either the character's progression or the audience's—without presenting a complementary movement from false illusions to disillusionment, a movement based on the antithetical structure I have been describing.[5] But it is quite possible to challenge the character's, and the audience's, assumptions about the world without substituting any more-authoritative knowledge, so that such stories constitute not a form of knowledge but a challenge to knowledge, that is, a way of debunking assumptions which are not really true. A great many American short stories, whose antithetical structures indicate movements toward disillusionment rather than teleological movements toward revelation and reintegration, constitute essentially a means of unknowing rather than a means to knowledge. To borrow the terminology of Susan Lohafer's *Coming to Terms with the Short Story*, I would suggest that each of these stories, whether or not it includes a homecoming, is preeminently a story of departure, of movement away from the known.[6] More specifically, these stories commonly debunk a particular subject: the concept of a public identity, a self that acts in such a knowable, deliberate way as to assert a stable, discrete identity. The American short story as a genre presents

5. See Charles E. May, "The Nature of Knowledge in Short Fiction," *Studies in Short Fiction*, XXI (1984), 327–38, on the "defamiliarizing" wisdom of the short story.

6. Susan Lohafer, *Coming to Terms with the Short Story* (1983; rpr. Baton Rouge, 1985), 95.

a critique of the notion of a stable and discrete personal identity constituted by an individual's determinate actions—a means to the author's unmaking, and the audience's unknowing, an active, determinate self that was only an illusion to begin with.

Critics have long recognized the importance of the debunking rhythm in stories about initiation, or the coming of age, of a fictional character. In Balzac's *Lost Illusions* and Flaubert's *Sentimental Education*, the heroes, who begin with high ideals and false assumptions about themselves, lose their ideals and illusions without gaining any compensating revelation or indeed anything more than experience of the world as it is. Short stories of initiation typically render the hero's identity problematic without substituting an equally stable conception of the world or of one's public identity. In Hawthorne's "My Kinsman, Major Molineux," Robin Molineux unlearns his country-bred certainties about the world, his kinsman, and his own identity without gaining any authoritative wisdom; he emerges from the callow certainties of youth without revealing anything like an equally stable maturity. When he beholds his uncle carried by torchlight through the street, it is impossible to tell whether his laughter is self-protective, contagious, or genuinely hilarious; when his companion invites him, now disabused of his youthful illusions, to remain in town, it is impossible to tell what his reaction will be. By unmaking his hero as a boy without remaking him as a man, Hawthorne indicates that men do not have identities as secure as boys'. In "The Man Who Became a Woman," Sherwood Anderson presents a hero whose experience of himself as female destroys his old certainties about himself without substituting any new certainties. Certainly he does not ultimately feel himself a woman, for his climactic encounter with a dead horse "burned all that silly nonsense about being a girl right out of me," but he can neither recapture the sense of himself as a boy nor articulate the sense of himself as an adult; he can only leave the world of horses for the more equivocal world of men.[7]

Great numbers of American short stories tend to produce in the reader an experience analogous to the character's experience in these stories of initiation. The structure of these stories is based on the process of unmaking or unknowing the stable, discrete self defined in opposition to the world of other selves and other experiences. The stories proceed to debunk the notion of personal identity by attacking

7. Sherwood Anderson, *Horses and Men* (New York, 1923), 225.

the assumptions on which it is based; when the attack is complete, the stories end, typically (though not invariably) providing the rhetorical satisfaction of terminal antithesis while withholding any more authoritative account of the self. The terms of this attack on the self vary widely from one author to the next, but each author's critique of the self is consistent throughout his short fiction, and the various critiques have striking similarities.

Poe's short fiction comprises perhaps the most single-minded attack on the unitary self in American literature. Poe's heroes—William Wilson, Prince Prospero, Montresor, Berenice's husband Egaeus, the anonymous narrators of "The Pit and the Pendulum," "The Tell-Tale Heart," "The Black Cat," and "The Imp of the Perverse"—present themselves initially as personalities who are defined on one hand by their actions and on the other by their perceptions, a psychological mode of existence uniquely their own. Yet Poe consistently undermines these claims to identity. Apparently active characters like Egaeus and William Wilson are eventually seen as driven by forces they can neither understand nor control; the will that produces such frequently catastrophic results as the murder of inoffensive people is not their own. The hero of "The Pit and the Pendulum," attempting to escape from a dangerous world about which he knows nothing, and fearing madness even more than death, is condemned to a moral passivity Poe's other characters, however apparently active, experience as well. Since they cannot choose other than to act as they do, Poe's heroes stake their identities more decisively on their unique sensibilities; but whether or not these sensibilities define stable identities is open to question.

Defining personal identity in terms of the individual's unique physical sensibilities produces, in extreme cases, the sensationalists who people so many of Poe's stories—those men and women whose physical sensations are, or have been made by a particular experience, abnormally acute. Roderick Usher, Egaeus, Ligeia's husband, and the narrator of "The Tell-Tale Heart" all claim to be abnormally sensitive to physical stimuli. But Poe persistently raises the question of whether their experience of the world, the unique sensitivity that sets them apart from ordinary people, is the product of visionary insight or of madness. To define one's identity in terms of one's sensibilities is to risk losing it entirely. And the fear of dissociation, of loss of identity, is at the heart of all Poe's short stories. Even the comic and satirical stories are organized around images or situations of lost identity: the comic doubling in "Lionizing," the dismemberments in "A Predicament" and "Never Bet the Devil Your Head," and the dilemmas of Lacko'breath in "Loss of Breath" and Brevet Brigadier General John A.B.C. Smith in "The Man That Was Used Up." Poe's growing interest in mesmerism toward the end of his life is a thoroughly logical development of his fascination with situations in which people are out of their minds—or literally not themselves.

The psychological focus of Poe's stories emphasizes his critique of personal identity as a function of either action or perception. But this critique is also apparent in writers whose focus is less resolutely psychological. Throughout Melville's work, the principals are characteristically exposed to people or situations that cause them to doubt their own views of the world, even the nature of the assumptions on which their own identities are based, without substituting any more authoritative view. The most famous example in Melville is of course the confidence man, a protean figure who challenges the identity of everyone he meets without establishing one of his own; but Melville's short stories enact similar patterns. In "Bartleby the Scrivener," the comfortable habits which have allowed the blandly unimposing narrator to make his way complacently through the world are challenged by the copyist Bartleby, whose identity remains mysterious, whose past is blank, and whose challenge consists entirely in preferring not to participate in a world that at once dehumanizes its citizens and confers on them the only human identity they can understand or accept. Benito Cereno, forced to confront the ultimate moral negatives of slavery and treachery, plunges into melancholia, despair, and death, whereas Captain Delano, more fortunate in his obtuseness, maintains his own command and his optimistic view of the world only because he cannot see the contradictions that destroy Don Benito. These stories are organized around a figure who claims a heightened sensitivity to the contradictions of the social order but whose sensitivity leads only to paralysis or death.

Similarly, Melville follows Poe in questioning whether a heightened sensitivity to the physical world is a sign of individual insight or dehumanizing madness even in such a slight story as "Cock-a-Doodle-Doo!" in which the rooster represents both Merrymusk's freedom from the travails of poverty, illness, and death, and the irresponsibility with which he courts those travails and which he bequeaths to the narrator. Is neglecting one's worldly duties because the crowing of a cock fills one with transcendent joy a sign of liberation from the world which constrains one's identity or of crippling alienation from a world in which, for better or worse, everyone must live? The story pointedly declines to answer this question. In "The Encantadas," worldly experience is decisively set against the very possibility of identity, the whole idea of the human. Melville's sailors and natives explore the enchanted isles for signs of transcendent meaning and play out their anecdotal dramas against them, but the isles themselves resist any attempt to impose a meaning on experience: as in Poe's stories, neither action nor perception can establish an identity that is not in constant danger of challenge, erosion, or loss of faith in the world as a reflection of oneself.

Stephen Crane's characters, like Melville's in "The Encantadas," are constantly attempting to establish identities their worlds do not support. Fred Collins, in "A Mystery of Heroism," acts heroically in crossing a battlefield for a bucket of water and, finally, in giving water to a dying officer, but feels certain that his deed, the response to a dare, does not make him a hero. Although he remains convinced that there is such a thing as a hero, the story, as its title indicates, serves to debunk the very possibility of heroism. In "The Open Boat," the shipwrecked men vainly attempt to establish an intelligible connection between their identities and the forces threatening them; although the survivors feel at last that when they hear the sea's voice from the shore, "they could then be interpreters," they are left with no reason why they were spared and the oiler was not.[8] One's actions and perceptions evidently have little to do with one's identity.

The elemental settings of Crane's stories of war and shipwreck, in which men facing the ultimate danger of meaningless death find that their assertions of identity—"Yes, but I love myself"—have become meaningless, may seem responsible for the existential emphasis of the stories, but the problem of personal identity remains pivotal even in the suburban setting of "The Monster," which focuses on the question of how much Doctor Trescott owes to Henry Johnson, who saved the doctor's son Jimmie from a fire but was horribly burned himself.[9] Is Trescott obliged to take care of Henry at the price of complete social ostracism, or has Henry become such a monster that the doctor owes him nothing he can pay? Henry's lumbering idiocy, set against the petty savagery of the townspeople in Whilomville, suggests that bio-

---

8. Stephen Crane, *Prose and Poetry* (New York, 1984), 909.
9. *Ibid.*, 902.

logical and social accounts of human identity are equally brutalizing, and that Trescott's humanity, represented by his sense of responsibility toward Henry, is doomed.

Perhaps Crane's most far-ranging critique of identity as a function of experience is in "The Blue Hotel," in which melodramatic incidents constantly hinting at a deeper meaning turn out to have none. The Swede is apprehensive about the West for no good reason; he becomes expansive and aggressive for no good reason; Johnnie Scully cheats in their card game for no good reason. After the Swede has outfought Johnnie, he walks out of the blue hotel into a snowstorm in which "it was hard to imagine a peopled earth. . . . The conceit of man was explained by this storm to be the very engine of life."[10] The Swede, failing to realize how tenuous are the customs and beliefs that keep him alive, walks into a saloon, bullies a stranger, and is killed. The blue hotel, whose color has been chosen to attract attention without providing any significance, is an appropriate figure for the condition of Crane's isolated principals, whose identities most often turn out to be a function of their capacity for self-delusion.

Poe, Melville, and Crane all debunk accepted notions of identity because of an existential suspicion that human existence is meaningless: one's identity is either forced on one or is the product of vain illusion. The critique of human identity reappears, though with a different resolution, even in such an optimistic writer as Flannery O'Connor, whose work, like Poe's, constitutes a thoroughgoing attack on the very notion of the self as stable, discrete, and knowable. "You aren't who you think you are," Julian tells his mother in "Everything That Rises Must Converge." His observation is true of all O'Connor's principals, including Julian himself, who after his mother's stroke finally realizes that he is "looking into a face he had never seen before" and that the self-righteously liberal clichés which have governed his own idea of himself are shockingly inadequate.[11] "Everything That Rises Must Converge" ends, like so many of O'Connor's stories, with a resolution recalling that of "My Kinsman, Major Molineux," a moment of grace during which all of Julian's old certainties burn away without being replaced by any new ones. O'Connor main-

10. *Ibid.*, 822.

11. Flannery O'Connor, "Everything That Rises Must Converge," in *The Complete Stories of Flannery O'Connor* (New York, 1971), 410, 420, copyright © 1961, 1965 by the Estate of Mary Flannery O'Connor.

tained that such a moment was the pivot of each of her stories. Her heroes—the grandmother in "A Good Man Is Hard to Find," Mrs. Cope in "A Circle in the Fire," Mrs. Shortley and Mrs. MacIntyre in "The Displaced Person," Hulga in "Good Country People," Thomas in "The Comforts of Home," O. E. Parker in "Parker's Back"—all begin by assuming that they (usually they alone, in all their world) know who they are; each story turns on a challenge to their certainties in the name of a transcendent certainty, a conception of one's identity as an incarnation of God's grace; each story ends with the acceptance of that grace; and in almost every case this acceptance is literally annihilating.

Because the focus of prose fiction (unlike that, for instance, of Dante's *Commedia*) is typically mundane rather than transcendent, it is not surprising that O'Connor would focus more sharply on the debunking challenge of her heroes' conversions than on their transcendent reintegrations. Even her rare stories with happy endings (such as "The Artificial Nigger" and "Revelation"), which typically conclude with a visionary description of this reintegration, however, emphasize the loss of what the characters have taken to be their individuality, so that Mr. Head and Nelson, in "The Artificial Nigger," become interchangeable, and Mrs. Turpin, seeing herself as a hog in "Revelation," observes of the souls ascending to heaven that "even their virtues were being burned away."[12] The mystery of identity in O'Connor is so consistently set against the illusion of individuality that many of O'Connor's critics, ignoring the author's frequent and explicit averrals that her work was organized around the experience of religious conversion, have followed John Hawkes in reading her as a secular ironist.[13]

The examples of Poe, Melville, Crane, and O'Connor suggest that just as the anecdotal story is a subset of the story of teleological revelation, the revelatory story and the debunking story are in turn complementary subsets of the antithetical story, the story which proceeds from an illusory initial way of knowing to a critique of or challenge to that order. In the revelatory story, the illusions implicit in the story's opening are displaced by a teleology that takes the form of some posi-

12. *Ibid.*, 508.
13. See John Hawkes, "Flannery O'Connor's Devil," *Sewanee Review*, LXX (1962), 395–407. For a representative expansion of Hawkes's reading, see Josephine Hendin, *The World of Flannery O'Connor* (Bloomington, Ind., 1970).

tive wisdom—a moral, a more stable model of the world, a deeper insight into the story's thematic material. The debunking story, by contrast, displays as its point and purpose the process of unknowing a false or delusive sense of individual action or perception as basis for a stable sense of personal identity.

The stories I have been examining all employ an antithetical structure to launch an attack on the self. But these stories may seem exceptional or unrepresentative. Surely, it might be objected, the stories magazines have carried for a hundred years—stories like O. Henry's "Strictly Business," F. Scott Fitzgerald's "The Offshore Pirate," and J. D. Salinger's "Down at the Dinghy"—are structured by ironies whose terminal force is less challenging and which therefore have helped establish the short story's status as an illustrative anecdote, or, more formally, what Mark Schorer has called "an art of moral revelation." [14] But each of these authors' most successful works—O. Henry's "A Municipal Report" and "An Unfinished Story," Fitzgerald's "May Day" and "Babylon Revisited," Salinger's "Pretty Mouth and Green My Eyes" and "A Perfect Day for Bananafish"—emphasizes the antithetical structure of challenge over any concluding integration or resolution.

More generally, no short story, however modest its aims, can achieve a sense of resolution or closure without mounting a challenge to the way its world is first adumbrated, even if that challenge takes the form of an ironic joke, as it does in so many of O. Henry's stories. Evidently the challenge itself is logically prior to the resolution, as the stories which present a conceptually open antithesis—a challenge without resolution—suggest. Examples from other authors could be multiplied to support my claim that the characteristic structural feature of American short fiction is the debunking rhythm—that even if stories which proceed to a revelatory teleology may outnumber stories which simply debunk the assumptions of their audiences, the most significant American short stories are organized around a conceptually unresolved challenge to the self.

If American short fiction is characterized by the debunking rhythm as a subset of the more general structure of antithesis, the question naturally arises to what extent that rhythm is characteristic of American fiction in general or of short fiction in general. Richard Chase, for

14. Mark Schorer (ed.), *The Story: A Critical Anthology* (Rev. ed.; Englewood Cliffs, N.J., 1950), 330.

example, has argued in a widely influential formulation that American literature in all its forms has more often focused on "the broken circuit," the contradictions and discontinuities of human experience, than on the possibilities of normative integration typical of British fiction.[15] Is the debunking tendency I have been ascribing to American short fiction more truly characteristic of American literature as such?

The attempt to make the debunking rhythm an exclusive characteristic of American fiction, rather than of short fiction, would raise many problems. Chase himself notes that *Wuthering Heights*, with its complete lack of interest in the resolution or social integration characteristic of most English novels, seems more like an American novel. Similarly, the stories of such non-American authors as Chekhov, Joyce, and Kafka seem to display the same challenge to assumptions about the self without supplying anything akin to the moment of revelatory wisdom commentators like Schorer have led us to expect—or, put more fairly, the revelation of "Gooseberries," "A Painful Case," and "The Hunger Artist" is a negative one, a debunking of inadequate certainties in favor of what Charles E. May has called "the immediate truth of intuition, emotion, and dreams."[16] Nonetheless, many American novels as well as short stories are structured by unresolved challenges rather than revelations of wisdom. Arthur Dimmesdale's neighbors never do agree about why a scarlet A appeared on his breast, or indeed whether it was really there after all; Ahab strikes through the mask to make a discovery whose nature remains mysterious; Huckleberry Finn lights out for the territory on his own; Quentin Compson pieces together the history of Thomas Sutpen's design only to end with the frantic assertion that he doesn't hate the South; Oedipa Maas, suspecting herself alternately of paranoia and hallucination, sits at the end of her novel still awaiting the crying of lot 49. Because the structure of conceptually unresolved antithesis is characteristic of so many American works, both short and long, it seems safest to argue only for tendencies; just as American fiction tends in contrast to British fiction to emphasize unresolved contradictions, so the same emphasis tends to appear in short stories in contrast to novels.

To the oppositions between American and non-American fiction and between short fiction and long must be added a third: the opposi-

15. See Richard Chase, *The American Novel and Its Tradition* (Garden City, N.J., 1957), 1–12.

16. Charles E. May, "The Unique Effect of the Short Story," *Studies in Short Fiction*, XIII (1976), 297.

tion between modern and premodern fiction. Antithesis is a primary structural principle in premodern short fiction, for example in the *Decameron*, which includes so many stories depending on reversals, unmaskings, or emotional contrasts (for example, the tragic love stories of Day 4). But because Boccaccio's antitheses characteristically debunk his principals' pretensions in the name of exemplary habits of justice, forgiveness, or love, and frequently for the sake of a new community based on a more open expression of sexuality and tolerance, his stories customarily end either with the establishment of this larger, more generous community or with the unhappy lovers' reaffirmation of the love which has defined them from the beginning. The debunking tendency of the modern short story allows it to present a rhetorically satisfying conclusion while maintaining a much greater degree of thematic openness.

But this contrast between premodern resolution and modern irresolution is equally apparent in other modes of discourse besides the short story. In particular, nonnarrative works contemporaneous with the development of the modern short story—the work of playwrights like Ibsen, Pirandello, and Georg Büchner, poets like Baudelaire, Whitman, and Eliot, and essayists like Freud, Jacques Lacan, and Michel Foucault—often seem equally to attack the conception of a nuclear self. The range of assaults on the self is evidently too wide to be limited to either a particular national literature or a particular generic mode. But if the tendency toward conceptually unresolved closure, the debunking rhythm I have been describing, is more prevalent in modern discourse than premodern, in American fiction than non-American, and in short stories than novels, then it should be possible to indicate a range of relations and dependencies between these oppositions. Although examining the full range of these relations is outside the scope of this essay, I should like to conclude by considering one of them—the relation between American fiction and short fiction—in some detail and venturing a brief suggestion about another, the relation between short fiction and modernism in general. My premise is that in the tradition of American prose fiction, the short story occupies a much more prominent place than in, for example, British fiction—that it is indeed the unmarked mode of American fiction.

This premise requires some justification in view of a persuasive essay to the contrary by Mary Louise Pratt, who contends that the relation between the short story and the novel is "a hierarchical one with the novel on top and the short story dependent. . . . Between these paired genres, relations of long to short coincide with relations of un-marked to marked, of major to minor, of greater to lesser." Hence "facts about the novel are necessary to explain facts about the short story, but the reverse is not so." Although Pratt acknowledges that "in the establishment of a modern national literature in Ireland, the short story emerges as the central prose fiction genre," and that "its role has been comparable in the emergence of the modern literature of the American South," she would probably argue that the greater power and prestige of the novel, and its historical independence from definition in terms of the short story, would preclude the establish-ment of the short story as the central or unmarked mode of American literary narrative.[17]

Pratt describes several differences between short stories and nov-els, including the short story's greater openness to formal experimen-tation and the exploration of new subject matter, its tendency toward orality, its retention of such older narrative traditions as parables, ani-mal fables, and fairy tales, and its status among critics and practi-tioners alike as a skilled craft (as against the sublime and unteachable "art" of the novel). Apt as these observations are, they apply almost equally well to the differences between American and English narra-tive fiction. Ever since Melville, American novels have been more of-ten experimental than English novels and more adventurous in their search for new subject matter. The tendency toward orality appears in a great many of Twain's and Faulkner's novels, in Salinger's *Catcher in the Rye,* and in all of Kurt Vonnegut's novels (indeed, Salinger and Vonnegut are far more conspicuously oral in their long fiction than in their short). Older narrative traditions survive in Hawthorne's novels (whose author kept apologetically describing them as romances), in the ironic allegories and exempla of Nathanael West, and in the encyclopedic fables of John Barth and Thomas Pynchon. As to the distinction between high and low art that Pratt finds characteristic of the difference between historical attitudes to short stories and to long, it is doubtful that until the 1950s academic criticism in America had much use for any writers currently active; even if short story writing has been taught as a craft, it has been equally true that ap-prentice writers have commonly had their sights on the great Ameri-

17. Mary Louise Pratt, "The Short Story: The Long and the Short of It," *Poetics,* X (1981), 180, 187.

can novel as a commodity to be duly produced and marketed; and if academic criticism has recently been more respectful of novelists like Saul Bellow and John Barth, the novel itself, as Thomas Whiteside points out, has at the same time become exceedingly commercialized by its producers and distributors.[18]

The similarities between the characteristics Pratt ascribes to the short story and those we may reasonably ascribe to American narrative fiction of any length help to explain the primary importance of the short story in American fiction. And when we consider the canonical American novelists, the dependence of American fiction on models of the short story becomes even clearer. It is true that the short story served as a training ground for many authors—Hawthorne, James, Hemingway, Flannery O'Connor—who went on to write novels. But writers like Melville, Stephen Crane, and Fitzgerald reversed this pattern, beginning with novels and only later writing short stories. Poe, Crane, and Hemingway all wrote many more short stories than novels, and the short stories of Poe, Hawthorne, Hemingway, and Sherwood Anderson excel their novels. Poe and Hemingway, for example, are major figures in the development of the short story whose novels are far less important and critically esteemed—a situation surely not to be explained by the "inferior" status of the short story. The fact that a surprising number of distinguished American novelists seem to have been storytellers at heart suggests that, for them at least, the short story, despite a generic name which presupposes the novel as the unmarked, "non-short" narrative mode, was itself the unmarked, and the novel the deviant, mode.

This is true even of such a major novelist (and relatively minor short story writer) as William Faulkner, whose longer works are based on transformations of the forms of short fiction. Faulkner's habit of incorporating previously published short stories (for example, "Barn Burning," "Wash," "Spotted Horses," and "Centaur in Brass") into his novels is well known. What is less widely appreciated is that with few exceptions (of which the most important is *Sanctuary*), Faulkner's most characteristic and successful novels are structured either as manifold perspectives on a single story (*The Sound and the Fury, As I Lay Dying, Absalom, Absalom!*) or as a network of analogous stories (*Light in August, The Hamlet, Go Down, Moses*). Since Faulkner con-

18. See Thomas Whiteside, *The Blockbuster Complex: Conglomerates, Show Business, and Book Publishing* (Middletown, Conn., 1981).

tinues, both within individual novels and in the Yoknapatawpha saga as a whole, to return repeatedly to the same situations and motifs, embodied either in the same characters or in their analogues, the line of development to which he subjects his material seems more properly ruminative and discursive than teleological and revelatory. *The Sound and the Fury* may be an investigation into the implications of a single image—Caddy's muddy drawers seen from below as she sits in the pear tree looking in the window and learning of her grandmother's death—but it is an investigation that ramifies endlessly; it concludes only with a parody of teleological resolution ("cornice and façade flowed smoothly once more from left to right; post and tree, window and doorway, and signboard, each in its ordered place") whose combination of terminal force with thematic irresolution is much more characteristic of short stories than of novels.[19]

Indeed, Faulkner is unique in having written several works (*The Unvanquished, The Wild Palms, Go Down, Moses*) whose status as novels or volumes of stories continues to be debated. His fondness for returning to the same setting, even the same characters and situations, over and over in novels and stories alike, and his determination to tell the whole truth about the world he presents, adding sequels (*The Town, The Mansion, Requiem for a Nun*) and filling in gaps once left open (Quentin Compson's experiences in *Absalom, Absalom!*), justify Malcolm Cowley's assertion that "he is not primarily a novelist: that is, his stories do not occur to him in book-length units of 70,000 to 150,000 words. . . . Faulkner is best and most nearly himself in long stories . . . or else in the Yoknapatawpha saga as a whole."[20] Evidently the short story is a unit of composition more stable and congenial for Faulkner than the novel over which he achieved such a personal mastery.

Faulkner's work suggests that the formal relation between short stories and novels is more problematic than is usually acknowledged. Faulkner's novels are surely more peculiar structurally than Jane Austen's *Emma* or George Eliot's *Mill on the Floss,* but no more peculiar than *Ulysses,* which Joyce first conceived as a short story, or Kafka's novels, which read like short stories run amok. Although theorists of

19. William Faulkner, *The Sound and the Fury* (New York, 1929), 401, with the permission of Random House, Inc., and Curtis Brown Agency.

20. Malcolm Cowley, Introduction to Cowley (ed.), *The Portable Faulkner* (New York, 1946), 18, copyright 1946 by The Viking Press, Inc., renewed © 1974 by The Viking Press, Inc., All rights reserved. Reprinted by permission of Viking Penguin Inc.

fiction, when they debate the nature of the short story, tend to measure it against an unmarked novelistic norm, that norm—represented, for example, by the single-plot linear narratives of Austen and Eliot— is inadequate even for the novel itself. Ever since the rise of the novel, the genre has spawned works (*Tristram Shandy*, Machado de Assis's *Dom Casmurro*, Gide's *The Counterfeiters*) whose digressiveness, self-reflexiveness, and episodic resistance to closure have set them apart from the norm.

In American fiction, the counter-tradition of what might be called nonnovelistic novels—novels whose linear structure is obscure, whose imagined world is unusually thin or whose compass of time unusually short, and whose unity is equivocal—has in fact been the dominant tradition, as it has been the dominant tradition of modern fiction generally. For the two hundred years following Defoe, the novel was indeed, as Pratt contends, the dominant form in Western narrative. Since the rise of modernist narrative in the work of Joyce, Kafka, Gide, and their contemporaries, however, the short story has exercised a decisive influence over the form of the novel. Even though we continue to read novels in preference to short stories, novels themselves have become to a great extent story-novels. Just as the short story represents the unmarked mode of American narrative, its structural affinities with recent longer fiction suggest that it may have replaced the traditional novel, with its linear plot, psychologically expressive overt action, and teleological revelation, as the unmarked mode of modern narrative.

Of course, the novel has been and continues to be the dominant mode of literary narrative in terms of economics and prestige. But the short story, far from defining itself purely in contradistinction to the novel, has established formal patterns which have been crucial to the development of the modern novel. And the foremost of these patterns is the debunking rhythm characterized by conceptually unresolved antithesis. In the work of English novelists between Scott and Trollope, the challenge to received ideas of personal and historical identity is typically incarnated in characters who end in death (Fergus MacIvor), compromise (Dorothea Brooke), or expulsion from the community (Lady Laura Standish), but whose challenge makes the range of reference—the novel's world—broader and truer. In the novels of Hardy, Lawrence, and Conrad, the challenge becomes more insistent and finally impossible to assimilate into the novel's represented world; and novels like *Ulysses*, Woolf's *To the Lighthouse*, and Forster's *A Pas-*

sage to India pose challenges to accepted notions of identity without providing complementary resolutions. In more radically experimental American novels (William Gaddis' *The Recognitions*, Pynchon's *V.*, John Barth's *Chimera*), antithesis appears plainly as what it has implicitly been all along: the constitutive trope of narrative fiction. Novels like Balzac's *Lost Illusions* and Stendhal's *The Red and the Black* often mitigate their challenge of unexamined ideals by presenting a world so detailed and extensive that its worldly wisdom is worth having; but American short stories, declining to evoke such a world, characteristically conclude with a debunking challenge to conventional assumptions about personal identity—a challenge coeval with the rise of modernism itself.

ROBERT M. LUSCHER

The Short Story Sequence: An Open Book

With some consternation, Hortense Calisher notes that the
separate identity of the short story can be threatened by the
context its neighbors within a collection provide: "A story is an
apocalypse, served in a very small cup. Still, it wants to be considered
in its company only. The presence of neighbors changes it. Worlds
meant to be compacted only to themselves, bump. Their very sequence can do them violence. Even when all the stories are by the
same hand."[1] Significantly, her remarks occur in the preface to her
Collected Stories, a volume in which she takes advantage of this "bumping" by rearranging the contents of her previous collections into four
sections of related stories. Although a sequential arrangement of
short stories may indeed do violence to the compact world we expect
to explore in each, such bumping and the ensuing binding cannot be
avoided; indeed, this phenomenon has been exploited since the in-
ception of the short story as a genre—especially when the stories
have been by the same hand.

Calisher's attempt to organize the canvas of her collected stories is
only a mild manifestation of the ongoing interest in the form I call the
short story sequence: a volume of stories, collected and organized by
their author, in which the reader successively realizes underlying patterns of coherence by continual modifications of his perceptions of
pattern and theme. Within the context of the sequence, each short
story is thus not a completely closed formal experience. Each successive apocalypse in some fashion prepares us for the next, shedding
light on the compact worlds to follow. The volume as a whole thus

1. Hortense Calisher, *The Collected Stories of Hortense Calisher* (New York, 1975), ix.

148

becomes an open book, inviting the reader to construct a network of associations that binds the stories together and lends them cumulative thematic impact.

Various names for this literary form have been suggested, but none emphasize the reader's progressive development of meaning as well as *short story sequence*. Dallas Lemmon's hybrid term *rovelle*—a blend of *roman* and *novelle*—refers to the form's dual impulses but suggests the presence of a causal and temporal narrative dimension most sequences do not possess. Joel Silverman's "short story composite," Joseph Reed's "short story compound," and Pleasant Reed's and Timothy Alderman's "integrated short story collection" all suggest the static unity of combined independent parts but fail to indicate the importance of the stories' sequential nature or the recurrent elements that provide more dynamic unity.[2]

Forrest Ingram's term, *short story cycle*, which critics most commonly use, draws attention to the recurrence of theme, symbol, and character, but does so at the expense of deemphasizing the volume's successiveness.[3] While Ingram's name evokes a distant kinship with epic cycles, the term *short story sequence* suggests the form's kinship with the sonnet sequence and the modern poetic sequence, thus highlighting the close alliance between the short story and lyric poetry. Since the reader's dominant experience as he negotiates the text and tentatively assembles its patterns is sequential, the term *short story sequence* is thus more accurately descriptive. As in a musical sequence, the story sequence repeats and progressively develops themes and motifs over the course of the work; its unity derives from a perception of both the successive ordering and recurrent patterns, which together provide the continuity of the reading experience.

Within a sequence, the individual stories do not lose their distinctiveness but rather expand and elaborate the contexts, characters, symbols, or themes developed by the others. These works should be

2. Dallas Marion Lemmon, Jr., "The Rovelle, or the Novel of Interrelated Stories: M. Lermontov, G. Keller, S. Anderson" (Ph.D. dissertation, Indiana University, 1970); Raymond Joel Silverman, "The Short Story Composite: Forms, Functions, and Applications" (Ph.D. dissertation, University of Michigan, 1970); Joseph W. Reed, Jr., *Faulkner's Narrative* (New Haven, 1973), 176; Pleasant Reed, "The Integrated Short Story Collection: Studies of a Form of Nineteenth and Twentieth Century Fiction" (Ph.D. dissertation, Indiana University, 1974); Timothy C. Alderman, "The Integrated Short Story Collection as a Genre" (Ph.D. dissertation, Purdue University, 1982).

3. Forrest L. Ingram, *Representative Short Story Cycles of the Twentieth Century: Studies in a Literary Genre* (The Hague, 1971).

viewed, not as failed novels, but as unique hybrids that combine two distinct reading pleasures: the patterned closure of individual stories and the discovery of larger unifying strategies that transcend the apparent gaps between stories. Constructed without the novel's more rigid narrative skeleton, the short story sequence relies on a variety of textual strategies to provide unity and coherence. Simple technical devices such as a title, a preface, an epigraph, or framing stories may be used; in addition, more organic unities such as common narrators, characters, images, locale, and themes may be present. Finally, structural patterns involving counterpoint, juxtaposition, or a loose temporal sequence can bring the stories together.

The successful evolution of this form has been closely linked with the continued vitality of the short story. Even Irving's *Sketch Book*, with its fictitious narrator Geoffrey Crayon, illustrates the early impulse to produce something beyond a miscellaneous collection of independent tales. Similarly, both Poe and Hawthorne attempted to publish volumes of stories unified by narrative frames, but met with no success.[4] In a more favorable publishing environment for short story collections, regional authors such as Hamlin Garland (*Main-Travelled Roads*, 1891) and Sarah Orne Jewett (*The Country of the Pointed Firs*, 1896) complemented the unity of place with other forms of coherence before Sherwood Anderson (in *Winesburg, Ohio*) and his contemporaries during the short story renaissance of the 1920s and 1930s developed the form further. Modernism provided an artist such as Faulkner with greater opportunity to loosen generic constraints in his novels and in his short story sequences *Go Down, Moses* and *The Unvanquished*. The recent resurgence of interest in the short story has fostered experimentation in the short story sequence by such established writers as John Updike and Peter Taylor, as well as by such newer artists as Gloria Naylor, Alice Munro, and Susan Kenney.[5]

4. On Poe's plans for "Tales of the Folio Club," see Alexander Hammond, "A Reconstruction of Poe's 1833 'Tales of the Folio Club,'" *Poe Studies*, V (1972), 25–32, and G. R. Thompson, *Poe's Fiction: Romantic Irony in the Gothic Tales* (Madison, Wis., 1973), 40–44. Concerning Hawthorne's plans and publishing difficulties, see Arlin Turner, *Nathaniel Hawthorne: A Biography* (New York, 1980), 49–58, 70–80, and James R. Mellow, *Nathaniel Hawthorne in His Times* (Boston, 1980), 33, 46–47, 70–71, 81–82.

5. A corresponding surge of critical interest in the form seems to be occurring. While this book was in press, two important resources appeared: a 1988 special issue of *Journal of the Short Story in English*, edited by J. Gerald Kennedy, and *The Short Story Cycle: A Genre Companion and Reference Guide* (Westport, Conn., 1988), by Susan Garland Mann.

Nevertheless, the short story has usually been a solitary creature. Nurtured by the periodicals since its beginnings, it has most often appeared singly, even though publication in book form is its final guarantee of immortality. The short story's major appeal as a genre has been its status as a brief, unified work with a certain formal wholeness. As Hollis Summers remarks: "We only assume that our interest in the short story is satisfied by its action, its people, or its theme. We stay with the story for the form itself." Yet if the short story offers us a complete and satisfying experience, then its incorporation into a larger aesthetic whole presents some problems. Brander Matthews, concerned primarily with establishing the short story as a distinct genre, felt that "its formal totality impresses the reader with the belief that it would be spoiled if it were made larger, or incorporated into a larger work. . . . Now it cannot be said too emphatically that the genuine Short-story abhors the idea of the Novel. It neither can be conceived as part of a Novel, nor can it be elaborated and expanded to form a Novel."[6] Matthews' overwhelming insistence on the short story's unity of effect grants it separate dignity but unnecessarily limits our perception of intertextuality. Although the single short story may abhor the novel, a group of stories joined in a volume need not do so. To approximate the diverse but harmonious effect that Matthews reserves for the novel, a writer need not expand and elaborate each story so much that it loses its distinctiveness; simply by judicious arrangement (or, if necessary, minor revisions and additions) he may shape a work in which each story elaborates upon and expands certain contexts, actions, symbols, or ideas developed independently by the others.

Such a possibility, however, may require a less restrictive conception of the short story; it also asks that we recognize a loose but comprehensive interrelationship among a writer's stories, especially if he has chosen to publish them as a volume. Henry Seidel Canby, who attempts to sketch the essential selectivity of the short story, nonetheless suggests that it might be an independent manifestation of a larger current of thought: "[the short story writer] looks only for the episode, which, like the bubble on the stream, is part of yet distinguished from the main current. . . . He foregoes in completeness and gains in force, and this by a change in the standpoint from which he

6. Hollis Summers (ed.), *Discussions of the Short Story* (Boston, 1963), vii; Brander Matthews, *The Philosophy of the Short-Story* (New York, 1901), 17, 26.

views his world of fact and fancy."[7] In collecting several of these "bubbles" from various sites and arranging them in some spatial order within a volume, the writer allows us not only to sound the depths beneath each bubble but also to feel the thematic current that flows through his "world of fact and fancy." While each short story probes a select and seemingly isolated episode in some depth from a particular standpoint, it may still be part of some larger conceptual whole, one indication of a wider truth or thematic current that a single short story cannot chart completely.

It might seem that a short story sequence demands a special type of story—some generic renegade which violates the prescriptions of unity laid down by Poe and Matthews. Such rules, however, are neither comprehensive nor totally descriptive; because of the wide variety within the genre, the behavior of the short story is hard to classify. "The 'short story' is a highly elastic term, after all," Joyce Carol Oates observes. "Poe's remarks are inappropriate to our time, and in fact to the marvelous modern tradition of the story that begins with Chekhov, Joyce, Conrad, and James." Poe required that everything the writer put *in* the story be directed toward the unified effect, whereas Chekhov, along with the other "moderns" Oates names, was concerned with what was left *out* of the story and its effect on the outcome. In his letters, Chekhov reiterates the short story's necessary incompleteness: "Long detailed works have their own peculiar aims, which require a most careful execution regardless of total expression. But in a short story, it is better to say not enough than to say too much."[8] In the interest of compression, a certain amount of subjective activity must be left to the reader, who participates by supplying what the author leaves out. Although this activity helps reinforce the concentration of the reading experience, at the same time it involves a reach outside the story itself for a moment.

Taking advantage of this evocative quality, the short story sequence offers a readily available source for the reader's subjective contributions. Almost any short story, even the most self-contained and strikingly unified one, may be potentially enriched by the context that a

7. Henry Seidel Canby, "On the Short Story," in Eugene Current-Garcia and Walton R. Patrick (eds.), *What Is the Short Story?* (Rev. ed.; Glenview, Ill., 1974), 41.

8. Sanford Pinsker, "Speaking About Short Fiction: An Interview with Joyce Carol Oates," *Studies in Short Fiction*, XVIII (1981), 240; Anton Chekhov, "On the Problems of Technique in the Short Story," in Current-Garcia and Patrick (eds.), *What Is the Short Story?*, 21.

group of similarly oriented stories by the same author provides. In Garland's 1891 edition of *Main-Travelled Roads,* for instance, the six Middle Border stories—unified by a consistent narrative sympathy, a reformist stance, the return motif, the opposition between the land's beauty and squalor, and a series of epigraphs—present a complex portrait of the region that a single story such as "Under the Lion's Paw" cannot offer. As Donald Pizer notes, "The book as a whole is powerful and evocative and has an aesthetic effect far superior to that of any one story."[9]

Often, the individual units of a short story sequence grow out of a larger controlling idea that may either precede them or take shape during their creation. For the writer, such a controlling conception can be a mixed blessing; it can provide a clear sense of place, character, or theme for his stories but, at the same time, create formal problems by offering the tantalizing possibility of a novel. Although the short story sequence provides a sound solution to such a dilemma, until recently its status as an alternative was somewhat provisional. Chaucer, Boccaccio, and Homer provide historical precedents for uniting a related group of stories, but nineteenth-century short story criticism, which stressed the story's generic integrity, and traditional concepts of novelistic unity severely discouraged the generic border crossings involved in the short story sequence. The form's development has been spurred not only by Joyce and Anderson but also by the possibilities of unity demonstrated in American regional collections and by more recent experimentation with the novel.[10]

Still, as Chekhov's honest doubts about his task illustrate, a writer attempting to go beyond the limits of the single story may encounter problems:

> And so in planning a story one is bound to think first about its framework: from a crowd of leading or subordinate characters one selects one person only—wife or husband; one puts him on canvas and paints him alone, making him prominent, while the others one scatters over the heaven like small coin, and the result is something like the vault of heaven: one big moon and a number of very small stars around it. But the moon is not a success, because it can only be understood if the stars too are intelligible,

9. Donald Pizer, Introduction to Hamlin Garland, *Main-Travelled Roads,* ed. Donald Pizer (1891; rpr. Columbus, Ohio, 1970), xiii.

10. See Robert M. Luscher, "American Regional Short Story Sequences" (Ph.D. dissertation, Duke University, 1984), 1–59 *passim.*

and the stars are not worked out. And so what I produce is not literature, but something like the patching of Trishka's coat.

Chekhov's difficulties suggest that the complete realization of certain stories may require a more extended but nonnovelistic form. Expansion and elaboration within the story itself would produce a clumsy patchwork quite unlike the vault of heaven; on the other hand, increased luminosity of one or more of the "small stars" in their own distinct settings (that is, stories) would brighten the entire thematic sky. By answering the demands of subject matter and theme in the extended framework of the short story sequence, an artist such as Chekhov would be more comfortable writing a short story which could stand "solitary out in space," as Eudora Welty contends a successful story does. "[We see] this story as a little world in space, just as we can isolate one star in the sky by a concentrated vision"—a vision that temporarily ignores whatever place the story might have in a larger pattern.[11]

The fictional world an artist creates, as Henry James acknowledges in his preface to *Roderick Hudson,* ultimately depends on artistic manipulation for its illusion of completeness: "Really, universally, relations stop nowhere, and the exquisite problem of the artist is eternally but to draw, by a geometry of his own, the circle in which they shall happily appear to do so."[12] For the novelist and the short story writer, this circle concentrates the reader's vision on the work's aesthetic wholeness and continuity within. The artist who creates a short story sequence, on the other hand, draws a wide circle which contains a number of smaller ones, introducing another dimension into his geometry. He takes advantage of the fact that "really, universally, relations stop nowhere," in order to fashion a work that compels us to trace, by a geometry of our own, that wider circle which unites distinct but related centers of concentration.

In the process of searching for unity, as Wolfgang Iser observes, no two readers will discern exactly the same circle or figure: "Two people gazing at the night sky may both be looking at the same collections of stars, but one will see the image of a plough, and the other

11. Chekhov, "On Problems of Technique," 22; Eudora Welty, "The Reading and Writing of Short Stories," in Charles E. May (ed.), *Short Story Theories* (Athens, Ohio, 1976), 163.

12. R. P. Blackmur (ed.), *The Art of the Novel: Critical Prefaces by Henry James* (New York, 1934), 5.

will make out a dipper. The 'stars' in a literary text are fixed; the lines that join them are variable. The author of the text may, of course, exert plenty of influence on the reader's imagination . . . but no author worth his salt will ever attempt to set the *whole* picture before his reader's eye."[13] In the short story sequence, even more so than in the novel (the basis for Iser's theories of aesthetic response), the artist may set forth even less of the whole picture and rely on the reader's pattern-making faculties to formulate the variable connections and build textual consistency. Such is the case with Eudora Welty's *The Golden Apples*, which requires that we perceive the complementary relationships between characters, recognize the network of mythological allusions, weave together various imagistic patterns, and evolve a sense of place as we read the stories in sequence.

Such pattern-making faculties, Philip Stevick argues, manifest the same tendencies we employ in everyday experience: "The impulse to enclose is a basic property of the mind. And consequently, the impulse to shape narratives into patterns is simply the result of the human perceptions that lie at its basis."[14] This shaping impulse need not be confined to narrative alone; whether we read a poem or a poetic sequence, a single short story or a short story sequence, a traditional novel or an experimental one, we can assume that the author has already drawn (or at least tentatively mapped out) some happy circle within which we may exercise our pattern-making faculties to develop relationships between the enclosed parts. Although the author's intentions may be diffuse, even indeterminate, we assume that his text is connected in some fashion that will allow us to discern pattern and meaning. Our desire for unity and coherence is so great that we often use our literary competencies to integrate apparently unrelated material, as long as we are sustained by the faith that the work possesses formal wholeness. Given a title, a beginning, and an end, we will valiantly attempt to make sense of what initially seem disjunct images, unrelated incidents, or a static series of sketches. Even in such a work as J. D. Salinger's *Nine Stories*, at first glance a random story collection, critics have perceived symbolic connections, formal wholeness, and a sequential progression, arising from such features

---

13. Wolfgang Iser, *The Implied Reader: Patterns of Communication in Prose Fiction from Bunyan to Beckett* (Baltimore, 1974), 282.

14. Philip Stevick, *The Chapter in Fiction: Theories of Narrative Division* (Syracuse, N.Y., 1970), 10.

as the Zen epigraph, the common theme of alienation, repeated images and character types, and the volume's arrangement.[15]

Although an imagistic poem or a "slice of life" short story presents special difficulties to some readers, more extended forms such as the novel and the long poem lack a concentrated unity and make certain demands on memory that increasingly tax the pattern-making faculty. In "The Philosophy of Composition," Poe argues that the aesthetic wholeness of the long poem is undermined by the form itself:

> What we term a long poem is, in fact, merely a succession of brief ones—that is to say, of brief poetical effects. It is needless to demonstrate that a poem is such, only inasmuch as it excites, by elevating, the soul; and all intense excitements are, through a psychical necessity, brief. For this reason, at least one half of the "Paradise Lost" is essentially prose—a succession of poetical excitements interspersed, *inevitably*, with corresponding depressions—the whole being deprived, through the extremeness of its length, of the vastly important element, totality, or unity, of effect.

Although Poe's comments may be based on an overly rigid concept of unity, he nonetheless recognizes the type of ebb and flow that characterizes our experience of a longer work. This successive oscillation does not, however, constitute a structural breakdown; it merely emphasizes that in longer works there is a need for subordinate configurations to assist our active pattern-making faculty. Whether the signal of such configurations is a subtle shift of tone or an obvious chapter break, its disruption of the work's continuity only aids our quest for coherence. We normally expect to reconcile these disparate parts into some semblance of wholeness. We generally believe, as Austin Wright does about the novel, that "most works are better unified than they may seem at first, for the formal convention is strong, and apparent lack of unity is often a failure on our parts to recognize some unfamiliar possibility."[16]

Still, for most readers, the short story sequence is one such unfamiliar possibility. As a result, the sequence may be read somewhat leisurely, with the pattern-making faculty attuned to the unity within each story but dormant when it comes to the larger formal possibil-

15. See, for example, Paul Krishner, "Salinger and His Society: The Pattern of *Nine Stories*," *Literary Half Yearly*, XII (1971), 51–60, and XIV (1973), 63–78, and James Lundquist, *J. D. Salinger* (New York, 1975).

16. James A. Harrison (ed.), *The Complete Works of Edgar Allan Poe* (17 vols., 1902; rpr. New York, 1965), XIV, 195–96; Austin M. Wright, *The Formal Principle in the Novel* (Ithaca, 1982), 102.

ities. Although bound between the same covers, stories in a collection invite us to consider them singly, since each rewards us with a sense of closure. Like the "succession of brief poetical effects" Poe notes in the long poem, the rising and falling curve of a story sequence can obscure the larger totality. It only does so, however, if we focus our attention too exclusively within each of the subordinate parts, ignoring the possibility that a writer might exploit the fact that stories physically bound together can be the basis for a work formally bound together and integrated into a unified book. The threads that bind a short story sequence may be, as Dirk Kuyk argues about Faulkner's *Go Down, Moses*, "cable strong." [17] Faulkner's volume is unified not only by Ike McCaslin's role as both narrator and protagonist but also by the blood relationships among characters, the ritual of the hunt, the symbol of the delta, the common theme of exploitation that binds the seemingly disjunct hunting stories with those concerning blacks, and the structural symmetry between these two clusters of stories. On the other hand, these threads may be as thin and intricate as the filaments of a spider web, as are the symbolic and thematic unities that complement the ties between characters in *The Golden Apples*. Compared to that in other genres, however, the unity of the short story sequence will ultimately be a looser one, involving us in a more wide-ranging search for patterns of action and meaning—a more cooperative venture between reader and author than less open forms demand.

A loose form, Wright asserts, cannot be deemed an inferior mode of unity: "In tight forms, the integration of parts is greater because of the greater number of strong abstract forms that predict them; we can offer more reason for the presence and location of the parts. In the loose work we are more aware of the possibilities that have not been selected by the artist. . . . Virtually all works of any magnitude must be loose to some extent, and looseness may be easily compensated for, justified, or even necessitated by other powers in the work. The term is relative, useful for making comparisons, and by no means necessarily pejorative." [18] Our greater awareness of the unifying strategies not selected by the author should lead us to cast about for others; loose unity demands that our pattern-making faculties bristle with at-

17. Dirk Kuyk, *Threads Cable Strong: William Faulkner's "Go Down, Moses"* (Lewisburg, Pa., 1983).

18. Wright, *Formal Principle*, 103–104.

tention and seek to pull together material which might initially seem disparate. Thus, in a short story sequence, we experience not only the pleasure of patterned closure in each story but also the rewards of discovering larger unifying strategies.

Still, many readers experience some discomfort because of the form's kinship with disunity, which Wright defines as "the failure of artistic form to become visible or to promise to do so." According to most models of form that use the novel as their standard, tight unity and formal economy are the main sources of reader satisfaction, and looseness must be compensated for or justified because it might impede our realization of the work's controlling principle. Yet looseness has its own unique rewards, arising from what Iser calls "the integral ambivalence" of a more open form, which suggests "various possibilities of combination without giving them final shape, so that this task is left to the reader's imagination."[19] Similarly, the loosening of restraints lends the short story sequence appeal by perpetuating a greater awareness of alternative formal, rhythmic, and thematic possibilities and by engaging the reader in creating meaning and assembling its parts. Thus, the reconciliation of an apparent disunity into a loose coherence provides distinct satisfaction for the faculties which consistently seek form and pattern in artistic experience.

In a short story sequence, then, there is more room for subjective interpretation and active participation; the reader's task thus becomes simultaneously more difficult and more rewarding. Concerning the novel, at least, Wright agrees: "If the aim is to create form in the process of becoming visible, victory would be measured by the extent to which this process is made more difficult (yet not actually prevented) by the restrictive conventions."[20] By operating without the major narrative unities of the novel, the writer of the short story sequence courts disunity in order to achieve "victory" over it by setting up a new set of narrative ground rules that rely heavily on active pattern-making faculties.

Since not all short story collections are sequences, we must somehow recognize when to approach a volume with our synthesizing powers at full steam. Usually, a combination of signals, some of which are discovered only after proceeding into the volume, can provide clues to its sequential nature. A title different from that of any of

19. *Ibid.*, 106; Iser, *Implied Reader*, 76.
20. Wright, *Formal Principle*, 178.

the stories (for example, Welty's *The Golden Apples*), an epigraph with thematic implications (such as the Zen koan in Salinger's *Nine Stories*), a related series of epigraphs before each story (as in Garland's *Main-Travelled Roads*), and a map of the locale (as in Anderson's *Winesburg, Ohio*) can all suggest unity. An author's preface, such as the one Updike provides for *Olinger Stories*, may reveal certain recurrent concerns or structural arrangements. Similarly, a fictive prologue and/or epilogue can frame the stories, providing an introduction and a sense of closure, as do the two brief sketches "Dawn" and "Dusk" in Gloria Naylor's *Women of Brewster Place*. When a common setting dominates the stories, as in Joyce's *Dubliners*, we might be alert for other potential unities. Almost all of the major unities that characterize the novel can be employed—in modified fashion—as modes of coherence in short story sequences: related characters, common or complementary narrators, repeated themes, loose temporal structure, counterpoint, and recurrent images and motifs may become increasingly evident as we negotiate the text.

There is no uniform model for the short story sequence, however; each one exhibits a distinctive unity and aesthetic integrity, and grows from a unique creative impulse. Although publishers and editors often have a hand in encouraging the direction of an author's creativity, the hand of the serious writer shapes the finished sequence according to his own aesthetic intentions. William Saroyan, for example, in accounting for his collection *My Name is Aram*, acknowledges the financial encouragement of the *Atlantic Monthly* and the call of Edward J. O'Brien, editor of *The Best Short Stories*, for more stories about Armenians. Yet the resulting volume of stories was in no way molded by editors; their encouragement only allowed Saroyan the freedom to write without a detailed plan and trust his memory to shape the book into a loose chronicle of Aram Garoghlanian's life "from the time he was seven-years-old and was beginning to inhabit the world as a specific person to the time he was seventeen-years-old and had forsaken his native valley for some of the rest of the world." [21]

On the other hand, selections made by an editor, no matter how excellent his intentions or critical acumen, must be regarded somewhat differently. Even if such a collection possesses a high degree of

21. William Saroyan, *My Name Is Aram* (New York, 1940), vii, copyright 1940, 1968 by William Saroyan, reprinted by permission of Harcourt Brace Jovanovich, Inc., and The William Saroyan Foundation.

unity and coherence and seems to approximate an author's intentions, it has not benefited from the author's insight or his shaping spirit. Philip Young, for example, by grouping and arranging all of the stories concerning Hemingway's recurrent protagonist into *The Nick Adams Stories*, hopes to remedy what he perceives to be the fragmented impact and obscured coherence of the stories Hemingway scattered in various volumes: "Arranged in chronological sequence, the events in Nick's life make up a meaningful narrative in which a memorable character grows from child to adolescent to soldier, veteran, writer, and parent—a sequence closely paralleling the events of Hemingway's own life."[22] There are two problems with Young's sequence: first, the plan for the fictionalized "autobiography" is Young's, not Hemingway's; and second, Hemingway created his own short story sequence using a number of Nick Adams stories—*In Our Time*.

Using eight previously unpublished pieces, along with stories about Nick Adams from other volumes, and deleting the stories in *In Our Time* that do not feature Nick, Young attempts to create a linear narrative that presents Nick's life in five distinct stages. Although not a novel, *The Nick Adams Stories* offers its selections in a much tighter temporal structure than those in Hemingway's volume. As Hemingway remarked in a letter to Edmund Wilson, *In Our Time* is structured "with a chapter [of the earlier *in our time*] between each story—that is the way they were meant to go—to give the picture of the whole between examining it in detail. Like looking with your eyes at something, say a passing coastline, and then looking at it with 15X binoculars. Or rather, maybe, looking at it and then going and living in it."[23]

Besides this contrapuntal structure, which Hemingway uses to reflect the era's fragmentary nature, *In Our Time* has a linear dimension provided by the loose arrangement of stories sketching Nick's growth; the stories that do not feature Nick in the volume's latter half present adult characters for contrast. "Big Two-Hearted River," which serves as the volume's conclusion, contrasts Nick's resolution in the healing ritual of fishing with Krebs's less successful readaptation to society in "A Soldier's Home," placed near the volume's midpoint. Although a powerful story in its own right, "Big Two-Hearted River" provides a

22. Philip Young, Preface to Ernest Hemingway, *The Nick Adams Stories*, ed. Philip Young (New York, 1972), 5–6, with the permission of Charles Scribner's Sons.

23. Carlos Baker (ed.), *Ernest Hemingway: Selected Letters, 1917–1961* (New York, 1981), 128, with the permission of Charles Scribner's Sons and Grafton Books, a division of the Collins Publishing Group.

sense of closure with its portrayal of Nick's tenuous resolution amidst the burned-out wasteland of modern life and makes the closing vignette, "L'Envoi," into an ironic coda concerning idealistic dreams of escape.

With its unique alternating arrangement of vignettes from the 1924 collection *in our time* and of previously published stories (not all of which involve Nick), *In Our Time* is Hemingway's short story sequence; *The Nick Adams Stories* is not. Both an editor's and an author's volumes may engage similar pattern-making faculties, but the editor adds another dimension to the work, interposing yet another layer of critical interpretation between the reader and the stories.

John Updike's *Olinger Stories*, which gathers and arranges earlier material about a common locale into a sequence, reveals the potential difference between an author's and an editor's efforts. Although hesitant at first about his publisher's proposal to cannibalize previous collections to create a volume of stories set in the fictional town of Olinger, Updike found that a surprising galvanization can occur when an author takes his past productions in hand:

> [My doubts] succumbed to the hope that a concentration of certain images might generate new light or at least focus more sharply the light already there. I hope that this book is justified. I bind these stories together as one ties up a packet of love letters that have been returned. Olinger has receded from me. Composition, in crystallizing memory, displaces it, and the town and the time it localized have been consumed by the stories bound here. Not an autobiography, they have made one impossible. . . . I offer this book in the faith that it is a closed book.[24]

In the writer's hands, his stories may take on new life and illuminate new meanings for both himself and his readers when brought together in one volume. Updike's "crystallized" stories block his reimagining of a fictionalized past, but bound together as a book, they consume the subject by concentration and reflexive reference. Even though Updike has not rewritten the history of Olinger, he has, by arranging his semiautobiographical "love letters" into a sequence that chronicles the maturation of a young man, created a volume which offers a new aesthetic experience. For Updike, *Olinger Stories* is now a closed book; for his readers, it becomes an open book, with each segment about Olinger shedding new light on the others.

An arranged sequence such as *Olinger Stories* represents one

---

24. John Updike, *Olinger Stories: A Selection* (New York, 1964), vi, with the permission of Random House, Inc.

possible creative strategy for producing a unified volume. Forrest Ingram separates the genre he calls the short story cycle into three distinct types, each governed by a different compositional process: "Linked stories may have been *composed* as a continuous whole, or *arranged* into a series, or *completed* to form a set." Although Ingram's categories prove useful for describing the strategies involved in creating short story sequences, it is often difficult to place a collection squarely in one category. Even in *Olinger Stories*, which seems purely an arranged sequence, the last story, "In Football Season," was not previously included in Updike's other collections; along with his foreword, the added story completes the book. Conceivably, it could be argued that Updike was subconsciously composing just such a continuous volume as he returned again and again to the same locale and to similar characters, who are, he asserts, "at bottom the same boy, a local boy." Not many volumes, however, resemble Ingram's composed variety, "conceived as a whole from the time [the author wrote] its first story." Most fall under his heading of completed cycles, which "are neither strictly composed nor merely arranged. They may have begun as independent dissociated stories. But soon their author became conscious of unifying strands which he may have, even subconsciously, woven into the action of the stories."[25]

The very looseness of the short story sequence form seems to undermine its status as "strictly" or "merely" anything. Most sequences, at some point in their composition, partake of all three impulses Ingram attempts to separate. Although the sequence may not be built according to a blueprint, there usually exists some unifying compositional principle, whether it precedes the stories themselves, as in Steinbeck's *The Pastures of Heaven*, develops during composition, as in Anderson's *Winesburg, Ohio*, or is formulated later to unite a number of similar stories, as in Updike's *Olinger Stories*. All sequences undergo some arrangement (and possibly rearrangement), whether planned beforehand or envisioned afterwards; the resultant pattern may exhibit some temporal progression or simply be shaped with what Calisher terms "the natural rhythms of an audience" in mind: "the rise and fall of interest, the need to go from frivol to gloom, from dark to light, from female to male to the general, and from an untrustworthy reality to a joyously recognizable fantasy."[26] Ultimately, all sequences are completed to some extent, whether by the addition of new

25. Ingram, *Representative Short Story Cycles*, 17, 18; Updike, *Olinger Stories*, v.
26. Calisher, *Collected Stories*, ix.

stories, the revision of existing stories, the inclusion of a preface, or simply the selection of a title. The relative influence of these three shaping forces has no absolute control over the degree of unity; a sequence created primarily by arrangement may be more highly unified than one guided by a master plan. Generally, however, sequences that involve an extensive process of completion achieve the highest degree of coherence, since these completions most often spring from a clearly formulated compositional principle and a finely tuned arrangement.

For the sake of convenience in generically locating the short story sequence and establishing its degree of unity, we might draw a continuum ranging from the miscellaneous collection, on one end, to the traditional novel on the other. On such a continuum, Anderson's *Winesburg, Ohio* and Welty's *The Golden Apples,* which illustrate a balanced tension between the independence of each story and the unity of the collection as a whole, should serve as the midpoint. As a collection becomes more organically and technically unified, it approaches that expansive middle territory of the short story sequence; as the separate parts lose their individual integrity and are subsumed by a larger narrative scheme, the work assumes a novelistic quality.

At one end of the continuum, then, is the "mere collection," containing stories about diverse subjects, a variety of character types, and a wide range of themes. In such volumes, the author makes little or no attempt to bring the collection together, though a few stories may bear some resemblance. A volume of stories begins to assume a greater degree of unity when its stories treat similar subjects or conflicts. Many of the early local-color collections have thus taken the first step toward being cut from the same cloth, even if they compose but a ragged fabric. Marginally united collections may remain disjointed, as does Bret Harte's *The Luck of Roaring Camp,* or contain so many stories, as does Mary Wilkins Freeman's *A New England Nun,* that only a loose perception of unity results—an aggregate or composite portrait rather than a more complex sequence. Such collections can present a consistent regional portrait or a common theme; unlike a true short story sequence, however, they do so in an aggregate rather than a sequential fashion.

With a shorter table of contents, a clearer thematic thrust, and the development of links between individual stories, a collection is able to approach the unity and progression which characterize the sequential form. To cross into the middle range of the continuum, however, the volume must in some way be dynamic. In other words, the reader must perceive that thematic similarities and patterns of coherence ultimately forward the development of some larger theme, not just bind the work mechanically. Harriet Beecher Stowe's *Oldtown Fireside Stories* exemplifies how a volume may be technically united but finally no more than a group of weakly linked tales. Sam Lawson, the common narrator who provides a bridge from one story to the next, serves mainly an atmospheric role: his dialect and personality may engage interest, but he has little relation to the tales he narrates. A more fully developed narrative sensibility, more organically related to the collection or evolving as a character, could lend that volume a stronger unity. Given the weak, mechanical links in *Oldtown Fireside Stories*, we can only process the collection in the manner of the children who serve as Sam's audience: "Ye tell 'em one story, and they jest swallows it as a dog does a gob of meat, and they're all ready for another." [27] In a short story sequence, which possesses both organic and technical unity, we must digest the stories gradually, attentive to their progression and potential intertextuality.

As setting, theme, motifs, characters, and narrators come into focus, stories with common features take on a recognizable form, which the reader should clearly perceive as developing in a sequential fashion. The strength of the writer's unifying idea thus may determine the coherence of the volume as well as the successiveness of the stories. In Charles Chesnutt's *The Conjure Woman*, for instance, the narrator, Uncle Julius, is part of an ongoing narrative that develops between the stories he tells in response to specific incidents in his employer's life; without this presence, the volume would lose not only its narrative impetus but also a thematic commentary on the dominant metaphor of conjuring. Our full realization of the patterns weaving together such stories often evolves from several rereadings, since only after reading the whole collection and confirming schemes of coherence can we fully reconcile the parts to the whole. Nonetheless, in sequences that are both technically and organically unified, the potential for a dynamic sequential unity resides in the text for the reader to develop.

More obviously sequential are volumes loosely structured around or roughly composing the story of a character's (or character type's) growth and maturation. Slightly before the midpoint on the continuum would be sequences such as Hemingway's *In Our Time* and Joyce Carol Oates's *Crossing the Border*, which appear to have large lapses in a loose sequential progression but merely require a more as-

27. Harriet Beecher Stowe, *Oldtown Fireside Stories* (Boston, 1871), 6.

tute perception of the work's thematic unity. Oates's book focuses primarily on the literal and metaphoric border crossings of a young couple fleeing to Canada, but seems to shift emphasis when stories of other characters intervene. Yet these stories ultimately broaden the title metaphor's implications and our understanding of the central characters, although they are not tightly interwoven and as a group create a structural imbalance.

In more evenly balanced collections such as *Winesburg, Ohio, The Golden Apples,* and *Go Down, Moses,* the stories of George Willard, Virgie Rainey, and Ike McCaslin are major parts of their respective sequences but do not completely dominate them. Interspersed with their struggles are glimpses into the lives of others whose situations obviously complement those of the recurring characters; further unifying these volumes is a network of subtly interwoven recurrent motifs and symbols. These three sequences establish a near-perfect equilibrium between the conflicting demands of the independent story and those of the continuous narrative.

On the other side of this midpoint, the fate of the overall narrative begins to assume greater prominence, but the stories still remain independent units. While *The Conjure Woman* and *Winesburg, Ohio* both cover a recognizable time span, the temporal scheme remains loose. Linked episodic sketches, however, such as those which compose Sarah Orne Jewett's *The Country of the Pointed Firs,* can provide a more evident sequential organization. In chronicling the narrator's visits to various residents of Dunnet Landing, Jewett adapts the travel-book format, using the narrator's personality and temporal frame (as well as repeated characters and images) to unite her volume. One of the most common techniques in highly unified short story sequences is the recurrent protagonist, often because an author finds himself unable to confine a fictional protagonist to a single story. Faulkner, for example, conceived *The Unvanquished* as "a long series": "I realized that they would be too episodic to be what I considered a novel, so I thought of them as a series of stories, that when I got into the first one I could see two more, but by the time I'd finished the first one I saw that it was going further than that, and that when I'd finished the fourth one, I had postulated too many questions that I had to answer for my own satisfaction."[28] Faulkner's stories evolved into a chronicle of Bayard Sartoris' education; although looser than what

28. Frederick L. Gwynn and Joseph L. Blotner (eds.), *Faulkner in the University: Class Conferences at the University of Virginia, 1957–1958* (Charlottesville, Va., 1959), 252.

even Faulkner felt a novel should be, the seqeuence is chronological and, with the aid of some revision by the author, coherent.

As traditional concepts of the novel and the short story fade, boundaries of genre begin to dissolve. "At the present moment," James McConkey observes, "the differences are much less than formerly. . . . The novel clearly is losing, or perhaps has already lost, its lengthy backbone of causal action. The modern story and novel alike are composed of a variety of blocks, many of which look backward rather than forward." Although we must read either type of work sequentially, we continually cast a backward glance to formulate the relationships of the past to the evolving whole. Such narrative organization is primarily spatial rather than temporal, since it subverts strict chronological progression. In such a text, Jeffrey Smitten argues, we must "pay extraordinary attention to the synchronic relation among seemingly disconnected word groups. . . . The units of the narrative must be seen as juxtaposed in space, not unrolling in time." [29] Such juxtaposition, in both modern novels and short story sequences, must present itself sequentially as we negotiate the text; the text's diachronic dimension never disappears totally, but the synchronic or associative relationships become more prominent in assembling pattern and meaning. In such a shift, setting, theme, and nontemporal patterns of organization, such as recurrent symbols, leitmotifs, and counterpoint, which require greater reader collaboration, become major unifying forces in the reading experience.

Unlike a chapter in a novel, which we consciously read in expectation of what comes next and attempt to subordinate to the work's aesthetic wholeness, the short story within a sequence still maintains its formal integrity, even while we are recognizing its reiteration and development of pattern and theme. The concentration of the story gives rise to a greater internal resonance of its formal features, since we examine more closely how all the parts of the compact world work in relation to one another. Our closer attention to detail, combined with a deeper understanding within the formal limits, leads to a greater impact on both the parts and the whole of the single story.

Paradoxically, this characteristic of the short story—the unity of

29. James McConkey, Review of Joyce Carol Oates's *By the North Gate*, in *Epoch*, XIII (1964), 171; Jeffrey R. Smitten, "Introduction: Spatial Form and Narrative Theory," in Jeffrey R. Smitten and Ann Daghistany (eds.), *Spatial Form in Narrative* (Ithaca, 1981), 19.

effect which supposedly distinguishes it as a genre—helps make each story more accessible beyond its single significance, more open to the multiple significances that a context of related stories evokes. In a short story sequence, each apocalypse may still be served in its own cup; the collision by no means shatters the vessel of the short story, even if some of the contents do spill over. The story's status as a significant part of a progressive whole does not undermine its independence, but rather expands its function and significance within an open book.

IV

How Has Story Evolved?

SUSAN LOHAFER

Introduction to Part IV

Deconstruction. New Historicism. For many graduate students today, these are signs at a fork in the road. It doesn't matter so much that deconstruction is a head feeding on the tail of New Criticism; nor that historicism is only new in a Marxian sense. What matters is that these are the spotlighted paths. Into them flows, at the moment, the current of excitement in literary studies. Wandering down these avenues, spying into every face—like Robin Molineux in search of his uncle—would we find what we are seeking? A short story critic who is *au courant?*

For now, let's consider New Historicism. Like most new roads, it's in part a retracing. In a review-essay on Roy Harvey Pearce, Arnold Krupat explains why the "old" historicism of the fifties, vitally interested in marginal texts, was itself marginalized by the New Critical emphasis on the established canon.[1] Today, the resurgence and growing persuasiveness of historical frames indicate the widening gauge of literary study—including so much that was once extraliterary, overlapping, so often, the social sciences. Viewing literature embedded within, encoded through, and consumed by the socioeconomic world is viewing literature historicized. Did short story critics ever do this? Are they doing it now?

Recalling the affinity between story critics and New Critics, we might think, "Not likely." And yet there have been attempts to establish a history. In 1917, James Cooper Lawrence subsumes Poe within an older story of the tale, beginning by the campfire, emerging in bal-

1. Arnold Krupat, "Criticism and the Canon: Cross-Relations," *Diacritics*, XVII (Summer, 1987), 3–20.

lads, seeding the field of literary culture.[2] By now, however, such claims for the antiquity of story are all too familiar; as in Lawrence's case, they highlight the oral tradition and rely heavily on studies of folklore and histories of printing and literacy. What they have to offer is historicality (chronologies of change in the manner and matter of story) rather than historicism (explanations in terms of historical moments). The latter begins to emerge as critics look for the "Americanness" of stories.

In 1952, Ray B. West, Jr., offers his own "great tradition" of short story writers in *The Short Story in America, 1900–1950*. After grouping literary artists into two categories, the "naturalist" and the "traditionalist," he foregrounds those who respond to the dilemmas of their time by uncovering the oldest of human values. Notably de-emphasizing Poe, he traces a line from Hawthorne to Melville to James to Hemingway, and thence to Faulkner. So, for example, unlike the standard evolutionary history—which locates Hemingway among the modernist rebels—West's constructive history puts Hemingway among the traditionalists, those who strip away illusion to reach "decorum." Throughout his study, he balances the view of art as conditioned by history with the view of art as determined by genius.

A decade later, in *The American Short Story* (1964), William H. Peden is, truly, inside his time. While acknowledging all of the usual influences on the development of the short story in the forties—the literary quarterlies, the university writing programs, the modernist aesthetic—he sees the shadow of the Bomb in the fifties, of Vietnam in the sixties, and (in a 1975 update) Watergate in the seventies. Arguing that the short story is particularly sensitive to the world of the moment, he finds the stories after World War II exhibiting certain "tendencies," developing certain themes. Abnormal psychology, Jewish angst, black struggle, war and its aftermath—categories like these name the subgenres of story and the ills in our time. Peden's vast knowledge of stories in periodicals and collections is a cultural bank. But the checks he draws are personal; this is the world as he sees it; these are the many, many stories he wants to describe. If we are looking for what it means to write a "history" of the short story, we do not find a theory of art as cultural expression. We find, instead, an ethos, captured in a voice that describes other voices as it claims its own.

It isn't until the seventies that cultural context—carefully and de-

2. James Cooper Lawrence, "A Theory of the Short Story," *North American Review*, CCV (1917), 274–86, rpr. in Charles E. May (ed.), *Short Story Theories* (Athens, Ohio, 1976), 60–71.

liberately defined—ceases to be a more or less informal backdrop for artistic achievements and becomes a source of discipline—the critical perspective that *defines* achievement.

As is often the case, the first signs appear when a critic, committed to a program of intellectual reform, uses a short story as illustration. In 1978, for example, Barbara J. Rogers, in her discussion of "Young Goodman Brown" in "Entropy and Organization in Hawthorne's America," wove politics, economics, social sciences, anthropology, cognitive theory, and the fine arts together into a replete context for the story.[3] Her interdisciplinary method would once have been called an "American Studies" approach; now, some just call it responsible. But Rogers did not choose her text *because it was a short story*. Nor did she offer her vocabulary, so indebted to the social sciences, to short story critics in particular. She's not on our route. She may not even be known to the two people we're fast approaching: a specialist in British literary history and a fiction writer who's also a critic. Both have contributed essays to this collection, and both are committed to a sociocultural approach to a theory of short fiction.

Let's start with Suzanne Ferguson. Within this volume, she needs little introduction, for her contribution to short story theory has been noted in the opening essays by Norman Friedman and Mary Rohrberger. As the author of "Defining the Short Story: Impressionism and Form," published in 1982, she is always mentioned whenever short story critics knock heads over the old question: is the short story different from the novel in kind or only in degree? By answering "in degree," Ferguson joins Norman Friedman in the attack on Romantic, sui generis, essence-oriented definitions of the short story. It has been her contention that many of the supposedly definitive characteristics of the modern short story—fragmentariness, suggestiveness, foregrounded point of view—are indeed modernist tendencies, and more particularly impressionist techniques, which may also be found in the novel of the period. As a literary historian, interested in the shifting codes of authorship and readership, Ferguson brings a dispassionate, wide-ranging eye to the society of genres.

In her latest work, the social metaphor is brought up front. Ferguson argues that there is a class system of genres operating within and in relation to the social dynamics of the "real" world. Mining English literary history for examples, she explains why the short story

3. Barbara J. Rogers, "Entropy and Organization in Hawthorne's America," *Southern Quarterly*, XVI (1978), 223–39.

has been more dominant in some periods than in others, how it has played its part in both defining and bridging class distinctions in England, and how, within its own "society" of forebears and contemporaries, some of the hardier lowbrow forms have "married up" on the scale of literary prestige. In making her assessments, Ferguson draws upon the history of magazine publishing, her own wide knowledge of major and minor English writers of the nineteenth and early twentieth centuries, and a theory of readership as a form of socially coded consumption.

Once again, Ferguson is needling the pretensions of the short story chauvinist. Does he think his text a marvel of elusive reference, dark insight, and psycho-subtlety? Would he welcome its old relatives, the "Ooooh!" ghost story, the "Aha!" detective story? Ferguson gives us these pleasures of transformation and recognition, not as a series of effects, but as a rational argument. She is explaining the social history of the short story genre in England. For some of her readers, the limits of her study may be either too rigidly or too loosely observed. Some may find the references to the American short story too broad and presumptive, wishing them developed or removed. Others may find the notion of class relations too simple, too metaphorical, too nineteenth century; readers may be either charmed or provoked by the comfortableness of the essay, the feeling that the social dynamics are more Trollopian than Marxian. In the end, it seems that Ferguson is no bandwagon "culture critic," but in many ways a traditional scholar, a taxonomist of literary forms and features.

Imagine taxonomy with a vengeance, defiantly antitraditional, and get ready for William O'Rourke. Finding him in the path is a real surprise. A novelist and short story writer, O'Rourke comes to criticism the way tornados come to Kansas. He shakes things up. Drawing from biology, physics, and economics, he develops three analogies for the short story, inviting us to place each figure in turn over the others in order to arrive at a complicated model of the genre's uniqueness. Old concepts undergo a swift and dizzying rebirth into the world of *Scientific American:* so, for example, the hoary notion of brevity is now a matter of "space-time" relations; Poe's totality is "exoskeletal" form; cameo perfection, that special artistry of the short form, is "capital intensive." Yet O'Rourke is doing far more than translating our heritage into Modernese.

He is addressing questions of perennial interest—evolving form, aesthetic markers, readership—from a truly contemporary point of view. His complaint is that literary criticism is never as modern as the rest of the world. As a producer of literature himself, he doesn't want to see art embalmed in old-fashioned theory. Perhaps it is fair to say that, for O'Rourke, being up-to-date in genre studies is not a matter of choosing Terry Eagleton over Stephen Greenblatt over Jacques Derrida. It is a matter of seeing one's field in relation to the ideas that truly energize and define the world we all live in: Einstein's relativity, Gould's evolution, Samuelson's economics. O'Rourke wants us to re-conceptualize the features that make the short story distinctive, account for its survival, and link it with the real world of the natural and the human.

For the purist, the ideologue, or the skeptic, O'Rourke's essay is an inviting target. Like the wind that leaves one man's piano in another's garage, O'Rourke keeps dropping the insights of one discipline on the yard of the next. Is this a truly integrative form of criticism, banishing the prim and parochial in favor of the brash and broad-minded? Is it a savvy, postmodern exercise in high-tech imaging, where surface and style are all there is, anyway? Or is it a fiction writer fancying the brilliantly bad dream of a freshman agog with Intro. to Lit., Basic Bio., Hist. of Sci., and Econ. I?

O'Rourke's essay finds its way into this collection because it is probably none of the above, all of the above, and something else, too. It is an eye-opener, a mind teaser, a kaleidoscope of images and insights that, for many readers, may be the lasting legacy of their trip through this book. O'Rourke is a writer who links powerful ideas with memorable tropes for practical gains in understanding. His closest tie with Ferguson is clearly his interest in production-consumption models of thinking about genre. Like her, he sees literature as part of a larger social dynamic—though for him this is just one of several interrelated contexts. These essays fall together because their authors share a broad-gauge vision, a tendency to see the literary and the nonliterary as interinvolved and changing through time.

Yet, casting an eye back over these essays, we might say they look very familiar. Haven't we met them on the oldest roads of short story criticism? One leads to The Question of Status, the other to The Question of Brevity. Like poor Robin Molineux, we are always looking ahead to discover the past. Surely these two essays do not "do" New Historicism; though they are heading that way, they arrive somewhere else, uncannily drawn to the primal themes of short story criticism.

SUZANNE FERGUSON

The Rise of the Short Story in the Hierarchy of Genres

It is possible that some disputes over the history of the short story might be resolved by recognizing that the issue is not simply the formal development of a genre but also how and when the short story was accepted as a highbrow, or prestige, genre.[1] Like societies of people, the society of literary genres has its class system, in which, over time, classes reorganize themselves, accept new members, and cast old members into the dustbin. It has its aristocracy, its middle classes, and its proletarians, and the genres vie for status as people do, by adopting the manners of the upper classes, by "marrying up," and by working themselves in persistently at the fringes of the class to which they aspire. They fall by becoming "bankrupt" or simply passé. Changes in the encompassing human society in which the literary genres have their being influence this rise and fall, as do the energy and brilliance of individual writers and works.[2]

Ruling the cosmos of the genres are "gods": the socially powerful who use literary genres and the other arts to represent cultural meanings, to secure the class systems of the culture, and to reflect their own power and prestige. The powerful of the society expect literature to glorify them and their social structures, and to be especially understandable to them, written in codes illegible to outsiders. Throughout the history of Western European cultures (and, indeed, most other

1. A shorter version of this essay appears as "The Short Story as Parvenu in the Society of Genres," in *Visions critiques, revue sur la nouvelle de langue anglaise*, V (1988), 267–74.

2. Although I am concerned here with the English short story almost exclusively, much of what I say is applicable to other traditions as well. The English story, however, had no Poe or Hawthorne to dramatically alter its course in the nineteenth century.

cultures we know about), the powerful have used their wealth and prestige to promote artistic display as an attribute of their own pre-eminence and taste. Artists, not without complaint, but with a fine sense of how to balance their own compulsion to create art with the practical needs of living, have managed to flourish within this system.

While the upper classes promote a kind of art that is, generally speaking, technically complex and formally difficult, so that its appreciation requires a certain expertise, the lower classes have their own genres, the "popular" ones, which are generally simpler formally and which they use for entertainment and, sometimes, instruction in how to move into the higher classes. Their genres are related to those of the upper classes in many important ways—thematically, structurally—but individual works of popular art have an important difference as well: they are regarded by both their creators and their audience as consumable. Designed for immediate gratification, they are not expected to give pleasure and edification over a long period of time. In the case of narrative art, popular stories, long and short, are generally disseminated in less permanent media than highbrow fiction, now as in the past. The simple fact of physical preservation is often a piece of evidence for the prestige of a work in its own time.

Like literate cultures, oral cultures have a hierarchy of genres, "high" styles and formulas to recount their histories and legends, and "low" styles to tell stories about their families and neighbors. "High" style works tend to get handed down, whereas most "low" style narratives are continually superseded. No particular intrinsic value on individual works is to be inferred from my use of *high* and *low*. There are wonderful "low" style oral narratives and dreadful highbrow written ones, just as there are noble savages and despicable lords in human societies. The point is that certain characteristics of a genre are class related, and a genre is able to "rise" and "fall" in a culture as it is identified with the structures of the "high" social classes in that culture. Moreover, when a genre that claims the approbation of the elite in a culture also gains the esteem of the middle and lower classes—the drama in Renaissance England, opera in nineteenth-century Italy, the novel in the West for the past two centuries—we are justified in supposing that its generic characteristics have been embraced as somehow representative of or responsive to a profound aspect of the spirit of the age.

Ranks of "high" and "low" in aesthetics are similar to, but not totally synonymous with, "high" and "low" in society. Wealth and power to a great extent define "high" culture, but since ancient times the "power" of artistic rhetoric (in whatever genre or medium) has been accepted by the politically influential classes as having its own rules for excellence. The test of true nobility in society includes the ability to appreciate "high" art on its own terms (that is, the terms of the community of artists and intellectuals). Shelley's image of poets as "unacknowledged legislators" conveys a significant truth.

The actual process of documenting the relations between prestigious art and prestige in the culture demands space and extensive, meticulous historical research. For purposes of my argument, however, I wish only to suggest a perspective that may be helpful in understanding what happened to short fiction, primarily in England, in the nineteenth century. In ages of courtly and ecclesiastical patronage, a limited educated public, and expensive production of books, the links between prestige and power are simpler to discern than those in more recent, democratic cultures in which the middle classes are themselves relatively wealthy, powerful, well educated, appreciative of "fine" art, and able to print and distribute literature widely and relatively cheaply. When a larger class defines the highbrow, dissemination as well as preservation becomes a more significant factor in assessing status.

Consequently, technologies influence the prestige of genres: stage machinery was an important requirement of early opera; the sophisticated instruments of modern symphony orchestras had to exist for the symphony or symphonic poem to develop and gain acceptance; and novels had to be printed and marketed to achieve prestige. The short story would seem to have few requirements not already fulfilled by the technologies that produced the novel, but its economics are somewhat more complicated. Like short poems, short stories must be printed with something else to make their circulation profitable. What they come with—other stories or other kinds of printed material—may distract readers from perceiving them as discrete works of art.

Another problem for the prestige of the short story is its lack of "magnitude": like the lyric poem, it tends to be regarded as less serious and important than a longer work. A small work of art obviously cannot reflect as much glory on its patron as a large and imposing one. It commands less attention and less space; it is easier to "lose." Great historic or mythic themes seem incongruous in a single short story, although, of course, stories can be linked in longer works in which they reinforce one another's effect.

When we think of the prestige of genres, though, two factors go beyond the simple questions of technical production, length, and subject matter: aesthetic complexity and refinement, and the elusive spirit of the time. The latter has to do with the ethos of a society, with what people of upper and middle classes of a particular time and place are interested in, what, as a group, they are concerned about, and what they require from art to help them contemplate and feel. Most historical and critical studies of the short story are concerned with the former, as they seek the turning point at which the short story became "modern," and somehow "better" than it had been.

I would argue, however, along with some earlier historians of the short story, that short fiction has always been an artful genre. Edgar Hill Duncan, in a 1974 survey of medieval short fiction in *Studies in Short Fiction*, concluded that there is "abundant evidence of the conscious application of artistic (artful) craftsmanship on the part of the authors . . . in accordance with doctrines inculcated in late medieval manuals of style (the *artes poetriae*)." And Margaret Schlauch, writing on the Renaissance short story in an earlier issue of that periodical, claimed of such "modern" techniques as realism of detail, devices for creating *frisson* (in the supernatural tale), and use of colloquial conversation that "it will be salutary for us to remember that similar devices were quite familiar to writers of the sixteenth century. Purpose and milieu have changed . . . but the means employed are not so new as uninstructed contemporaries of ours may sometimes think."[3]

Techniques do develop and change, come into and go out of artistic fashion, and the modern short story is clearly different from earlier short fiction. But that is because it now appeals, in subject and style, to our modern taste, rather than because it has somehow radically changed in form. What has changed most is the reception of the short story as a genre. What makes the short story more prestigious now than earlier? Why do some important writers choose to compose their most profound and lasting work in this form? Why do cultural arbiters—professional critics, professors of literature—pay attention to the short story as an important locus of artistic value?

All Western cultures have written-down short stories, but except for those regarded as holy, they have never been demonstrably prestigious at any time prior to our own except the fourteenth century. In

3. Edgar Hill Duncan, "Short Fiction in Medieval English: II. The Middle English Period," *Studies in Short Fiction*, XI (1974), 241; Margaret Schlauch, "English Short Fiction in the 15th and 16th Centuries," *Studies in Short Fiction*, III (1966), 434.

antiquity, short stories appear as parts of longer, more prestigious works, but not separately. A few "detachable" stories were written into the relatively low-prestige prose ("Menippean") satires: "The Widow of Ephesus" into Petronius' *Satyricon* and "Eros & Psyche" into Apuleius' *Golden Ass*. And stories were used as exempla in religious works beginning quite early in the Middle Ages. Precisely why a moment of cultural power in the short story took place in the late Middle Ages, then waned, we can only speculate. It is easy enough to attribute the rise to the excellence of Boccaccio or some of the authors of romances and lais, or of Chaucer, or even to the authors' personal friendships with the rich and powerful. Clearly, it is as anthologies, not individual works, that these stories survive. *The Canterbury Tales* is a compendium of types of stories, a collection of exemplars with many common themes (like *Dubliners*), and the whole—including, of course, the frame—is greater than its parts. Boccaccio and Chaucer not only endowed us with great anthologies of the types of short story enjoyed by the upper classes of the Middle Ages but wrote into their frames the codes by which we might recognize the relative prestige of the various kinds of individual stories. That romances are more prestigious than fabliaux we know by who tells them, as well as by who populates them.

Perhaps there are similarities of ethos between the England of the fourteenth century and that of the late nineteenth which also might account for the prestige of the short story in both periods: a certain volatility in the class structure, which welcomed the fine differentiation in generic types and social classes so succinctly offered by the forms and content of short fiction; a simultaneous longing for the realistic and the idealized; a preoccupation with sorting ideas out, an intellectualizing of passion—all of which the short story embodies extremely well. I think it can be argued that similar conditions characterize the rise of the short story in America earlier in the nineteenth century and the flowering of the short story in mid- to late-nineteenth-century Russia, as well as in England and other European countries.

One apparent differentiating factor is that most, if not all, medieval short stories of any prestige are in verse, and thus are poems rather than short stories: the courtly romances and lais which seem to grow out of or at any rate parallel the ballads of oral tradition. Prose appears only in sermons and lowbrow narrative, as of Chaucer's Parson and his "pilgrim Chaucer's" "Tale of Melibee." But verse is simply a marker of the "high" style of the Middle Ages, and a work such as

Chaucer's "Shipman's Tale" is closer in structure and feeling to almost any of Chekhov's prose stories than to almost any verse narrative written in the centuries that separate them. Acceptance of prose as a prestigious literary medium came gradually, in the rise of prose romances, belles-lettres, and then the novel. Even now, verse has a nostalgic advantage: verse drama is automatically regarded "higher class" than prose drama, and laureates, though perhaps anachronisms, are always poets, not prose writers.

In England, the short story went back "underground" in the fifteenth through the seventeenth centuries, lost in the shuffle of the Wars of the Roses and subsequent struggles for dynastic sway, when the prestige genres of history, epic, and tragedy were recalled from the storage stacks of the past to celebrate the rise of the great families and modern aristocracy of England and continental Europe.[4] Short stories exist from this period, but primarily in association with the underclass of rogues and coney catchers; "serious" fiction is long, and in romance or apologue form.

In the eighteenth century in England, as in the nineteenth, many short stories were published both in journals and in book form, to appeal to all classes.[5] Oriental tales, moral apologues, and sentimental tales tilted toward highbrow tastes but rarely exhibited pretensions to prestige status as art. They were consumables, and literary "art" was still undertaken as poetry, then, gradually, the novel.

When the audience for literary art expanded in the eighteenth century, the English short story caught onto the coattails of the novel as that genre made its bid for high prestige. Ian Watt's durable identification of the primary types of novel—the mock-epic, highly plotted, stylized form of the Henry Fielding novel and the middle-class, psychologically realistic, and unpretentiously written Samuel Richardson novel—adumbrates the generic social ground the novel had to cover as it became the preeminent mainstream genre of the nineteenth and twentieth centuries. It had to make its middle-class readers—from the gentry "down" through the commercial and artisan classes—into its epic heroes and evolve a form and style that could be recognized as

4. An excellent study of the relation of genre to prestige in Renaissance England is Leonard Tennenhouse's *Shakespeare and the Politics of Genre* (London, 1986).

5. See Benjamin Boyce, "English Short Fiction in the Eighteenth Century: A Preliminary View," *Studies in Short Fiction*, V (1967), 95–112, and Edward Pitcher, "On the Conventions of Eighteenth-Century British Short Fiction," *Studies in Short Fiction*, XII (1975), 199–212, 327–41.

"high" class, as well as be "realistic" for its audience. Like the powerful of older times, the rising elite of democratic societies wished to see their prestige represented in art, and the novel, with its wealth of detail, its ponderous and loose development, and its opportunity for psychological analysis, was the genre these classes embraced as their own, not least because no previous power elite had been able to claim it.

The fact of serial publication, and the popularity of serialized novels among the English middle classes, inadvertently gave the short story its break. In addition to the serialized novels which presumably kept the reader coming back week after week, many short stories were published by magazines. It was not until well after the middle of the nineteenth century, however, that collections of short stories were recognized by the publishing industry itself as anything but "children's" literature. *The Bookseller*, a trade journal equivalent to *Books in Print* first published in 1858, lumped novels and stories ("tales") with children's fiction in 1860; by 1865 novels were separate and tales were in the category of "minor and juvenile fiction"; but by 1870 short fiction was listed alongside novels.

More than novels, nineteenth-century British short stories were of several distinguishable types. Many general kinds survived the Middle Ages and often resurfaced in the magazines of the nineteenth century. The correspondent types of the medieval knightly romances, themselves adaptations of epic, were adventure stories and the romances of the upper classes, the "silver fork" fiction of the time. Adventure stories became progressively associated with juvenile readers, more and more a genre of formula and lowbrow, consumable status. Thus, as stylish a writer as Robert Louis Stevenson is relegated to lower status than several less-gifted of his contemporaries, not simply because he uses young protagonists but because his subjects are adventures in exotic or historical settings rather than the domestic and social intrigues in urban, modern settings that characterize the novel. Similarly, the supernatural element associated with earlier romances was channeled into the Gothic romance (where it was often revealed to be malevolent chicanery rather than truly supernatural) and the specialized genre of the ghost or horror story, both less highbrow genres than the realistic novel or story.

If elements of adventure and the supernatural are ruled inadmissible, it may be argued, one can hardly contend that what is left *is* romance and not some new, indeed impoverished, form. The knightly romance, however, did frequently center on love and marriage as the basis of social relations, and the implications of individuals' love affairs extended well beyond the personal relationship. The very etymology of the term *romance,* which looks back to the "matter of Rome" as well as Romance languages, suggests the political and social ramifications of its subject matter. Although nineteenth-century criticism blurred the nature of romance as a genre by focusing on its nonformal characteristics—its subjectivism, its idealizing—and opposed these to realism, and in America particularly this opposition came to be seen as a generic opposition of romance to novel, the basic plot of romance as the story of love triumphing over opposition and bringing in its train social success (or, in its negative, "tragic" manifestation, failing to do so) remained central to the novel in England as in the rest of Europe.

The urban, domestic romance fit more closely with the aspirations of the rising middle classes than the historical or exotic adventure. The plots and milieux of domestic romances, both short and long, represented, in addition to love, instances of proper or improper behavior as determined by contemporary mores. These stories typically portrayed social questing and love as exemplifications of moral issues and ideas affecting both individuals and their social environment. The heroes and heroines typified the ideals of the society, whereas minor or negative characters might travesty or attack these ideals. As in the nineteenth-century novel, plots of marriage or of social mobility (often through marriage) were common in the short works of such writers as Mrs. (Catherine Mary) Gore, whose prolific output of over seventy titles in all literary genres included more than a dozen of short fiction.[6]

Throughout most of the period both the short story and the novel were clearly regarded as "consumables" and were lower in generic status than poetry, especially the long poem. At one end of the aesthetic spectrum—Jane Austen's novels—artistic finish was highly valued, and a typical, "realistic," rather than a highly idealized, society was the goal of representation. In less aesthetically presumptuous work, including most short fiction, a stronger didactic cast was evident. Emphasis on good behavior, from childhood on, was the purpose of Maria Edgeworth's short and longer fiction, with aesthetic considerations merely the sugar coating for the social pill. A more even balance between the aesthetic and the didactic characterizes

6. *Dictionary of National Biography,* VIII, 237–38.

Mrs. (Elizabeth Cleghorn) Gaskell's fiction. Stories by these writers and others were published both in journals and in anthology form, and collections were produced both by individual writers and by editors selecting from published periodicals and soliciting new works for "gift books." *Bentley's Miscellany* was screened for numerous anthologies which appeared from the 1830s on, as was the more highbrow *Blackwood's Edinburgh Magazine.* These were eclectic in their selection of story types, with *Bentley's* leaning more to the comic and adventure story than *Blackwood's,* and they provide telling information as to the general taste of the age in English short fiction: sentimental, amusing, exotic. Only rarely do the stories in them approach the psychological and social probing that Poe and Hawthorne were already achieving in short fiction in America.

The romance short story was a highbrow form when compared to other types, but the more overtly didactic a romance was, the lower its prestige value. (Didacticism I measure by authorial directives to the reader and the ready sacrifice of realistic representation to obviously stylized—often called "wooden"—characterization, plot, and dialogue in the service of some advised course of action.) Titles often give a clue to the teaching function of the story. "Out of Debt, Out of Danger," "Right at Last," "Hand and Heart," and "A Vain Self-Sacrifice" are examples from Edgeworth, Gaskell, and Gore. Even more peculiar to the modern sensibility are didactic stories of the type frequently published in *Household Words,* which give information on sanitation, health care, and household management, and even, in one case, advice about purchasing life and fire insurance. The most didactic forms of romance were directed toward young or working-class audiences. These stories were meant to teach "outsiders" how to enter the ranks of society (children) or how to accommodate themselves to their proper place in the social scale (parlormaids). The styles of the stories were adjusted to the audience: patronizing, perhaps simplified, but "high" enough to show the intended audience the gap between writer and reader.

The less didactic, more "representational" and "aesthetic" romances served as entertainment and gratification for those already "inside," manifesting a style and substance as à la mode as possible. This urban, domestic, quasi-didactic romance remains the essential base of the story in the twentieth century, though its details and characters have been modernized, along with those of the novel. Frank O'Connor's persuasive argument, in the 1963 volume *The Lonely Voice,* that the short story is about marginal figures on the outskirts of society, seems equally descriptive of the modern novel. In America, the tradition of the isolated hero, excluded from social acceptance because he cannot or will not play the corrupt social game, affected novel and tale even earlier, and contributed to the critical division between novel and romance noted above.

Another prominent type of short fiction that survived from the Middle Ages was the comic story, also popular in England in the nineteenth century. In keeping with Victorian mores, it lacked the open references to sex and scatology common in earlier comic writing, but it was similarly contemptuous of social climbers, hypocrites, misers, braggarts, domineering parents, and fops. Frequently inverted or parodic romances, many of the comic stories are ethnic background stories, particularly of the Irish, perennially outsiders and taking advantage of it through clowning. Particular subgenres of comic stories, such as the hunting story, the fishing story, and the military practical joke, throve throughout the century. R. S. Surtees' Jorrocks, combining the satire of the parvenu (as grocer-become-"gentleman"-hunter) with the pratfalls of inept hunting misadventures, is the quintessential nineteenth-century comic type.[7] Somerville and Ross's *The Irish R.M.* (1899 and later), now past its second series of dramatizations for American public television, is the early twentieth-century version of the comic hunting story, still having fun with Irish stereotypes (and, frequently, women). In its energy and stylishness, it is still popular with an audience that rereads the books many times with seemingly undiminished pleasure.[8] (That these same authors also wrote the dark and grimly critical study of Irish women's life entitled *The Real Charlotte*, now regarded a significant document in the feminist canon, seems at the least incongruous.)

Traditionally associated with carnival and social criticism, the comic story has never gained the prestige of some other kinds of short stories. Despite the enormous skill and polish of a Saki, P. G. Wodehouse, or Kipling (and such later writers as Frank O'Connor), comic stories have never laid claim to highbrow status; they retain as their domain from ancient times portrayal of the bumptiousness of the lower classes

7. The first collection of stories about this character, *Jorrocks's Jaunts and Jollities*, was published in 1838.

8. See, for example, Frank O'Connor, *The Lonely Voice: A Study of the Short Story* (Cleveland, 1963), 34–36.

and satire of meretriciousness in the upper classes. Comic forms of the story have also remained fairly stable, rarely exhibiting experimental tendencies (at least until the advent of the absurd). They may parody current upper-class social formalities and dialects of any age, but formally they take the essential contour of the joke (or a series of jokes), in which one or more characters get some sort of comeuppance in return for overreaching themselves. The elaborately detailed practical-joke stories found in Wodehouse and Kipling (among others) are the culmination of this strong tendency in the comic story, and these stories claim prestige only insofar as there is a serious underlying theme informing them. Kipling became less popular as a comic writer the more the complications of his stories suggested serious (often metaphysical) themes and manifested complexities of form. Becoming less popular, he also attained, several decades after his death, something of an elite status, at least among a particular circle of critics.

A third kind of nineteenth-century English story also has a long history: the ghost or horror story, now sometimes called, as by Valerie Shaw, the "sensation story."[9] Like comic stories, ghost stories tend to lack prestige as a subgenre and to appeal to the dark emotional or psychological, as opposed to the public, sociable, side of human nature. Paradoxically, the telling (or reading) of such stories was and remains frequently a public, social event, as "around the campfire." Ghost stories, tales dealing with the supernatural and meant to create a physical or psychological *frisson* in the reader, were popular all through the nineteenth century and appeared particularly frequently in collections as framed narratives, told "'round the hearth" by nurses to children, or clubmen to one another, as evening or Christmastime diversions. Mrs. Gaskell, Wilkie Collins, and Dickens all represent this practice. In thus framing the governess' tale of horror in *The Turn of the Screw*, Henry James is less modern than firmly traditional. The popularity of ghost stories is apparently universal and timeless. However, a "superior" form of the genre—so far as creating *frisson* is concerned—has emerged in "slasher movies" to fill the consumable, entertainment end of the spectrum. Ghost stories exploit the signifying power of words to evoke scenes and events that "make your flesh creep" (in the words of Dickens' Fat Boy), playing upon conscious and unconscious fears, guilt, and doubt in contexts resembling the

9. Valerie Shaw, *The Short Story: A Critical Introduction* (London, 1983). In my view, this is currently the best introduction to the short story.

settings of realistic fiction, rather than fantastic worlds (as in H. G. Wells). Inverting the comic formula of ridiculing the threatening, they take it seriously and thus—perhaps—purge it.

I would argue that the sensational element developed in the best of the nineteenth-century and early twentieth-century English ghost story writers—Sheridan Le Fanu, Wilkie Collins, M. R. James, and Kipling—contributed in a significant way to the rise of the highbrow, "mainstream" short story in the twentieth century. The techniques of description used to create the realistic setting in which the outré events take place, the symbolic character of the setting, and the psychological involvement of the protagonist were important in the development of significant settings and psychological plots in the twentieth-century short story. The effort, in Conrad, "to make you hear, to make you feel, above all to make you *see*" a situation, to experience vicariously and sensationally—phenomenologically—is more fully practiced in the ghost story than in any other short genre.

In addition to old forms revived and refurbished, two essentially new forms of short fiction, the local-color story and the detective story, emerged in the nineteenth century. But even these had forerunners in earlier ages. Both were originally "popular" genres appealing to the whole range of middle-class readers. The local-color story began as a sort of didactic story to teach the audience about different cultures, similar to narrative television documentaries today: long on scenery and description of local customs, and short on plot. Because the plots themselves, such as they are, customarily follow the general romance type, local color finally need not be seen as a separate type but as a variation of the romance, with other antecedents in earlier travel literature.

Beginning in the 1820s, Mary Russell Mitford established local color for England in her sketches and stories of a small English rural community in *Our Village*; during the thirties and forties, Mrs. Gaskell provided numerous examples from both urban Manchester and more usual rural local-color settings. Their stories differed from earlier travel and regional tales by dealing with domestic, small-group scenes and characters, usually from the middle and lower classes. J. M. Wilson's collections of his and others' stories in *Wilson's Tales of the Borders of Scotland* were extremely popular at midcentury and later, relating "scenes of cattle-flitting, love, murder, border warfare, and other exciting matters, but all of unexceptionable character." As this description in the 1858 *Bookseller* suggests, they tend to be adventures rather than what we usually think of as typical local-color stories. Aside from Irish comic stories, from the thirties on there were also Irish romances that exploited local color, by John and Michael Banim (publishing under the pseudonym "The O'Hara Family"), William Carleton, Anna Fielding Hall, and numerous others. Prefaces to collections reveal these were often written for the express purpose of recording customs and ways of living on the verge of extinction.

More exotic but still usually domestically oriented local color was published by Mrs. Gore in her *Hungarian Tales* (1829), *Polish Tales* (1833), and her appealing stories with a Brittany setting. By midcentury, translations of international stories, especially from Russian, caught the English public fancy (Turgenev, for example, appeared in *Household Words*), as did travelogue stories and American local color. The interest in international local-color fiction shows a broadening of taste and a developing curiosity and cosmopolitanism in the audience, as well as a kind of positivistic faith in the truth of empirical detail. As a people could be represented in a story, so were they judged to be: having universal human characteristics but often "quaint" and therefore interesting manners.

The detective story, in the work of Poe and Doyle and their followers, is closely related to the horror story but rationalizes and domesticates the horror by revealing that the seemingly uncanny is merely human evil after all. Here, too, a primary focus on setting and sensation is important, but deception of the reader and the reader's engagement in creating the true "story" which it is the author's business to conceal are the "modern" characteristics distinguishing it from earlier sensational fiction. The plot formula of the detective story, with its clues, gaps, suppressions, and final revelation, is reflected in that of some modern "mainstream" stories, such as Joyce's "The Sisters" and "A Painful Case," where a psychological crime is pieced together by the reader and a "guilty detective" narrator.[10]

The detective story established a new kind of contract between the writer and the reader that openly called for the reader's active participation in constructing meaning in the plot, and provided a way of "making a long story short," so to speak, through compression and elision. The tendency, in the modern highbrow story, to focus upon a

10. I argue this line more fully in my "A Sherlook at *Dubliners:* Analogues Between the Detective Story and the Modern Short Story," *James Joyce Quarterly,* XVI (1979), 111–21.

moment of illumination near the end of the story, a moment in which apparently disparate threads of the characters' experience are drawn together into an intelligible pattern, rather than a traditionally prepared plot climax, is very much dependent upon, and perhaps readable because of, the prominent popular success of the middlebrow detective story in the preceding decades.

Both of these relatively low-prestige forms contributed importantly to the grooming of the English short story for its assault on the generic high society. Local color did so by foregrounding the detailed local setting, with its emphasis on realistic natural and social scenes (and thus "atmosphere") and with its relative deemphasis on plot. The detective story left its trace in the assumption of the setting into the impetus of plot and in the omission of certain expected elements in the plot that were simply deduced and tacitly supplied by the reader, never actually told in the story. In both, the importance of setting seems to have influenced the modern short story, where it is frequently made to convey ideas about characters and feelings as well as merely place, simply through being given extraordinary prominence while other elements are left obscure and undeveloped. This very obscurity, which requires of the audience special reading techniques, became essential to the "glamor" of the short story for its modern writers and readers.

Emerging in the last two decades of the century, the aesthetic story put the finishing touches on the restyling of the English short story for modern tastes. Another variation of the romance, this type utilized the descriptive techniques and gradual heightening of psychological tension of the sensation story and the concealment of meaning associated with the detective story, along with "fine writing," to make an overt bid for high prestige. Its preoccupation with its own preciosity, together with its frequently morbid themes, earned it the epithet "decadent" as well as "aesthetic." [11] Writers and critics began to claim this type of story to be superior to the novel in artistry because the short story was more controlled, intense, and, finally, reflective of life itself.

Writers for glossy, arty magazines such as the *Yellow Book* and *Savoy*, many of the "aesthetes" were drawn to poetry as well as prose. Ernest Dowson, and even Yeats, on occasion, wrote stories utilizing what are

11. See John R. Reed, *Decadent Style* (Athens, Ohio, 1985), for a full discussion of the relationship.

usually considered poetic stylistic devices: figures of speech, meta-phorical imagery, purple descriptions, deliberately stylized rhythms and aural tropes. Others of this loosely identifiable group, such as Frederick Wedmore, Hubert Crackanthorpe, Ella D'Arcy, and George Egerton, concentrated on developing sketchy, psychologically com-plex plots in addition to poetic prose.[12] Influenced by Russian writers, especially Turgenev, George Moore wrote identifiably impressionist stories in his local-color collection, *The Untilled Field* (1901 in Gaelic, 1903 in English), which in turn inspired, or influenced, *Dubliners*. The self-consciousness of aesthetic artistry in the short story, encouraged by Flaubertian novelist-critics such as Henry James, Conrad, and Ford Madox Ford, influenced the next generation of short story writers, who "invented" for England the modern, prestige short story: Joyce, Mansfield, Lawrence, the later Kipling, and then the generation of Elizabeth Bowen, A. E. Coppard, V. S. Pritchett, and Sean O'Faolain. Significantly, James later wrote of the *Yellow Book,* in his preface to Volume XV of the New York Edition of his works, that it "opened up the millenium to the 'short story.'" Wells, in the preface to his collec-tion of short stories, *The Country of the Blind* (1911), approvingly char-acterized a catalog of short story writers from the nineties as "a mixed handful of jewels drawn from a bag."

More than any other single quality, artistry itself, as a highbrow value, pitched the short story genre above the popular, middlebrow status it had throughout most of the nineteenth century. The myste-riousness of the modern short story, its being written in a code of ge-neric and stylistic conventions that only the initiate of modern art could decipher, was part and parcel of this success. Although the highbrow novel for a time certainly shared not only the emphasis on artistry but the precise techniques of literary impressionism—frag-mentation, sketchiness, time shifts, exploitation of unusual points of view, stylistic foregrounding—its length permitted a fuller and ulti-mately more traditional development. I have contended that it is pri-marily that difference in length, and what goes into the impressionist novel to create that length, that differentiates it from the impressionist short story, rather than some essential difference in vision, form, or technique.[13] The elaboration of formal and stylistic elements in the

12. An art critic as well as a writer, Wedmore wrote an important essay on the artful-ness of the highbrow short story in his *On Books and Arts* (London, 1899), 1–24.

13. Suzanne Ferguson, "Defining the Short Story: Impressionism and Form," *Mod-ern Fiction Studies*, XXVIII (1982), 13–24.

smaller space of the short story contributed to a certain element of detachment, "coolness" in the aesthetic medium, that made clear to the story's audience the intellectual effort necessary to decipher its meaning, in contrast to the "warm" emotional milieu of the longer, more experiential novel.

Moreover, in the early decades of the twentieth century, moral uncertainties about existing class structures allowed rhetorically powerful "post-aesthete" writers and critics such as Ezra Pound and Ford Madox Ford the opportunity to argue for a modernist aristocracy in the arts, which, though not specifically concerned with the short story, benefited it as a modern form. In this view, artists and intellectuals rather than the politically or economically powerful are the possessors of a superior vision, which they exhibit in the secret, refined languages of their art. The codes of this art were so esoteric (and often so deliberately offensive to middlebrow taste) that the general public was sometimes moved to assault exhibits or performances verbally and even physically, in notorious outbursts that now seem merely quaint. A less public art than music, painting, or sculpture, the short story escaped such demonstrations. (Perhaps excepting the destruction of the plates and type for what was to have been the first edition of Joyce's *Dubliners,* in a printer's objection to its content, rather than its form.) Rejection by the lowbrow became a touchstone of high modernist art, and to be too popular, as Dickens was, or Kipling in his early years, was to court critical deprecation. Appreciation of the short story, along with that of other modernist art forms, became connoisseurship.

But beyond the formal changes, beyond the changes simply deriving from the short story's imitation of twentieth- rather than nineteenth-century behavior, speech, and details of everyday life, the preeminence of the short story as a modernist genre grew out of the modern, highbrow audience's acceptance of fragmentation as an accurate model of the world, with a concomitant focus on "being"—as in Woolf's "moments of being"—rather than the "becoming" that characterizes the plot of the Romantic and the Victorian novel. The brevity that marked "minor" to earlier generations became a badge of the short story's superior representational capacity. For a brief period, in English literature, at least, the short story became not just a prestige genre but the genre that could be said to best represent the essence of the age, as did drama at the end of the sixteenth century.

Thus, by persistently trying to move into the prestige circles of the genres, by marrying characteristics of several subgenres of the short story with characteristics of poetry, drama, and its own accommodating prose relative, the novel, the short story came into its own "social" success, producing a highbrow heir to lowbrow and middlebrow kin. The latter continue to thrive with "common" readers, though themselves threatened with obsolescence by a newer, easier, more sensational popular medium, television. The waning of modernism and the rise of creative writing as an academic discipline have located the short story as, often, the kind of work done by a young writer to prepare for a novel. Yet some writers continue to earn reputations based upon the short story alone, and the highbrow short story continues to hold a place as a prestige genre. One of the prime factors in this ranking of the short story is the continuing hold of New Critical principles in the college classrooms of the United States, where short stories, widely anthologized in textbooks, receive repeated threshing out and analysis, and are taught as literary artifacts to millions of students each year.[14] A canon of the short story has emerged, its traces recorded in succeeding editions of the popular teaching anthologies. The final accolade, of course, is the form's subjection to theoretical scrutiny, in its own scholarly periodicals, critical books, collections such as the one in which this essay appears, and symposia at professional meetings.

14. The relation of New Criticism to aestheticism and its heirs in the modernist period should not be lightly glossed over.

WILLIAM O'ROURKE

Morphological Metaphors for the Short Story: Matters of Production, Reproduction, and Consumption

I would like to offer a triptych of metaphors, three central analogies—appropriated from the worlds of the natural and social sciences—to suggest ways of seeing how the short story differs from the novel. They are all physical metaphors, and they can be extended to describe a variety of aspects of the short story form: its production, reproduction, and consumption.

The first metaphor is a model of the structural makeup of vertebrate and exoskeletal animals. Holding that a novel has a skeletal structure, is not, of course, a new concept. Alberto Moravia, in his essay "The Short Story and the Novel," speaks of a novel's "ideology, that is the skeleton of the theme from which the flesh of the story takes its form." He also claims that "the novel has a bone structure holding it together from top to toe, whereas the short story is, so to speak, boneless." It is this "absence of bone structure that makes a short story not a novel."[1] We are not using the same metaphor or, rather, Moravia does not extend the metaphor he employs. He contrasts skeletal with boneless, whereas I contrast the interior skeleton of large organisms with the exterior skeleton of some smaller creatures.

Zoologists often list size among the host of reasons explaining the evolution of vertebrates and exoskeletal animals. Animals with exoskeletons only grow so large—about the size of a giant lobster.[2] One

1. Alberto Moravia, *Man as an End: A Defense of Humanism* (New York, 1966), 180, translation copyright © 1965 by Martin Secker and Warburg Limited, reprinted by permission of Farrar, Straus and Giroux, Inc. Section rpr. in Charles E. May (ed.), *Short Story Theories* (Athens, Ohio, 1976), 149.

2. See the *Larousse Encyclopedia of Animal Life* (London, 1967), 156–59.

argues over the maximum length of the short story, but there are fewer arguments on about just how long a novel can be. Recall the jibe at Proust: Life is too short and Proust is too long.[3] How large can a vertebrate grow? The size of whales, dinosaurs? Nagging questions regarding maximum length and problems of definition apply to the novel as well as to the short story, except that since the novel inhabits the realms of excess, those questions are never so bothersome.

Size has other contingencies. The relationship of the reader to the short story is one of spectator to object. It is the same order of relationship found when a shell or a sculpture is viewed—but not a painting. One can walk around sculpture; it is whole, discrete, intact, three-dimensional. But painting is vertebrate, endoskeletal, two-dimensional; it expands toward all points of a compass, limited only by the size of the frame. A novel's vertebrate structure is necessarily interior, whereas its flesh, its text, is exterior. A novel is wrapped around its structure, stretched around it, as a canvas is fastened on its frame. But a short story's text is its structure and its structure is its text. Frank O'Connor's remark is apt: "One can put this crudely by saying that the form of the novel is given by the length; in the short story the length is given by the form."[4] Some would like a single sentence to qualify as a short story, but given my model, that is unlikely. In the building trades, is one I beam ever a structure?[5] Literature never seems to have too much structure: too little may be a fatal flaw.

A story, because of its size, is always (like a piece of sculpture) held in view; but it is difficult to see a whole novel (with all its parts), just as it is difficult to take in an entire painting at once. The experience of seeing a sculpture requires first seeing the whole: is seeing, or noticing, only part of a sculpture seeing the sculpture?

One usually knows the length of what one is reading before one begins. In all discussions of short story theory, the problem of length is duly noted. But, until recently, the notion of length was merely touched on and then abandoned, as if reading time were not, in and

---

3. How long can a novel be? 1,500 pages? One was recently published: Helen Hoover Santmyer, ". . . And the Ladies of the Club" (Columbus, Ohio, 1983).

4. Frank O'Connor, The Lonely Voice: A Study of the Short Story (Cleveland, 1963), 27, with the permission of Harper and Row Publishers. Section rpr. in May (ed.), Short Story Theories, 92.

5. Susan Lohafer's remarks about the sentence are useful here. See Coming to Terms with the Short Story (1983; rpr. Baton Rouge, 1985), 34–52. See also Stephen Fredman's Poet's Prose: The Crisis in American Verse (New York, 1983), 12–55.

of itself, an overwhelming fact. Although Albert Einstein postulated his theory of relativity in 1905, discussions of length—time—in literature are still framed in largely Newtonian terms. Critics pay a great deal of lip service to the post-Einsteinian world when they deal with modern literature, but what they offer is the few usual clichés—"entropy," "fragmentation," "flux"—all acknowledging that a general reassessment has taken place. Seldom, if ever, is there any direct application of the specific concepts involved.[6]

If post-Einsteinian science has seemed to describe nature as more chaotic, it has also made nature more concrete. My second metaphor, the middle panel of the triptych, is an application. The New Columbia Encyclopedia notes in its definition of *time*, "In the theory of relativity, the intuitive notion of time as an independent entity is replaced by the concept that space and time are intertwined and inseparable aspects of a four-dimensional universe, which is given the name SPACE-TIME."[7] For my analogy the concept of length (when thinking of a short story or a novel) must be replaced by the concept of space and time intertwined. It is not the length of a short story that is critical but its space and time: not the length of time (one sitting, for example) needed to read it, but the distance from the observer it creates. The greater the space, the more time it takes to comprehend, to see. To see all the parts of a novel requires great distance, therefore more time, but not so the short story: the reader is always close enough to see a short story whole. It is simpler if we picture a short story's space and think of size, not length.

In a comparison of the first sentence of a short story with the first sentence of a novel, the overall "size" (the story's space-time continuum) usually reveals itself. Let us consider, for instance, the first sentence of Hemingway's "The Short Happy Life of Francis Macomber": "It was now lunch time and they were all sitting under the double green fly of the dining tent pretending that nothing had happened."

6. See James M. Mellard, *The Exploded Form* (Urbana, Ill., 1980), 38–39. Mellard's is an instructive discussion, though he too avoids direct application of post-Einsteinian theory. One game attempt is Anne Mangel's "Maxwell's Demon, Entropy, Information: *The Crying of Lot 49*," *TriQuarterly*, XX (1971), 194–208.

7. Many definitions of *relativity* are available. In one discussion, the physicist Robert H. March remarks, "Normally it takes a physicist about five years of contact with the ideas of relativity to feel comfortable with them" (*Physics for Poets* [Chicago, 1984], 104–17, 108, copyright © 1984 by McGraw-Hill Book Company, reprinted by permission).

There is a very short focal length of vision; something entire is being seen from a relatively short distance. Compare that sentence to the first sentence of Hemingway's novel *A Farewell to Arms:* "In the late summer of that year we lived in a house in a village that looked across the river and the plain to the mountains."[8] There is a long focal length in that sentence; the reader is asked to look at a great distance of space-time.

Flannery O'Connor claimed, "The major difference between the novel as written in the eighteenth century and the novel as we usually find it today is the disappearance from it of the author."[9] And when authors began to disappear from their novels, they had been absent from short stories for some time. Without authorial standing, the narrator's point of view (be it persona, pseudodocumentary, or unreliable) becomes an extension of the reader's point of view; the reader becomes the surrogate narrator. In this way, the reader "tells" the story, just as those viewing a play tell the story to themselves.

One reason the short story shares structural similarities with drama is that the reader's position (vis-à-vis the short story) is the same as the playgoer's. Looking. Observing from a short distance. This retention of the spectator's point of view is the principal vestige of the modern written short story's oral roots. The oral tale teller would often adopt a persona, take on a role and pretend not to be there, although the listener could see the narrator pretending; in this way, the listener objectified the story as an entity told, as well as a serialized telling.

My earlier assertion that a short story's text is its structure and its structure is its text proceeds directly from the exoskeletal metaphor; and such exoskeletal structure accounts for much of the recent critical language that has been used to describe the short story. Archaeologists can reconstruct a pot from a shard: the part will have some overall defining shape. It will reveal the size of the whole. My contention is that a piece of a short story will also reveal the curve of its shape,

8. Ernest Hemingway, *The Fifth Column and the First Forty-Nine Stories* (New York, 1938), 102, and Hemingway, *A Farewell to Arms* (New York, 1929), 3, reprinted with permission of the Executors of the Ernest Hemingway Estate, Jonathan Cape Ltd., and Charles Scribner's Sons.

9. Flannery O'Connor, "The Nature and Aim of Fiction," in Sally and Robert Fitzgerald (eds.), *Mystery and Manners* (New York, 1974), 74, copyright © 1957, 1961, 1963, 1964, 1966, 1967, 1969 by the Estate of Mary Flannery O'Connor, reprinted by permission of Farrar, Straus and Giroux, Inc.

the size of its whole, because of its space-time configuration, its exo-skeletal, microform elements. Short stories are akin in their geometry to fractals, shapes that look more or less the same on all, or many, scales of magnification. Any number of essays on the poetics of the short story, and on closure in particular, buttress this view.[10] The literary physics involved in the difference between exoskeletal and vertebrate structure can be compared to the difference between calculus and algebra: algebra describes linear relationships (such as in a novel), and calculus describes rates of change along curves (as in a short story). Four-dimensional space requires calculus to describe it. Novels are products of literary algebra; short stories are examples of literary calculus.

My metaphors, at their hearts, distinguish between large and small. The third metaphor of structure I want to introduce is one used most by economists, but, significantly, it is also used by physicists in quantum theory; it is the concept of micro and macro forms.[11] In my analogy, the short story is a micro form and the novel is a macro form. The micro/macro model reveals more fully the space-time attributes of the short story. One household, one factory, one individual is studied in microeconomics; the relationship between many households, many factories, many individuals is the subject of macroeconomics.[12] A short story is a micro-form, space-time, exoskeletal phenomenon and can be explained most completely by the intertwining of these metaphors; as in quantum theory, each metaphor needs to be laid atop the others.[13]

Relativity is often illustrated by picturing one object (such as a planet) and many observers situated at different points from the object. Time is influenced by space, the distance from the object that is

10. Lohafer, *Coming to Terms*, 10–33, 82–86.

11. C. J. S. Clarke's essay, "The Hinterland Between Large and Small," in *The Encyclopaedia of Ignorance* (New York, 1978), 111–18, discusses "the central distinction between the physics of the large and the physics of the small" that is pertinent to my model. See also B. M. Eikhenbaum, *O. Henry and the Theory of the Short Story*, trans. I. R. Titunik (Ann Arbor, 1968), 4, quoted by Charles E. May, "The Nature of Knowledge in Short Fiction," *Studies in Short Fiction*, XXI (1984), 328: "The difference [between the novel and the short story] is one of essence, a difference in principle conditioned by the fundamental distinction between *big* and *small* form."

12. For a discussion of these principles, see Michael Parkin, *Macroeconomics* (Englewood Heights, N.J., 1984), 228–29.

13. Clarke, "The Hinterland Between Large and Small," 112.

observed. In my model, the exoskeletal short story is observed from a much shorter distance than the novel and, in almost every case, from just one point of view. It is therefore represented by a single equation. A novel is viewed, because of the distance (the space) involved, from many points of view (or, one might say, many points of view are seen); and novels often use multiple points of view. Because of its space-time components, the novel can be defined as a macro-form, multiple-equation phenomenon with vertebrate elements.

These three metaphors can be further intertwined and extended to elucidate another aspect of the short story: its survival as a form—the survival, perhaps, of the fittest. Since the short story has an exoskeletal structure, it displays wonderful adaptive skills (of the sort that make it hard to kill). And, ancient as it is, it survives to the present, whereas some younger vertebrate forms totter, it is alleged, toward extinction.[14] No one ever talks of the death of the short story. In *Coming to Terms with the Short Story*, Susan Lohafer makes two relevant remarks prompted by those of Nadine Gordimer and William Carlos Williams: "The short story, because of its brevity and concentration, is the most usable form left to literature," and "[Both Gordimer and Williams] view the short story as the survival form of fiction. It can shape itself to the particles of reality without unduly falsifying them or losing its own entirety."[15]

The exoskeletal structure of the short story (its brevity and concentration) may well leave it, like the hardy cockroach, the chief survivor of our blasted literary age. Even though academic critics continue to describe the short story as the poor relation of the novel, neglected at every turn, the short story is, nonetheless, the current contemporary form in fashionable ascendancy.[16] It is, ironically, specialists in the short story who most vocally announce its neglect. Such complaints seem to boil down to the fact that short story studies wasn't an approved specialty long before they chose it themselves. Susan Lohafer comes the closest to describing the nub of the complaint: "There is an aristocracy of genres in which the short story is forever in the train of the novel, classified by author, subcategorized as text. For every course

14. Mellard, *Exploded Form*, 5. See also Leslie Fiedler, *What Was Literature?* (New York, 1982), 73–82. I am here speaking of the modern novel and short story.

15. Lohafer, *Coming to Terms*, 29.

16. See Charles Champlin, "The Great American Short Story Rides Again," *The Book Review*, Los Angeles *Times*, June 30, 1985, p. 1, and David Leavitt, "New Voices and Old Values," *New York Times Book Review*, May 12, 1985, p. 1. Even *USA Today*, May 17, 1985, Sec. 4D, devoted a whole page to "Short Stories in Review."

in 'the realistic novel,' how many courses, do you suppose, are taught in 'the lyrical short story'?"[17] What is being objected to is the hierarchy, the "aristocracy of genres"—and the shunting of practitioners of short story criticism to the "subcategorized" world outside the limelight.

This has been the plight of the short story from the beginning of the form. Edgar Allan Poe, when he wrote his review of *Twice-Told Tales*, was attempting to accomplish the same, necessary task for the short story as Tom Wolfe, in the last decade, accomplished for the so-called New Journalism. Poe was both publicist and practitioner of a new form, and needed (like Wolfe) to stake out unclaimed theoretical territory for it. They both sought justifications of their respective forms in order to make them fashionable and profitable.[18] But the irony is that as fewer commercial magazines publish it and the general public continues to avoid it, the short story rises in critical favor, not only among professors but among literary reviewers.

Regardless of the short story's oral antecedents, it is no longer a "popular" form, but an art form. As the number of outlets for commercial short story publication has dropped, the number of outlets for noncommercial publication of short stories has soared. The list of publications in *The Best American Short Stories of 1965* filled two-and-a-half pages, whereas the list found in a recent volume of *The Pushcart Prize* occupied thirteen and a half. The 1934 volume of *The Best American Short Stories* contained one-and-a-half pages of publications; in the 1984 volume there were over six pages—and the substantial majority of stories came from small presses and academic journals.[19] These fluctuating numbers suggest the special economics of the short story form.

Its market is consumers of writing. The mass audience finds most of its entertainment in forms that are overwhelmingly oral (television, movies, and popular literature). One of the requirements of the oral form is not stopping and thinking about what has been said (or read),

17. Lohafer, *Coming to Terms*, 4. Charles E. May, in "A Survey of Short Story Criticism in America," in May (ed.), *Short Story Theories*, 3, voices the typical complaint: "Although the short story is respected by its practitioners, it is largely ignored by both the popular and the serious reader."

18. Edgar Allan Poe, "Review of *Twice-Told Tales*," in May (ed.), *Short Story Theories*, 45–52. See Tom Wolfe's discussion in *The New Journalism* (New York, 1973), 3–52.

19. Martha Foley (ed.), *The Best American Short Stories of 1965* (Boston, 1965); Bill Henderson (ed.), *The Pushcart Prize, IX: Best of the Small Presses* (New York, 1984); E. J. O'Brien (ed.), *The Best Short Stories* (Boston, 1934); J. Updike and S. Ravenel (eds.), *The Best American Short Stories* (Boston, 1984). See John Updike's remarks in this last volume's introduction, xiv–xv.

lest we lose the thread of the narrative, miss what is said next. The written form allows readers to influence the space-time equation: to think, reflect, ponder, if they choose. Researchers looking into the differences between comprehension and memory of oral versus written discourse have discovered that "readers and listeners may tend to extract different kinds of information from oral and written statements. Listeners may tend to recall more of the gist of the story and readers may recall more of *the surface structure* or verbatim features of the story." And in "oral language, the point, intention or significance of the language, the 'speaker's meaning' is preserved in the mind of the listener; as the actual words, syntax, and intonation are ephemeral, they are rapidly exchanged for those interpreted meanings which can be preserved. In written language, the words and syntax, the 'sentence meaning,' is preserved by the artifact of writing, and mental recall becomes the precise reproduction of that artifact."[20] To what audience is this feature attractive? The oral always posits a group audience; the written assumes most often one person.[21]

One of the audience difficulties that besets the contemporary novelist, it is claimed, is that "he" does not know for whom "he" writes. In "The Post-Modern Aura," Charles Newman remarks, "I think it's fair to say that no serious fiction writer in America today can tell you whom he is writing for." Newman is speaking primarily of novelists; even so, I suspect that "she" has a better idea to whom "she" is writing.[22] But because of the nature of the short story—given the fact that its place of publication assumes a particular audience—it is still audience directed. Much more than a serious novelist, a short story author can envision the reader of the story: the demographics are more clear-cut.

John Updike has addressed this issue and, along the way, made tantalizing use of an economic metaphor: "But there also has to be a genre, a pre-existent form or type of object to which the prospective artist's first relation was that of consumer, the pleasure of his consumption extending itself into the ambition to be a producer."[23] Short

20. Angela Hildyard and David R. Olson, "On the Comprehension and Memory of Oral vs. Written Discourse," in Deborah Tannen (ed.), *Spoken and Written Language* (Norwood, N.J., 1982), 19. Emphasis added.

21. An interesting discussion of the social qualities of the short story is found in Edward J. O'Brien's *The Advance of the American Short Story* (New York, 1923), 21–23.

22. Charles Newman, "The Post-Modern Aura," *Salmagundi*, LXIII–LXIV (1984), 150. See my "Response to Charles Newman" in *Salmagundi*, LXVII (1985), 183–85.

23. John Updike, "The Artist and His Audience," *New York Review of Books*, July 18,

story writers not only know for whom they are writing but take their place in the economic history of literary consumption and production. Over time, the story has changed from the oral to the written tradition, whereas the modern novel remains divided, both traditions still in active competition. That the modern short story has completed this evolution is partly due to its least discussed literary progenitor, the sermon.[24]

In many ways, the sermon is the missing link between the oral and written traditions. For while the preacher uses oral rhetorical devices, he, at the same time, asks the audience to think about what the sermon says, to ponder, while it listens. That is why, in sermons, there is so much repetition, circular movement, tightly woven rhetorical threading—exoskeletal structure, I would claim—in order to compensate for the major fact of its oral form: the relationship of the spectator to the teller, just the oral element that the modern written short story retains. And that is why the exoskeletal structure of the short story is so critical—because the limited size retains that close space-time, spectator-to-object relationship. The short story, like the sermon, asks readers to contemplate what they experience while experiencing it; in other words, they are asked to be reflective, self-examining, conscious of their apprehension of the story they read: the hallmark of the written form.

What was held against the short story by literary critics decades ago was the genre's popular appeal, its association with mass taste, the slicks, the formulaic, and the romantic, in the heyday of magazine publishing, back before the advent of the paperback book. Today, the large numbers of romance readers have abandoned the short story and taken up with the commercial romance novel. And the oral traditions of the tale (which were found abundantly in the popular short story of the twenties and thirties) now find themselves cozily at home in the empty mansions of the best-selling romance novel.[25]

Jayne Anne Phillips writes in the introduction to the 1984–85 *Push-*

1985, pp. 14–18, reprinted with permission from *The New York Review of Books,* copyright © 1985 by Nyrev, Inc. See also Corinne Demas Bliss, "The Short Story: Writer's Control/Reader's Response" (Ph.D. dissertation, Columbia University, 1980), 1–37.

24. For connections with the sermon see May's remarks about the sacred in "The Nature of Knowledge in Short Fiction," 327, and Valerie Shaw, *The Short Story: A Critical Introduction* (London, 1983), 9, 16, 128, 141, 145. The short story is becoming the contemporary secular sermon.

25. See my discussion of this audience in "Catholics Coming of Age: The Literary Consequences," *New Catholic World,* CCXXVIII (1985), 148–52.

cart Prize volume: "It is a paradox that much of what is evolving in current American writing evolves in relative secrecy, unreflected in the obvious media: television and film, and the handful of commercial magazines which continue to publish fiction and poetry and essays. Even in such magazines, space is limited, and what fills the space is often dictated by marketing considerations. The climate fostered by such conditions, especially for young writers, is daunting. . . . Since [small presses] have no 'target' readerships [other than the "literary"-minded] and few advertisers, [they] often publish work that is unconventional in subject matter or technique."[26]

Today the short story is fashionable, but not popular. An explanation for this seeming paradox can be found by extending the third of my metaphors, micro and macro forms, more deeply into economics. Put simply, the modern short story is now a micro form which is highly capital intensive. Indeed, one reason for the recent ascendancy of the short story has been the rise of the small press movement during the last two decades and the concurrent growth of graduate writing programs. Both phenomena I hold to be capital intensive.

Some simple illustrations of capital and labor intensivity in production and consumption will explain what I mean. Sending someone a birthday card is capital intensive; sending someone a letter on a birthday is labor intensive. What is being produced is a greeting. Here is an illustration of consumption: the Concorde airplane and the Super Chief passenger train are both modes of transportation. The Super Chief (in my analogy) is macro-form, vertebrate, long in space-time, and labor intensive. The Concorde is the opposite: micro-form, exoskeletal, compact in space-time, capital intensive. What can be consumed by means of both modes is a trip. But they are utterly different, despite the fact that they are both ways to move from one place to another. The Super Chief can be compared to the novel; the Concorde the short story.

Short stories take less time to produce than novels; they take less time to consume. But the paradox is that the short story, though no longer the popular form, is the fashionable form. "Fashionable" is capital intensive, whereas "popular" is labor intensive. The short story is fashionable because it is produced and consumed by those whose time is valued—thus used sparingly. Time is conserved and capital investment (education, formal training) increases in the production (and consumption) of the densely structured, written short

26. Henderson (ed.), *The Pushcart Prize*, 25.

story. Romance novels are the popular literary form; they are read by people who in essence want to *kill* time—those whose time is much less valued. (Sophisticated readers sometimes resort to escape literature—detective novels, for example—for the same reason.)

The modern short story requires a great deal of personal investment (sophisticated training), but also the shortest amount of initial reading time. It is the density of the modern story's exoskeletal structure that requires sophisticated training (offered by capital-intensive universities) to master and enjoy. Certain literary novels, on the other hand, use large amounts of both capital and labor and, consequently, are never popular, since in an industrialized market society either capital is substituted for labor or vice versa, depending on which of the two is more dear. Both capital and labor are lavishly expended only when there is a surplus (and, where literature is concerned, fashionableness can create a sort of surplus). Occasionally, capital- and labor-intensive novels will be kept alive in the hothouse environment of a university—*Finnegans Wake*, for example.

The short story form is a more elemental form than the novel and, therefore, is more successfully armored for the rigors of evolution, which makes it a veritable laboratory for measuring fundamental changes in the nature of contemporary literature.[27] Throughout history the short story has continued to be the fruit fly of literature, insofar as it mutates through generations much faster than any other form. Because of its elegant but less extensively modifiable structure (one difference between exoskeletal and vertebrate forms), the short story is the form most attempted by amateurs.

It was a chestnut of the fifties that everyone had one novel in him or her. It is now the fact of the eighties that it is possible for anyone to write one good short story. A frivolous definition of a short story could be: a piece of literature of which a good example can be produced by accident—or by an amateur. Writing a good novel by accident is impossible, though the chance of writing a good short story is within the realm of possibility. Anyone who has had any connection with writing programs, or writing students, over the last fifteen years will attest to such an occurrence.

The fact that men and women of letters are disappearing provides us with another reason for the short story's increasing regard. Al-

27. See May, "The Nature of Knowledge in Short Fiction," 328. May quotes Eikhenbaum's distinction between "elemental" and "primitive" forms. See also the *Larousse Encyclopedia*, 206. In evolution the exoskeleton is a more elemental form; the vertebrate results in the possibility of extensive modification.

though a handful of aspirants to the title still exist, the number of writers of the post-1945 generation who want to, hope to, write in all genres is shrinking. Younger writers have seen the future, and what appears to work is specialization—a capital-intensive phenomenon. Their careers must start up quickly; a premium is put on time.[28]

It is more likely these days for a young writer to acquire reputation and advancement through the writing of short stories than through the writing of novels. Literary journalists and academic critics are in business; their time is money. So they value its expenditure. Depending on where the short story has appeared, some prejudging has already occurred; magazine editors do some of the critics' work. By reading three or four stories by the same author, the critics will feel that they have a true sense of that writer's abilities. It is not the same if the critics or reviewers peruse a few pages of a novel. This fact is another testament to the difference between exoskeletal and vertebrate form. The reading of short stories is capital intensive and allows the critics to become experts more quickly.

With novels, the role of the publishing house is analogous to that of magazines, but not as directly indicative; in publishing there is certainly an aristocracy of imprint. A novel brought out by a high-caste house will immediately seem more literary regardless of the novel's content. Some books are announced by their covers.

A novel can be published, not even reach bookstores, and be pulped. That is the most extreme case, but if a novel is not bought by libraries or individuals (or, most importantly, by a paperback house), it disappears, is not available, becomes an instant rare book. A novel must gather at least four reviews from a list of over seventy periodicals to be included in the venerable reference *Book Review Digest*. Quite a few novels by important writers of my generation, for example, did not gather the necessary four reviews and, subsequently, do not even exist as references. Magazines and periodicals have more life, dog-eared in waiting rooms, on shelves in libraries, in bound collections of quarterlies which academics and critics can get to, or stumble over, eventually. And the small press movement has published hundreds upon hundreds of short stories, but only a handful of novels.

An inspection of the last nine volumes of *The Pushcart Prize* reveals the extent of this phenomenon. A few "small presses" have become not-so-small presses and have taken to reprinting novels originally published by trade presses but which have lapsed from print (for

28. See Leavitt, "New Voices and Old Values," 1.

example, Graywolf Press and Thunder's Mouth Press). University presses retain the same ratio of short story collections to novels. The universities of Missouri, Illinois, and Pittsburgh (among others) have short stories series, but with one or two exceptions, university presses have not, in the past, issued many novels. And, once published, short stories are reprinted in anthologies, win prizes, and (depending on where they are published) immediately link one writer to other writers, making *ad hoc* groups critics do not need to gather independently—one such being the so-called *New Yorker* writers.

The *New Yorker*'s influence on the contemporary short story has been immense, if for no other reason than it has remained a glamorous holding pen for the genteel tradition. (John Updike, for one, will write two sorts of stories: one that is published in the *New Yorker,* and one that is published in *Playboy.*) When Poe became a spokesman for what eventually became the commercial (oral-based, labor-intensive) short story, and when Tom Wolfe beat the drum for New Journalism, each did so because his form was, in its time, not yet acceptable for genteel publication. Oddly, where New Journalism was concerned, it, more than fiction, profited from the striking down of obscenity statutes. Fiction had already won that battle, since there have always been two traditions in fiction, the genteel and nongenteel. And that is yet another reason for the current high esteem given to the short story. It is now, much more than the novel, the inheritor of the genteel tradition.

Roger Angell, senior fiction editor of the *New Yorker,* has remarked: "There's a great national factory out there. If you open the windows, you can hear the sound of typewriters driven by people writing stories all over the country. It may tell something about the state of the novel that this seems to be a particularly good time for the short story."[29] What the sound of typewriters should tell Angell is that the writing of novels in the "national factories"—serious, literary (written, rather than oral) novels, macro-form, labor-intensive, vertebrate as they are—is an unprofitable enterprise, a fact which the newest generation of writers has (unconsciously, at least) assimilated, and that is why all those typewriters are pounding out micro-form, capital-intensive, exoskeletal short stories.

29. Robert Angell, interviewed by Herbert Mitgang, in "A New Life for the Short Story," New York *Times,* March 20, 1985, p. 24, copyright © 1985 by The New York Times Company, reprinted by permission.

V

How Is Story Processed?

SUSAN LOHAFER

Introduction to Part V

Deconstruction is no longer a password, but it is still the key to
certain doors in literary study. Turned in, say, a feminist or
Marxist direction, it is a way into the gap between words and
Word, readers and Reader. It leads to a place—some might say a job—
for the critic. Traveling in that direction are the followers of Derrida
and Paul De Man, and among them do we find, *could* we find, a short
story critic?

What we are likely to find is that certain stories like Poe's "Pur-
loined Letter" have been famously deconstructed—but not in the interests of genre criticism, and not for the sake of short story theory.
Pressing in upon us at the start here is a question I've raised several
times: why are self-styled short story critics, as a group, so indifferent
to the fashions of narrative theory? There are pejorative answers, of
course, based on the notion of stories as "easy" material, a safe preserve for the tried and true. Perhaps that is why the pages of the *Explicator* will always be full, but there is no legion of short story theorists, marching along in yesterday's path. There are only a handful,
wandering on and off the roads we've been searching. As I suggested
earlier, if short story theorists have neglected the highroads of the
eighties, it may be because they prefer the off ramp on principle. Or,
as I hinted in the previous introduction, our efforts may have their
own story. Whoever its heroes and heroines may be—and their names
have been scattered throughout this book—the plot is recursive; we
are forever struggling with the same questions—definition, brevity,
and status—and forever discovering what we already know. Where,
then, is this story heading?

Home. Back to basics. Yet I don't mean to imply that the future of short story theory is either limited or compromised. On the contrary, I believe it is breathtakingly open and inviting. The possibilities that lie ahead do not exclude the work encountered so far in this book. Those essays test viewpoints, ask questions, propose strategies that can (and we hope will) lead to further work by their authors, by other authors represented here (for we are in the business of trading ideas with all due credit but no strings attached), and by readers. By the same token, the four essays gathered in this final section are hardly closural. They are another way to carry on the story. They illustrate a powerful new way to tell it, a way that gives short story theory new connections in the academic world and shows, once again, that in its unassuming way, it occasionally winds up ahead of the crowd.

For, among certain short story critics, there is a developing interest in what we might call the deconstruction of the reading process. Yet it bears little relation to what we usually mean by that catchword. The guidelines for this project do not come from the French so much as the Dutch—the Netherlands school of discourse analysis headed by Teun A. van Dijk. But the real inspiration for this work lies deeper. It is part of a far larger and more significant shift in paradigms in the academic world. This shift has been described in many ways, often broadly as a move from positivist to constructivist theories of meaning and knowledge. Many disciplines have been affected, but we are concerned here, in particular, with psychology. Having struggled throughout much of its history for respect as a science, it is now, in some areas, turning to the humanities for models of experience, for new concepts of data. Chief among these models is narrative or, more particularly, story.[1]

Psychologists who are studying cognition, particularly as it develops in children, and discourse analysts who are studying how texts are "generated" (told or written) and "processed" (understood, remembered, used) clearly have much to say to one another. Stated most simply, both psychologists and discourse analysts have come to regard "storying" as a form of cognition, highly privileged and discrete in the set of human adaptations to experience. By the manner in which stories are created and consumed, much can be learned about this highly significant form of cognition. In the seventies and eighties,

1. For an excellent survey of the role narrative is coming to play in psychological research, consult Theodore R. Sarbin (ed.), *Narrative Psychology: The Storied Nature of Human Conduct* (New York, 1986).

the most visible results of study in this area were the variety of narrative grammars presumed to guide both the creating of new stories and the processing of all stories.

Structuralist critics had, of course, been there before, via their association with anthropology and the structures, or grammars, that codify meaning. What was new was the attempt, by some developmental psychologists, to locate the source of these grammars experimentally. The question of whether story grammar was a preprinted circuit, a substructure of the nervous system, or whether it was an acquired competence, a social skill, was never decided. Theories based on Jean Piaget's stages of cognitive development tended to support the first view, arguing that the ability to make and recognize stories depends on certain specific cognitive functions (such as the concept of repetition) which develop naturally in a particular sequence at a known rate. Theories based on social context tended to support the second view, arguing that story competence derives from experience with play situations, "event knowledge," and/or stories told or read by adults. More and more, however, the old nature-versus-nurture debate gave way to the overwhelming influence of new technology, the powerful new model of artificial intelligence. In the late eighties, story grammars have been challenged on many grounds, often pushed aside for theories based on the goal-directed "plans" of stories, their cultural emplotment, or the structure of the affects triggered in the reader.[2] Once again, short fiction theorists are catching up with a trend—in this case, interdisciplinary study; however, by leaning in the direction of cognitive theory, we may be, after all, in the vanguard. It seems that almost everyone can agree on one thing: cognition is a matter of "framing" input. "Storying" is one of the, if not *the*, most significant, earliest developed, most usable, and most culturally embedded of the mind's framing capacities. Story is the human frame for experience.

Cutting-edge theory—or ancient tautology? Both, say short story critics. Some of the essays in the previous sections, and especially those in Part II, are evidence of frame theory at work. What we are going to see now is the more technically developed and foregrounded use of

2. See the *Journal of Pragmatics*, VI (1982), a special issue focusing on story grammars and related topics; also, William F. Brewer and Keisuke Ohtsuka, "Story Structure, Characterization, Just World Organization, and Reader Affect in American and Hungarian Short Stories," *Poetics*, XVII (1988).

that concept. Why is it so appealing? I think because it *is* so new—and so old. One of the enduring themes in short fiction studies is the unified, irradiating, and finally ineffable salience of story. Metaphors abound in the writings of Poe, Welty, May, Rohrberger, Shaw . . . all aimed at describing the way stories "get" to us, aligning themselves with the roots of our being. How can we capture this sense of primacy within an intellectual framework suitable for research? For many of us, the answer seems to lie, at least for now, in cozier relations with fields already on good terms with one another, and on the move in our direction: cognitive science, developmental psychology, and discourse analysis. They have helped us understand "storyness" as a cognitive frame. With this knowledge, we have begun to investigate, to demystify, and to deconstruct—in what we might like to think of as a less capricious, more conserving way—our experience with stories.

Four essays lie ahead. Each, in specific and technical ways, draws upon theories of discourse processing, making this exciting new field relevant to the work of short story critics. Suzanne Hunter Brown and I are particularly interested in the cognitive aspects of reading, of processing story; Armine Kotin Mortimer and Ian Reid aim their theory at critical functions, the interpreting of story. All of us are mediators between a technical apparatus and a familiar goal—the subtler understanding of literary short stories.

Brown's essay, "Discourse Analysis and the Short Story," is exactly what its title implies. It is a work of orientation, a digest of important ideas and research, sorted and explained for the reader who would put down an article at the mere hint of a node diagram or a *macro* prefix. As a storywriter herself, this author is no cold clinician in the lab of discourse. Theory is only a route back to art. She takes us along. And yes, she is the same Brown without whom no survey of short story criticism would be complete. Indeed, the final section of this book may well be the ripple effect of her 1982 essay comparing a slice from *Tess of the D'Urbervilles* read as part of a novel with virtually the same text read as a short story.

Her conclusions there—that we read identical texts differently, depending on whether our genre frame is "novel" or "short story"—are perhaps debatable, but they are unforgettable. They suggest that the more we learn about the general laws of cognition, and how they apply to discourse processing, the more rationally and precisely we can explain the effects of brevity in short fiction. Brown's essay in this section makes good that suggestion, and prepares the way for future experiments and discoveries. Yet some readers may resist the jargon, may feel we have little to gain from those who do not privilege the literary text. Others may grant the validity of cognitive science, yet believe it has no more relevance to problems in aesthetics and hermeneutics than *Gray's Anatomy* has relevance to the *Laokoön*. Brown would, of course, disagree, pointing to the applications of her work in Appendix A. At the very least, her essay is controversial in a good cause, making us ask what, indeed, it means to be up-to-date as a short story critic.

Can I say as much for my own essay? "Preclosure and Story Processing" makes no claim to scientific method or validity, though it draws upon fields where those concepts are respected. It is much more like a personal experiment. I'd been convinced for many years that concepts of closure, such as those developed in Barbara Herrnstein Smith's study of closure in poetry, were particularly central to short fiction studies. This idea runs through my book *Coming to Terms with the Short Story*, and informs many of the strategies I use in the classroom. More recently, I'd been finding the concept of preclosure equally, if not more, useful as a heuristic in teaching. Nudged toward theory, I wondered if the study of preclosure might not link traditional ideas of form with modern text-grammars. From reader-chosen points of preclosure, I hoped to learn more about story schema, and perhaps eventually about "storyness" as a primal perception.

Both Brown and I are interested in the way short stories are cognitively processed (maybe because we write them ourselves). Yet despite some new terms, we are looking for answers to the same old questions: how do brevity and wholeness together create an experience for the reader that is genre-specific? Brown's aim, finally, is to enrich the field of short story criticism by naturalizing concepts and methods deemed sciencelike and alien. My own aim is to see what happens when we bring some of these concepts home with us, making them interact with old friends like reader-response theory and rhetorical and stylistic analysis. The liabilities here are obvious. Experts in the fields I've plundered may think I've played fast and loose with many of their concepts, to suit my own taste. Skeptics will wonder if I haven't made a short story long, belaboring the simple to retrieve the obvious. But perhaps a few readers will come away with new words for the ineffable, and a willingness to try a similar experiment.

Something of the same urge toward theory-in-practice is evident in Armine Kotin Mortimer's essay "Second Stories." There she examines a particular class of texts that encode a "second" (unwritten but entailed) story which must be processed in order for the written text to be understood. For example, a tale of a husband's discomfiture leaves out, but requires us to fill in, the "story" of a wife's behavior. How do readers know there is a second story, and how do they piece it together? In explaining the kinds of story competence required for such work, Mortimer verges on the topics of narrative grammar, story schema, and frame theory to be found in Brown's essay and my own. All three of us are assuming that adult readers of stories use cognitive strategies of a very basic and imperative kind.

To demonstrate, Mortimer offers a detailed exegesis of five stories. She explains the way a second story can be retrieved from each, and how necessary, how definitive, is that reconstruction. Her examples come exclusively from Maupassant, although she mentions stories like Katherine Mansfield's "Bliss" and Edith Wharton's "Roman Fever" in passing. Readers more familiar with the British and American canon may wish Mortimer had not limited the scope of her examples. They may think she runs the danger of limiting her theory, making the second story seem an embellishment of French wit rather than a narrative staple. Yet her choice is deliberate, perhaps a way of forcing us to read our canon more broadly, to fill in the gaps of an Anglo-American bias.

A committed and instructive work, Mortimer's essay is narratological in the classic structuralist tradition. Her model of processing is detection, the breaking of codes rather than the chunking of data. The cognitive strategies are not so important in themselves; what matters is their usefulness. What matters is a better interpretation of a given story or a class of stories.

This literary goal is shared by Ian Reid, whose essay "Destabilizing Frames for Story" is a perfect marriage of technical theory and literary insight. Here, finally, we have a detailed explanation of frame theory. Its several meanings are noted, and its relevance to genre issues thoroughly explored through the example of Daudet's "Monsieur Seguin's Goat." The critical history of this story relegates it to the categories of "charming," "little," and "tale," leaving open the question of whether it is a short story at all. Reid walks us through the cognitive perceptions that frame the text, both externally (in relation to the book which contains it, other texts to which it refers) and internally. What emerges is a highly complex set of relationships dependent on the network of frames. What looks like a simple tale is really an "unstable area of textual play," calling for the most alert and sophisticated reading we can manage.

The old question of definition, of what *is* a short story, is subsumed within the larger problem of genre itself. Within the field of literary study, Reid is making us aware of that larger paradigmatic shift I mentioned earlier: in this case, genre is not a term that points unequivocally to some set of features in the text; rather, it is a construction, an inference from the play of features associated with a variety of genres. Reid is correcting for the sort of "underreading" that fails to encode the myriad ways in which text is conditioned by context. To what end? To make us subtler, more responsible readers and much better critics.

It might be easy to say that the ways in which cover blurbs frame books, neighboring texts frame a given story, and so on, are either trivial for the purposes of literary criticism or already taken into account by the normal processes of careful reading. After all, one does not need to be consciously aware of frame theory in order to revise one's view of a literary text, finding it richer than others have thought. Hasn't that process been the making of sundry articles, if not careers, since the dawn of the profession? Yet of course that awareness can be enhanced and systematized. Hasn't that been the burden of what we teach our students? Reid is offering a clarified, orderly, fundamental, and universally applicable way of looking at texts—and particularly those narratives small enough to be always embedded, always enframed, in prominent ways.

All four of the essays in this section ask how we read short stories and how we can understand the reading process better by considering its cognitive structure. All of us have been willing to test our readers' patience with terminology that has no inherent appeal or cherished history for the literary critic. Yet, by contrast with the narratological rigors of a Vladimir Propp or a Gérard Genette, or the diagrammatics of a Gerald Prince, these essays are notably informal. Each has a voice that speaks warmly and directly to people who love short stories and for whom reading is a vocation. We are free to wonder at Brown's fascination with gestalt experiments, at my own lapses from critical decorum, at Mortimer's shared eurekas, or the genial force of Reid's persuasion.

In earlier introductions, I have sketched out the history of short story criticism and commented here and there on the reasons for its rather eccentric development. I have hinted at a certain recalcitrance, a dislike of orthodoxy, that marks our writings, past and present.

Mainly, though, the explanations of the field's development have to do with the status of short stories within the system of genres, with the prevalence of what we've called "practitioner" criticism by short story writers, and with the case-by-case, pedagogical bias of many critics attracted to the genre. Have any of these conditions changed, or could we expect them to do so in the future? To answer that question, we would have to have some idea of what we want short story criticism to be. We would have to have some sense of a developmental destiny.

Mary Rohrberger has likened the short story critic to the pogonophore that rewrites its own sign. What if all we are doing is rewriting Poe? Definition, brevity, status. The circuit of short story criticism. It is adaptable to the times, certainly, as we can see in the essays collected here. It is responsive to shifting paradigms of knowledge. It is maybe even a little in advance, here and there. Maybe a little proud of its primal subject. Fond of its need to be personal. Haunted, in the midst of complexity, by a pure simplicity: story is the human frame for experience. With such a premise, who can say where the story will end?

SUZANNE HUNTER BROWN

Discourse Analysis and the Short Story

> Who can remember, well enough to pronounce upon it critically, all
> of *War and Peace*, or *The Wings of the Dove*, or even *Death in Venice*, the
> small enclosed world of which ought at least to do something to aid
> our memories? I have re-read all three of these books in the past year;
> yet for the life of me I could not pretend to know them as wholes, and
> without that knowledge I lack the materials of criticism.
> —ALLEN TATE

> Lucinda can't read poetry. She's good
> Sort of, at novels, though. The words, you know,
> Don't sort of get in like Lucinda's way.
> —GEORGE KHAIRALLAH

Allen Tate suggested in 1955 that our understanding of literary works
is intimately linked to our representation of them in memory. This
representation is the result of our "packaging" material in short-term
memory (STM) for storage in long-term memory (LTM). STM has a
limited capacity: 7 ± 2 units. Since STM is also the "working" memory—the place where understanding and organizing of material takes
place—our perception of a text is affected by the limited capacity of
STM. Our memory for works is also influenced by the storage capacity of STM, since we store in LTM only material packaged in STM:
Teun A. van Dijk writes, "The representation of stories in episodic
memory will be a function of the structures assigned during comprehension." The verbatim structure of a text—the pattern of phonemes
and morphemes—is generally quickly converted in STM into a series
of propositions, which are in turn combined into macro-propositions
that will be remembered. Macro-propositions are formed according to
macro-rules. Van Dijk claims that macro-rules *reduce* propositions,
eliminating those that are deemed irrelevant, *generalize* sequences of a
superconcept ("dogs" becomes "pets"), and *organize* socially well-

known episodes (various sequences of events like "cutting a cake" combine in "birthday party").[1]

This process must involve interpretation; it is impossible, for example, to discard less important propositions without employing a hierarchy that provides a basis for such ranking. Thus Michael Townsend writes, "During the reading process the reader must engage an appropriate cognitive structure in order to comprehend the material."[2] Our reading of texts usually is—and to some degree, because of processing limitations, must be—reductive. We do not remember a text; we remember the macro-propositions we form as we read. And as Tate knew, criticism, and the meaning a text has for a reader, are more a product of this reductive version than of the text itself. Because of STM limitations, we must encode the text according to some schema, and we do not remember—do not in fact truly apprehend—those elements of a text that are not important to the various macro-propositions of the schema. Moreover, this tendency to encode is a stronger characteristic of "good" readers—that is, experienced readers—than of poorer, or less experienced, ones.[3]

Such encoding operations at the textual level are analogous to the encoding operations at the sentence level that linguists have analyzed in the past twenty years.[4] In the seventies and early eighties, most research on the global processing of stories emphasized narrative schemata—story "grammars" and narrative episodes. Jean Mandler summarizes the results of this line of inquiry: "Mandler and Johnson (1977), following work by Rumelhart (1975) and earlier work by Propp (1968) and Colby (1973), characterized the underlying structure of

1. Teun A. van Dijk, "Story Comprehension: An Introduction," *Poetics*, IX (1980), 18, with the permission of North-Holland Publishing Company, Amsterdam, and "Cognitive Processing of Literary Discourse," *Poetics Today*, I (Autumn, 1979), 147.

2. Michael Townsend, "Schema Activation in Memory for Prose," *Journal of Reading Behavior*, XII (1980), 52, with permission of the National Reading Conference. Various researchers employ different terms for the frameworks readers may construct in order to process texts, among them *scaffolds, macro-structures, global structures, macro-propositions, frames,* and *scripts.*

3. See Patricia R. Martinez, Elizabeth S. Ghatala, and John A. Bell, "Size of Processing Unit During Reading and Retention of Prose by Good and Poor Readers," *Journal of Reading Behavior*, XII (1980), 90, and Douglas B. Eamon, "Selection and Recall of Topical Information in Prose by Better and Poorer Readers," *Reading Research Quarterly*, XIV (1978–79), 247.

4. For a discussion of the relation between sentence-level factors and text-level factors, see Karl Haberlandt, Claire Berian, and Jennifer Sandson, "The Episode Schema in Story Processing," *Journal of Verbal Learning and Verbal Behavior*, XIX (1980), 635.

simple stories as a set of basic nodes in a tree structure, each of which is either causally or temporally connected to other nodes of the tree."[5] But most of these studies employed stories for children or the folktales of an oral tradition—"simple" stories. We might suppose that the global structures adults use to apprehend written texts that they regard as literature might be in some ways different and more complex. Indeed, story researchers were puzzled when they found that different readers applied alternate schematic structures to the same text.[6] Nevertheless, the application of *some* schema is a powerful aid to memory, and we can assume that experienced readers of complex written literature also employ such a structure to comprehend the text.

Readers' uses of schematic structures are related to the primacy effect. Once people have activated a particular framework for meaning, they are more likely to apprehend following material if it is intelligible within the frame. In one demonstration of this effect at the sentence level, subjects were better able to recognize the words *who, brought, some, wet,* and *socks* through distracting noise when these sounds were presented in a "meaningful" order.[7] Moreover, the adoption of a particular meaning for a sequence influences interpretation of any element in it. The same effect holds true for the visual arts. In Robert Leeper's experiment, subjects who first saw Figure B below were likely to see the same young girl in A, whereas subjects first given C perceived an image of the old woman when presented with A.[8]

A   B   C

5. Jean M. Mandler, "A Code in the Node: The Use of a Story Schema in Retrieval," *Discourse Processes,* I (1978), 15.

6. See Lucy Pollard-Gott, Michael McCloskey, and Amy K. Todres, "Subjective Story Structure," *Discourse Processes,* II (1979), 270.

7. For a discussion of this study, see Peter H. Lindsay and Donald A. Norman, *Human Information Processing: An Introduction to Psychology* (New York, 1972), 134.

8. For a discussion of this experiment, see Menakhem Perry, "Literary Dynamics: How the Order of a Text Creates Its Meanings," *Poetics Today,* I (Autumn, 1979), 51.

Menakhem Perry relates this experiment to the perception of literary texts: "The first stage of the text-continuum serves as a sort of heading for those following it. It creates a perceptual set—the reader is predisposed to perceive certain elements and it induces a disposition to continue making connections similar to the ones he has made at the beginning of the text. What was reconstructed from the text as the reading began affects the kind of attention paid to the subsequent items and the weight attached to them." The activation of a frame involves expectations; if these predictions are not fulfilled, a reader can of course shift frames. Townsend calls "schema shifting" a "cognitive process that underlies the comprehension of continuous prose." And Perry claims that a literary text "is based on the tension between forces resulting from the primacy effect and the material at the present point of reading": "When the reader expects the appearance of specific material at a given point in a text, there is, at first, a tendency to assimilate what has actually appeared to what had been expected, to make it conform as much as possible to the expectation. When this proves impossible, and the expectation is not fulfilled, there is a sharp confrontation between the expected and the actual, which may sometimes lead to reexamining the particular place in the text where this expectation arose, and correcting it in retrospect."[9]

Yet as Perry mentions later, there is a problem in supposing that readers can construct new frames for past material in instances where previously chosen schemata become unsatisfying; the reader is likely to have forgotten the words of the text and will remember only the gist he has abstracted from them:

> To what extent should the "backward" action, especially when directed at distant parts of long texts, take into consideration principles of recall? Ordinarily a reader well advanced into the text would draw upon the frames he has constructed rather than on the items that went into their construction. To read is to "label" (Perry, 1967), and it is these "labels" to which we come back. The sequel may—as often happens—create difficulties for old frames, in which case one must go back and re-think the grounds for having constructed them, dealing once more with individual items.[10]

The implication for short stories is clear: in briefer texts, readers depend less on previously created schemata and have easier access to

9. *Ibid.*, 50, with the permission of North-Holland Publishing Company, Amsterdam; Townsend, "Schema Activation," 52; Perry, "Literary Dynamics," 52.

10. Perry, "Literary Dynamics," 54–59. Perry cites the 1963 work of N. H. Anderson

actual verbatim content of the work. No part of a short story will be "distant" from the present point of reading.

The process by which verbatim information is forgotten is complex and is still a subject of debate for researchers. This loss is not a simple function of the limited capacity of STM; some lexical information is retained in memory. Frank Yekovich and Perry Thorndyke report that subjects who processed a short narrative text "were able to distinguish statements that had occurred in the texts from meaning-preserving paraphrases of these statements," both immediately and after a one-hour delay. Yet there is evidence that had the text been longer, subjects would not have had access to so much verbatim content. Verbatim recall is based on "item-specific processing" rather than "relational processing," which refers to the encoding of similarities among a class of events. R. Reed Hunt and Gilles O. Einstein have found "preliminary evidence that relational information decays less rapidly than item-specific information." Verbatim recall is subject to what is called the "list length effect": the longer the list of items in which a target item is presented, the lower the probability that this item will be recalled. Maria F. Dal Martello concludes that "unless some other overriding factor is present, a statement from a short text will be remembered better than a statement from a long text, and that this result holds both for recall and recognition."[11] Martello found, however, that global memory is not subject to the list length effect; recall of main points is not affected by text length.

A 1985 study by Morton Ann Gernsbacher suggests that the very process of frame shifting may cause the loss of exact verbal content, which psycholinguists call "surface structure."[12] Incoming information stimulates memory cells to transmit information through enhance-

---

and S. Hubert, who claim there are separate memory systems for impressions produced by words and for words themselves.

11. Frank R. Yekovich and Perry W. Thorndyke, "An Evaluation of Alternative Functional Models of Narrative Schemata," *Journal of Verbal Learning and Verbal Behavior,* XX (1981), 454; R. Reed Hunt and Gilles O. Einstein, "Relational and Item-Specific Information in Memory," *Journal of Verbal Learning and Verbal Behavior,* XX (1981), 513; Maria F. Dal Martello, "The Effect of Illustrative Details on the Recall of Main Points in Simple Fictional and Factual Passages," *Discourse Processes,* VII (1984), 489.

12. Although I accept the basic distinction between "the pattern of phonemes and morphemes" and the "gist" a reader abstracts from this pattern, it seems misleading to suggest that one aspect of the text is "above" the other. Therefore, I will refer to "verbatim" rather than to "surface" structure except when quoting material from the many researchers who do use this terminology.

ment and suppression: information deemed important to the cognitive frame is enhanced while less relevant information is suppressed. Thus, "after a processing shift occurs, information represented in the previous substructure becomes more difficult to access."[13]

The research of Susan D. Baillet and Janice M. Keenan indicates that even if a reader recognizes that he has activated an inappropriate frame, he may lack access to verbatim content in creating a substitute; even if a researcher "prompts" the retrieval of particular information, subjects are less likely to remember it if it has not been encoded as important within the framework activated during initial reading: "The present results demonstrate that even though the retrieval framework can operate selectively in making certain information more accessible for output, it is ultimately constrained by the accessibility of information as determined by the encoding framework." Furthermore, this effect may hold more for longer texts processed over a greater period of time than shorter ones: "Because information irrelevant to the encoding schema does not get processed as deeply as relevant information, it is less available after a delay" ("delay" in this study was one week; the researchers considered recall after twenty minutes "immediate"). Warren Fass and Gary M. Schumacher confirm this result in their study: "The results indicated that during immediate recall, either an encoding or retrieval perspective influenced recall. However, *when recall was delayed*, only the encoding perspective influenced recall."[14] In short, a reader of *War and Peace* will have a more difficult time creating new relationships among the exact words of the text than will a reader of Ambrose Bierce's "An Occurrence at Owl Creek Bridge," even if both readers are prompted by new, incompatible information to do so.

This distinction between short and long texts is, of course, complicated by the possibility of rereading. For in a written text of any length, a reader has perpetual access to exact wording. Perry assumes that when frames in long works present difficulties readers will pause to reread earlier sections; thus he declares, "This is why research into the problem of how simple texts are remembered after one reading is of little relevance to describing the process of concretizing the literary

13. Morton Ann Gernsbacher, "Surface Information Loss in Comprehension," *Cognitive Psychology*, XVII (1985), 346.

14. Susan D. Baillet and Janice M. Keenan, "The Role of Encoding and Retrieval Processes in the Recall of Text," *Discourse Processes*, IX (1986), 247, 266; Warren Fass and Gary M. Schumacher, "Schema Theory and Prose Retention: Boundary Conditions for Encoding and Retrieval Effects," *Discourse Processes*, IV (1981), 17, emphasis added.

text."[15] But is this always true? If a selected frame produces no radical incompatibilities, how likely are readers to interrupt the narrative flow of a novel in order to reread for verbal detail? It is in general more likely that readers will immediately reread a short story of ten pages than a novel of four hundred, because the necessary investment of time and energy is less. Not only is a reader more likely to recall the verbatim structure of a shorter text so that he can organize it on that basis, but the shorter the text, the more likely he is to regain access to verbal details by rereading.

Moreover, the connections we make on first reading probably affect the relationships we perceive on subsequent readings. Knowledge of how readers rely on schemata, particularly in longer works, shows why the experience of a first reading might partially control the perception of relationship even on rereading. If a chosen global schema disappoints our expectations, the resulting tension may of course force us to choose another. (Whether we will actually reread or whether we will rely on those details we can remember to effect this substitution is another matter.) But if the first macrostructure does allow us to connect the elements of the text in a comprehensible way, we are less likely to perceive other possible relationships, even on rereading. For this reason, the initial experience of reading a text is not irrelevant to the "process of concretizing a literary text."

At any rate, we are left with schemata, not words, when we read. Although a written document seems to offer constant access to verbatim content, active interpretation, as well as retrospective interpretation, relies on memory, since reading is a temporal activity. Exact verbal content is the first aspect of a text to be lost. Moreover, according to Thorndyke and Yekovich, this tendency increases at the most important parts of the text assigned by the interpretive schema: "The available evidence suggests that memory for the surface structure of a proposition is inversely related to the proposition's importance." We should consider this fact when we speculate about a reader's response to a text. Stanley Fish, for example, claims that "it is impossible to mean the same thing in two (or more) different ways, although we tend to think that it happens all the time. We do this by substituting for our immediate linguistic experience an interpretation or abstraction of it, in which 'it' is inevitably compromised."[16] One

15. Perry, "Literary Dynamics," 59.

16. Perry W. Thorndyke and Frank R. Yekovich, "A Critique of Schema-based Theories of Human Story Memory," *Poetics*, IX (1980), 36, with the permission of North-

wonders why Fish, who bases his idea of meaning on reader response, refuses to include in his concept of meaning such a basic fact of reader behavior as the tendency to encode in exactly such a reductive way. Fish implies that we should not compromise "it," but psycholinguists have demonstrated that we must in order to comprehend at all.

One might object that reductive cognitive tendencies do not apply to literary discourse because experienced readers of literature expect to focus special attention on the verbatim content of a text that they regard as literature. According to this argument, increased attention to this aspect of the text would result in better memory of exact wording. Certainly attention to verbatim content is part of the convention experienced readers of literature evoke in approaching a work "as literature." Van Dijk acknowledges that we should "search for some particular aspects in the ways the general procedures are applied or used in the interpretation of literary discourse. This is not, or at least not primarily, due to possible specific structures of literary texts, but rather to the pragmatic and socio-cultural functions of literature in communication interaction." [17]

To approach a work "as literature" is to supply a special context, and this context will affect the way in which the text is understood. Randolph Cirilo and Donald Foss postulate "regular relations between the proposition being processed and its context which can serve as cues to the proposition's role in the structure." Such special literary expectations affect the framework a reader will adopt in comprehending a text. Perry describes the process of adopting such a frame: "Any reading of a text is a process of constructing a system of hypotheses or frames which can create maximal relevancy among the various data of the text—which can motivate their 'co-presence' in the text according to models derived from 'reality,' from literary or cultural conventions, and the like." [18]

Thus we should consider the influence that regarding a work as literature might have on the frame a reader chooses. Since it is conventional for readers of literature to attach importance to the verbatim con-

---

Holland Publishing Company, Amsterdam; Stanley Fish, "Literature in the Reader: Affective Stylistics," *New Literary History*, II (1970), 131.

17. Van Dijk, "Cognitive Processing," 151.

18. Randolph Cirilo and Donald Foss, "Text Structure and Reading Time for Sentences," *Journal of Verbal Learning and Verbal Behavior*, XIX (1980), 106; Perry, "Literary Dynamics," 43.

tent of a work, Fish justly complains that linguists such as Chomsky ignore occasions when a reader's goals may be concerned with this aspect of a text, which linguists oppose to "deep" or semantic struc-ture: "Presumably the 'correct processing,' that is, the uncovering of the deep structure and the extraction of deep meaning, is the only goal, and whatever stands in the way of that uncovering is to be tolerated, but assigned no final value." In short, linguists assume that all readers are like Lucinda, that "words get in their way." Using Chomsky's examples "John is eager to please" and "John is easy to please," B. G. Campbell notes that the "surface structure" of the two sentences is similar, whereas the "deep structure" is not. In nonliter-ary reading we would indeed be likely to ignore the sound similarity. Yet if the sentences occurred in a poem, experienced readers of litera-ture would be likely to consider the sound repetition in their analysis. Indeed, most poets would expect readers to do so. Campbell himself acknowledges at the conclusion of his description of the process of "normal"—that is, nonliterary—reading: "Yet there do seem to be certain poetic or aesthetic conventions that transcend what is usually thought of as 'normal' syntactic transformations. It is obvious that we do respond to poetic meaning over and above those aspects of mean-ing encompassed by the model."[19]

Regarding a work "as literature" can affect a reader's "cognitive set," inclining him to focus his attention on a text's verbatim content. Van Dijk notes that concentrating attention differently can increase readers' memory for verbatim content, though he is more concerned with "tasks" than with "conventions": "One of the factors of the cog-nitive set, for instance, is the specific task or problem the reader has when reading a text. Thus, a reader may, in general, have the task of detecting a certain theme. But he may also be required to focus at-tention on certain words, grammatical constructions or spelling, as is the case for a student of grammar or style, a proof-reader. . . . This kind of task will be called *non-normal*, because it does not focus on the global semantic and pragmatic themes (macro-structures) of the discourse."[20]

Despite the above argument, van Dijk suggests why cognitive facts must hold to some degree for literary texts as well as for others; he contends that work on discourse processing is relevant to literary in-

19. Fish, "Literature in the Reader," 144; B. G. Campbell, "Aspects of Meaning," *Journal of Reading*, XXIV (1980), 51–53.
20. Van Dijk, "Cognitive Processing," 153.

terpretation because "our cognitive mechanisms will simply not allow us to understand discourse or information in a fundamentally different way," so "we strictly deny the completely 'specific' nature of so-called 'literary interpretation' as it is normatively postulated in traditional literary scholarship." Patricia Gildea and Sam Glucksberg's study of readers' processing of metaphors also suggests that perception which we regard as literary shares important properties with nonliterary perception: "The apparent ease with which people seem to use contextual information to disambiguate metaphors suggests that nonliteral comprehension mechanisms share important functional properties with literal comprehension mechanisms."[21]

Van Dijk suggests that the very complexity of literary texts might increase the need for readers to rely on the creation of macro-propositions at the expense of attention to exact verbal content: "The complexity of (literary) narrative, however, requires that semantic processing also take place at the global level: the formation of macro-structures is necessary, otherwise we do not know what the story is about. In principle the same macro-rules operate as for other kinds of discourse."[22] Forming macro-propositions from the words of a text and relinquishing verbatim content accommodates the limitations of STM. Focusing on verbatim detail—which van Dijk calls "local" as opposed to "global" processing—does not. Consequently, while directing attention to exact words can increase our memory for them, our ability to recall a text verbatim can only be stretched so far by this adjustment in the cognitive set.

Processing literary discourse, then, involves a fundamental tension between the psychological necessity to repackage words according to some schema and the convention of artistic discourse that disposes experienced readers to remember "surface" features of a text when they regard it as literature. Van Dijk points out this conflict: "The paradox of this fact is that our memory for literary discourse will first of all affect those properties which are usually considered to be of primary importance in literary communication: we will tend to recall of a novel its global plot, and not (each of) the stylistic surface structure manifestations of the story at the local level. At most we have a *global* memory for the major stylistic properties, or incidental memory for *salient detail*."[23]

21. *Ibid.*, 151; Patricia Gildea and Sam Glucksberg, "On Understanding Metaphor: The Role of Context," *Journal of Verbal Learning and Verbal Behavior*, XXII (1983), 588.
22. Van Dijk, "Cognitive Processing," 156.
23. *Ibid.*, 157.

Significantly, van Dijk's example of a text that we process globally (according to plot) and not locally (according to verbatim content) is a novel. The length of a work obviously affects the tension he describes: the shorter a literary text, the better able an experienced reader of literature will be to fulfill the literary convention of focusing on the verbatim content of the text. A reader of a long work such as a novel must overcome memory limitations in order to retain some verbatim content and even then must rely on reductive global structures to an extent. For this reason, van Dijk believes novels are processed in a more "normal," less "literary" way than are poems: "That is, many kinds of literature, e.g., novels, will not exhibit structures which would require different semantic processes of comprehension. Whereas certain literary texts, e.g., certain forms of modern poetry, which do not seem to have such structures, may share such structures with all kinds of non-literary texts, such as advertisements and everyday conversation."[24] Short stories are thus a curious hybrid. Like novels, they exhibit narrative features that would allow a reader to process them globally. But like lyric poems, they are brief and enable *local* processing, close attention to verbatim text structure, and need not rely on overarching narrative schemata to be retained.

This distinction between local processing in short texts and global processing in long texts should be qualified. It would be absurd to suggest that readers are unaffected by the "surface" aspect of novels and other longer texts. Van Dijk suggests that literary texts can overcome limited memory for "surface" detail if reader attention is focused on salient detail. We can, for example, gear our perception to a single "surface-level" repetition; a New Critic, ignoring the plot and counting the occurrences of *common* in George Eliot's *Middlemarch*, will of course organize the text in terms of the selected feature. Although normally we remember macro-propositions rather than structural details, van Dijk acknowledges that if "such a 'structural detail' is linked with much information in our cognitive set, e.g., a certain task, interest, attitude, value, etc., this detail may nevertheless become 'salient,' and be easily retrieved."[25] We have seen that regarding a novel as literature inclines readers to focus attention in this way, expanding memory resources to some degree.

Although a long text may help readers expand verbatim recall by rehearsing a verbal pattern, in a lengthy work such foregrounding

24. *Ibid.*, 151.
25. *Ibid.*, 150.

of selected structural detail must be intense and, to some degree, rather uneconomical to distract the reader's attention from the macro-propositions of the plot. Noting the problem of the "reader's forget-fulness," Susan Rubin Suleiman predicts that "the longer the text the more it will need to multiply its redundancies," adding that "the de-gree and the type of redundance in a given text are a manifestation of its genre."[26] Even if the number of repetitions necessary to make "sur-face design" a major organizational principle in a long novel does not overwhelm the reader, studies measuring recall of word lists indicate that such rehearsal of a verbal pattern in a text may have limited power to enhance a reader's memory for the repeated item.[27]

Novels that fragment narrative structure *may* incline readers to rely less on schemata; Thorndyke has found that readers are more likely to retain works verbatim if familiar plot structures are absent: "When the passages contained identifiable plot structure, much of the de-tailed surface information was forgotten. However, when the pas-sages are less structured, more surface information from the passages is retained." (Thorndyke, of course, demonstrated this effect only for short texts. And it is possible that disrupting narrative continuity in novels may sometimes actually focus reader attention on re-creating such a global schema, for example, in certain works by Faulkner.) Gernsbacher confirms this result and extends it to stories. He reports that memory for verbatim detail is significantly worse "when the in-put sentences formed a cohesive story than when the sentences were semantically unrelated. . . . more synonym substitutions occurred when recalling sentences originally processed as a thematic story than when the sentences seemed completely independent." Verbatim in-formation may be more available in seemingly incoherent texts be-cause "surface information is no longer more rapidly changing than thematic information; therefore, it would be less likely to be sup-pressed or more likely to be enhanced."[28] Moreover, even when the

26. Susan Rubin Suleiman, "Redundancy and the 'Readable' Text," *Poetics Today*, I (Spring, 1980), 122.

27. See Tore Helstrup, "Presence and Absence of Serial Position Effects in Short-term Memory," *Scandinavian Journal of Psychology*, XIX (1978), 301–307; Karl Haberlandt and Geoffrey Bingham, "Verbs Contribute to the Coherence of Brief Narratives: Read-ing Related and Unrelated Sentence Triples," *Journal of Verbal Learning and Verbal Behav-ior*, XVII (1978), 419–25; and John B. Black and Hyman Bern, "Causal Coherence and Memory for Events in Narratives," *Journal of Verbal Learning and Verbal Behavior*, XX (1981), 267–75.

28. Perry W. Thorndyke, "Cognitive Structures in Comprehension and Memory of

text is coherent, this same effect may hold if the coherence is "difficult" to perceive. Most literary texts, and most obviously many modernist works, would exhibit for many readers a "difficult" coherence.

Thus, despite the possibilities for some increased attention to the verbal patterns in longer texts, the basic psychological limits remain important factors. Wolfgang Iser writes that "what has been read shrinks in the text to a foreshortened background"; though an item can through repetition be "evoked" in a new context, it cannot return in full, "for then memory and perception would become indistinguishable." According to Iser, "That which is remembered becomes open to new connections," and *only* what is remembered. Van Dijk agrees that perception of literary texts is subject to memory limitations:

> Here the tendency will be that our memory and processing resources are able only in a very restricted way to store and retrieve these kinds of surface structural information, even if the communicative conventions require specific attention on such structures. Thus, no normal reader of literature will be able, after reading a literary text of some length, to reproduce it verbatim. He will not even be able to recognize most of the sentences used in the text, even if locally he paid particular attention to them. Only occasionally, viz., as a so-called salient structural detail, the choice of certain words and a syntactic structure may be recognized or even recalled.

Allen Tate, speculating about the influence of memory on the criticism of a literary work, notes that imaginative works differ from philosophical works, "which our minds apprehend and retain almost as wholes through the logical and deductive structures which powerfully aid the memory."[29] He did not, of course, suggest that narrative schemata, plots, might to some degree aid our memories in the case of literary works.

Although van Dijk presents a convincing case for considering the significance of length, he reverts to the distinction between poetry and prose when discussing genre:

> Typical for many kinds of poetry, then, is that the kind of predominantly local processing allows a lower organization degree at the global level. Al-

Narrative Discourse," *Cognitive Psychology*, IX (1977), 97, with the permission of Harper and Row Publishers, Inc.; Gernsbacher, "Surface Information Loss," 343, 352.

29. Wolfgang Iser, *The Act of Reading: A Theory of Aesthetic Response* (Baltimore, 1978), 111; van Dijk, "Cognitive Processing," 153; Allen Tate, *The Man of Letters in the Modern World* (New York, 1955), 79.

though we may perhaps assign one fragment of a global theme (a "theme concept," such as "life," "death," "love," "misery," etc.), it is not always possible to normally summarize a poem in the same way as we can summarize the global meaning of a novel by its "plot." This means that a poem may well have no macro-structure, because its processing is (i) short term, (ii) surface structural and finally (iii) predominantly locally semantic. . . . The cognitive interpretation of narrative prose has quite different properties. With the exception of certain kinds of modern prose, the interpretation of sentences and sentence connections will seldom be partial: at the local level we mostly know what the story is about.

Van Dijk lays the groundwork for supposing that the brevity of the short story would allow the sort of local processing he associates with poetry, but he does not mention the form. Work on memory and discourse processing has explained why words are more likely to get in Lucinda's way when she reads a poem than when she reads a novel; the only danger is in allowing *novel* to become shorthand for "all literary prose." It has also explained the phenomenon noted by Elder Olson, namely, that "appropriate" size may differ according to individual genres, "the parts and wholes of which impose different burdens upon the memory." [30]

We can now see why a lyric poem may be too long to be properly structured in memory, though it may be the same length as a tragedy which can be easily recalled. Van Dijk's work suggests that the tragedy can be packaged according to its global structure, or plot, in a way that the poem cannot be:

This explanation of the possibility of processing specific kinds of information from texts also explains why most poems are relatively short, a question we seldom ask when we talk about poetry. As soon as we need extra memory resources for the processing and storage of (surface) structural information, memory for those particular words, phrases, sentences—and the various phonological, graphemical, syntactic operations based on them—is possible only when the amount of information is rather low. And, for the same reason, literary conventions require that poems are read more attentively, more repeatedly (learned by heart), than, for instance, novels. In longer poems or in novels we will, in general, expect or require additional forms of organization, e.g., a narrative schema and, of course, themes and topics at a more global level. [31]

30. Van Dijk, "Cognitive Processing," 154, 156; Elder Olson, "An Outline of Poetic Theory," in R. S. Crane (ed.), *Critics and Criticism* (Chicago, 1952), 559.

31. Van Dijk, "Cognitive Processing," 154.

The short story, like the poem, can make greater demands on our re-call for exact verbal content because it is brief, even though it may have a plot like the tragedy.

The primacy effect also helps explain why brief works in general are likely to be read more slowly and with greater regard for verbal texture than longer ones. The beginning of any text must be read slowly and processed locally because the reader has not yet deter-mined an appropriate frame to use in "reducing" the words to sche-matic chunks. Perry writes: "At the beginning of a text there are no dictates from earlier stages in the text; there are as yet no expectations other than cultural ones as to what is to be expected of texts in general or of a particular kind of text. This is why the most intensive closing of options occurs at the early stages. The reading tempo of actual read-ers is far slower at the beginning of novels than at the middle or end." Studies show that reading times for later sections are faster because attention lapses. When subjects process word lists, they exhibit what Perry calls "passive attention decrement": "The subjects pay more at-tention to words at the beginning of the list while they are first at-tempting to form some impression, but once a first impression has been formed, they pay less attention to the rest of the list. According to this explanation there is no interaction between the meaning of ini-tial words and those occurring at the end of the list." [32]

Thus disoriented processing at the beginning of texts, when read-ers have not yet activated a frame, resembles of necessity the non-schematic approach van Dijk believes readers bring to poetry:

> Apparently, some literary texts do not have a semantic structure, or only a very fragmentary kind of macro-structure. In certain kinds of poetry this "lack" of global coherence may be counterbalanced by specific semantic processing at the local level. It may be the case, for instance, that (i) surface structure cannot easily or unambiguously be translated into propositions and (ii) that these propositions from the respective (semi-) sentences can-not easily be connected by explicit conditional relations (involving e.g., identical referents), or by propositional information drawn from memory. This is possible only when the reader has enough time, resources and at-tention to "decode" the sentences and local sentence connections anyway, e.g., by neglecting the construction of the global theme of the text. [33]

One can see why it is that the opening sentences of so many novels are famous and memorable. We are inclined to devote special atten-

32. Perry, "Literary Dynamics," 53, 56.
33. Van Dijk, "Cognitive Processing," 154.

tion to them, and careful authors design them to reward this close scrutiny by readers. The foregoing observations suggest that because short stories are brief, their readers spend a much higher percentage of reading time in this disoriented, word-by-word type of processing than do readers of longer works such as novels.

If brevity promotes slow reading and attention to individual words, we would expect short story writers to recognize and exploit this tendency. Their comments suggest that they do. Writers of short stories often mention verbal demands on their readers' attention. Mark Helprin, a contemporary short story writer, connected this attention with slow reading in an interview with Anatole Broyard. He said of the English language: "I don't like the speed, the effect of speed, with which it is sometimes written. I want to slow it down, to make it more considered. . . . In the kind of writing I like, it is not possible to get something for nothing. The reader must work. Vision and redemption do not come quickly, but, after a time, overwhelmingly."[34] John Cheever agrees: "With a short story, you have to be in there on every word; every verb has to be lambent and strong. It's a fairly exhausting task, I think."[35] In 1902, Henry Seidel Canby wrote of the short story that "for a satisfying exposition of the full power of words, it is much superior to the novel, and can rank only below the poem. But the novel and the Short Story are distinct instruments, differently designed, for diverse needs. And with such a point of view it is impossible not to grant to the latter a separate use and classification." Close verbal connections, "local processing," are made possible by brevity; thus short stories with intricate, tight verbal structures are likely to please us because they reward the tendency to process brief works in this way. Thus we can explain the verbal density often attributed to short stories and also the fact observed by Randall Jarrell about extremely short narratives: "When we try to make, out of these stories life gives us, works of art of comparable concision, we almost always put them into verse."[36]

34. Mark Helprin, as interviewed by Anatole Broyard, "Mysterious Short Story," *New York Times Book Review*, March 1, 1981, p. 35, copyright © 1981 by The New York Times Company, reprinted by permission.

35. Remarks by John Cheever made during the panel discussion "Is the Short Story Necessary" held October 18, 1966, in May (ed.), *Short Story Theories*, 102. Reprinted from *The Writer's World*, p. 260. Elizabeth Janeway, ed. Published by McGraw-Hill Book Company. Copyright © 1969 by The Authors Guild, Inc.; reprinted by permission.

36. Henry Seidel Canby, *The Short Story* (New York, 1902), 30; Randall Jarrell, "Stories," in May (ed.), *Short Story Theories*, 37.

Attention to local or global processing, "slow" or "fast," or "under" or "over" reading, is in turn related to a central tension in the way we may organize and perceive any given work. Various critics and theorists have employed numerous pairs of terms to designate this basic distinction. Linguistics provides us with quite technical terms. Robert Scholes offers his own version of Ferdinand de Saussure's point: "Any particular phenomenon in language (and in many other studies) can be examined in either of two ways. It may be seen as part of a total system simultaneous with itself, or as part of a historical sequence of related phenomena." [37] Saussure called these two approaches "synchronic" and "diachronic" respectively.

Roman Jakobson extended Saussure's distinction in a way important to structuralism in literature; he postulated that literary, in addition to grammatical, units connect according to the same distinction and that different literary styles may be classified by their preference for metaphor or metonymy. Relationships of similarity and difference are of course most easily perceived, in Scholes' terms, as "a total system simultaneous with itself," whereas cause-and-effect relationships are perceived when a system is organized as "a historical sequence of related phenomena." Tzvetan Todorov cites temporality as the basis for "horizontal," metonymic order: "We know that poetry is based essentially on symmetry, on repetition (in a spatial order), where fiction is constructed on relations of causality (in a logical order) and of succession (a temporal order)." Jakobson's theory resembles Boris Tomashevksy's outline of two ways of arranging thematic elements, "that in which causal-temporal relationships exist between the thematic elements, and that in which the thematic elements are contemporaneous or in which there is some shift of theme without internal exposition of the causal connections." Other theorists refer to "paradigmatic" and "syntagmatic" structures. For my own purposes, I prefer the informal terms *configuration* and *succession* that Paul Ricoeur suggests:

> Every narrative combines two dimensions in various proportions, one chronological and the other nonchronological. The first may be called the episodic dimension, which characterizes the story as made out of events. The second is the configurational dimension, according to which the plot construes significant wholes out of scattered events. Here I am borrowing from Louis O. Mink the notion of a configurational act, which he interprets as a "grasping together." I understand this act to be the act of the

---

37. Robert Scholes, *Structuralism in Literature* (New Haven, 1974), 17.

plot, as eliciting a pattern from a succession. . . . Anti-narrativist historians and structuralists thus share a common prejudice: they do not see that the humblest narrative is always more than a chronological series of events and that in turn the configurational dimension cannot overcome the episodic dimension without suppressing the *narrative structure* itself. . . . The temporal dialectic, then, is implied in the basic operation of eliciting a configuration from a succession.[38]

Although many of these theorists attribute successive structure to fiction and characterize poems as configurations, I suggest that brevity inclines readers to organize works as configurations rather than as successive structures. This proposition is in accord with the common insistence of short story writers that their genre "works" more like poetry than like the novel.

The two modes of organization I have just described have also given rise to a more controversial set of terms. *Temporal* is often equated with *succession* and is then opposed to *spatial* (Todorov in fact associated repetition and spatial order in the above quotation). The question of spatial form has vexed literary criticism since Joseph Frank's 1945 essay on the subject ("Spatial Form in Modern Literature"). Theorists object that *spatial* is a misleading metaphor; literature is a temporal art, so the objection runs, and to suggest that it can resemble visual art is inaccurate. W. J. T. Mitchell writes, "An almost universal objection is that spatial form is a 'mere metaphor' which has been given misplaced concreteness and that it denies the essentially temporal nature of literature."[39] Mitchell, however, contends that spatial perception is no less metaphorical in the visual arts than in literature. A more detailed investigation of the ways in which we "decode" texts and paintings is useful in understanding the perceptual facts that may cause a perceiver to emphasize either the successive or the configurational aspect of a system.

It is customary to distinguish literature, a temporal art, from painting and sculpture, spatial arts, by maintaining that we spend time decoding the former but that our perception of the latter is "timeless." Iser, for example, writes: "In our attempts to describe the intersubjec-

---

38. *Ibid.;* Tzvetan Todorov, *The Poetics of Prose,* trans. Richard Howard (Ithaca, 1977), 136; Boris Tomashevsky, "Thematics," in Lee T. Lemon and Marion J. Reis (eds. and trans.), *Russian Formalist Criticism: Four Essays* (Lincoln, Nebr., 1965), 66; Paul Ricoeur, "Narrative Time," *Critical Inquiry,* VII (1980), 178.

39. W. J. T. Mitchell, "Spatial Form in Literature: Toward a General Theory," *Critical Inquiry,* VI (1980), 541.

tive structure of the process through which a text is transferred and translated, our first problem is the fact that the whole text can never be perceived at any one time. In this respect it differs from given objects, which can generally be viewed or at least conceived as a whole." Gotthold Lessing, however, described the apprehension of visual art as a distinctly temporal process: "How do we attain to a distinct conception of an object in space? *First*, we look at its parts singly; *then* at their combination; and, *lastly*, at the whole." For that matter, as Mitchell points out, a text is a spatial form: "The physical text is an 'order of coexistent data,' and the reading process is a conventional procedure for transforming this spatial form into a temporal one." He claims: "If we examine our experience of such unquestionably literal spatial forms as paintings, statues, buildings, and landscape gardens, we readily acknowledge that it takes time to experience and 'decode' them, that we never apprehend space apart from time and movement. . . . The argument, then, that literature differs from the plastic arts by its 'reading time' and by its presentation of narrative or fictive time crumbles on any close inspection." Northrop Frye supports him in this view:

> Some principle of recurrence seems to be fundamental to all works of art, and this recurrence is usually spoken of as rhythm when it moves along in time, and as pattern when it is spread out in space. Thus we speak of the rhythm of music and the pattern of painting. But a slight increase of sophistication will soon start us talking about the pattern of music and the rhythm of painting. The inference is that all arts possess both a temporal and a spatial aspect, whichever takes the lead when they are presented. The score of a symphony may be studied all at once, as a spread-out pattern: a painting may be studied as the track of an intricate dance of the eye.[40]

Comparison and contrast can be based on three different aspects of an artwork's mode of existence in space and time. The first is narrative, the possibility of the work's relation to a sequence of fictional events. Although most obviously an attribute of written stories, paintings, too, often involve some relation to an imaginary event chain. Paintings of familiar subjects may evoke to some degree the well-known stories in which such figures take part. A given observer may utilize

40. Iser, *The Act of Reading*, 108; Gotthold Lessing, *Laokoön*, trans. E. C. Beasley, in Edward Bell (ed.), *Selected Prose Works of G. E. Lessing* (London, 1879), 98, emphasis mine; Mitchell, "Spatial Form," 544; Northrop Frye, *Anatomy of Criticism* (1957; rpr. Princeton, 1973), 77.

such knowledge in understanding the artwork. Some paintings even divide the canvas in such a way as to portray more than one moment in a fictional story. And, as Lessing pointed out, some seemingly static frames may actually contain by implication the preceding or following moment in the fall of a drapery.[41]

The second aspect is order of "telling." Meir Sternberg insists that only in literature does order of presentation interact with an inferred sequence of fictional events:

> The temporal potentialities of literary art as a whole have particularly complex and potent manifestations in texts with a narrative backbone. For here the textual dynamics deriving from the sequential nature of the verbal medium as a continuum of signs necessarily combines and interacts (as it does not do in music or descriptive poetry) with the dynamics of at least two other sequences or processes, informed by a largely extraverbal logic that relates to the semantic referents of those signs: the two-fold development of the action, as it objectively and straightforwardly progresses in the fictive world from beginning to end (within the fabula) and as it is deformed and patterned into progressing in our mind during the reading-process (within the sujet).[42]

But we have seen that painting may involve narrative, and program music such as *Pictures at an Exhibition* or *Peter and the Wolf* does as well. And various cultures "read" pictures from left to right or top to bottom; most designs contain lines and emphases that draw the eye in a sequential order.

A third consideration, the order a perceiver is likely to employ in organizing a work in memory, is the one central to our discussion of configuration and succession. This organizational pattern need not directly reflect either a sequence of events inferred from a work (*fabula*) or the order in which we encounter those events in perceiving the work (*sujet*). "Narrative" painting may be organized by the perceiver as a spatial construct; even though an artwork—such as a painting—may evoke a narrative element (Saint Paul's conversion), we may perceive as more significant its static design, the echo of one line, one curve, in another. Nelson Goodman, for example, writes of Memling's *Life of Christ*, which depicts many incidents in a single landscape, "This pictorial organization of events of a lifetime is spatial, atemporal, motivated perhaps both by considerations of design and by regard-

41. Lessing, *Laokoön*, 104.
42. Meir Sternberg, *Expositional Modes and Temporal Ordering in Fiction* (Baltimore, 1978), 34.

ing these events as eternal and emblematic rather than as episodic or transient." He discusses the scenes as creating "only different spatial patterns." The same tendency may hold in other cultures. Goodman writes of a "picture biography" of the Japanese Buddhist prince Shotoku Taishi, painted by Hata no Chitei in 1069, "If there is some factor at work here other than an unworldly and atemporal or even antitemporal outlook along with a concern for all aspects of design, I have yet to discover it." [43] We may well ask ourselves why Goodman opts for a spatial, configurational interpretation of this painting.

The remembered organization of a work need not reflect the order of presentation—Goodman is not foregrounding scenes in *Life of Christ* either as we may infer events "happened" to Christ or as they occur from left to right in the painting. Immersed in the critical tradition distinguishing *fabula* and *sujet*, we have focused on the relationship between order of "telling" and inferred or imagined order of "occurrence" (for, of course, fictional events never actually occur), neglecting the order which is likely to predominate in a reader's memory, an order which need not coincide with either *fabula* or *sujet*. Goodman suggests that order of telling in itself does not control the reader's tendency to supply other sorts of connections than those of sequence:

> Some stories when reordered in certain ways are no longer stories but studies. . . . Aldous Huxley's brilliant short piece on the abominable British painter Benjamin Robert Haydon contains enough reports of events in Haydon's life from childhood to death to constitute a brief biography; but the arrangement of these reports is strikingly at variance with chronology. . . . Now displacements in order of telling, as we have seen, are not in general incompatible with narrative; but here, rather than heightening the story, they work against it, being guided by how the reported incidents document and illuminate various aspects of Haydon's character. . . . The result is no biography but a character study, no story but an essay on self-deception and other matters. The order of telling so groups incidents reported as to bring out kinships and contrasts that cut across and obliterate—or at least blur—the story line. Narrative gives way to exposition. [44]

Perry notes that the famous division of *fabula* and *sujet* has resulted in an assumption of narrative order as a norm from which the telling may deviate. The possibilities of other norms are obscured by a confu-

43. Nelson Goodman, "Twisted Tales; or, Story, Study, and Symphony," *Critical Inquiry,* VII (1980), 110, 114, and rpr. in Goodman, *Of Mind and Other Matters* (1984).
    44. *Ibid.*, 115–19.

sion between the order of telling and the order likely to establish itself in the reader's memory:

> Examples of "distorting the order of the *fabula*," signalled by researchers, are usually cases where the text does conform to a "natural" chronological sequence, only this does not happen to be the one signalled by the researcher.
>
> Moreover, the distinction between *fabula* and *syuzhet* confers upon temporal order an exclusive role in the organization of narrative sequence. But there is no reason to separate temporal types of order from other frames relevant to the text, which also possess orders that the text may maintain or distort. Non-temporal ordering principles which are reconstructed, and against which the textual sequence is matched, are no less significant for the description of a literary text and even for the description of narrative prose.[45]

Boris Eikhenbaum's discussion of two stories may serve to illustrate the difference between order of presentation and order emphasized in memory. Eikhenbaum compares Tolstoy's "Three Deaths" to O. Henry's "Roads of Destiny." In the former, the essential parallelism of three events is superimposed by the reader upon a seemingly straightforward narrative. In the latter, however, the configurational structure is divorced from succession in the actual presentation: the poet David Mignot takes three separate forks in a road, is part of a different story on each, but each time dies by the pistol of the Marquis de Beaupertuys: "The plot is presented straight off in its three possible versions—in the form of pure parallels, without their being brought together, as is usually done, into a single whole with the aid of one or another motivational device. For comparison, one can take, for instance, Tolstoy's 'Three Deaths,' where the parallelism (the lady, the peasant, the tree) is presented in a specially motivated consecutive order of events (the halt on the road, the driver and the boots of the dying peasant, the promise to erect a cross, etc.)." Eikhenbaum also writes of O. Henry's story, "We have three tales joined together, but the joining is done not on the principle of the consecutive order of the hero's adventures (as it would be in the adventure novel) but on the principle of comparison and contrast."[46] In Tolstoy's story, the textual order of presentation is sequential; in O. Henry's tale, it is not.

---

45. Perry, "Literary Dynamics," 40.

46. B. M. Eikhenbaum, *O. Henry and the Theory of the Short Story*, trans. I. R. Titunik (Ann Arbor, 1968), 11–12.

Yet Eikhenbaum refers to the underlying parallelism of both—he perceives and organizes the two works in the same way, though in the case of Tolstoy's story he must depart from sequential textual presentation to do so.

Even the most straightforward chronological narrative may be restructured in a reader's mind in ways that subordinate chronology in interpretation. Goodman writes:

> The classification that supersedes or subordinates chronology is not always in terms of topical features. Sometimes, rather, it is in terms of expressive or other aesthetically relevant qualities. . . . In such cases, a story becomes more a symphony than a study.
>
> In all these examples, of course, what nullifies narrative is not the order of telling itself but the resultant alignment with certain categories that are—or are to be made—highly relevant in the context and for the purpose at hand. World structure is heavily dependent on order of elements and on comparative weight of kinds.

In any case, interpretive order is a matter of the reader's foregrounding some relationships among elements and subordinating others. Goodman declares: "In other cases, narrative status rather than being nullified is merely subdued. And where order of occurrence itself happens to yield a sorting into prominent categories, we may have what is both a story and a study or symphony. These types of discourse, though distinct, are not mutually exclusive."[47]

It is obviously the reader who may or may not "subdue" narrative. What causes a reader to favor one pattern or the other? Perry's description of the interaction between reader and text is perceiver oriented, yet he implies that text structures are the primary factors in a reader's experience of a work: "Here the text is grasped as a message which is supposed to be experienced. The sequence is justified through its effect on the reader; its function is to control the reading process and to channel it in directions 'desirable' for the text, so as to induce the reader to opt for the realization of certain potentialities (e.g., impressions, attitudes) of the material rather than others." The notion that certain texts "impose" spatial or temporal form on the reader has resulted in some confusing distinctions. Mitchell points out the many guises assumed by this opposition; it has been described "as a generic opposition (the novel is linear in contrast to the spatiality of poetry or drama); as a historical 'progression' (nineteenth-century literature is

47. Goodman, "Twisted Tales," 119.

linear and temporal in contrast to modern or eighteenth-century literature which is spatial); as an intrageneric distinction (novels of plot and story are linear while lyric novels are spatial)." He notes that a logical last step is to declare that literature shows aesthetic (that is, spatial) form and nonliterary discourse is characterized by "straightforward linear procedures."[48]

It is clearly more useful to adopt Goodman's suggestion and view sequential or configurational organization as a tension in every work. Thus the psychological tendencies and limitations of readers are also important factors in interpretive choices. Thorndyke and Yekovich's insistence on the question's two sides is therefore useful: "If readers are able to use any of several organizational schemata for a text, then what characteristics of a text *or of the reader* trigger the adoption of a particular organizational form?" The degree of choice that readers exercise in ordering textual structures as configurations or successive plots surprised psychologists who found that the same text was grouped in different ways by individual readers. Lucy Pollard-Gott, Michael McCloskey, and Amy Todres discovered that story episodes from the same text were sometimes combined by similarity of function and at other times by temporal relationships showing cause and effect.[49] Thus influences such as generic size which might incline readers to favor one form of organization over another in a given situation should be considered.

Lessing explored the perceptual facts which may underlie spatial, configurational patterning. Frank bases his aesthetic approach and his concept of spatial form on the ideas of *Laokoön;* he writes, "For Lessing, as we have seen, aesthetic form is not an external arrangement provided by a set of traditional rules. Rather, it is the relation between the sensuous nature of the art medium and the conditions of human perception." Although no act of perception is in fact timeless, Lessing pointed out that we may well have this *illusion.* The illusion of instantaneous apprehension is central to configurational patterning, and Lessing believed that the effect of simultaneity was possible only when a perceiver could process all the parts of an artwork quickly in order to unite them into a whole: "The different operations are performed by our senses with such astonishing rapidity that they appear

48. Perry, "Literary Dynamics," 40; Mitchell, "Spatial Form," 560.

49. Thorndyke and Yekovich, "A Critique of Schema-based Theories," 45, emphasis mine; Pollard-Gott, McCloskey, and Todres, "Subjective Story Structure," 270.

to us to be but one." Mitchell maintains that the same illusion may occur in reading: "The reading experience may produce in us the sense that no real time is passing, that we are in an eternally timeless realm where everything occurs simultaneously. Or it may produce the illusion of temporal sequence, with distinct stages like beginning, middle, and end." [50]

If Lessing is correct in linking rapidity of perception with what Mitchell calls the illusion of "an eternally timeless realm where everything occurs simultaneously," it follows that this effect can be more easily achieved in brief texts. The distinction Lessing makes between painting and poetry is one of degree; the parts of a visual design are apprehended separately, then united into a whole, but this process is faster for a visual object than for a poem we must read. We can extend Lessing's point: although we cannot "take in" the whole of a brief text as a verbal construct nearly as rapidly as we can a visual object, we can certainly apprehend and organize it far more quickly than we can the parts of a long one. The three seconds in which we may decode a Titian canvas may make the painting a very different experience from the lyric poem it takes us three minutes to read, but so may the twenty minutes we spend perusing a short story mark its effects off from those of a novel read in numerous sessions over the course of a week.

As important as initial processing time (we may study a Titian canvas for hours) is our ability to review rapidly the individual units of an artwork. Lessing praised this advantage of visual art: "To the eye the parts once seen are continually present; it can run over them time after time." He believed that in verbal art the role of the eye is assumed by memory; the poet must rely on "the ear," which "entirely loses those parts it has heard, if they are not retained in the memory. And even if they are thus retained, what trouble and effort it costs us to renew their whole impression in the same order, and with the same liveliness; to pass them at one time under review with but moderate rapidity, in order to attain any possible idea of the whole." [51] Aristotle and Olson also related memory in verbal art to vision in spatial art and considered the limitations of memory relevant to the proper size of an artwork. All these theorists insist that forgetfulness most

50. Joseph Frank, *The Widening Gyre: Crisis and Mastery in Modern Literature* (New Brunswick, N.J., 1963), 8; Lessing, *Laokoön*, 98; Mitchell, "Spatial Form," 544.

51. Lessing, *Laokoön*, 98–99.

affects our ability to perceive a work as a whole—in other words, to organize it as a configuration.

The analogy between memory and the eye, which is based on the "simultaneous" apprehension of a configuration by the two, also underlies Frye's distinction between the *mythos* and *dianoia* of a work. Frye harks back to Aristotle for his terms, but the similarity to Ricoeur's *succession* and *configuration* is obvious:

> Works of literature also move in time like music and spread out in images like painting. The word narrative or *mythos* conveys the sense of movement caught by the ear, and the word meaning or *dianoia* conveys, or at least preserves, the sense of simultaneity caught by the eye. We *listen* to the poem as it moves from beginning to end, but as soon as the whole of it is in our minds at once we "see" what it means. More exactly, this response is not simply to *the* whole *of* it, but to *a* whole *in* it: we have a vision of meaning or *dianoia* whenever any simultaneous apprehension is possible.

Mitchell notes that *dianoia*, as Frye has defined it, is similar to what other critics have called spatial apprehension: "This familiar pattern in literary criticism—the claim that we do, at least for a moment, 'see the meaning' of a work, coupled with our inability to state it in a verbal paraphrase—seems to me a phenomenon that rises out of a spatial apprehension of the work as a system for generating meanings."[52]

In summary, any work can be organized as a configuration or as a successive structure, and both possibilities are probably utilized to some degree in the perception of any art form. There are two reasons, however, to believe that brevity inclines readers to foreground an achronological model, or at least makes it easier for them to do so. First, it is obviously easier to "grasp together" units in a synchronic "reflective act" when there is less material for our memories to deal with. Configurational interpretation clearly makes special demands on memory that can be offset by brevity. Second, we can process the parts of a short text more rapidly, and Lessing pointed out that "this rapidity is indispensable, if we are to form an idea of the whole, which is nothing more than a resultant of the ideas of the parts and of their combination."[53] Because a sense of the whole is more vital to configurational than to successive patterning, the length of a text will influence our organizational choice. The faster we are able to ap-

52. Frye, *Anatomy*, 78–79; Mitchell, "Spatial Form," 553.
53. Lessing, *Laokoön*, 98.

prehend the separate parts of a work and "grasp them together" into a whole, the freer a work is to reinforce nonsequential structures, even when a narrative order is present.

The inclination to "get on with" the story that characterizes Lucinda's reading is a strong one; readers need all the added resources of attention that brevity can supply if they are to emphasize nonsequential connections instead. In general, then, readers will prefer linear relationships in long texts. The additional ease of eliciting a configuration from a succession when texts are short is important if readers are to prefer this way of organizing a work, precisely because the human disposition for processing in sequential, cause-and-effect modes is so strong. Faced with integrating a large amount of material, the reader is even more likely to find it irresistible. Frank Kermode speaks of "the comforts of sequence, connexity" and believes that "we cannot do without them." He concludes his discussion of Joseph Conrad's *Under Western Eyes* by noting that readers will attend *either* to sequence or to configurational patterns. Although *spirit* is repeated "well over a hundred times in the novel," he admits, "we may ignore this aspect if we choose. . . . It is a question of the form of attention we choose to bestow; of our willingness to see that in reading according to restricted codes we disregard as noise what, if read differently, patiently, would make another and a rarer kind of sense. And the text, almost with 'cynicism,' tells us what is there, confident that we shall ignore it." We ignore such configurational patterns in a novel because "all this adds up to a quantitatively quite large body of text which on the face of it contributes nothing to sequence—clogs it, indeed." [54] We have seen that novel-length texts may have excellent reasons for such "confident cynicism."

Kermode's opposition of recurrent features ("key words") and "sequence" implies the way in which configurational patterning interacts with local processing. When we discuss the way, as readers or viewers, we unify parts of an artwork into a whole, we need to consider the size of the unit treated as such a "part." Frank notes the importance of this issue and treats it as a generic matter when he discusses the spatial patterning of the county fair scene in *Madame Bovary*: "In Flaubert's scene, however, the unit of meaning is not, as in modern poetry, a word-group or a fragment of an anecdote; it is the totality of

54. Frank Kermode, "Secrets and Narrative Sequence," *Critical Inquiry*, VII (1980), 87, 98, 100.

each level of action taken as an integer. . . . [T]he novel, with its larger unit of meaning, can preserve coherent sequence within the unit of meaning and break up only the time-flow of narrative."[55] Frank thus points out that the novel's larger unit of meaning makes it easier to miss the spatial aspect of patterning because it is opposed to the overriding sequential principle.

Ralph Freedman, in his study of the lyric novel, never deals with the question of unit size. (We have seen that *lyric* sometimes designates "dense verbal patterning" and sometimes "a pattern of heightened emotional response"; it is also used to indicate configurational patterning. The fact that one term covers three different features of texts probably indicates that these three features reinforce one another and are often found in the same texts.) Frank attributes a preference for configurational, lyrical organization to modern novelists such as Virginia Woolf and Djuna Barnes: "These writers ideally intend the reader to apprehend their work spatially, in a moment of time, rather than as a sequence." Yet whatever these authors may intend, readers clearly cannot organize lengthy texts as configurations in precisely the same sense that they can pattern lyric poems in this way. If, as Freedman maintains, we do experience a sudden sense of configurative patterning at the end of a modern novel, it is unlikely that this sense of simultaneous design will involve recall of any great percentage of words or other small verbal units, since the very process of reading the novel necessitates relinquishing most words in favor of larger, more abstract narrative "chunks." Moreover, as Frye points out, when we subordinate our "local" experience of a text, it is generally in favor of some version of plot: "A considerable amount of abstraction enters at this stage. When we think of a poem's narrative as a description of events, we no longer think of the narrative as literally embracing every word and letter. We think rather of a sequence of gross events, of the obvious and externally striking elements in the word-order. . . . We may use the word 'plot' or 'story' for the sequence of gross events."[56]

We can focus on larger units even when the narrative sequence is most severely disrupted. It is again useful to recall Olson's declaration that genres differ as to appropriate size, "the parts and wholes of

55. Frank, *Widening Gyre*, 15–16.

56. Ralph Freedman, *The Lyrical Novel* (Princeton, 1963), *passim;* Frank, *Widening Gyre*, 9; Frye, *Anatomy*, 78–79.

which impose different burdens upon the memory." If a lengthy work reinforces processing in terms of units more appropriate to a smaller genre, it may then become too long to be remembered as a whole. Frank expressed misgivings about *Ulysses* on exactly this count.

> The reader is forced to read *Ulysses* in exactly the same manner as he reads modern poetry, that is, by continually fitting fragments together and keeping allusions in mind until, by reflexive reference, he can link them to their complements. . . . This, it should be realized, is the equivalent of saying that Joyce cannot be read—he can only be reread. A knowledge of the whole is essential to an understanding of any part; but unless one is a Dubliner, such knowledge can be obtained only after the book has been read, when all the references are fitted into their proper places and grasped as a unity. The burdens placed on the reader by this method of composition may well seem insuperable. But the fact remains that Joyce, in his unbelievably laborious fragmentation of narrative structure, proceeded on the assumption that a unified spatial apprehension of his work would ultimately be possible.

Research in discourse processing again indicates that recall limitations hold to some degree even if a reader is "forced" to read in a particular way. E. Z. Rothkopf and M. J. Billington found that readers' ability to expand recall in order to integrate text elements is dependent on text length: "When attempts at integrative linking are possible, such as in self-paced reading, they are more easily exercised with shorter than longer texts. This is because either (a) shorter passages contain fewer elements, or (b) fewer other sentences are interposed between critical components in smaller than in longer texts." [57]

Thus the short story form involves a peculiar tension: short stories, like most novels, offer us the possibility of sequential narrative structures, but like lyric poems and other short works, they also afford opportunities to seize upon verbatim content and nonsequential relationships of equivalence or contrast, because brevity makes it easier for readers to process locally and to organize texts as configurations in terms of minimal units. The tension between temporal and configurational organization can be observed in the history of the short story. It is suggestive that in Russian, American, and German literature, all traditions that have produced short story masters, an essentially

57. Frank, *Widening Gyre*, 18–19; E. Z. Rothkopf and M. J. Billington, "Passage Length and Recall with Test Size Held Constant: Effects of Modality, Pacing, and Learning Set," *Journal of Verbal Learning and Verbal Behavior*, XXII (1983), 667–81.

static, nonnarrative written form has merged with an oral action tale to produce the short story. In American literature we find the sketch; in Russian, the feuilleton; in German, Ludwig Tieck's *Die Gemälde*. Ray West makes this point in discussing Washington Irving's sketches and *Die Gemälde*: "It would seem more reasonable to say that both the sketch and the tale (if there ever was a real distinction) have been absorbed into our modern concept of the short story."[58]

Since the length of a work affects the size of the unit treated as a "part" in configurational patterning, there is an additional reason why brevity reinforces attention to the individual word-unit at the expense of "grosser" episodic "chunks." Although he does not consider generic size a relevant factor, Frye notes that various literary movements and critical methods focus attention on different aspects of a text. Processing in terms of minimal units emphasizes literature as "centripetal verbal patterning," whereas processing in terms of "a sequence of gross events" encourages us to respond to a text as a "representation of life." According to Frye, the former view characterizes the methods of New Criticism and the techniques of *symbolisme*, whereas the latter dominates naturalism: "In the documentary naturalism generally associated with such names as Zola and Dreiser, literature goes about as far as a representation of life, to be judged by its accuracy of description rather than by its integrity as a structure of words, as it could go and still remain literature."[59] We can easily understand why Zola has been attacked as the enemy of the short story and why some critics believe that essentially synchronic formalism cannot isolate the diachronic organizational modes more important to our experience of long works.[60]

58. Ray B. West, Jr., "The American Short Story at Mid-Century," *The Short Story in America; 1900–1950* (Chicago, 1952), 5, rpr. in Hollis Summers (ed.), *Discussions of the Short Story* (Boston, 1963), 131.

59. Frye, *Anatomy*, 79–80.

60. Brander Matthews, for example, alludes to Zola's declaration that "the novelist of the future will not concern himself with the artistic evolution of plot: he will take *une histoire quelconque*, any kind of a story, and make it serve his purpose,—which is to give elaborate pictures of life in all its most minute details." Matthews comments, "It is needless to say that the acceptance of these stories is a negation of the Short-story" ("The Philosophy of the Short-Story," in May [ed.], *Short Story Theories*, 56). Sean O'Faolain also sees Zola as the enemy of the short story and praises Chekhov for avoiding the dullness of strict naturalism (*The Short Story* [Old Greenwich, Conn., 1974], 86–95).

The foregoing would lead us to expect that critical methods which isolate synchronic verbal patterns are most often applied to brief texts. Although no New Critic ever suggested that his tools were more appropriate for one genre than another, in practice New Critics gravitated toward poems and short stories. It is no accident that the New Critical primer on prose narrative, *Understanding Fiction*, is actually a textbook on reading the short story. Cleanth Brooks and Robert Penn Warren certainly advocate local processing at the expense of more "global" considerations. West suggests that New Critical "close reading" is particularly effective in revealing how short stories work; he remarks, "The writing of the New Critics has affected our attitude toward the short story as a form," resulting in "increased awareness of the problems of craftsmanship on the part of the American short-story writer." No doubt this school of criticism has influenced and modified our general tendencies in reading, encouraging us to read novels more like short stories. But Frederic Jameson objects to concentrating on static verbal designs in novels. According to Jameson, Russian Formalism "finds its privileged object in the smaller forms, in short stories or folk tales, poems, anecdotes, in the decorative detail of larger works. For reasons to which we cannot do justice in the present context, the Formalistic model is essentially synchronic, and cannot adequately deal with diachrony, either in literary history or in the form of the individual work, which is to say that Formalism as a method stops short at the point where the novel as a problem begins."[61] Jameson's charge that Formalist critics isolate designs which are central to small forms but which are "decorative" in longer works implies that such patterns are subordinated to developmental, diachronic structures in long works. Although, as a Marxist critic, Jameson has an ideological bias toward diachronic readings, he does not state that diachronic organization is inherently superior but only that it is more relevant to our experience of long works. He implies that synchronic models are more suitable for isolating patterns central to our reading of brief texts.

Not only particular critical approaches but also certain literary styles may interact more effectively with the psychological tendencies engendered by short or long works. For example, the naturalist's pre-

61. West, "American Short Story," 37–38; Frederic Jameson, "Metacommentary," *PMLA*, LXXXVI (1971), 12.

tense of including all the "facts" and eschewing "artificialities" such as contrived verbal patterns frustrates the local processing we tend to accord brief works. Although all genres are affected to some degree by movements such as naturalism, a particular literary style can have greater or lesser impact on an individual form. West finds "the photographic reproduction of the actual" alien to the short form: "It might be said that literary naturalism made less of an impression upon the history of the short story than it did upon the history of the American novel. In the first place, the short story because of its length demanded a greater preoccupation with literary techniques than the naturalist, who was in an important sense antiliterary, was willing or able to grant." [62]

Jameson's preference for global, sequential readings and the naturalist's distaste for contrived verbal patterns and for aesthetic configurative form suggest that these distinct ways of processing texts have implications for values and meaning. These two interpretive processes lead to distinct modes of resolution. When we organize a text as a sequence of episodes, we tend to resolve an active conflict in terms of time, thus assuming a historical reality rooted in the particulars of time and place. When we organize a text as a configuration, however, it is more likely that we will render all details symbolic and view the text as revealing an eternal conflict or a timeless truth.

Appendix A provides extended examples of the application of discourse analysis to specific stories, demonstrating that changing the way we process a text not only adds to, but potentially modifies or even reverses, our response to the text. Each of the two texts I discuss exploits the tension between local and global processing and shows to some degree a self-conscious awareness of the ways in which evaluation is tied to processing and thus to genre. Indeed, what discourse processing has to offer short story theory and genre theory in general is an emphasis on the ways in which reader perception underlies both the meaning of individual texts and a useful definition of genres as categories of cognitive and cultural significance.

62. West, "American Short Story," 33.

SUSAN LOHAFER

Preclosure and Story Processing

When I teach a story, I sometimes "back up" the ending. On a ride from first word to last, I get off early, at an interim stop. "Suppose the story ended *here*," I say. It's a common strategy. The false ending highlights the true ending, isolating what we mean by resolution, by fulfillment of design, by the achievement of a vantage point from which the whole story reveals its contour and point. For the exercise to work, the mock ending must have a certain feasibility, must strike the students as intuitively or logically possible. In other words, it must have some, if not many, of the same features as actual closure.

In recent years, a lot of short story criticism has focused on closure.[1] Looking at how stories end has let us concentrate on what is undeniably distinctive about short fiction—the nearness of the end—and has let us practice a generally informal kind of reader-response criticism, as we study the effects of that imminence on our experience of a text. For me, paying attention to preclosure seemed just another way of applying theories of closure. My perspective changed, however, when I turned to discourse analysis. Derived from psychology and linguistics, rather than from aesthetics, the notion of processing a text takes something away from the privilege of endings (as the definitive constituent of unity) and brings each increment of text into focus as both the "now" and the "end" of the process-so-far.

For the reader caught up in the flow of the process, what would cause the feeling that "things could end here"? Would such triggers exist locally in the text, or would they be the effect of some higher-

1. See the introduction to Part III.

level step in the processing? Would such preclosures be perceived as errors, to be overridden, or would they form an enduring part of the assimilated meaning? And, indeed, assuming that such responses could be determined for any one person, how much agreement could be expected from reader to reader? How would agreements in the recognition (or choice) of preclosure points correlate with kinds of training as readers, and with the kind of "yield"—interpretive facility—that matters to teachers of literature, as opposed to cognitive scientists?

Keeping these larger questions in mind, I asked 180 readers to answer some questions about their experience with Kate Chopin's story "Aunt Lympy's Interference." With 169 sentences, this *conte* is short enough to be read and reviewed within a 50-minute class period. It is a simple yet artful story, accessible and interesting to a wide range of people, from high school sophomores to literary critics. Because it is relatively unknown, readers are not likely to be influenced by previous encounters or critics' opinions. And it is a gauge for certain readerly skills. Composed in the nineteenth century, by a writer whose themes have a sly new timeliness, the story both demands and measures readers' savvy, their grasp of historical context and literary convention.

Why did I choose 180 readers? Again, the answer is part convenience and part design. I used my own students, at every level from freshman to doctoral candidate, and asked for the help of two high school teachers, with students in "developmental reading" and in creative writing.[2] The total sample divided roughly in half between high school and college students, and also included me and one other teacher. Responses to questions were sorted with a simple data-base program for the IBM personal computer, with relationships noted in simple percentages. There is no pretense here of scientific method. This is a tentative sally across those wavy lines between narrative theory, discourse analysis, and classroom practice—reported in a language, and for a purpose, aimed at short story critics.

Readers were given the complete Chopin text, with each sentence numbered from S/1 to S/169 ("S/" for "Sentence," as opposed to "P/"

---

2. Karen Acton, chair, and Judy Griffith, former member, of the English department, West High School, Waterloo, Iowa, were kind enough to take an interest in this project and to carry out exercises with their students, the high school readers who represent half of the population for this study.

TABLE 1
Preclosure Points Chosen by Readers

Cluster	Sentence	% of readers
A	[S/53]	4%
	S/54	8%
		12%
B	S/105	9%
	S/107	17%
		26%
C	[S/137]	6%
	S/140	11%
		16% (overlap of one person)
D	S/162	19%
	S/163	20%
	S/164	23%
	S/166	21%
	S/167	16%
	S/168	24%

for "Proposition"). While reading, each person was to mark any sentences that, in his opinion, *could* end the story. Up to five of these choices were then recorded, starting with the one closest to the actual end of the story and working back toward the beginning.

I wanted first to know which sentences were preferred—and to what degree. Technically, all sentences except the final one (actual closure) were candidates for choice. As it turned out, though, only 80 of the 168 (or slightly less than half) were regarded as feasible. Of these 80 I am going to use only 12: the 10 most frequently chosen preclosure points, and the 2 more (in brackets in Table 1) located near a preferred sentence (at most three sentences away) and receiving the highest share of votes within a range of 21 sentences on either side of the preferred one. The twelve sentences are arranged in Table 1 in order of their occurrence in the text. Perhaps it is surprising that no one sentence was chosen by more than 24 percent of the readers. I would have welcomed higher percentages—and might have gotten them, had I used readers with more in common. But I had reasons for wanting diversity in age and training. Under the circumstances, it may be remarkable that nearly a fourth of the readers *did* agree on at least one sentence. In any case, what matters for this study is *relative* agreement.

The D cluster represents the final group of sentences in the story, omitting S/165 (which is a one-word sentence, "Why?" entailing an answer—and hence an unlikely preclosure point). As the percentages indicate, and as we might guess, the sentences near the end of the story were most often chosen as preclosure points. I will call these six sentences the "outer-shell" preclosure points. Clusters A, B, and C are scattered within the story. They emerge from the data less predictably—and more revealingly—to claim our attention. I will call these sentences, as a group, the "inner-shell" preclosure points.

Had I devised this study to confirm some notion of "completed storyness," I would have tried to predict the results, especially the location of the "inner-shell" points. I have, however, worked as inductively as possible, letting the readers take their pick, and only *then* asking what these choices could tell me. My own students, of course, had heard the term *preclosure* before. Having been exposed to my way of teaching short fiction, they might be expected to "give me what I wanted." But I could never have predicted the exact location and distribution of preclosure choices. To make sense of them, we must turn to the story.

"Aunt Lympy's Interference" belongs to the major, late period of Chopin's work. Written in 1896, it is bracketed by "The Story of an Hour," 1894; *The Awakening*, 1897; and "The Storm," 1898. The scene is Acadian Louisiana, with its caste society and plantation economy. We meet a girl of "good" family, on the verge of maturity, drawn to her window on a soft spring day. As in her better-known work, Chopin deftly penetrates the tangle of half-understood feelings, resistances, and yearnings of the female psyche in an era when neither sexuality nor independence of mind and pocket was "respectable" for women.

Now that her parents are dead, the young heroine, Melitte, is living with her brother's family, in somewhat reduced circumstances. Her social status is further jeopardized by her new occupation as a schoolteacher for the local children. Melitte enjoys the work; it gives her an indefinable sense of worth. Quite the opposite view is taken by Aunt Lympy, whose visit is the precipitating event in the story. She is a woman of color, a former servant in the family (the title "Aunt" is conventional), who sees herself as the guardian of that family's welfare and honor. In her eyes Melitte's occupation is a degradation, a reproach to the males in the family—especially to the father's brother, who is a wealthy member of New Orleans society.

Aunt Lympy's "interference" is a gesture of meddlesome goodwill. Since Melitte is stubbornly happy in her work, Aunt Lympy goes behind her back to appeal to the girl's uncle, picturing Melitte in "misery." Sentimentally contrite, he writes to Melitte, inviting her to join his family and share in a life of parties, leisure, and money. Melitte seems to have two options: remain a schoolteacher or become a socialite.

What gives the story its complication is the existence of another choice not so clearly defined. Although hardly aware of the nature of her feelings, Melitte is attracted to a young Creole neighbor, Victor Annibelle, a childhood playmate who has recently returned to manage his family's estate. Every day that Melitte walks to school, she passes the Annibelles' house. Every day, Victor is working on the fence that borders her route. They barely speak a word to each other. They are in love, though hampered by shyness, by uncertainty about each other's feelings, and by the social conventions of the time. Melitte never acknowledges it to herself, but her third option—and the one yearned for by her affectionate nature and budding desire—is marriage to Victor.

What is so modern about Chopin's story is her dramatization of the pressures bearing upon Melitte as she confronts these three options, these three adult roles: self-supporting worker, perpetual "daughter," and lover/wife/mother. Of course, we might wonder whether teaching is really a role; it might be just a way of staying home, close to Victor. But Chopin calls our attention to Melitte's salary, and specifically her desire not to "contaminate" it with gift money from her uncle. Having her own money represents to her, fairly consciously, a kind of independence, something earned, not bestowed. She really is being pulled three different ways.

And the pressures increase. Society urges Melitte to accept her uncle's offer; self-esteem keeps her working; nature (she's young; it's springtime) draws her to Victor. Yet it's important to notice that neither Melitte nor Chopin overtly identifies or weighs these alternatives. Instead, the story foregrounds Melitte's chagrin, her pouting sense of hurt because no one begs her to stay where she is. The hurt is half real, half cultivated; she wants to feel needed where her heart is attached. Transparently, yet innocently, she's lovesick.

When Victor, driven by the fear of losing her, does speak out and declare his need, Melitte responds temperately, even coolly, but with evident relief and deep satisfaction. We know she will marry him. The story ends, however, with a summary of others' reactions to Melitte's decision. Some sympathize; some don't. The final sentence (actual closure) focuses on Aunt Lympy: "[She] was not altogether dissatisfied; she felt that her interference had not been wholly in vain."[3] The compounding of negatives, the hint of wryness, may be taken a number of ways. Aunt Lympy *did* set in motion a chain of events that will get Melitte out of the schoolroom. Furthermore, in marrying Victor, Melitte will be choosing the kind of fate Aunt Lympy had in mind—a respectable, "womanly" place in the world.

This is a story about a girl awakening to herself and finding a mate; the imagery of "freshness," "dewiness," the "hot, sweet scent of flowers and sometimes the good smell of the plowed earth," needs no Freudian gloss. It is also a story about the possibilities for a young, intelligent, warm-hearted girl at the end of the nineteenth century in the American South. I do not mean to rewrite the story as social critique; the hints are all too muted, all too musing. Besides, Melitte's case is hardly a test of "career" versus "home"; teaching young children is, in this story, essentially surrogate mothering. And yet something is at stake for Melitte. She gains her heart's desire, abides by nature—yet loses something, too.

With this sketch of the tale in mind, let me now identify the preferred preclosure points. Readers will encounter the A cluster first. These are the sentences marking the end of Aunt Lympy's visit. Here is the favored S/54, with the sentences on either side of it:

S/53. She [Aunt Lympy] said good-by, with solemnity, as we part from those in sore affliction.

S/54. *When she had mounted into her ramshackle open buggy the old vehicle looked someway like a throne.*

S/55. Scarcely a week after Aunt Lympy's visit Melitte was amazed by receiving a letter from her uncle, Gervais Leplain, of New Orleans.

Eight percent of the readers thought the story could end at S/54; 4 percent chose S/53. About one-eighth of the readers, then, found preclosure here. The visit is over; Melitte has held firm.

3. Kate Chopin, "Aunt Lympy's Interference," in Per Seyersted (ed.), *The Complete Works of Kate Chopin* (2 vols.; Baton Rouge, 1969), II, 511–17. All quotations are from this edition.

The B cluster portrays Melitte, in defiant self-pity, thinking she *will* leave.

S/105.   "Oh, I'll go!

S/106.   I will go!" Melitte was saying a little hysterically to herself as she walked [toward school].

S/107.   *The familiar road was a brown and green blur, for the tears in her eyes.*

S/108.   Victor Annibelle was not mending his fence that morning; but there he was, leaning over it as Melitte came along.

As Table 1 illustrates, 17 percent of the readers thought the story could end at S/107, and 9 percent chose S/105, for a total of 26 percent. In other words, a full fourth of the readers sensed preclosure just where Melitte gives up on herself and on Victor.

Next, the C cluster arrives. Victor makes his confession.

S/137.   "Oh, I can't bear to have you go, Melitte!"

S/138.   They were so near the school it seemed perfectly natural that she should hurry forward to join the little group that was there waiting for her under a tree.

S/139.   He made no effort to follow her.

S/140.   *He expected no reply; the expression that had escaped him was so much a part of his unspoken thought, he was hardly conscious of having uttered it.*

S/141.   But the few spoken words, trifling as they seemed, possessed a power to warm and brighten [Melitte's day in school.]

In this case, 11 percent of the readers found S/140 a convincing stopping place, and 6 percent identified S/137, for a total of 16 percent of the readers, since the two groups overlapped by one person. In other words, about one-sixth of the readers thought the story could end with Victor's confession of love. He phrases it in the very words Melitte has been longing to hear; if we back up to S/102, we find her wondering, "Why should she stay where no soul had said, 'I can't bear to have you go, Melitte?'" In cluster C, her words, her dreams, are realized.

Now that we have identified the "inner-shell" preclosure points, it will be a simple matter to list the "outer-shell" points. They are simply the last six sentences of the story, minus one. At this moment of the story, Victor has waited all day for the children to go home, coming up just as Melitte tries to close the school window. He admits to hoping she will stay if he begs her, taking her hand and asking "Would you, Melitte—would you?"

> S/162.   "I believe I would, Victor.
> S/163.   Oh—never mind my hand; don't you see I must shut the window?"
> S/164.   So after all Melitte did not go to the city to become a *grande dame.*
> [S/165. Why?]
> S/166.   Simply because Victor Annibelle asked her not to.
> S/167.   The old people when they heard it shrugged their shoulders and tried to remember that they, too, had been young once; which is, sometimes, a very hard thing for old people to remember.
> S/168.   Some of the younger ones thought she was right, and many of them believed she was wrong to sacrifice so brilliant an opportunity to shine and become a woman of fashion.

On the average, about one-fifth of the readers chose each one of the sentences in cluster D, and many of these people chose several from this group—making it impossible to add up the percentages in any meaningful way. The cluster is sharply set off from preceding sentences; S/161 was chosen by only 2 percent of the readers; S/162 by 19 percent. The preference is understandable. S/162 (". . . I would, Victor") declares Melitte's will; we know now what path she will take. S/163 may seem a less likely choice. Concerned with shutting the window, it seems humorously off the point, but the play on open and shut windows, on sills as barriers or bridges, harks back to earlier imagery. The story begins with Melitte dreaming at an open window that looks out on the Annibelle place and is a portal for the sounds of life and the "hot, sweet" smells of the earth. Nature has claimed her, and now, at the end, her primness hides a concession that's really a gain but also a loss (who's "victor"?).

S/164 ("So after all . . .") and S/166 ("Simply because . . .") are obvious choices because of their declarative, summationlike quality. S/167 fared less well than S/168, perhaps because readers saw these two sentences as a pair and declined to separate them: the "old" think this; the "young" think that. Finally, S/168 received the most attention of all. It *does* complete a pair and cap a series of comments. Also, for readers who see society (rather than Victor or Aunt Lympy) as "the problem," this sentence is a confirmation of sorts. The most influential factor, however, may be simply position. S/168 fills the penultimate slot in the text as a whole.

How many readers chose the same *sequence* of preclosure points? Four-place and five-place agreement occurred only when people counted down from S/168 to S/164 in order; evidently, these readers (four altogether) did not understand the exercise and chose a mechanical answer. Two-place agreement occurred so often as to tell us little more than we already know from the overall tally of preferences. Three-place agreement occurred about twenty times. The particular sequence S/137, S/163, S/164 recurred only once. I found it in the choices of the student who (weeks before I tallied these results) earned the highest grade in my class, and I found it in my own list of choices.

Although flattered by a coincidence that was, finally, not much of a surprise, I did not intend grades to be a factor in the study, and did not include them in the data. I did not want to correlate performance in the exercise with performance in a given class (where the "distortions" of teaching style and subject matter would be even more of a problem). Rather, I wanted to correlate performance in the test case with "training" in the gross but standard terms of school levels, and in the special terms of fiction-writing experience.

Using the nine most frequently chosen preclosure points (I omitted S/105 from the base group of ten, so that each "inner-shell" cluster would be represented by only one point), I sorted the readers by their level in school: high school junior (54 students) and senior (34); college sophomore (18), junior (29), and senior (21); graduate school and professional (19). To reach the total number of readers represented in Table 2, I also counted two high school students who listed themselves as sophomores and three college students who listed themselves as freshmen. Ranking the preclosure choices (counting overall number of mentions) made by readers at each school level, I found no clear-cut correlation between level and preferred choices. However, when I compared the high school readers as a whole with the readers having college-level schooling, I did see some differences worth noting. Obviously, the degree of agreement is higher among readers with more formal schooling. In Group I, only one preclosure point (S/164) received more than 20 percent agreement; in Group II, as many as five preclosure points received at least 20 percent agreement, and a third picked S/168.

TABLE 2

Preclosure Choices of High School and More Advanced Readers

Cluster	Preclosure point	Group I: High school readers (90)	Group II: College-level readers and above (90)
A	S/54	13%	3%
B	S/107	17%	17%
C	S/140	10%	13%
	S/162	11%	28%
	S/163	10%	32%
	S/164	23%	23%
D	S/166	11%	30%
	S/167	17%	15%
	S/168	16%	33%

Now let's look at those preclosure points receiving significantly different recognition from the two groups. The percentage of Group II favoring S/163 is more than three times higher than the percentage of Group I choosing that point. S/163 is the sentence about shutting the window; coming in the middle of the final exchange between Victor and Melitte, it is low in event-related preclosure signals, but high in image-related signals. The window returns us to the opening of the story, when the distant sounds and sights of the spring and of Victor's life came through Melitte's open window; now he literally reaches through a window to take her hand and offer her what those images heralded. Melitte's shutting the window is a gesture of reserve, but also a close to her life as a teacher. As we might expect, college-trained readers were more likely to sense the preclosure function of a recycled image, and more likely to respond to the intrinsically closural force of the verb *shut*.[4]

On the other hand, the percentage of readers choosing S/54 is four times lower for readers with college training than for high school readers. This is the sentence in which Aunt Lympy departs, full of

4. In *Poetic Closure: A Study of How Poems End* (Chicago, 1968), Barbara Herrnstein Smith identifies certain words (like *end* and *final*) that have intrinsic closural significance.

sorrow and dignity, after her visit to Melitte. The sentence *is* rich in imagery, as the buggy becomes a "throne" for Aunt Lympy. But the imagery only underscores a potential for rule, for governing people's fates; we have not yet seen that power in action. In other words, the imagery opens up possibilities; it doesn't close them (as in the window sentence). So preclosure here is probably not triggered by image-related signals.

To think the story could be over when Aunt Lympy leaves is to give preference to event-related signals, to the closural function of the visit's end *as such* (many stories *are* coterminal with a visit); it is to respond to a crude but fundamental correlation between a physical encounter and a significant unit of experience. High school readers were more likely to make this response. Readers with more schooling seemed to realize that the visit by Aunt Lympy had, as yet, effected no change in the status quo of the story world. (Not until something disrupts the equilibrium—the arrival of the letter—is there a conflict of the sort students are taught to recognize.) Knowing that stories read in class contain nothing extraneous, these readers may also have noted that Victor, obviously an important character, isn't mentioned in the interview; hence the story can't end here.

Overall, then, the information in Table 2, which compares the choices made by high school students with those made by readers with college-level schooling, gives some concrete particularity to generalizations about "training." Students with more experience in "academic" reading were more likely to pick up on cues embedded in the local linguistic fabric of the text or encoded in classroom talk about unity and conflict. Readers with less experience were more likely to be satisfied by cues conveyed by larger, event-related, structural units per se. If there is, as some claim, a "maturation calendar" for kinds of aesthetic perception, we may be seeing some evidence of it here.

We *can* identify varying degrees of experience with the practical aesthetics of story composition. I asked all the readers to assign themselves to one of the following categories of experience with fiction writing: 1) "Have never tried to write a story," 2) "Have tried, but no formal training," and 3) "Have had formal training and/or publication." I assumed that more experience in writing fiction would tend to correlate with more advanced schooling in general (though I knew creative writing was taught in one of the high school classes). If the assumption held, we would expect Group III in Table 3 to make the more sophisticated choices—to be most alert to S/163, the window

TABLE 3

Preclosure Choices and Writing Experience

Cluster	Preclosure point	Group I: No experience	Group II: No formal training	Group III: Trained
A	S/54	3%	10%	7%
B	S/107	9%	18%	22%
C	S/140	19%	8%	11%
	S/162	19%	19%	22%
	S/163	3%	25%	20%
D	S/164	28%	25%	18%
	S/166	31%	23%	11%
	S/167	19%	17%	13%
	S/168	38%	17%	33%

sentence, and least inclined toward S/54, the sentence marking the end of Aunt Lympy's visit. Neither expectation was quite fulfilled, for Group I was most alert to *both* S/163 and S/54, whereas Group II was *least* interested in these sentences. Furthermore, the findings, when placed next to those in Table 2, suggest that the readers with formal training as writers did not always tend toward the same choices as the readers with the greatest amount of schooling in general. In fact, the trained writers paid more attention to S/107 (near "Oh, I'll go!") and S/162 ("I believe I would, Victor") than they did to S/163. In other words, they focused slightly more on event-related signals (decision to go; decision to stay) than on the closural function of particular images. We cannot conclude that they were less sensitive to imagery, but perhaps, when it came to preclosure, they were more responsive to blocks of experience.

In the area where the trained writers *did* share a preference with the more schooled readers in Table 2, there is a new quirk in the results. The trained writers gave overwhelming preference to S/168, the sentence that "ends" the story with an echo of the choice foregone ("Some of the younger ones thought she was right, and many of them believed she was wrong to sacrifice so brilliant an opportunity to shine and become a woman of fashion"). But in making this decision, they were suddenly, and by a large margin, aligned with the least experienced writers! To my mind, this is one of the most striking, because least predictable, of the findings so far.

It suggests that when the variable is experience in fiction writing, the responses of trained writers correlate most highly with the responses of readers with no experience in writing. If we are trying to predict the overall favorite preclosure point, the people who say they have never tried to write a story turn out to be as reliable a guide as the people who have taken writing courses (and in some cases published their stories)—and both are a better guide than the people who have tried to write stories but are schooled only as readers (and critics). This is not, of course, to say that writers are superior readers. What is intriguing here is the bonding of naïveté and sophistication.

Story rhythm, the sense of what closes the "period" of a story, may be among the most primitive of the story conventions we all internalize. Group I seemed to "go by the gut." On the other hand, "doing" endings is part of the craft of storytelling; Group III knew this consciously and well. Yet Group III followed the lead of Group I. The favoring of S/168 joins innocence and experience, intuition and calculation, artlessness and artfulness. The same has been said of the short story genre.[5]

In the course of reviewing how experience affects preclosure choices, we have made a start in seeing how the choice of preclosure points correlates with certain processing activities, such as the recognition of event-units and of locally embedded signals of closure. Now I'd like to explore further the relationship between preclosure recognition and understanding a story. Putting the preclosure points back in context, we can see right away that certain features are shared by the "inner-shell" points while certain other features are shared by the "outer-shell" points. Beginning with the "inner" points, we note that all exhibit these features: 1) location at the end of a paragraph (though the action or theme of the paragraph may be vested in an earlier sentence, which turns up as the second-favored choice in the cluster— S/53, S/105, and S/137); 2) correlation with a shift in physical place (S/54, Aunt Lympy moves off in her carriage; S/107, Melitte sets out for school; S/140, Melitte walks away from Victor toward the children under the tree); 3) correlation with the end of a debate (S/54, end of discussion between Aunt Lympy and Melitte about her teaching;

5. Valerie Shaw, in *The Short Story: A Critical Introduction* (London, 1983), pairs two chapter titles: "'Artful' Narration" and "'Artless' Narration." In my own book, *Coming to Terms with the Short Story* (1983; rpr. Baton Rouge, 1985), I open Chapter I with a section entitled "The Artless Art."

S/107, end of Melitte's debate with herself about going or staying; S/140, break in a conversation with Victor); 4) correlation with a bent toward one of Melitte's choices as a woman (S/54, Melitte affirms the option of teaching school; S/107, Melitte accepts the option of going to New Orleans; S/140, Melitte receives the option of marrying Victor— which we know she will take).

It seems that the feeling of preclosure is enhanced, if not triggered, when these features coincide. What do they tell us? It is not surprising that the visual break between paragraphs should be a powerful signal, overriding, for many people, the more logical choice of a sentence in the body of a paragraph. It also may be that the choice of preclosure points rests not so much on a sense of ending as on a sense of beginning—found in the sentence *after* the chosen one. In other words, it is possible to conceive of another study, replacing each S/x with S/x + 1.

The value of the preclosure sentences emerges again, however, as we note the other correlations, with place, speech-act, and orientation toward one future rather than another. As readers of Donald Barthelme and others, we may forget how much our sense of fictional world is tied to place and how necessarily a change of venue means a change in state. More to the point in short fiction, a movement from here to there, a route taken, a home-leaving and/or a homecoming, is often the physical emblem of what's directing a life (Hawthorne's "Young Goodman Brown" and Welty's "A Worn Path" come easily to mind). Melitte is vacillating along several paths we can draw on a map—of Louisiana or of womanhood.

The correlation with the end of a discussion confirms and strengthens other signals of preclosure, and might yield more to an approach based on speech-act theory. But far more interesting, for now, is the fact that each of the "inner-shell" clusters privileges a different one of the three options Melitte is facing. At cluster A she is confirmed in her teaching; at B she's conceding to her uncle; at C she is joining up with Victor. At A it is *her* will in force; at B it is Lympy's (and society's); at C it is Victor's. This is as much as to say that this charming little story zigzags through several turns, driven by the forces of convention and desire, with each turn a potential end to the series.

The very fact that preclosure choices do cluster at these points tells us that readers intuit, or look for, the impress of will, that they sense "storyness" in those phases of experience that are rounded out by desire and fulfillment. We have always known that "storyness" has this shape, but perhaps we have never had so simple a proof that students perceive it before teachers abstract it. Nor have we had such clear evidence that readers, left to their own devices, "chunk" a story this way.[6]

Surely local signals such as change of place do influence the preclosure choices, but the larger sense of "storyness," coincident with the victory of one of Melitte's options, is harder to talk about. These options are nowhere spelled out in the discourse itself. I arrived at them through a simple critical analysis of the story. But many readers involved in the preclosure exercise may not have conceptualized them at all, though apparently confirming them in the choice of preclosure points. (This "guess" is not entirely without foundation, since the story summaries the readers wrote were in no case clearly and prominently organized around the three options as such.) We can assume, then, that it is not only, and perhaps not primarily, the overt, locally processed features of the discourse that signal preclosure—but that the signals are coming from, or through, a more complex part of the reading process.

To take us above the level of the word-by-word text, we can use the concept of macrostructure, defined and applied in various ways by different discourse analysts, but prominently advanced in the work of Teun A. van Dijk. Macrostructures are identified by statements that do not necessarily appear in the text but are generated—according to certain processing rules—by the propositions within the text. These rules simulate or stand in place of the cognitive operations we perform as we read, for "macrostructure formation in complex discourse is a necessary property of cognitive information processing."[7] As we read a story, we process it into macropropositions that identify macrostructures. Van Dijk's rules insure a systematic, more or less objective way of replicating this process—moving up the ladder of generalization by dropping out redundancies, subsuming details, and reducing a large number of propositions (impossible to hold in memory) to a smaller number, easier to retain.

6. There *have* been studies of story recall that identify the level (within a hierarchy of generalization) of those propositions retained in a summary of the story. A pioneering work here is Perry W. Thorndyke's "Cognitive Structures in Comprehension and Memory of Narrative Discourse," *Cognitive Psychology,* IX (1977), 77–110.

7. Teun A. van Dijk, *Macrostructures: An Interdisciplinary Study of Global Structures in Discourse, Interaction, and Cognition* (Hillsdale, N.J., 1980), 46–48, and *Text and Context: Explorations in the Semantics and Pragmatics of Discourse* (New York, 1977), 158.

Informally identifying the proposition as subject plus finite verb plus complements, I rewrote the 169 sentences of the story as 387 propositions. So, for example, S/52–S/54 became the following propositions:

P/120. But Aunt Lympy would not eat
P/121. [She would not] drink
P/122. [She would not] unbend
P/123. Nor [would she] lend herself to the subterfuge of small talk
P/124. She said good-by with solemnity
P/125. [She parted] as we part from those in sore affliction
P/126. She mounted into her old ramshackle open buggy
P/127. The old vehicle looked someway like a throne

I then turned to van Dijk's rules of deletion (omitting details that do not condition future states or actions), generalization (grouping individual details under a covering umbrella), and construction (building a stereotypical configuration), as well as the zero rule (importing a microstructure into the macrostructure unchanged). The resulting macroproposition was:

M/x. Aunt Lympy departed in state.

I carried out the application far enough to determine that a macrostructure statement never swallowed up a preclosure point; that is to say, it always netted propositions up to, but not across, the preclosure point. This discovery confirmed the prominent role of preclosure points in the processing of the story text. Since I already knew, however, that these points were associated with gaps in the discursive continuum—authorially signaled by the break between paragraphs—my experiment with macrostructures gave me only a more generalized version of what the sentences had told me. I needed to look "higher."

Van Dijk does identify another level of cognitive organization, called the superstructure. It reduces and generalizes the macrostructures even further and is specific to various genres or types of discourse.[8] Thus, for scientific argument, the superstructure might identify a fundamental relationship between evidence and inference; for

8. Van Dijk, *Macrostructures*, 107–32.

narrative, it would involve certain relations between events. By definition, the superstructure of a story is a conventionalized grammar of narrative, usually represented as a causally connected chain of events by means of which one state of affairs is transformed into another.[9] It might, therefore, be interesting to see whether a superstructure derived from "Aunt Lympy's Interference" shows any correlation with the favored preclosure points.

Van Dijk uses a much-simplified (and very conservative) model for his tree diagram of story superstructure.[10]

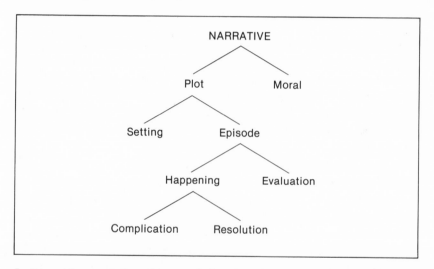

In "Aunt Lympy's Interference," the plot consists of S/1 through S/164 ("So after all Melitte did not go to the city to become a *grande dame*"), and S/165 through S/169 (summarizing reactions) occupy the moral slot. Setting may be instantiated by S/1 through S/19, if we take setting in the broadest sense to include the norms of Melitte's life. It is here that the imagery of spring and youth is established. "Aunt Lympy visits Melitte" is the first happening of the story, extending from S/20 to S/54; evaluation as such is not overt, though the image of Aunt Lympy moving off in her thronelike buggy sums up the importunate and judgmental tone of her visit. This series of sentences ends in the A cluster of preclosure points.

A causal connection leads into the next happening, "Melitte re-

9. For an example of such a grammar, see, for example, Gerald Prince's *A Grammar of Stories: An Introduction* (The Hague, 1973).

10. Van Dijk, *Macrostructures*, 116.

ceives a letter from her uncle." What follows is a "complication" of responses, as everybody puts pressure on Melitte, ending in a resolution: S/105, "Oh, I'll go!" Here we arrive at the B cluster of preclosure points. The third happening is the encounter with Victor, complicated by Melitte's coyness, resolved by his passion, and ending in the C cluster. No further events are dramatized, though Melitte's implied marriage and the summary of reactions to it are the subject of comment on all sides—the D cluster. In short, the statements of the superstructure, following van Dijk's model, divide up the text in exactly the same way as the preclosure clusters do, following the free choices of 180 readers.

A very general truism can be inferred from this correlation: young-adult and adult readers of short fiction have internalized certain broad conventions of narrative structure, and therefore intuitively recognize as wholes those portions of a story that can be blocked out as events and hence retained on the superstructural (most conventionalized, paradigmatic) level. It seems that both the macrostructures and the superstructures, as representations of how a story is "chunked" in the act of processing, confirm my sense that preclosure choices are another way of arriving at some of the same information—and by means of a simple, direct, nontechnical exercise any teacher can use. But "chunking" is only a rudimentary step in processing.

To learn more about what, and how much, a reader understands, we need to look between the macrostructure and the superstructure. We need to identify the interim-level strategies for processing, configuring, and making sense of the propositions in the story. Discourse analysis draws heavily here upon the concept of frames—those stored configurations of knowledge that allow us to process information more efficiently.[11] A frame labeled "office," for example, stores the common denominators of our experience with offices. Top levels of the frame carry the most general information—the presence of a desk, associations with work rather than pleasure, and so on. Lower-level terminals are less stable, filled with "default assignments" such as paper clips, wastebaskets, typewriters.[12] These are the things we expect to find in an office. If we read that "Mary was told to file it," we

11. The following works offer a good introduction to frame theory: John Frow, "The Literary Frame," *Journal of Aesthetic Education*, XVI (1982), 25–30; Dieter Metzing (ed.), *Frame Conceptions and Text Understanding* (New York, 1980)—especially W. G. Lehnert, "The Role of Scripts in Understanding," M. Minsky, "A Framework for Representing Knowledge," and S. T. Rosenberg, "Frame-based Text Processing."

12. Minsky, "A Framework," 2.

don't have to be told there's a file cabinet. On the other hand, in the case of any given office, some of the default information will be missing, and some will be false—let's say there is a computer with a printer, rather than a typewriter. An easy substitution. But if we say there is a bed in the room—information that clearly doesn't fit—then the processing becomes more complex (is it an office with a bed, or a bedroom with a desk?). When the stereotyped information involves a series of actions in a setting (such as a job interview going on in the office), the term *frame* is often replaced by *scenario* or *script*. And now, finally, we return to narrative, to story.

Readers of "Aunt Lympy's Interference," like the readers of any other story, will be constantly employing frames and scripts to help in the processing of the text. Indeed, one gauge of understanding may be the recognition of, and ability to use, frames that are either employed by characters within the story or required of the reader who processes the story. Obviously, the number and complexity of such frames defy any kind of exhaustive listing or study. The "young love" frame, for example, helps us process the encounters between Melitte and Victor, helps us guess right away that they are in love, for many of the default features of the frame are instantiated: the physical beauty of the couple, the awkwardness and indirection of their speech, their humorously transparent excuses to meet, the springtime setting, and so on.

How could I learn what frames were available to my readers and which ones they were actually using? My method here was, admittedly, indirect, for I did not want to introduce a new focus into the questionnaire. I simply asked each reader to summarize the text in a space about 3 1/4" by 6 1/2". I shifted, too, from an inductive to an a priori method. Instead of reading the summaries to collect a roster of frames (worth doing, but far too big a task at the time of the study), I began with a list of ten frames I knew would be useful for coding the information in "Aunt Lympy's Interference." Of these I chose four to work with.

In each of these four cases, there is a clear difference between a nineteenth-century "southern" filling of the frame and a contemporary "eighties" filling of the frame. My intention was to isolate fairly simple and predictable kinds of misunderstandings—those that could come from an inability to recognize frames, or differentiate between features relevant to the story, and those not—in order to learn something about levels of understanding among my readers.

Let us call the four frames "mulatto," "family servant," "working woman," and "female psychology." As I read through the summaries of the story, I coded three possibilities for each frame: (Y) recognition, (X) simple absence of recognition, and (N) misconstruction or error traceable to a fault in recognizing or applying the frame. I was dismayed to find how many readers mistook Aunt Lympy's status, missing both her probable mulatto status (S/25, "she was light-colored"; S/26, "Two heavy bands of jet-black hair showed beneath her bandanna and covered her ears down to the gold hoop earrings") and her stated role as old family servant (S/46, "Melitte felt the inutility of trying to dislodge the old family servant's deep-rooted prejudices").

Recognition of the servant frame for Aunt Lympy (and hence the perspective in which her concern must be placed) appeared in only 2 percent of the summaries written by high school sophomores, and (still only) 42 percent of the summaries by college graduates with further schooling. Overt errors (such as the assumption that Lympy was a blood relation, or that Melitte, herself, was black) occurred from 32 to 46 percent of the time in each of the high school and college categories! Such misreadings, in the face of explicit statements in the text, seem clearly due to a lack of familiarity with the norms and conventions of the nineteenth-century South, particularly as they are encoded in the literature of that period and place. If the frames are unavailable, the information is bypassed and replaced with default information from other, more familiar frames (for example, *aunt* in the literal sense).

What is interesting about the working-woman frame is that it carries different default features, depending on the century in question. In Melitte's world, a default reading includes "necessitated by poverty" and "socially compromising," whereas in the twentieth-century world to which most contemporary readers belong, a default reading might include "personally fulfilling" and "self-respecting." Melitte's story is, in a sense, the story of an old-fashioned woman who instantiates this frame in a protomodern way—and therefore runs head-on into prejudice.

A surprising number of readers did comment, in their summaries, upon Melitte's being out of step with the norm, struggling with the assumptions of others and her own desires. Thirty-four percent of the high school sophomores recognized the conflict within this frame, and 74 percent of the college graduates with advanced schooling did. The two youngest groups, however, also exhibited a high incidence of error (missing the prejudice), with 36 and 46 percent, respectively, while no one in the post-graduate group made this mistake. The younger readers may simply have been paying more attention to the foregrounded issue of Melitte's need for love, while the advanced readers were juggling more themes.

Finally, I checked to see how readers responded to Chopin's portrait of female psychology. Melitte's vacillations, hurt feelings, and self-pity all may be viewed as either finely realistic or dated and sexist. Is Chopin merely the naturalist, displaying behavior, or is she the subtle critic, showing us how a girl like Melitte is victimized by emotional dependencies often thought to be typically and charmingly feminine?

What concerned me here was whether a reader noted the confusion and conflict Melitte was experiencing under the pressure to give up her job. As much as 27 percent of the youngest group did; 68 percent of the group with the most schooling did. The percentage of error (missing the turmoil) was highest among high school sophomores (20 percent) but overall was quite low (zero among college seniors and only 10 percent when percentages in all six groups were averaged together). In other words, the more schooled readers were much more likely to *use* the frame, but most readers were able to recognize the psychodynamics of Melitte's case—enough to avoid the kinds of misreadings found with the mulatto and family servant frames. Human psychology doesn't "date" quite so fast.

I was curious to see whether the gender of the reader affected the recognition and use of the working-woman and female psychology frames. In both cases, the percentage of recognition was about the same for male and female readers (all within a range of 38 to 43 percent). Men, however, were more likely to misread the story in ways related to a failure to recognize the frame: for the working-woman frame, the percentages of misreadings were 20 percent for female readers, 28 percent for male readers; for the female psychology frame, the percentages of misreadings were 11 percent for female readers, 15 percent for male readers.

Having determined that recognition and use of frames correlate positively with increase in schooling and modern currency of the frame, we can ask, finally, whether they correlate with any pattern of preclosure choices. We will put aside the mulatto and family servant frames, for they don't emerge crucially at any of the preclosure points. The working-woman frame *is* evoked, to some extent, in all of the points. Those who recognized the working-woman frame chose preclosure points correlating closely with the choices of the readers over-all. For example, 23 percent of them chose S/168; 24 percent of all readers did the same. The percentages are similarly close (within a few points) in the other clusters. It seems that recognition of the working-woman frame did not sensitize readers to any particular pre-closure points. But this frame is more nearly standard equipment for most readers in the eighties and therefore not likely to affect the data by itself. Other speculations are possible, too. Perhaps we are seeing evidence that the issues raised by Melitte's job are never finally worked out in the story. I believe, for instance, that Chopin leaves implicit the loss Melitte suffers in giving up her job. The issue is *not* "closed."

Those who recognized the female psychology frame, however, did show greater sensitivity than the group at large to certain points of preclosure. They showed a greater preference (32 as opposed to 17 percent) for the C cluster of preclosure points (S/137, S/140). This is where Victor echoes—and satisfies—Melitte's yearning to be wooed: "I can't bear to have you go." These same readers were also more likely (32 as opposed to 21 percent) to favor S/166, which confirms Melitte's apparent capriciousness but really deep need: "Simply be-cause Victor Annibelle asked her not to." Is there some significant re-lation here?

I went back to the total group of readers and sorted out those who had chosen either S/137 or S/140, to see whether they were especially likely to use the female psychology frame in their summaries of the story. Unfortunately, only 28 percent of them recognized the frame, as opposed to 42 percent in the group at large. It would seem, there-fore, that use of the frame tends to correlate with sensitivity to the preclosure points that particularly invoke that frame; however, choice of those points does not necessarily mean one is more likely to em-ploy the frame.

The reason may be that the points evoking the female psychology frame also exhibit many signals of preclosure. Actions are resolved there. Preference for these points may depend more on perception of the plot (girl gets boy) than on sensitivity to the frame in question (girl wants to be needed). Having students choose preclosure points in this story doesn't necessarily show us which students are aware of which frames; however, checking to see which frames are at work does help explain a greater-than-usual sensitivity to certain preclo-sure points.

If, as teachers, we take for granted the need to make outdated frames available, comprehensible, we may find ourselves simply delivering this information as "background." What we've seen here is that such information *can* be tied in with perceptions of "storyness." If, as critics, we think eternal issues and desires (such as women's dignities and rights) need no cultural framing, we may be dulling our sense of what Chopin accomplished.

Literary criticism is always reinventing itself with the language of other disciplines. This volume itself came about because a significant number of short story critics are pushing at boundaries, looking over fences, trying to redefine the nature and aims of their study. With Suzanne Hunter Brown, I believe discourse analysis is particularly suggestive for short story critics. My own interest might almost be called survivalist. Discourse analysis can take the formalist's concern for word order and affective stylistics, and reinvest it in a study of text grammar, text processing, and culturally derived meaning. In an era of New Historicism and ideological commitments (feminist, Marxist, Lacanian), this kind of study offers a middle ground between an elite aesthetics and a respect for readership in a broad sense. We may not need the technical language, but we can use the standpoint.

But why discourse analysis instead of, for instance, reader-response criticism? The crudity of the "responses" captured by my experiment would dismay a Stanley Fish or a Wolfgang Iser. Besides, I am dealing with variously trained readers. The "informed" reader is not a standard in my experiment, but simply a variant. There is also the issue of first readings versus rereadings. Trained readers are rereaders; my study assumed a first-reading experience, overruling, perhaps, the very kinds of responses trained readers have been taught (and prefer) to give.[13] One person, among the most sophisticated readers in my sample, said she had not even considered preclosure points in the body of the text (the "inner-shell" points) because, as a reader of short fiction in particular, she privileged "the whole" and resisted preclosure.

Good readers ignore preclosure. They do so on principle. In asking readers to "break training," I was asking them to deconstruct not so much the web of language (the focus of hermeneutical studies), not so

13. For relevant discussions, see Menakhem Perry, "Literary Dynamics: How the Order of a Text Creates Its Meanings," *Poetics Today*, I (Autumn, 1979), 35–64, 311–61, and Armine Kotin Mortimer's essay in this volume.

much the joints of narrative (the focus of narratology), but the habits of academic reading. In other words, I was short-circuiting, if not subverting, the materials of reader-response criticism. I was asking readers to look for minimal, short-term "storyness," at the expense of duration and complexity. I was making primitives of them.

Does that mean I was making children of them? Let's look, for a moment, at some of the work done in the last decade on the developmental psychology of reading. Much of it rests on a surprising change of view in the field of psychology itself. R. L. Gregory makes the point that "organisms are controlled by fictions rather than stimuli." Even on the neurological level, "storying"—making predictive scenarios—controls adaption, survival. And according to James Britton, "it requires an act of the imagination to construct any situation in which we actually find ourselves." [14] In other words, storytelling is not only a recreation, an art, a social activity, but a primary mode of cognition. A fundamental way of managing experience is to encode it as story. Recognizing story is therefore perhaps the most basic, least sophisticated, least *literary*, of our responses to fiction.

It is not news that stories may be expressions of fundamental drives or ways of interacting with the world. In the late fifties, Randall Jarrell defined *story* in Freudian terms as "a wish, or a truth, or a wish modified by a truth." What he did not say, and what I'd like to add, is that "storying" is a way of "chunking" fictively represented experience for purposes *not* just of self-expression, *not* just of vicarious living, but primarily of cognitive management. Here I am following closely D. W. Harding's view of literature's cultural function. He rejects the idea that literature offers mainly opportunities for emotional identification with characters (the basis for much teaching) and says, instead, that "in entering into the 'virtual experience' of influential works of literature, a child is offered a flow and recoil of sympathies that accords with the culture pattern in which he is growing up." [15]

Elsewhere, Harding explains the position of the reader as an "onlooker" who maintains "a non-participant relation [to the contents of

14. R. L. Gregory, "Psychology: Towards a Science of Fiction," in Margaret Meek, Aidan Warlow, and Griselda Barton (eds.), *The Cool Web: The Pattern of Children's Reading* (London, 1977), 396, and James Britton, "The Role of Fantasy," *ibid.*, 41, with the permission of The Bodley Head.

15. Randall Jarrell, "Stories," in Charles E. May (ed.), *Short Story Theories* (Athens, Ohio, 1976), 32; D. W. Harding, "Response to Literature," in Meek, Warlow, and Barton (eds.), *The Cool Web*, 379.

a story-world] which yet includes an active evaluative attitude."[16] Tracking the "flow and recoil," or marking the oscillation of attitudes in any great detail, might lead us to a sentence-level, reader-response concern with affective stylistics. On the other hand, identifying attitudes in larger contexts brings us back to the way we implement frames. In talking about the socializing function of literature, Harding seems to be saying that readers not only use frames in reading but learn, or at least reinforce, frames *through* reading.

As we have seen, frames may determine not only what "facts" we do or do not recognize (for example, Aunt Lympy's blackness) but also what issues we think are engaged (for example, society's view of working women). We could say that "storyness" is itself a frame, though I would argue that it is more aptly described as a cognitive mode in which frames are deployed. It is a primary mode of "chunking." "Storyness" inheres in a chunk of virtual experience (or a segment of text) that can be perceived as modeled by (not necessarily imitating) a unit of actual experience in which well-being is at stake—that is, may be either lost or gained (or sustained).

Such a definition keeps the focus on cognitive management, without moving too far away from either the expressive language of Jarrell or the technical language of discourse analysis. "Storyness" often enough inheres in a rhythm of excitation and release to echo the language of "organic" approaches. It can also be said to inhere, at least most of the time, in an event, an "E_1" or "E_2," to quote the grammarians. In the case of "Aunt Lympy's Interference," "storyness" inheres in those segments of the text beginning with $S/1$ and ending with any one of the preclosure points.

Let us return to the four traits shared by all of the interior preclosure points: location at the end of a paragraph, correlation with a shift in physical place, correlation with the end of a debate, and correlation with a bent toward one of Melitte's choices as a woman. The end of a paragraph is, of course, a visual marker of closure. Change of location (requiring a new "scene") and end of verbal exchange (delimiting a "dialogue") are old conventions of drama. No one of these markers, by itself, is enough to signal "storyness," though the presence of all three close together is highly reinforcing to the sense of "storyness." The really operant feature here is the fourth—that unit

16. D. W. Harding, "Psychological Processes in the Reading of Fiction," in Meek, Warlow, and Barton (eds.), *The Cool Web*, 59.

of virtual experience in which we can see well-being either gained or lost in a definitive way.

The interest in Chopin's story is in seeing the conflicting options for, and kinds of, well-being considered. As the traits listed above reveal, Chopin has written a conventionally structured story. In doing the experiment again, I would use an unconventional story, one in which, for example, it is harder to recognize the E1's and E2's. I would look for one in which fewer markers reinforce one another. For now, however, I can say that preclosure choices in Chopin's story do reflect the notion of "storyness."

And so I return to the somewhat subversive results of my study. I wanted to deconstruct not the story but the reading of story. I wanted to surprise that primitive sense of story in the act of underwriting the reading of a literary text. Yet there was shockingly small agreement on these "simple" recognitions. Does that mean a primitive sense of "storyness" is, paradoxically, far from universal? Does it mean that "literary" reading, even on beginning levels, dulls or disorients that sense? Is there any way to strengthen that sense, and is there any point in doing so? Granted its limits, I think my study answers yes to all of these questions.

Certainly the short story form, with its oral, tale-ended beginnings, still draws much of its peculiar force from its primitive connection with a mode of knowing. Under the present educational system, we misname or abuse the sense of "storyness" when we talk only of plot; we forget or underrate it when we privilege either New Critical or New Historical approaches exclusively. I do not mean that we should teach the sense of "storyness" per se; if the ability to "chunk" stories in this way exists at all, it is already learned by the time students read Chopin—or any other literature *as* literature. Rather, we may want to invoke that sense, respect it, and build on and from it.

Those whom our system identifies as creative writers, those who have tried to make stories, may, through that process, have come round again to what the untrained reader still relies on—a way of configuring experience as story. Perhaps that is why the story writers in my sample seemed to have such a surprising degree of correlation with the naïve readers in the group. Again, I am not suggesting that we teach story writing in aid of story reading. Rather, we may want to keep retying discussions of theme to decisions of structure (how differently would the story "mean" if it ended here, if it began there, if this happened before that, if this were left out). Above all, we may want to keep our students asking what is at stake, and for whom.

Many people have noticed that some of the most influential statements about the short story come from short story writers. A kind of practitioners' criticism coexists with, and may dominate, the body of formal, academic criticism. Much of what these writers have to say is impressionistic; as they attempt to get back to fundamentals, their statements verge on the ineffable, because elemental "storyness" is pre-effable, centered not in language but in a cognitive strategy. Folk-tales, anonymous and conventionalized, have their roots in the un-spoken and unspeakable. Modern stories thrust their language upon us, in all the signatures of style—signing our presence, our desire to be well. Poe, Anderson, Welty, Bowen—when it comes to the short story, we turn to them, to the makers and shapers. Perhaps that is because we have not yet found a critical vocabulary that is simple enough.

ARMINE KOTIN MORTIMER

Second Stories

> It is the *excess* of the suggested meaning—it is the rendering this the
> upper instead of the undercurrent of the theme—which turns into
> prose . . . the so-called poetry of the so-called transcendentalists.
> —EDGAR ALLAN POE, "The Philosophy of Composition"

Poetry is not alone in having an undercurrent of suggested meaning
that risks platitudes as soon as it is exposed. I have been collecting
examples of short stories that owe their "wow" to the careful embedding of a second story in the first.[1] Indeed, the action of these stories
on the reader is such that the reader is actively solicited to recognize
that undercurrent, encoded in diverse ways, and in so doing to create
a second story that is not told outright. The second story may be in
addition to the first, occurring after it; it may be prior or simultaneous; it may remain quite hidden or erupt full-blown into the first story
(Katherine Mansfield's "Bliss" or Edith Wharton's "Roman Fever"). In
the most frustrating examples, it never comes to light, though it leaves
clues (Maupassant's "En Voyage" and Barbey d'Aurevilly's "Le Plus
Bel Amour de Don Juan"). It constitutes a complete narrative, and it is

---

1. Portions of this essay overlap with "Second Stories: The Example of 'Mr. Know-
All,'" *Studies in Short Fiction*, XXV (1988), 307–14. I am borrowing the notion of the
"wow" from Ernest Hemingway and adapting it to my discovery of second stories.
Hemingway was referring to that clotural tag that neatly wraps up an anecdote, and
that the reader expects: "*Old lady:* And is that all of the story? Is there not to be what we
called in my youth a wow at the end? [*Narrator:*] Ah, Madame, it is years since I added
the wow to the end of a story. Are you sure you are unhappy if the wow is omitted? *Old
lady:* Frankly, sir, I prefer the wow" (*Death in the Afternoon* [New York, 1932], 182, reprinted with permission of the Executors of the Ernest Hemingway Estate, Jonathan
Cape, Ltd., and Charles Scribner's Sons).

not secondary. In all cases, the second story is necessary to the intelligibility of the first.

To distinguish this narratological construction from other forms is not always easy. It is not a simple *mise en abyme,* in which an embedded story reflects on the outside story, because in that construction a second story is not told; for the same reason, it is different from the frame of a narrative that also tells a story. Nor is this a matter of metaphoric treatment of the plot, or allegory, in which the reader may well treat the entire story as symbolic and translate it to another dimension. Detective activity, which does in a sense characterize the reader of second stories, is aimed at uncovering the first story in the case of mystery stories; they do not usually have second stories as well. Many stories with second-story construction also have surprise endings, but not all stories with surprise endings have second stories. And fantastic stories, in which the plot may seem to refer to another story that is made to account for the unexplainable phenomena, differ in that the other story *never happened.* Finally, unlike an open-ended structure, or a threshold closure, the second-story construction does not leave the outcome up in the air; quite to the contrary, the action of the second story often brings closure to the first. This construction is particular to short stories, although it can also enter as an element into parts of longer narratives. Translated to the scale of a novel, however, this narratological device would lose some of its definition.

Ernest Hemingway had a utopian view of the writer as one who must know everything, the better to omit things: "If a writer of prose knows enough about what he is writing about he may omit things that he knows and the reader, if the writer is writing truly enough, will have a feeling of those things as strongly as though the writer had stated them." He meant, of course, knowledge about things like marlins and bullfights ("A writer who omits things because he does not know them only makes hollow places in his writing"), and he called this the principle of the iceberg: "The dignity of movement of an iceberg is due to only one-eighth of it being above water." [2] And I would add its beauty and awesomeness, its fascination and attraction, and also its risks. Borrowing Hemingway's term, and adapting it to the second-story writer and reader, I would say that the writer of second-story constructions submerges things because he knows them, leav-

2. *Ibid.*, 192.

ing the tip of the iceberg as a clue that there is something more to reckon with, that there is more than meets the eye; the reader must know that icebergs are mostly hidden, and must know almost as much as the writer. The writer does something to give the reader a feeling for that story just as surely as if the writer had stated it. The reader's role is to complete the hidden part of the story by using whatever clues the writer has given and by matching the writer's degree of cultural competence, the writer's knowledge. We will now look at some examples of second-story construction, all taken from Maupassant, and then consider the implications for theories of reading.

"La Chambre 11" (1884)

Wife of a provincial magistrate, Marguerite Amandon, whose life is above reproach, "savait . . . trouver de l'argent pour les pauvres et distraire les jeunes gens par mille moyens" [knew . . . how to find money for the poor and amuse young people in thousands of ways].[3] Under a discreet demeanor, this "petite provinciale délurée, avec son air de bourgeoise alerte, sa candeur trompeuse de pensionnaire, son sourire qui ne dit rien, et ses bonnes petites passions adroites, mais tenaces" [cunning little woman from the provinces, with her brisk bourgeois manner, her deceptive schoolgirl's candor, her smile that said nothing, and her good little deft but tenacious passions] hides feminine ruses more inventive than "toutes les Parisiennes réunies" [all the women of Paris combined] (394). It is the point of this story to reveal how she satisfies her tastes without awakening the least small-town scandal.

Mme Amandon's invention is to find a lover in the army and keep him three years, the time the regiment stays in town: "Dès qu'un nouveau régiment arrivait à Perthuis-le-Long, elle prenait des renseignements sur tous les officiers entre trente et quarante ans—car avant trente ans on n'est pas encore discret. Après quarante ans, on faiblit souvent" [As soon as a new regiment arrived in Perthuis-le-Long, she would inquire about all the officers between thirty and forty—for one is not yet discreet before thirty. After forty, one frequently slackens] (394). With sureness of purpose and practicality of

3. Louis Forestier (ed.), *Contes et Nouvelles [de] Maupassant* (2 vols.; Paris, 1974, 1979), II, 393, hereafter cited parenthetically by page and, if necessary, volume number in the text. Translations are my own.

method, she makes her selection, invites him to a ball, and, "en val-
sant, entraînée par le mouvement rapide, étourdie par l'ivresse de la
danse, elle se serrait contre lui comme pour se donner, et lui étreig-
nait la main d'une passion nerveuse et continue. S'il ne comprenait
pas, ce n'était qu'un sot, et elle passait au suivant, classé au numéro
deux dans les cartons de son désir" [while waltzing, carried away
by the rapid movement, intoxicated by the frenzy of the dance, she
would press herself against him as if to give herself to him, and would
squeeze his hand with a nervous and continuous passion. If he did
not understand, he was just a fool, and she would go on to the next
one, filed under number two in the folders of her desire] (395). With
equal practicality, she has taken a room in a hotel, where she meets
her chosen officer: "Elle disait, en dînant, devant les domestiques: 'Je
vais ce soir à l'Association des ceintures de flanelle pour les vieillards
paralytiques.' Et elle sortait vers huit heures, entrait à l'Association,
en ressortait aussitôt" [She would say, while dining, in front of the
servants, 'Tonight I am going to the Association of Flannel Belts for
Paralytic Old Men.' And she would go out about eight o'clock, enter
the Association, and come right out again] (396). Disguising herself as
a little maid under the suggestive name of Mlle Clarisse, she would
make her way to "la chambre 11" and the satisfaction of her "senses."
This continues eight years without a problem until, inevitably, given
that a story can be made of it, she is discovered.

That disclosure is the very result of her discretion: "Jamais Mlle
Clarisse ne venait à ses rendez-vous deux soirs de suite, jamais, étant
trop fine et trop prudente pour cela" [Never would Mlle Clarisse
come to her rendezvous two nights in a row, never, being too clever
and too prudent for that] (397), so the hotelkeeper sometimes uses
her room the day following an assignation. But one July when "Madame avait des ardeurs" [Madame is hot with ardor] and her husband
is out of town, she plans to come back a second night. The same heat
has brought cholera to town, and a traveler allowed to rest in her
hotel room dies there on the very day Mme Amandon rejoins her
lover. Intending to remove the body under cover of darkness, the
hotelkeeper leaves it in the bed, where our provincial *belle-de-jour*
finds it and mistakes it for her sleeping lover: "Une minute, mon
chéri, j'arrive" [Just a minute, darling, I'm coming] (398). Dressed
only in her "chemise de soie rouge" and her "bas de soie noire à jour"
[red silk slip and black silk net stockings], she jumps into bed, "en
saisissant à pleins bras et en baisant à pleines lèvres, pour le réveiller

brusquement, le cadavre glacé du voyageur!" [clasping fully in her arms and kissing fully on his lips, in order to wake him up instantly, the glacial cadaver of the traveler!] (399). At last Mme Amandon's prudence and discretion fail her, as she runs screaming into the hall, arousing the entire hotel, to fall finally into her lover's arms crying: "Sauvez-moi, sauvez-moi, Gontran. . . . On a tué quelqu'un dans notre chambre" [Save me, save me, Gontran. . . . Someone has been killed in our room] (399).

When the police commissioner arrives, "[il] leur rendit la liberté, mais [il] ne fut pas discret. Le mois suivant, M. le Premier Amandon recevait un avancement avec une nouvelle résidence" [(he) gave them their liberty, but (he) was not discreet. The next month, Magistrate Amandon received an advancement with a new residence] (400). On this elliptic last sentence ends the tale, thereby purporting to accomplish the intention of the opening sentences of the story, in which there is the mere hint of a frame. There, a knowledgeable but unnamed narrator in dialogue with an unnamed narratee offers to supply the missing explanation of the magistrate's promotion out of Perthuis-le-Long: "Comment! vous ne savez pas pourquoi on a déplacé M. le premier président Amandon? —Non, pas du tout. —Lui non plus, d'ailleurs, ne l'a jamais su" ["What! you don't know why presiding magistrate Amandon was relocated?" "No, not at all." "Neither has he ever known, for that matter"] (393). The last statement, upon reflection, is an enigma worth recalling at the end of the tale. For it is clear that the answer to the initial question—why the magistrate was relocated—is a further riddle, to which only a second story will supply the correct answer. Inserted neatly between the "indiscretion" of the police commissioner, which would be the first line of the second story, and the promotion and new residence of Amandon, its outcome, the second story is one the narratee tells himself.

In truth, only an indiligent reader would fail to fill in the missing lines of the second story, which establishes the connection between the downfall of the wife and the elevation of the husband. So common a story is it that our narrator need only give its opening and its closure; he assumes that the narratee will competently supply the rest (although it must be admitted that seven out of eight modern-day seminar students who read this story needed a short course in feminine ruses and masculine politics of the past): Mme Amandon has surrendered to pressure from high places—if she has not, indeed, offered herself, for the police commissioner's leniency had to be rewarded, and the receiver of his indiscretion placated.

Beyond these repayments of sorts, one has to adduce that Mme Amandon has so well pleased her husband's boss that he has rewarded her by promoting him. Although the details (the how, the where, the when) are completely up to us, the competent reader must at least acknowledge the existence of the system of exchange practiced by women for whom a husband's career and advancement justify any measures. Such a reader must be learned in the cynical literary tradition that presents this reality as one of the common variants on feminine strategy or masculine ascendancy. This dialogue from a Balzac story, about an elegantly dressed, unknown young woman, succinctly translates that tradition to an aristocratic salon: "Comment, Martial, tu n'as pas deviné la femme de quelque sous-préfet de la Lippe ou de la Dyle qui vient essayer de faire un préfet de son mari? —Oh! il le sera" ["What, Martial, haven't you guessed that it's the wife of some subprefect of Lippe or Dyle who has come to make her husband into a prefect?" "Oh, he'll be that all right"].[4] It is an old story and one whose multiple variations do nothing to obscure the essential fact that what a woman can offer will be rewarded. And in this case, the reward is of stature, testifying at least to Madame's talents.

The fact that the narrator acts as if it is completely unnecessary to add the details of the second story only underscores how obvious it is and that it is well-enough begun with the short phrase indicating that the police commissioner was not discreet. With that beginning, the second story suggested here seems to be the only one possible or, more precisely, the only one that the narratee can possibly understand, retroactively, after the ending ("Le mois suivant, M. le Premier Amandon recevait un avancement avec une nouvelle résidence" [The next month, presiding magistrate Amandon received an advancement with a new residence]). The narratological implication is that only one kind of story has that kind of ending, so common and well known as to require no recounting, for the narration leaves the main point of the story, the entire answer to the opening question, in the second-story mode. In other words, for a complete answer to why Amandon was promoted one must supply the second story. It is probably *because* the events of that story are so predictable that it is a second story, and not a first, for as a first story it would be dull reading— hardly a story worth telling. Thus it has its piquant flavor, or its

---

4. Honoré de Balzac, "La Paix du ménage," in P.-G. Castex *et al.* (eds.), *La Comédie humaine* (12 vols.; Paris, 1976), II, 99. My translation.

"wow," only because it is a second story, which stands in a particular relation to the first.

Because of the second-story construction, a good deal of authority is placed in the hands of the narratee, an obvious double for the reader. With that authority, we can devise the scenarios suggested by the police commissioner's two actions: giving Mme Amandon and her lover their freedom, and revealing his discovery to the unnamed person of power. Mme Amandon will have instantly recognized the terms of the contract offered by the first of these acts; the second she can anticipate. In that sense she is an excellent reader. For the actual reader of the story, however, a question that may never be satisfactorily answered is who makes the first gesture engaging the system of exchange that is the necessary prelude to the promotion the following month. The indications provided in the first story require only that Amandon never learn of "la chambre 11," so that we must assume discretion by whoever is in a position to promote him—but this identity cannot be ascertained. The very rapid ending and the absence of any further commentary, in particular by the narratee, require the reader's reconstruction and completion of the story by the insertion of the second story, so that the closure of the first story depends entirely on the reader's skill in "writing" the scenes with the police commissioner and the magistrate's boss, and on the desire for completion.

The second story is completely embedded in the first, and it is necessary to the complete intelligibility of the first. The discovery of the second story, parallel to the discovery of the first, requires a competent reader willing to shed his innocence to achieve this end, for in order to find a secret, one must first believe that a secret exists and that it is secret because it is unavowable. Thus we may perhaps affirm that any second story will refer to something better left unsaid—an adulterous love affair, murder, incest, perversion.

The competence called for here might well be considered a particular case of Jonathan Culler's "literary competence," or even the "semantic competence" Stanley Fish asks for.[5] Yet little more is demanded of the reader than to be guided by Mme Amandon's own competence; nor is there much to say about the tip of the iceberg here. The second

5. Jonathan Culler, *Structuralist Poetics: Structuralism, Linguistics, and the Study of Literature* (Ithaca, 1975), Chap. 6; Stanley Fish, "Literature in the Reader," in Jane Tompkins (ed.), *Reader Response Criticism: From Formalism to Post-Structuralism* (Baltimore, 1980), 84–85.

story functions as if it were self-evident, and most readers will be in complete agreement about it. Indeed, "La Chambre 11" is a straightforward example of second-story construction. The "wow" in this case exists only because of the second-story construction, because the reader enjoys proving his competence and skill, and because the real point of the story lies not in why Amandon was promoted, even though that is the point the narrator claims to be making, but in evoking and engaging the second-story tradition and the reader's competence in it. Our amusement and pleasure lie more in the detection of the hidden second story than in the subject of that story.

"Un Million" (1882)

"Un Million" calls for a similar competence and stands in tandem to "La Chambre 11." Here a young couple, the Bonnins, must produce a child in order to inherit a million dollars from M. Bonnin's aunt, but Bonnin's most laborious efforts only prove his sterility. So ill does he become that he is obliged to abandon the attempt. A fellow employee, Frédéric Morel, "le harcelait d'allusions, de mots grivois, se faisant fort, disait-il, de le faire hériter en vingt minutes" [badgers him with allusions, with bawdy words, boasting to turn him into an heir in twenty minutes] (I, 615). Bonnin comes to see how a wife might adroitly help her husband along, and he makes mysterious allusions to "femmes d'employés qui avaient su faire la situation de leur mari" [employees' wives who had known how to get their husbands a position] (617), giving the example of a man who has "une femme intelligente. . . . Elle a su plaire au chef de division, et elle obtient tout ce qu'elle veut. Dans la vie il faut savoir s'arranger pour n'être pas dupé par les circonstances" [an intelligent wife. . . . She was able to make herself attractive to the division chief, and she gets everything she asks for. In life, one has to know how to arrange things so one won't be the victim of circumstances] (618). The last sentence is like a maxim, a statement of the common sense, the cultural know-how, that makes these mysterious allusions into a law of "life" as seen by employees. Knowing how to "s'arranger" may well include adultery if that will prevent one from being the victim of unfair circumstance.

These lines are followed by three questions: "Que voulait-il dire au juste? Que comprit-elle? Que se passa-t-il?" [What exactly did he mean? What did she understand? What happened next?] (618). Through them the narrator marks his distance from the second story:

he will tell us neither what kind of social sense Bonnin was alluding to nor what his wife does. These questions are the narratological index of the existence of a second story, again "unavowable" because adulterous and second because untold, though understood without difficulty by anyone sharing that social sense. These falsely ingenuous questions mark the narrator's explicit refusal to tell the second story. Like rhetorical questions, they point to their simple answers unproblematically. We successfully read between Bonnin's lines, just as Mme Bonnin does to determine what to do; like this good and faithful wife, we acquire competence in the cultural context Bonnin has first learned of, and has allusively passed on to his wife. For not only does Mme Bonnin become pregnant, but she succeeds in remaining a good wife, and this is the delightful point of the story's closure.

The tale might have ended with the couple rich but unhappy, for the child is clearly Morel's. Many another Maupassant tale has thus doomed a marriage. Instead, Mme Bonnin adroitly reveals both the origin of the baby and the proof that she will never again commit adultery, thereby concluding the story on a moment of union:

> Or, un soir, comme M. Bonnin rentrait chez lui où devait dîner son ami Frédéric Morel, sa femme lui dit d'un ton simple: "Je viens de prier notre ami Frédéric de ne plus mettre les pieds ici, il a été inconvenant avec moi." Il la regarda une seconde avec un sourire reconnaissant dans l'oeil, puis il ouvrit les bras; elle s'y jeta et ils s'embrassèrent longtemps, longtemps comme deux bons petits époux, bien tendres, bien unis, bien honnêtes.
>
> [Then, one evening, as M. Bonnin came home, where his friend Frédéric Morel was to dine, his wife said to him in a simple tone, "I have just asked our friend Frédéric not to set foot here again, he has been improper (*inconvenant*) with me." He looked at her for a second with a grateful smile in his eyes, then opened his arms; she flung herself into them and they kissed for a long, long time, like two good little spouses, very tender, very united, very honest.] (618–19)

Mme Bonnin's simple sentence, with the understated *inconvenant*, "tells" the second story in retrospect, just as Bonnin's mysterious allusions "told" it in prospective narration. Bonnin's grateful smile, implying his forgiveness, also furnishes the index of his successful reading of her second story, which remains even for the characters a second story. Here the second story that is untold is essentially similar to the one in "La Chambre 11," at least to the extent that a wife obtains something good for her husband through an otherwise immoral act. What is interesting is the different reasons why the stories are second. What in "La Chambre 11" is treated as so common and well known as to require only a beginning and an ending, that any competent reader will enjoy filling in, is treated in "Un Million" as if it were morally reprehensible, not of course to Maupassant's readers, who on the contrary are amused, but to the *bons petits époux*, who prefer to keep the story second.

In "Un Million" the characters themselves are involved in providing the clues to the second story, and not just the narrator; this difference with "La Chambre 11" is significant. It would not be far-fetched to claim that the couple's happiness depends on their shared competence as readers; they are tenderly united, *honnêtes*, and *bons époux* at the end only because each has read with equal skill the second story alluded to by the other. No such shared competence marks the Amandons' marriage, in which the second story is kept entirely secret from the husband. There, the reader's only guide is the narratee faintly evoked in the opening few lines, the one who is curious to know why Amandon was promoted. Here, in contrast, both spouses are our models and, indeed, know more, in a sense, than the narrator.

"La Serre" (1883)

Just who knows a second story is treated comically in "La Serre." Mme Lerebour, middle-aged, seems dissatisfied with her husband and has become increasingly bitter and discontented; in bed, she makes veiled reproaches that Lerebour fails to understand and that only make him feel more guilty, and about which he can do nothing. One night, hearing a noise, Lerebour goes out to investigate and returns forty-five minutes later, laughing as he hasn't laughed for years: at the far end of the garden, in a greenhouse, the maid Céleste has rendezvoused with her lover. Significantly, all Lerebour can bring himself to tell his wife is "Si tu savais ce que . . . ce que . . . ce que j'ai vu . . ." [If you knew what . . . what . . . what I saw . . .] (I, 859). Sex is obviously not an open topic of conversation between the spouses. That, of course, is what the reader is meant to understand from Mme Lerebour's veiled references to her dissatisfaction.

The second story is simple: through the glass of the greenhouse Lerebour watched Céleste making love with her lover. This leads to a dramatic change in the Lerebours' sex life. Madame stops her bitter reproaches, and Monsieur loses weight. Furthermore, Céleste gets a pay raise, for the spouses often creep furtively out into the garden on clear nights: "Et ils restent là blottis l'un près de l'autre contre le vitrage comme s'ils regardaient au-dedans une chose étrange et pleine d'intérêt" [And there they stay, pressed one next to the other against the glass as if they were watching, inside, something strange and full of interest] (860). Maupassant's mocking irony at his prosaic characters provides much of the fun in this story, but it is the gesture of withholding knowledge that puts the second story into play. At no time does Lerebour tell his wife just what he saw that first night, although it has turned a souring marriage into "le rebours"—the opposite—of what it was. His teasingly repeated "Si tu savais! Oh! si tu savais!" [If you knew! Oh! if you knew!] (860) even after Mme Lerebour no longer has the slightest doubt what he saw—has indeed seen for herself—calls attention to the fact that he alone *knows* what happened that night; she had to guess it from these few words and especially from his laughter and his subsequent lovemaking. Thus he makes of her a reader of a second story, and in a particularly concrete way her happiness depends on her skill as a reader.

In a similar manner, Céleste guesses something different has happened the next morning when, the couple failing to appear for breakfast, she is astonished to see them billing and cooing in bed. Here the reader follows Céleste's guide in supplying the remainder of the second story—the new and enduring sexual relations between husband and wife. This is not difficult—neither for the two female characters nor for us. This is a case in which a character exploits a superior knowledge of a second story to reach a satisfying conclusion—for Mme Lerebour as well as for the reader—for it is by playfully withholding the details of what he knows that Lerebour entices his wife to pleasures she has not enjoyed before. Thus the story thematizes the parallel pleasure that an author prepares for a reader by withholding the details of a story that remains second. We may have here a clue to the motives for second-story construction.

"Décoré!" (1883)

In "Décoré!" Jeanne Sacrement achieves a quite opposite purpose by withholding a second story from her husband. The theme is again like that of "La Chambre 11," and the untold story is nearly identical: Jeanne obtains a decoration for her husband by sleeping with a man in a position to grant it. Sacrement's single passion in his otherwise foolish, idle, and otiose life is to obtain the Legion of Honor, and to this effect he asks his wife to speak of him to the deputy M. Rosselin, himself decorated, "sans qu'on sût quels motifs lui avaient valu cette distinction" [without anyone's knowing what reasons had earned him this distinction] (I, 1068). This she does. The deputy takes quite an interest in Sacrement, gives him all sorts of practical advice, and comes to lunch frequently.

In order to have some sort of accomplishment that might deserve recognition, Sacrement has taken to writing pamphlets on educational reform (for example, "L'instruction des enfants par les yeux" ["The Education of Children Through the Eyes"]), which all go unnoticed, except by Rosselin, who obtains for his friend a special mission. The "comité des travaux historiques" [Committee on Historical Works] sends Sacrement on a tour of libraries throughout France, where he rummages through dusty books and endures the hatred of the librarians. Finding himself one night in Rouen, he decides to take the nine o'clock train to Paris and surprise his wife. He lets himself quietly into the house, then finds he has to knock on her bedroom door, which is locked. Jeanne eventually opens the door: "Quelle surprise! quelle joie!" But on a chair is an overcoat that poor Sacrement must recognize is not his own, because there is a red ribbon in the buttonhole!

For the terrified Jeanne, there is only one way out of this predicament, and that is to tell Sacrement that he has been decorated, that it was to be a surprise, that it would be announced in a month to six weeks, and that she had prepared this new overcoat for him. It is Rosselin who has obtained this singular honor for him, she adds. When a card falls from the pocket bearing Rosselin's name, it only confirms what she has just said: "Tu vois bien" ["You see!"] (1070). There follows the wonderful punch line: "Huit jours plus tard l'*Officiel* annonçait que M. Sacrement était nommé chevalier de la Légion d'honneur, pour services exceptionnels" [Eight days later the *Officiel* announced that M. Sacrement was named chevalier in the Legion of Honor, for exceptional services] (1070). It has taken Mme Sacrement only a week to obtain the little red ribbon, and the "services exceptionnels" are clearly those she has offered!

Several details, however, are not immediately obvious, on first reading. A careless or rapid reader will not pay particular attention to the frequency of Rosselin's lunchtime visits or register the fact that it is Rosselin himself who has obtained the library research mission for his "friend," or reflect on the reasons behind that generous action or the importance of the incidentally mentioned decoration ("d'ailleurs") that Rosselin possesses. The significance of this tidbit of information becomes clear to the reader only when the overcoat is discovered in the bedroom, at which point the reader's delight stems from the knowledge of the truth Mme Sacrement is doing her best to disguise. Furthermore, the process of the narration is such that the crucial scene in the bedroom is told entirely through Sacrement's naïve vision, thus making of the reader a knowledgeable spectator of his discomfiture:

> Elle dut avoir grand-peur, car il l'entendit sauter du lit et parler seule comme dans un rêve. Puis elle courut à son cabinet de toilette, l'ouvrit et le referma, traversa plusieurs fois sa chambre dans une course rapide, nu-pieds, secouant les meubles dont les verreries sonnaient.

> [She must have been very frightened, for he heard her jump out of bed and talk to herself as if in a dream. Then she ran to her closet (*cabinet de toilette*), opened it and closed it again, crossed the room several times on the run, barefooted, shaking the furniture whose glasswork tinkled.] (1069)

That the single most damning proof, Rosselin's calling card, should function for Sacrement as the verification of his wife's story, rather than as the confirmation of the second story the reader has by now successfully narrated, only lends a greater pleasure of discovery to the reader's effort. The reader, of course, knows more than the poor husband. It is partly this skillful distribution of knowledge that makes "Décoré!" more amusing in its conclusion than "La Chambre 11." It is also less subtle, but who would think to complain?

"Bombard" (1884)

In "Bombard" the art and authority of the second-story reader are put seriously to the test, for the elliptical ending is considerably more enigmatic than the one in "La Chambre 11." So obscure is the enigma, indeed, that lacking the account of the second story, one finds the first inconclusive and thus nothing more than a somewhat whimsical portrait of two amusing character types, a lazy, wily Norman womanizer and a demanding, rich English widow.

Simon Bombard, who found any mental effort beyond his powers, "se l'était coulée douce" [had been taking it easy], hoping that his red whiskers, flourishing vitality, and "élégance tapageuse de provincial en fête" [noisy elegance of the provincial on holiday] (II, 365) would make it possible for him to find the wife whose fortune would guarantee more of the same till the end of his days. And so he does: a caricature of an Englishwoman, "assez grande, un peu maigre, l'Anglaise audacieuse dont les voyages et les circonstances ont fait une espèce d'homme" [rather tall, somewhat thin, the audacious Englishwoman of whom trips and circumstance have made a kind of man] (367) and one whose wealth can compensate for a certain lack of charm. They marry. "Mme Bombard jeune n'était plus jeune, assurément, et sa fraîcheur avait subi des atteintes; mais elle avait une manière d'exiger les choses qui faisait qu'on ne pouvait les lui refuser" [Mme Bombard the younger was assuredly no longer young, and her freshness had suffered some attacks; but she had a way of demanding things that made it impossible to refuse] (368). Some of these demands are conjugal: "Elle disait . . . 'Oh! Simon, nô allons nô coucher,' qui faisait aller Simon vers le lit comme un chien à qui on ordonne 'à la niche'" [She would say . . . "Oh! Simon, we ah goin' to bed," which made Simon go toward the bed like a dog that one orders "to your place"] (368). Imperious but calm, never raising her voice, never irritated or hurt, she speaks with a tone that admits of no refusal.

Clearly, for a man who considers that "la vie était faite uniquement pour bambocher et plaisanter" [life was made only for joking and fooling around] (365), this is not the woman to satisfy Bombard's desires, and with the means in his pocket he easily finds others. "Mme Bombard s'en aperçut, sans qu'il devinât à quoi" [Mme Bombard found out, without his being able to tell how] (368), and she announces one day that they are moving to another town. In their new home Bombard conceives a plan worthy of the calculating Norman: he hires a maid whom he carefully prepares for his intentions. While Mme Bombard retires early, Simon plays whist at the Café du Commerce till exactly 9:30 P.M. Victorine, the maid, waits in the corridor, on the steps of the vestibule, in the dark, and Bombard has at most five minutes: "Mais enfin cinq minutes de temps en temps suffisaient à son ardeur, et il glissait un louis, car il était large en ses plaisirs, dans la main de la servante" [But then, five minutes from time to time was sufficient for his ardor, and he would slip a *louis*, for he was generous in his pleasures, into the hand of the servant] (369). To compensate for the imperfection of this arrangement, Bombard has the solitary pleasure of fooling his wife: "Fichue dedans, la patronne" [Foiled her again, the boss] (370).

In less than a page, two final scenes bring a denouement to this comedy of manners. One night Victorine seems "plus vive, plus animée que d'habitude" [more lively, more animated than usual] (370), and Bombard dallies all of ten minutes, only to find, to his horror, that his wife is not in bed. But as she returns, she calmly explains she had gone to the kitchen for a glass of water. The next day at lunch, however, when Victorine serves the chops,

> Mme Bombard lui tendit un louis . . . et lui dit . . . "Tené, ma fille, voilà vingt francs dont j'avé privé vô, hier au soir. Je vô les rendé." Et la fille interdite prit la pièce d'or qu'elle regardait d'un air stupide, tandis que Bombard, effaré, ouvrait sur sa femme des yeux énormes.
>
> [Mme Bombard handed her a *louis* . . . and said: "Here, girl, here ah the twenty francs I deprived you of last night. I'm givin' them back." And the speechless girl took the gold coin, which she looked at stupidly while Bombard, aghast, stared at his wife with enormous eyes.] (370)

These are the last lines of the story, and they pose the enigma in definite economic terms—a payment or compensation that was waylaid is returned to its proper recipient. Since the conditions of payment are quite precise—last night; twenty francs; Mme Bombard preventing Victorine from getting the money, and now returning it—they must correspond to some equally precise situation, which the reader has only to ferret out to bring about the closure of the tale. This the reader does by "writing" a comical retelling of the night before: in the darkened vestibule, Bombard has failed to recognize his own wife, who has sent Victorine away and taken her place on the steps.

This story was in the dark. To bring it to light (as the French say, *tirer au clair*) is to adopt the role of detective. The reader must bring to its reading not only a superior recall but also a store of knowledge of a specific kind. One must remember not only the mentioned obscurity of the corridor but also the exceptional animation of "Victorine," Mme Bombard's absence from her bed, her calmly demanding manners in general and in conjugal matters in particular, her uncanny ability to discover Bombard's infidelities, the fact that she never raises her voice, and so on, not to mention the difficulty of noticing her dramatically understated way of informing Bombard that he is found out. It would be an exceptional reader who would have retained all these bits of evidence and combined them in the correct way when first reading the last lines of the tale. The last scene functions most strikingly by referring back to these proofs to complete the unstated, thus making of the reader a true participant in the closure of the story. The second story—Bombard unknowingly making love to his own wife and finding it better than his infidelities with his maid—is indeed a well-known, classic one; numerous fabliaux and tales present exactly that motif, known as "the wife who takes the place of her servant" (often to the satisfaction of all three parties). This is the special knowledge the reader must have, just as Maupassant undoubtedly did.

The revelation of the second story to the reader is accomplished by the lunch-table scene, the laconic matter-of-fact action by Mme Bombard, and its mute reception by Bombard and Victorine. In this wonderful closure, with extraordinary economy and hilarious pathos, Mme Bombard tells her husband not only that she knows he has been unfaithful (again) but also that it was indeed she on the steps the night before—a fact that he hasn't been able to figure out for himself.

The very curious relation of the second story to the first is different from that in "La Chambre 11." There the second story is completely unsaid except for its opening and closing lines, and must be inserted by the reader just before the final paragraph explaining Amandon's promotion. In "Bombard" the second story takes place under our very eyes—but is disguised. In this disguise, the role of the third-person, largely omniscient narrator is crucial, since it is he who fools the reader by stating that Bombard "trouva *comme d'habitude Victorine* l'attendant sur les marches" [found *Victorine as usual* waiting for him on the steps] (370, my emphasis). It would be more correct to say that there is a lapse of omniscience, without warning: the narrator suddenly knows no more than Bombard himself, and there is no clue that the narrator is fooled as well. (Such a clue does exist in "Décoré!" in the obvious disjunction of the narrator's and Sacrement's vision.) It would have made a considerable difference, for instance, if this sentence had read, "Il trouva une femme l'attendant sur les marches" [He found a woman waiting for him on the steps]. The narrator has us see things through the eyes of Bombard, and this limited vision is defective without our knowing it.

For the same reason, we are misled into being reassured just as Bombard is when his wife tranquilly explains her absence from the bedroom: "Il s'efforça de calmer les soupçons qu'elle pouvait avoir; mais elle semblait tranquille, heureuse, confiante; et il se rassura" [He strove to calm any suspicions she might have; but she seemed tranquil, happy, confiding, and he was reassured] (370). Just as *comme d'habitude* [as usual] and *Victorine* in the previous case are traps for the unknowing reader, so Bombard's anxieties about his wife's possible suspicions are designed to distract the reader from the real events of the darkened vestibule. With Bombard we consider a false possible outcome—something on the order of Mme Bombard's confronting her husband with eyewitness proof of his infidelity. And we are just as falsely led to lay aside these anxieties when Bombard is reassured by his wife's tranquil, confiding happiness—which upon reflection (and rereading) is actually a further clue: Madame is happy because of what has just taken place! Roland Barthes would say there is both a "snare," here a pretense addressed both by the discourse to the reader and by Mme Bombard to Simon Bombard, and a "blockage" of the hermeneutic code in the crucial scenes just described.[6] Almost certainly, a retroactive reading is necessary to unmask the event of the second story, and that retroactive reading is called for only by the last scene, the return of the *louis* into the hands of the maid. It is a joke on the misled reader that he, like Bombard, will see this second story only when he opens *sur sa femme des yeux énormes*. If like Victorine we look at the gold coin *d'un air stupide*, we will not be able to piece together correctly the events of the night before.

Thus vision—false, defective, or limited, and finally true—is crucial to the narratological point of the story, as its last two words hint. With "enormous eyes" wide open, we will not fail to interpret the second story correctly.[7] Imagine that the nighttime scene has been told entirely omnisciently, or from the point of view of Mme Bombard. Although Bombard would still be unaware of the truth, readers would know that the exceptionally animated woman with him is really Mme Bombard; they would know Victorine has been sent away under some false pretense (for clearly Mme Bombard has not told Victorine she knows of the maid's habitual station in the vestibule—that is indexed by Victorine's *air stupide*); they would know Mme Bombard expects

6. Roland Barthes, *S/Z* (Paris, 1970), 215.

7. Menakhem Perry's remarks on retroactive, or second, reading are pertinent here. The hypotheses the reader will have constructed on a first reading must be revised on a second reading: "Many of the patterns indispensable for an adequate concretization of a literary text cannot be discovered in an actual first reading, but only in additional readings," in "Literary Dynamics: How the Order of a Text Creates Its Meanings," *Poetics Today*, I (Autumn, 1979), 59. Perry was discussing, not second stories, but the reading action in any story.

more from her husband on the steps than in her bed; they would know she would limit her revenge to the simplest of strategies for proving once again that she wears the pants in the family, by demonstrating that the *louis* Bombard habitually gives to Victorine actually does come from her purse, for her sexual satisfactions are more important yet than her desire to dominate. Yet all of this knowledge, if it were patently obvious to readers through such a narrator, would destroy most of their pleasure, which depends on and results from the unraveling of the economic enigma—why does Mme Bombard give Victorine twenty francs, thereby finally opening Bombard's eyes? Without this clue that there is more to the story than the comical clash of two incompatible stereotypes, more than the small disaster barely averted, that pleasure would remain out of reach. A delicate balance between telling all and not hinting enough makes all the above knowledge available, but not without requiring the reader's significant involvement, for the reader "authors" the fragments of the second story. In both "Bombard" and "La Chambre 11" (unlike other stories such as Somerset Maugham's "Mr. Know-all"), there is no character who, "reading" the second story, acts as a model or guide to our reading. Only the nameless recipient of the narrator's account of "La Chambre 11," mentioned in a brief opening line, and Bombard's newly opened eyes, a last-minute guide that is retroactive at best, hint in the direction of a reading competence that we might emulate. "La Serre" plays at guiding the reader ("If you knew, if you knew . . ."), who nevertheless "knows" almost as readily as Jeanne Sacrement's reader does. The very sharing of readerly competence in "Un Million" allows for its perfect ending (the couple is both rich and happily married). But when a story lacks such a reader's model, a developed character whose skill as a reader orients or contrasts with ours, we naturally question our own competence in reading the second stories.

Our accurate reading of second stories depends on four factors: interest, skill, knowledge, and integrity. By *interest* I understand a particular interaction between text and reader that allows the former to involve the latter; the reader must be open to its influence to recognize the existence and the narrative of the second story. I include this factor on the basis of experience: a first reading does not necessarily alert us that a second story exists, and a desire to see more by delving deeper is prerequisite to the competence to find it. *Skill* means the ability to combine available clues so as to achieve a result, to see what things mean by implication or deduction. Logical reasoning is required; the reader must share with the author the ability to weave a narrative fabric out of given elements. By *knowledge* I mean the necessary background information the reader must have, a kind of cultural competence that the writer assumes in the reader, as in all the Maupassant tales here. As for *integrity*, this is a necessary characteristic of the reader's construction of the second story: it must account for all clues, all indications, all information available. In an ordinary sense, it must have unity and wholeness, opening and closure. The reader who would be competent must hold integrity as a value, almost as a check against excess as well as against deficiency. A kind of paranoia is perhaps called for by these stories: we must not take them at face value; worse, we must take pleasure in a delirium of interpretation.

In the limited space of a *nouvelle* or short story misleading clues are unlikely. A mystery novel (even a mystery short story) abounds in misleading directions to the reader. Their very purpose is to tantalize, to bewilder, to lead astray; they are essential to the creation of the sense of mystery; they constitute the *modus operandi* of the puzzle the mystery reader seeks. Any reader of mystery stories knows he is being misled, and his pleasure as a reader consists in playing a game with the writer. But by the end of the mystery narrative, every clue will have been dealt with and classified permanently, as either part of the solution or a red herring. Such a classification is possible because the mystery story tells only one story.

In contrast, any unexplained items of a first story must be accounted for in the second story. Where there is a glitch, there may be a second story. Michael Riffaterre calls the presence of such things in poetry "ungrammaticality"—obstacles to a simple interpretation, aggravating difficulties, unaccountable statements or words, or, more narrowly, "a deviant grammar or lexicon (for instance, contradictory details)." He remarks, wherever "there are gaps or compressions in the text—such as incomplete descriptions, or allusions, or quotations—it is . . . literary competence alone that will enable the reader to respond properly and to complete or fill in according to the hypogrammatic model." The return of twenty francs to Victorine and Amandon's promotion are such "ungrammaticalities"; they are *not* red herrings. Perry writes somewhat analogously, "Items that were there from the start but that could not be easily reconciled with the old frame, raising difficulties for it (but not enough to undermine it), now do accommodate to the new frame." Although Stanley Fish warns the reader, "Clues, after all, are sometimes misleading and give rise to 'mistakes,'" clues such as these, the necessary elements of the hidden second story, the tips of the second-story iceberg, are not misleading in themselves. Of course Fish considers the "mistakes" that may result from misreading clues heuristically valuable and encourages them in his students. In like manner, the unexplainable factors, forgotten unimportant details, and incidentally mentioned facts are the raw elements out of which the reader builds the second story.[8]

We might eventually establish an inventory of the kinds of clues there are to second-story constructions—rhetorical, symbolic, syntactic or mechanical, codal or subcodal, and so on. When Bombard understands something, in the final sentence of the story, that the reader has not yet grasped, this is a clue and the impetus to look for the story to which it refers. It is a syntactic code in that it refers us to the mechanics of the story; it tells us something did happen beyond the portrayal of two clashing types. The narrator's promise to explain Amandon's promotion in "La Chambre 11" and his apparent failure to do so, at least in supplying the complete story, are syntactic clues that an element of the story has to be supplied by the reader. In "Un Million," it is a rhetorical moment—the litotic *inconvenant*—that opens the door to the entire second story, doubling the laconic narrator's feigned ignorance in his three rhetorical questions. The clue to a second story can be a symbolic if concrete item—such as Rosselin's overcoat in "Décoré!"—which simultaneously confirms the second story for the reader and keeps it hidden from the unknowledgeable character. All the elements of the "code" that reigns in the second story (such as the systems of exchange in "La Chambre 11" and "Un Million") provide a way to organize it into an integral whole. Subcodal clues are elements of the first story that cannot be organized by any of its codes and so remain deviant, or "ungrammatical." The extraordinary animation of "Victorine" is such a clue.

When such clues are lacking or inadequate, the second story may never reach the reader. Such is the case with Maupassant's "En Voyage" (the one beginning "Le wagon était au complet depuis Cannes"). Here a character in the frame knows something about the narrated story, which remains enigmatic, but she is too overcome with emotion to complete her sentence. "Ces deux êtres-là ont été moins fous que vous ne croyez . . . Ils étaient . . . ils étaient . . ."

8. Michael Riffaterre, *Semiotics of Poetry* (Bloomington, Ind., 1978), 2, 5; Perry, "Literary Dynamics," 60; Fish, "Literature in the Reader," 86.

[Those two people were less crazy than you think. . . . They were . . . they were . . .] (I, 815) is all she can say before dissolving into tears; this is both the clue that there is some other story making the first intelligible and at the same time the author's refusal to give it. One might suppose that the other clues in the story itself were sufficiently enlightening to knowledgeable contemporaries of Maupassant—and I mean a close circle of friends—for them to complete this hanging clue, perhaps even by supplying names; but the second story is forever lost to us. In Barbey d'Aurevilly's "Le Plus Bel Amour de Don Juan," a systematic set of rhetorical, symbolic, and codal clues is put into place, but it never goes far enough to allow a construction from them. The reader is intended to fail, to be left with an unsettling sense of mystery about a "reality" behind the story that will always be hidden.

Second-story construction puts other aspects of reader dynamics into play. There is not only the question of the narrator's reliability— as in "Bombard" and "Un Million"—but also the parallel and much more fascinating question of the *narratee*'s reliability, for our reading depends on it, and our creativeness as critics. To the extent that the reader doubles the narratee, and I have referred to a reader's model (the implied or real narratee) who informs our own reading, we can question the degree of authority granted to the reader when he is recounting the second story. The second-story reader is a special case of the "reader in the text"; he is an active reader more explicitly defined than the interpreter in general. His stage directions are often directly encoded in the text, in the form of a created model, an obvious guide.

The reader actually writes the second story, constructs it from the first, using the same stones to build a different building, appropriating authority, hallucinating a new text. Second-story constructions propose a special task and make a different point: the subject or plot of these stories is doubled by another plot, which concerns the process by which the second story comes to light; the reader is involved in reading and writing that plot as much as the first. He is like the detective, but also like the actual writer of the detective story.

The question of the validity of second-story constructions is relevant here. Tzvetan Todorov writes that if readers' constructions of stories are right, they are all alike.[9] It would be interesting to see if the

9. Tzvetan Todorov, "Reading as Construction," in Susan Suleiman and Inge Crosman (eds.), *The Reader in the Text: Essays on Audience and Interpretation* (Princeton, 1980), 79.

second stories readers tell themselves are indeed all alike. But what governs the readings we make? Are there conventions for second stories, parallel to those for first stories? Is the plotting we do as readers rigorously analogous to the plot's plotting?[10] Jonathan Culler speaks of structural conventions, which would determine our acceptance of the second story; for instance, some stories have a quick point or a reversal, such as "La Serre" and "Un Million." Christine Brooke-Rose writes that there are few semes of any one code in a short story, but they are repeated often; this is certainly true of the second story in "Bombard," in which the semes accounting for Mme Bombard's behavior there are repeated throughout the first story. These semes are used by the reader retroactively to validate the second-story construction. Perhaps more than for a first story, second-story conventions are determined; there are encoded directions for writing them.[11]

Such issues will raise questions and propose responses to E. D. Hirsch and other critics of value hermeneutics, and require some measure of agreement on the extent to which interpretations must be "stable" (to use Riffaterre's term) and have closure. Indeed, the analysis of second stories will perhaps shed a different light on the validity of interpretation, in that such constructions are usually more determinate than interpretation in general, although just as dependent on cultural, literary, and semantic competence.[12]

Finally, it would be interesting to trace the course of the second-story reader's inquiry, in which we should recognize the capital role played by pleasure. Barthes, in *Le Plaisir du texte*, proposes four types of readers—fetishistic, obsessive, paranoid, and hysteric—whose pleasure depends on a hallucinated form of the text. Of these four, the reader of second stories cannot be fetishistic or hysteric. He can

10. I am making the same distinction Peter Brooks has made in *Reading for the Plot: Design and Intention in Narrative* (New York, 1984), 35.

11. Jonathan Culler, "Prolegomena to a Theory of Reading," in Suleiman and Crosman (eds.), *The Reader in the Text*, 62; Christine Brooke-Rose, "The Readerhood of Man," *ibid.*, 137–38. Stanley Fish might disagree: see Susan Rubin Suleiman, "Introduction: Varieties of Audience-Oriented Criticism," *ibid.*, 20n29: "[Fish] has shifted his position about texts; whereas even in 1972 he spoke of reading a work 'correctly,' that is, as the author intended . . . in 'Interpreting the Variorum' he explicitly rejects the notion that there is a 'correct' reading, or even that texts contain any 'encoded' directions for how to interpret them."

12. Michael Riffaterre, "Hermeneutic Models," *Poetics Today*, IV (1983), 7–16. On determinate versus indeterminate interpretations, see Jonathan Culler, "Stories of Reading," in *On Deconstruction: Theory and Criticism after Structuralism* (Ithaca, 1982), 64–83, especially his discussion of Fish, Riffatere, and Umberto Eco.

be somewhat obsessive: "The obsessive would have the voluptuous pleasure of the letter, of secondary, unhooked languages, metalanguages (this category would bring together all the logophiles, linguists, semioticians, philologists: all those for whom language *returns*)." But he is mostly paranoid: "The paranoid would consume or produce twisted texts, stories developed like reasonings, constructions proposed like games, secret constraints." Obsessively, the reader of second stories counts clues and looks for secondary, unhooked languages—languages other than the apparent surface story. But mostly he engages in a kind of delirium of interpretation, proposing constructions of secret stories, producing texts that are not there, twisting things to make new stories. The hysteric reader lacks the discipline to recount the second story, though he undoubtedly sees it: "As for the hysteric (so contrary to the obsessive), he would be the one who takes the text at *face value*, who enters into the bottomless, truthless comedy of language, who is no longer the subject of any critical gaze and *throws himself* across the text (which is completely different from projecting himself into it)."[13] It is our reader's models here who are hysteric: Sacrement, Bonnin, and Lerebour. In watching them, in watching the second story emerge from our reading, we are perhaps neither fetishistic, obsessive, paranoid, nor hysteric, but voyeuristic.

13. Roland Barthes, *Le Plaisir du texte* (Paris, 1973), 99, 100. The translations are my own.

IAN REID

Destabilizing Frames for Story

Whether in scholarly publications or in classroom practices, short story criticism has generally operated with scant recognition of two important points: that stories become meaningful only within particular acts of reading, and that the acts of reading are always—but variously—framed. Why is it important to be aware of these points? Unless the intricate processes of framing are brought fully into critical consciousness, they will cramp and distort interpretation. This can be an acute problem in teaching situations, which often frame students' reading narrowly; and it can be a special hazard in dealing with short stories, since they provide the staple of so many introductory courses in literary study and their generic status is normally supposed to be definite and clear-cut.

In itself, the notion of framing is unavoidably abstract. Even when it includes specific material elements, what these signify must still depend on processes of interpretation. This is the meaning I take from an enigmatic remark by Jacques Derrida in an essay on aesthetics: "Framing occurs, but there is no frame."[1] Frames, in other words, are in the eye of the beholder. But by no means does this make them unimportant; after all, reading itself is in the eye of the beholder as well.

The term *frame* has been variously used in literary criticism and related fields with no systematic analysis of the different senses involved, which extend from that which is current in cognitive linguistics (a mental schema or ideational format used for organizing information) to that which is current in narratology (an embedded structure of tales within tales).[2] My attempt to sort out and clarify

1. Jacques Derrida, "Parergon," in *La Vérité en Peinture* (Paris, 1978), Pt. 2, p. 8. My translation.

2. For an overview of the term's use among cognitive linguists, see Dieter Metzing

these usages can be summarized in advance, and in very general terms: there are ways in which narratives virtually frame themselves, and there are ways in which they get framed by textual mediators (notably publishers, editors, and teachers) and by a whole range of assumptions that readers may bring to bear. A fundamental task for short story criticism is to ensure that due attention is paid to the varieties of framing, to their complex interrelations, and to their destabilizing of generic markers.

At least four kinds of framing should be differentiated, though they are not entirely discrete, and indeed their overlap and interplay are often generically significant. For convenience, and with due contrition for augmenting the technical lexicon, I shall label these as circumtextual, intratextual, intertextual, and extratextual frames. All have some bearing on the way a text's genre is perceived; all are capable of disconcerting certain categories of orthodox short story criticism. These frames are considered here with reference to the supposedly distinct genre of the short story, particularly "Monsieur Seguin's Goat," in Alphonse Daudet's *Letters from My Windmill.* Even such a famously "simple" little tale reveals how intricate the processes of framing can be.

The most palpable reading frame is constituted by the material bor-

---

(ed.), *Frame Conceptions and Text Understanding* (New York, 1980); Teun A. van Dijk, *Macrostructures: An Interdisciplinary Study of Global Structures in Discourse, Interaction and Cognition* (Hillsdale, N.J., 1980); Umberto Eco, *Semiotics and the Philosophy of Language* (London, 1984), 70–78. Some would distinguish between *frames* and *scripts*, though both terms refer to remembered data patterns and hypotheses about textual organization; *cf.* Robert-Alain de Beaugrande and Wolfgang Dressler, *Introduction to Text Linguistics* (New York, 1981), 90. Among related usages in other disciplinary areas are those current in philosophy (*cf.* Adam Morton, *Frames of Mind: Constraints on the Common-Sense Conception of the Mental* [Oxford, 1980]) and sociology (*cf.* Basil Bernstein's chapter "On the Classification and Framing of Educational Knowledge" in his book *Class, Codes and Control* [2 vols; London, 1971], I). The discussion of certain composite texts in terms of an outer frame that encloses several stories has long been common in accounts of Chaucer's *Canterbury Tales,* Boccaccio's *Decameron,* and other such collections, but some recent studies of such texts use the term *frame* with a fuller awareness of the complicated reading operations that can be involved; *cf.* Joy H. Potter, *Five Frames for the "Decameron": Communication and Social Systems in the "Cornice"* (Princeton, 1982). Additionally, within a given individual story, there may be a technique of embedded narration; *cf.* Angela S. Moger, "Narrative Structure in Maupassant: Frames of Desire," *PMLA,* C (May, 1985), 315–27. This last aspect of texts has of course been analyzed also in a number of important studies that do not use the term *frame; cf., e.g.,* Ross Chambers, *Story and Situation: Narrative Seduction and the Power of Fiction* (Minneapolis, 1984).

ders of a text. These will include details of its physical format, cover
and prefatory information, title, opening and closing formulas, authorial ascriptions, and other such circumtextual (or paratextual) markers.[3] Now whereas the form of the novel is closely aligned with the
form of the book, and indeed hardly conceivable without it, those
texts that we call short stories are almost always either in tension with
the book (being physically less than the whole) or quite outside it (appearing, for example, in magazines). By that token they tend to emphasize the instability of any frames through which they are interpreted.[4] Consider the following example.

Above a harvest scene brightly reproduced from a Van Gogh painting, a book's black-framed front cover announces that it is the Penguin Classics version of Daudet's *Letters from My Windmill*.[5] The back
cover tells us a few things about the author, and about the suitability
of the translation and illustrations done for this edition. (There are
also some incidental trade details; but exhaustive description is unnecessary here.) Some of the cover material is repeated inside on the
preliminary pages. The contents listing adds certain information, notably that the book comprises a sequence of parts, most of them numbered and individually titled. (They are unnumbered in my French
edition, which differs in other respects as well; but we already have
enough complications on our hands without going further into that
set of comparisons.) Then come various prefatory materials from author and translator, then three of the letters themselves—whereupon
I reach, as the fourth numbered item, "Monsieur Seguin's Goat." Beyond that lie a score of other "letters," and the book is rounded off by
a few pages of advertisements for other Penguin Classics translated
from the French, such as Flaubert's *Three Tales* and Hugo's *Notre Dame
de Paris*.

In some ways, then, "Monsieur Seguin's Goat" is surrounded by
concentric rings, from which it is marked off sharply by certain details
of layout: it has a separate set of pages to itself, a new section number,
and its own title; and what we tend to think of as "the story itself" is

3. *Cf.* John Frow, "The Literary Frame," *Journal of Aesthetic Education*, XVI (1982),
25–30.
4. See Adena Rosmarin, *The Power of Genre* (Minneapolis, 1985), 7–8, 163–64nn22–
24, for a discussion of Maurice Blanchot and others on the relation between genre
and book.
5. Alphonse Daudet, *Letters from My Windmill*, trans. Frederick Davies (Harmonds-
worth, U.K., 1978).

introduced by an epistolary formula, a quasi-postal address ("To Monsieur Pierre Gringoire, / Lyrical Poet, / Paris"). And yet the dividing lines are not at all clear-cut. On the one hand, the inner text's available meanings are partly dispersed among those outer casings that seem at first glance to enclose it so neatly, while on the other hand it is less easy than one might at first suppose to fix the boundaries of "the story itself," which comes to seem more and more onionlike in its internal structure.

As a brief example of the textual dispersion outwards through the circumtextual frame, consider a passage from Daudet's preface in which he recounts how he would dream away the hours in his hillside windmill until sunset, when, "at the call of a marine conch, the horn of Monsieur Seguin calling home his goat, I used to return for the evening meal." He would return, that is, to the farmhouse, where he would spend the evening listening to a hospitable old dame as she reminisced about such things as dancing a farandole with a handsome officer who "made her skip like a goat . . . all night long."[6] What happens here, passingly and partially, is a proleptic framing of the yet-to-come story about the goat's failure to return and nightlong tussle: the reader is being encouraged to place it in relation to either of these possible (but different) terms of reference that concern the old lady and the narrator himself. These suggestions, though casual and undeveloped, work somewhat against any detachment of "Monsieur Seguin's Goat," as an autonomous short story, from the *Letters* as a book.

Not only do textual limit-markers shift somewhat in the circumtextual framing, but there is also a converse shiftiness *within* the story itself. This is a matter of intratextual framing because it operates within the terms on the page. A text will sometimes seem to comment on aspects of its own genre through some little embedded episode, image, or situation that serves as a part-for-whole-mirror, an inset reading model; this frames it intratextually. Consider the phrasing used at the very end of Daudet's text: "Hear well these words, Gringoire: '. . . then in the morning the wolf ate her.'" This concludes the little epilogue, which links up with the preamble to form a layer of direct admonition to the narratee, who is supposedly a contemporary Parisian poet and for whose benefit the inset cautionary tale from Pro-

6. *Ibid.*, 38, copyright © 1978 by Frederick Davies, reproduced by permission of Penguin Books Ltd.

vence is being told. Yet epilogue merges back into tale through a repetitive device of embedding. The formula "then in the morning the wolf ate her" occurs three times: not only is the last line a variant of the sentence that ends the inset narrative recounting the demise of Blanquette, but it is also a virtually exact repetition (transposed into Provençal dialect) of the words used earlier about one of Monsieur Seguin's previous escapees, Renaude, whose sad fate has been recounted (ineffectually) to Blanquette as a deterrent. That "story of old Renaude" comes belatedly to the younger victim's mind when she herself eventually meets the wolf, and it is as a conscious reenactment of Renaude's nightlong struggle and subsequent capitulation that Blanquette completes her own plot. In a sense, then, the story of "Monsieur Seguin's Goat" is an episode from a larger implied tale. It suggests a series of reiterations, with Blanquette substituted in this instance for Renaude—who in turn was just another in the long line of lost goats. Regarded thus, Blanquette is not so much an individual delinquent as a creature whose sacrifice the narration itself requires. When the narrator uses the formula *"To cut a long story short,* Monsieur Seguin's goat spent a wonderful day," the reader's attention is drawn intratextually to the way this text much curtails the substitutive pattern by which it proceeds: the replacement of one figure by another and then another, successively, is itself a figure for the narrative impulse that pulls against the generic tether.[7]

As well as the tales-within-tales variety of intratextual framing, further elements may also serve implicitly as embedded models for the relation between reader and text. In doing so they may trouble our generic expectations; Mary Ann Caws remarks that inwardly mirrored images and passages of this sort "often enable the intrusion of another genre into the narrative text."[8] The built-in tale of Blanquette's compulsion to seek out a dangerous freedom is supposed to be specifically relevant to the situation of a writer, pointing a moral about the destructiveness of *la vie bohème.* But though ostensibly an epistolary fable as far as Gringoire the narratee is concerned, it becomes perhaps a rather different sort of text for the implied reader, who wants to go beyond the purported simplicity of tone and reference to consider further allegorical possibilities along the following lines. An explicit parallel is drawn, certainly, between Gringoire and the goat; but in

7. *Ibid.*, 69, 67, emphasis added.
8. Mary Ann Caws, *Reading Frames in Modern Fiction* (Princeton, 1985), xi.

that case, what might the other characters, Monsieur Seguin and the wolf, stand for? In some respects the former resembles the narrator, whose admonitions to Gringoire are like Seguin's to Blanquette. To accept that equivalence is, of course, to regard the narrator's tale as misconceived (at least in terms of its apparent cautionary purpose), since Seguin is said to be ignorant of goatishness and his warnings do no good at all. For all Seguin's didactic injunctions, and the narrator's likewise, goats will be goats—and writers, writers. This may even be taken to imply that in not recognizing the incorrigible nature of the artist's self-destructive impulses, the narrator is no true writer himself. The overt moral is not to be taken at face value, then; and accordingly this is no straightforward Aesopic tale after all. And what about the figure of the wolf? Given that Blanquette repeats "the story of old Renaude" as if acting out a scripted role, does it not follow that she is *textually* consumed—that the wolf represents the irresistible force of storytelling compulsions, with the goat standing as much for a reader as for a writer?

Such considerations are further complicated by the third kind of framing, which is intertextual. This should be understood as involving more than just passing allusions or traces of "influence"; intertextuality comprises devices by which a text signals how its very structure of meanings depends on both its similarity to and its difference from certain other texts or text types. Sometimes the signaling is unmistakable, as when the narrator pauses in his description of Blanquette to say, "She was nearly as charming as Esmeralda's little goat—you remember, Gringoire?"[9] The reference is to Hugo's *Notre Dame de Paris*, in which the gypsy girl Esmeralda has a small white goat, and the poet Gringoire rescues it. What larger significance does this passing mention have for the story? For one thing, Hugo's poet-character was in turn based on an actual writer of three centuries earlier; so Daudet's narrator, by conflating his supposedly contemporary addressee with a historical figure already fictionalized in a prior text, acknowledges that Gringoire is a type rather than a person and that the modern address-frame is just as fictive as the story it contains. At the same time, the reader is implicitly invited to notice how different the cheeky semiconversational mode of "Monsieur Seguin's Goat" is from the massive nineteenth-century historical novel typified by *Notre Dame de Paris*. Quite another kind of characterization is at work, through

9. Daudet, *Letters from My Windmill*, 64.

quite another kind of text, and the intertextual frame can help a reader to recognize this.

More discreetly intertextual is an echo from Charles Perrault's "Little Red Riding Hood." Again, this should not be understood in terms of the empty notion of the "influence" of one writer on another. Rather, it is a matter of what a semiotician would call the passage from one sign system to another. A text type, such as a traditional fairy tale, can be thought of as a sign system in the sense that it generates meanings in a particular set of ways—for instance, through highly conventional plot structures. The final sentence of Daudet's story (apart from the epilogic return to Gringoire), "Alors le loup se jeta sur la petite chèvre et la mangea," follows the fairy tale's well-known concluding formula so closely that a French reader could hardly miss the link: "Ce méchant Loup se jeta sur le Petit Chaperon rouge, et la mangea."

A further precursor, less specifically invoked but obviously pertinent nevertheless, is the beast fable, and there is a specific link through La Fontaine's "The Dog and the Wolf." Of the several fables that bear some relation to "Monsieur Seguin's Goat," among them "The Wolf and the Lamb," it is "The Dog and the Wolf" that shares a particular emphasis on the comparative attractions of perilous freedom and safe tethering. But much more is involved, for the intertextual field includes previous adaptations by Daudet himself of both "Little Red Riding Hood" and "The Dog and the Wolf." [10] These were among the satirical fantasies published during his apprentice days, in the decade before the *Letters*, and both of them anticipate "Monsieur Seguin's Goat" in evoking the dangerous delights of bohemian freedom for a writer. But they do so in surprising ways. In Daudet's version of "The Dog and the Wolf," it is the wolf that is equated with the willful free-lance poet. And in his version of "Little Red Riding Hood," which brings in additional characters drawn from Shakespearean and other sources, the closing moral about the sticky outcome of blithe hedonism is attributed to Polonius—whereas Little Red Riding Hood herself, cheerfully accepting her death as destined, advises everyone to seek pleasure without regret.

While on the one hand "Monsieur Seguin's Goat" reworks some things written by Daudet before the *Letters*, on the other, it figures as

10. *Cf.* Murray Sachs, *The Career of Alphonse Daudet: A Critical Study* (New Haven, 1965), 40–43.

an insertion in one of his later texts. Produced in 1872 with music by Bizet, the play *L'Arlésienne* (*The Girl from Arles*), which is itself a dramatized expansion of a story from the *Letters*, incorporates virtually word for word the ending of "Monsieur Seguin's Goat." The play opens and closes with an account of Blanquette's surrender to the wolf, narrated by a shepherd; and just as the goat in the *Letters* seems to confront her death in conscious compliance with narrative exigencies, following the same pattern of nightlong resistance and then death in the morning as in "the story of old Renaude," so also in the playscript version of *L'Arlésienne* the lovesick youth, immediately before his suicide, draws a direct parallel between his situation and the end of the goat's struggle.[11]

What, then, are we to make of these several possibilities for intertextual framing? Surely they should make us cautious of any tendency to assign this text to a neat generic monotype. If we want to continue to use a term such as *short story*, it must be with an awareness that, as Anne Freadman remarks in an important essay on genre theory, "the rules of a genre and the formal properties of a single text will not correlate" since "texts may, and frequently do, play several games—and thus, several partners—at once."[12] (By "partners," she means other texts.)

"Monsieur Seguin's Goat" presents itself, then, less as a told story than as an adaptable set of storytellings, directly affiliated with a play, a novel, a fairy tale, a fable, and more—for through other intertextual devices, too, the text signals its status as a meetingplace for various generic tendencies. Although ostensibly aligning itself with homespun Provençal folktales ("If you ever come to Provence, our farmers will talk to you often about Monsieur Seguin's goat") in explicit contrast to the manner of Parisian journalists, it goes on to show that this opposition between provincial and metropolitan forms is not at all simple. Some oral features of the tale are recognizably derived from the Parisian newssheet, or *chronique*, which, as Matthew MacNamara has remarked, often sought a style based on the personal voice; Daudet's stylistic choices here amount to a "refusal to separate the anecdote from the actions of its telling and its hearing, from an identifiable

11. Alphonse Daudet, *L'Arlésienne*, in *Théatre I* (Paris, 1930), 359–435, vol. XIX of Daudet, *Oeuvres Complètes Illustrées*, 20 vols.

12. Anne Freadman, "Anyone for Tennis?" in Ian Reid (ed.), *The Place of Genre in Learning: Current Debates* (Geelong, Australia, 1987), 98.

narrator telling it in an identifiable situation." And as Murray Sachs has pointed out, the tone of ironical observation is characteristic of the "Parisian boulevard wit"—and of the pieces Daudet had been writing for years in city magazines, where indeed the *Windmill* letters themselves first appeared. Or, moving beyond contemporary affinities, one could attempt to trace the story's intertextual relations further back—only to find, once again, that origins remain elusively deferred and that one is no closer to fixing the generic nature of Daudet's text. This was A. H. Krappe's discovery many years ago when he investigated the resemblance between "Monsieur Seguin's Goat" and the tenth-century Latin poem *Ecbasis Captivi*, written in a Lorraine monastery; he could only hypothesize a common source for them in French folklore.[13]

Finally, extratextual frames include the range of knowledge and expectations that, observing the cues provided by the other three sorts of textual frames, a reader brings to the interpretation of a particular text. Among them are generic understandings, pedagogic habits, and notions about literariness. Although a genre may be signified circumtextually, intratextually, and intertextually, it will go unrecognized unless a reader can draw on appropriate extratextual information. On the other hand, it may happen that a text is inappropriately framed, its particular contours willfully disregarded, if a reader's assumptions are too rigid. Extratextual framing has not been well theorized or empirically studied hitherto; as H. Verdaasdonk remarks, "Still unanswered questions are: how frames are activated, how they are acquired, to what extent they embody detailed 'knowledge,' etc. For these reasons it is unclear what it means to 'understand' a text . . . with the help of a frame."[14]

What is clear, however, is that these extratextual frames always carry an ideological freight, albeit inconspicuously and unwittingly. Foremost among them is likely to be a set of assumptions based on the perceived status of the author and the supposed nature of his writings. In the present case, knowing that Daudet long ago lost his once-prominent place in the ranks of "major" writers and is generally

13. Daudet, *Letters from My Windmill*, 69; Matthew MacNamara, "Some Oral Narrative Forms in *Lettres de mon Moulin*," *Modern Language Review*, LXVII (1972), 291–99; Sachs, *The Career*, 41; A. H. Krappe, "'La Chèvre de Monsieur Seguin' de Daudet et l'*Ecbasis Captivi*," *Revue de Littérature Comparée*, V (1925), 339–42.

14. H. Verdaasdonk, "Conceptions of Literature as Frames," *Poetics*, XI (1982), 87–104.

regarded as just a sentimental humorist specializing in bucolic vignettes, most readers take it for granted, perhaps unconsciously and as if naturally, that "Monsieur Seguin's Goat" is a lightweight piece that does not need any of the careful scrutiny one would expect to bring to a tale by Flaubert or Gérard de Nerval, for example. Sachs notes that "Daudet has for some time been considered too simple in his techniques, and too obvious in his meanings, to challenge an age which takes particular pride in penetrating the hermetic world of the 'difficult' obscure artist."[15]

To sharpen this point, one need only entertain the possibility of arguing that "Monsieur Seguin's Goat" is a work of parody or pastiche—that its mixture of fable, folktale, letter, and *chronique* accentuates the elusiveness of those generic types on which it teasingly touches. If that seems an implausible reading, it is only, I suggest, because of the particular expectations that one brings to bear on Daudet's *Letters;* for parody is not so much a quality inherent in a text as an extratextual frame through which a reader construes or subdues the other framing elements. Daudet does not have a reputation as a subtly self-reflexive parodist; in recent times, hardly any critic has taken him up at all, let alone in a deconstructive spirit attentive to textual play. In short, there is little to dissuade anyone from underreading "Monsieur Seguin's Goat" as merely an artless, moralized piece of rustic nostalgia.

Indeed, the "almost umbilical attachment to Provence" that the Penguin Classics cover blurb attributes to the author, and the associated notion that these "letters" are essentially reminiscences ("to invent, for him, was to remember"), is so unquestioned an orthodoxy that Daudet's work has become fixed in an ideological frame through which it seems both thematically and formally organicist. I apply this term in the sense used by Terry Eagleton, "to signify social and aesthetic formations with the supposedly spontaneous unity of natural life-forms."[16] What organicism involves here is a tacitly assumed link between these propositions: 1) the "letters" are cohesive in subject matter, representing an integrated community's "natural" way of life; and 2) accordingly (as it were), there is a "natural" unity of form that shapes each piece individually and the book as a whole.

Regrettably, a remark of my own, made more than a decade ago in

15. Sachs, *The Career*, vii.
16. Terry Eagleton, *Criticism and Ideology* (London, 1978), 103.

my monograph *The Short Story*, seems to endorse that way of reading Daudet's text; I mentioned his *Letters* as one of the "notable nine-teenth-century prototypes" of modern "short-story cycles . . . [which] locate their unity of place in some rural region." In part I amended this statement by going on to observe that the *Letters* is too much of a miscellany to fit that unificatory pattern neatly, since it "seems casu-ally conjoined, and comprises a heterogeneous assortment of nar-rative types—sketches, yarns, fables, 'ballades en prose'—set into an informal frame." But a more careful reading would have gone further, to show (among other things) that the organicist notion of a rustic "unity of place" is itself ironically treated within the *Letters*. It would be a mistake to think that the tone of the first section, celebrating the harmony of the Provençal countryside and its pastoral routines in ex-plicit contrast to "noisy, dirty Paris," pervades uniformly the rest of the sections as well. After all, the narrator confesses on the book's last page that Paris haunts him in his rural retreat; he acknowledges that it is through "the Paris newspapers" that he reaches his readership; and the "memories" on which his final emphasis falls are not of the little regional community but of that beloved city, now distant: "Oh, Paris! . . . Paris! . . . Always Paris!"[17]

Pedagogic habits are often involved in our framing of texts. Edgar Allan Poe's notion that the chief formal property of "a short prose tale" is "unity of impression" lends itself all too readily in the class-room to a reductive preoccupation with eliciting a theme or message. Such an approach to "Monsieur Seguin's Goat" would ignore latently ironic elements that run counter to its own overt moralizing. To ask "Quelle est la morale de l'histoire?" (as the editor of the Classiques Larousse edition does) is to err by supposing its point *can* be consid-ered unitarily as that of *une histoire*, a single story with a single mes-sage, rather than as an unstable area of textual play.[18] The slim Clas-siques Larousse paperbacks, with their pedagogic apparatus of notes and questions, epitomize the impact of certain extratextual norms on material, circumtextual frames in ways that can powerfully constrain particular generic expectations; and the same is true of many a college anthology of short fiction.

Extratextual framing is unavoidable. No text can be understood

17. Ian Reid, *The Short Story* (1977; rpr. New York, 1979), 49, 51–52, with permission of Methuen and Co.; Daudet, *Letters from My Windmill*, 220.

18. Alphonse Daudet, *Lettres de mon Moulin* (Paris, n.d.), 47.

apart from what readers bring to it. The important thing is not to be locked preclusively into one or two kinds of extratextual framing. Instead of fixing on the idea that Daudet's tale is a moralized fable, for example, one could foreground gender issues: what does it mean that Blanquette is a pretty and wayward female who disobeys her male custodian and therefore falls prey to the male wolf? This linking of the text with sex-role socialization would give significant recognition to elements noted in the intertextual frame, particularly "Little Red Riding Hood" and *L'Arlésienne*.[19] When problems arise in short story criticism, often the cause is that extratextual framing has not been adjusted attentively to other framing possibilities within and around a given text.

19. *Cf.* Jack Zipes, *The Trials and Tribulations of Little Red Riding Hood: Versions of the Tale in Socio-Cultural Context* (South Hadley, Mass., 1983).

SUZANNE HUNTER BROWN

Appendix A: Reframing Stories

Here I will discuss two texts, one classical and one modern. Both present the reader with characters interpreting the story of a central female figure where choices of local or global processing, sequential or configurative organization, have impact on meaning and affect their view of the woman's behavior. We will see that questions of value and evaluation have become questions of genre.

"The Widow of Ephesus," by Petronius

In order to demonstrate how local processing and configurational, "spatial" patterning affect meaning, I will organize a story from the *Satyricon* in two ways. I assume in these readings of "The Widow of Ephesus" that both sequential and configurational organization are potential ways of structuring this work; I accept W. J. T. Mitchell's view that spatial organization is not an exclusively modern phenomenon. He writes, "I propose, therefore, that far from being a unique phenomenon of some modern literature, and far from being restricted to the features which Frank identifies in those works (simultaneity and discontinuity), spatial form is a crucial aspect of the experience and interpretation of literature in all ages and cultures."[1] We cannot say that one mode of organizing this text is right and the other wrong; we *can* say that readers are more likely to prefer configurative patterning when they bestow on the text the kind of close verbal attention

1. W. J. T. Mitchell, "Spatial Form in Literature: Toward a General Theory," *Critical Inquiry*, VI (1980), 541.

311

engendered by brevity. Sequential patterning is more likely if readers process the text not as a short story but as a piece of the *Satyricon*. Translation will be an issue here, for to the extent that verbatim structure is vital to patterning, important aspects of works are "untranslatable." Next to poems, short prose narratives lose the most in the transition to another language.

Considered episodically, the tale is cynical and ironic. A married woman, renowned for her virtue, proclaims eternal devotion to her dead husband and follows him into his tomb, intending to starve herself. A soldier, charged with keeping watch over the bodies of crucified robbers to prevent their burial, hears her groans and discovers the faithful wife mourning over the corpse with a loyal maid. Moved by the widow's beauty, the man first tempts the servant woman to eat and drink, then, with the maid's help, induces the mistress to succumb also. He and the widow become lovers. While they are together in the tomb, one of the bodies the soldier was to guard is stolen and buried. Certain that he will be punished for leaving his post, the soldier prepares to kill himself. Instead, the faithful wife offers her husband's body as a replacement for that of the thief.

This reductive version mocks the widow's supposed virtue. It emphasizes the reversal of her intentions, with its movement from her lonely fast to three days of feasting and lovemaking in the tomb of her husband. It ends with her decision to make use of the body she has sworn to mourn forever. Indeed Eumolpus, entertaining his party on board ship, precedes this story with "many taunts at the fickleness of women," and the claim that "no woman was so chaste that she could not be led away into utter madness by a passion for a stranger." When he finishes this narration, the soldiers receive this tale with a roar, and one listener, Lichas, declares, "If the governor of the province had been a just man, he should have put the dead husband back in the tomb, and hung the woman on the cross."[2]

Yet attention to the exact Latin words, to verbal repetitions, and to the binary opposition of word clusters creates quite another meaning for the tale. The Latin words can be sorted into two groups, the one clustered around life, light, common human nature, beauty, food,

2. Petronius, "The Widow of Ephesus," in E. H. Warmington (ed.), *Petronius*, trans. Michael Heseltine (1913; rev. ed. and rpr. Cambridge, Mass., 1969), 269, 277, hereafter cited parenthetically by page number in the text. Text and translation appear on facing pages in the original.

wine, crowds, health, love, and sensuality; the other concerned with uniqueness, separation from "common" people, death, mutilation, grief, fasting, and deprivation.

Falling in the first division are words expressing the widow's dissatisfaction with the common custom (*non contenta vulgari more*) of mourning through primarily ritualistic self-mutilation (beating her breast, loosening her hair). She is not content merely to accompany her husband's body to the tomb but wishes to follow it in. The soldier whose curiosity leads him to follow the groaning sounds is moved by a very human weakness (*vitio gentis humanae*). He tells the woman that her grief is pointless, for death is the common end and home of all men (*omnium eundem esse exitum [sed] et idem domicilium*). Although in Michael Heseltine's translation the maid is described as responding to the soldier's "kindly invitation," *humanitatem* in the phrase *ad humanitatem invitantis victam manum* significantly echoes the *humanae* above and reverberates with its secondary meaning of common human nature. When we come upon the final instance of this word in the three-page narrative, in a sentence that Heseltine renders as "Well, you know what temptation generally assails a man on a full stomach," the pattern culminating in *humanam satietatem* suggests that the woman's preference for lovemaking over death is a reflection of common human nature and not such an occasion for scorn as Eumolpus makes it (273). Other important repetitions are variants of *light* (*lumen, lumen, clarius fulgens, lucis commodis frui*), uniting the blessings of life and light outside the tomb; *living* (*vivam, vivere, reviviscere, vivas*); *food* (*cenulam, cibum, vini, potione et cibo, cibum sumere aut vivere, cibo*), as that which sustains life; *love-pleasure-beauty* (*pulcherrima muliere, placitone etiam pugnabis amori?, delectatus miles et forma mulieris et secreto*); and *senses* (*odore corrupta, sentire, avide*).

Opposing patterns in the first group referring to general human nature are words expressing the widow's desire to be a unique example removed from the crowd (*singularis exempli*). Life words are contrasted with terms of death (*cadaver, corpus, corpus, vivum occidere*) and insentient ash (*cinerem aut manes sepultos*). Opposing the food patterns are words centering on starvation and sensory deprivation (*inedia, sine alimento, inedia, abstinentia*). Reminders of beauty alternate with references to self-mutilation (*faciemque unguibus sectam*); pleasure with grief (*dolore supervacuo ac nihil profuturo gemitu*).

We might produce from the short text a spatial chart showing its configurational design in two columns:

Common human nature	Uniqueness
non contenta vulgari more	*singularis exempli*
vitio gentis humanae	
omnium eundem esse exitum [sed] et idem domicilium	
ad humanitatem invitantis victam manum	
humanam satietatem	
Light, life	**Death**
lumen	*cadaver*
lumen	*corpus*
clarius fulgens	*corpus*
lucis commodis frui	*vivum occidere*
vivam	*cinerem aut manes sepultos*
vivere	
reviviscere	
vivas	
Food	**Starvation, deprivation**
cenulam	*inedia*
cibum	*sine alimento*
vini	*inedia*
potione et cibo	*abstinentia*
cibum sumere aut vivere	
cibo	
Love, pleasure, beauty	**Self-mutilation, grief**
pulcherrima muliere	*faciemque unguibus sectam*
placitone etiam pugnabis amori?	*dolore supervacuo ac nihil profuturo gemitu*
delectatus miles et forma mulieris et secreto	
odore corrupta	
sentire	
avide	

Perceiving the story in this way vies with the sequential effect. When the widow declares at the end, "Malo mortuum impendere quam vivum occidere" ("I prefer to hang a dead man rather than to kill the living"), the first set of associations does seem more attractive than the second, and we are inclined to understand her response to this opposition (277). The maid herself sounded the central contrast earlier: "Ipsum te iacentis corpus commonere debet, ut vivas" ("The very body of the one lying there should persuade you that you ought to live"), and her argument too seems sound when we read the story in light of its verbal repetitions (273). Local processing of this text, resulting in an atemporal configuration, not only adds to but potentially modifies or even reverses our responses to the text as a sequential plot unfolding in time. Spatial patterning reveals the power of common human life to overcome a morbid and perverse loyalty to death; temporal patterning demonstrates that "in time" the most faithful woman is fickle.

The type of interpretive process embodied in the chart is more likely to take place when the brevity of a text makes local processing and configurational organization easier for readers. Kermode might be pleased to realize that if this three-page narrative is isolated as a short story, readers are unlikely to ignore the extreme density of key words in favor of sequence. We can in fact represent the findings of this interpretive process as a spatial chart precisely because sequential organization is subordinated. In a configuration, words are seen as part of a "centripetal verbal pattern"; it is not important how they occur in terms of an inferred order of events (*fabula*) or in actual textual presentation (*sujet*). The order preserved by the chart is bipolar—it arranges verbal units in terms of perceived similarity and difference. Morse Peckham contends that such contrast is basic to spatial organization: "It will become apparent that when we look at art from the point of view of the classical division of the arts into spatial and temporal, that the spatial arts tend to present these signs as contrasting, while the temporal arts are particularly useful for presenting primary signs as continua."[3]

In my configurational reading, I organized an ancient prose narrative in the spatial mode Joseph Frank attributes only to modern poetry:

> Since the primary reference of any word-group is to something inside the poem itself, language in modern poetry is really reflexive. The meaning-relationship is completed only by the simultaneous perception in space of word-groups that have no comprehensible relation to each other when read consecutively in time. Instead of the instinctive and immediate refer-

3. Frank Kermode, "Secrets and Narrative Sequence," *Critical Inquiry*, VII (1980), 87, 98, 100, rpr. in W. J. T. Mitchell (ed.), *On Narrative* (Chicago, 1981), 83, 94, 96; Morse Peckham, *Man's Rage for Chaos: Biology, Behavior, and the Arts* (New York, 1965), 115, copyright 1965 by the author, reprinted with the permission of the publisher, Chilton Book Company, Radnor, Pa.

ence of words and word-groups to the objects or events they symbolize and the construction of meaning from the sequence of these references, modern poetry asks its readers to suspend the process of individual reference temporarily until the entire pattern of internal references can be apprehended as a unity.

Frank's last point is an important one—since readers must retain much verbatim information until the end of the text if they are to prefer this mode of organization, a text's brevity seems a more vital factor in the way it is perceived than either its modernity or its classification as poetry or prose. Indeed, my chart embodies something like Frank's description of *The Waste Land:* "Syntactical sequence is given up for a structure depending on the perception of relationships between disconnected word-groups. To be properly understood, these word-groups must be juxtaposed with one another and perceived simultaneously. Only when this is done can they be adequately grasped; for, while they may follow one another in time, their meaning does not depend on this temporal relationship."[4]

When we consider the word groups polarized by the widow's conflict, we may well wonder how new are the "new patterns of story development" that Eileen Baldeshwiler discovers. She credits Turgenev and Chekhov with initiating "the circling around a central dilemma or set of feelings, the record of a moment of intense feeling or perception which contains its own significant form." The following might be said of Petronius *if* we process his text locally and organize it as a configuration: "Turgenev and Chekhov consciously exploited language itself to express more sharply states of feeling and subtle changes in emotion. With these authors, the locus of narrative art has moved from external action to internal states of mind, and the plot line will hereafter consist, in this mode, of tracing complex emotions to a closing cadence utterly unlike the reasoned resolution of the conventional cause-and-effect narrative."[5]

The episodic reading of "The Widow of Ephesus" answers an action question in terms of time: Will the widow keep her vow? When we organize the text as a configuration, however, it is conventional to accord our interpretation the status of an eternal conflict and a time-

4. Joseph Frank, "Spatial Form in Modern Literature," *Sewanee Review,* LIII (1945), 229–30, rpr. in *The Widening Gyre: Crisis and Mastery in Modern Literature* (New Brunswick, N.J., 1963), 13, 12.

5. Eileen Baldeshwiler, "The Lyric Short Story: The Sketch of a History," *Studies in Short Fiction,* VI (1969), 446, rpr. in Charles E. May (ed.), *Short Story Theories* (Athens, Ohio, 1976), 206.

less truth: human nature "naturally" prefers life to death. Baldeshwiler is correct in suggesting that these two interpretive processes lead to distinct modes of resolution.

"A Rose for Emily," by William Faulkner

Here we will consider some aspects of the critical tradition surrounding William Faulkner's "A Rose for Emily" in order to see how the criticism reflects and embodies the tension between sequence and configuration, between global and local processing, which I have described as central to the short story. I assume, as does Dieter Freundlieb in his analysis of interpretations of Poe's tales, that "one major aspect of the analysis of interpretations, rather than literary texts themselves, is an explanation of how ascriptions of global meanings to texts come about." This approach emphasizes the ways in which reader perception underlies both the meaning of individual texts and a useful definition of genre. As Marie-Laure Ryan writes: "Once we realize that genres are a matter of communication and signification, generic taxonomy becomes tied to the same type of assumption that underlies current linguistic theories: namely that the object to account for is the user's knowledge. . . . The significance of generic categories thus resides in their cognitive and cultural value, and the purpose of genre theory is to lay out the implicit knowledge of the users of genre."[6]

I have chosen Faulkner's story, a war horse of high school anthologies, for two reasons. First, we have a tremendous body of material recording and analyzing the responses of various readers to the text. This material covers not only the views of professional literary critics but also those of presumably less experienced readers.[7] Second, the text is self-reflexive. Faulkner comments within it on the possible ways in which readers may organize the information provided and implies the ways in which various interpretive strategies may affect meaning.

---

6. Dieter Freundlieb, "Understanding Poe's Tales: A Schema-theoretic View," *Poetics*, XI (1982), 28, with the permission of North-Holland Publishing Company, Amsterdam; Marie-Laure Ryan, "On the Why, What and How of Generic Taxonomy," *Poetics*, X (1981), 111–12.

7. This story has attracted the attention of a large number of critics concerned with reader response. See Norman Holland's *Five Readers Reading* (New Haven, 1975), which includes the responses of undergraduate English majors to the text.

The narrator of "A Rose for Emily" contrasts a reading of Miss Emily's story which emphasizes chronology with one which does not. He comments explicitly on the way in which the old men who attend the heroine's funeral view her past and their own. These Civil War veterans talk of Miss Emily as if she had been a contemporary, "believing that they had danced with her and courted her perhaps, confusing time with its mathematical progression, as the old do, to whom all the past is not a diminishing road, but, instead, a huge meadow which no winter ever quite touches, divided from them now by the narrow bottleneck of the most recent decade of years."[8] This quotation suggests Faulkner's preoccupation in his famous story with the way in which interpreters—the southern townsmen, Miss Emily, the narrator of the story, and, finally, the readers of the text—construct Miss Emily's story. Faulkner opposes two alternatives: a linear, sequential organization ("a diminishing road") and a configurational, spatial patterning ("a huge meadow"). As Dennis Allen observes, "In contrast to the 'diminishing road' of chronological time, memory is non-linear, a space in which the present and the various areas of the past exist simultaneously, eternally immune from death and decay."[9] Each interpreter of Emily's story is caught between these two ways of making sense.

Other reader-response critics have already noted that the text depends on the foregrounding of achronological patterning to achieve one of its major effects, though they have not discussed the way in which the brevity of the short story form may reinforce Faulkner's careful control of the connections readers make. Menakhem Perry remarks that the surprise ending would scarcely be a surprise if readers ordered the events in the story as a cause-and-effect sequence unfolding in time; if a reader put together that Homer Barron was heard to say he was not a marrying man, that Miss Emily then bought arsenic, that her lover was next seen entering her house at dusk and was never seen again, that shortly thereafter a terrible smell of decay appeared around her house, he might well have his suspicions long before he reads that the townspeople break open a sealed room after her funeral and discover the body she had slept beside. Perry notes that Faulk-

8. William Faulkner, "A Rose for Emily," in *Collected Stories of William Faulkner* (New York, 1943), 129, with the permission of Random House, Inc. Hereafter cited parenthetically by page number in the text.

9. Dennis Allen, "Horror and Perverse Delight: Faulkner's 'A Rose for Emily,'" *Modern Fiction Studies*, XXX (1984), 688.

ner deliberately scrambles the chronology of the *fabula* and substitutes analogical connections leading to perception of Miss Emily's qualities, her static "character," for those of time.[10] The episode in which Miss Emily buys the arsenic, for example, is introduced as an example of her imperviousness; it is like other occasions (regardless of time) when she demonstrates this same quality: "It was as if she demanded more than ever the recognition of her dignity as the last Grierson; as if it had wanted that touch of earthiness to reaffirm her imperviousness. Like when she bought the rat poison, the arsenic" (125). Similarly, the incident of the smell is linked by analogy to an incident many years afterwards: "So she vanquished them, horse and foot, just as she had vanquished their fathers thirty years before about the smell" (121).

Although Perry's article supplies a valuable analysis of the foregrounding of configurational links instead of sequential ones, Perry does not fully consider that it is the narrator of the story who supplies these achronological connections. Most critics see the story's unusual point of view as highly significant. Faulkner's narrator uses the pronoun *we*, emphasizing his role as a spokesman for the town and insisting that his information about the heroine is assembled from the gossip around Jefferson. It is this embodiment of town opinion that suppresses the sequential unfolding of Miss Emily's story. If Faulkner's sole purpose were to distract the reader from his surprise ending, he would be singularly unsuccessful. Junior high school students may indeed be pleasantly shocked by Miss Emily's crime, but for years my college students have reported that they saw through the whole affair early on (though they may still be surprised by the infamous strand of hair). Compared to Agatha Christie, Faulkner, then, is a failure. He seems almost to be colluding with the reader behind the back of the dull narrator, who ignores the significance of chronology. In each of the two cases cited above, after the narrator has emphasized the timeless nature of Miss Emily's character, he presents the reader with the significant timing of the event, though the narrator himself seems not to catch on: "That was over a year after they had begun to say 'Poor Emily,' and while the two female cousins were visiting her" (the purchase of the poison) and "That was two years after her father's death and a short time after her sweetheart—the one we believed would marry her—had deserted her" (the smell) (125, 122).

10. Menakhem Perry, "Literary Dynamics: How the Order of a Text Creates Its Meanings," *Poetics Today*, I (Autumn, 1979), 35–64, 311–61.

In fact, the narrator, and by extension the people of Jefferson, are not dull, but are deliberately repressing time and sequence when they consider Miss Emily. Throughout the story, the narrator compares Miss Emily to timeless and immortal symbols. She is a "fallen monument," an "angel in a colored church window," a "strained flag," an "idol in a niche." It is he who offers the "rose" for Emily, the story, which, unlike real roses, cannot fade and die. No wonder the townspeople are shocked; no wonder they have the story all wrong until they break open the door of her chamber and discover that the last Grierson was also a mortal woman existing in time. The townspeople's suppression of sequence in Miss Emily's story is linked to their static view of history. As Allen points out, the townspeople "not only recognize the social taxonomy but actively work to maintain it," since it is they who call in the Alabama cousins when they believe their monument is "fallen." [11] They are understanding of, even pleased by, Miss Emily's more dramatic demonstrations of her "Griersonness." In her, they find the unnatural natural; the narrator says of her denial of her father's death: "We believed she had to do that. . . . [W]e knew that with nothing left, she would have to cling to that which had robbed her, as people will" (125). Not only do the townspeople find that her status necessitates her denial of mortality; they are not surprised by her repression of sexuality. They expect her to marry Homer after the departure of the cousins, but when he disappears and she closets herself in the house, the narrator says, "We knew that this was to be expected too; as if that quality of her father which had thwarted her woman's life so many times had been too virulent and too furious to die" (127).

But these statements also suggest that the townspeople are simultaneously aware of the sequential nature of Miss Emily's story: she has been "robbed" and "thwarted." Besides seeing her as the last Grierson, they see her as a young girl who has been denied suitors by her father and has then lost that father through death. She may have been a Grierson in the past, but she has now become a poor woman. When they think of her sequential history and not of her eternal status as a monument, the townspeople feel pity: "Poor Emily." Furthermore, this sequential reading of Miss Emily's story is linked to a progressive view of history and, as Allen points out, a new democratic ideology. The townspeople are pleased when Miss Emily becomes

11. Allen, "Horror and Perverse Delight," 693.

like them in knowing "the old thrill and the old despair of a penny more or less," the ladies are not surprised when the smell of decay links "the gross, teeming world and the high and mighty Griersons" (123, 122), and they are pleased when they believe Miss Emily has married the "Yankee day laborer"—thus, Allen claims, siding "with Emily's recognition of her sexuality, the sign of her similarity to her neighbors." [12] What they do not see is their own role in "robbing" and "thwarting" Miss Emily through their ambivalence about her status as icon.

The younger generation of townspeople is allied with the forces of progress. Indeed, the town has adapted to the gasoline pumps, cotton gins, and other "eyesores" of modern industrialism that Faulkner describes with distaste. The new generation is more interested in a dollar than in preserving Miss Emily's symbolic exemption from taxes. Yet it is precisely because the townspeople refuse to live in the past that they need a symbol of that past. Ambivalent about their own alliance with Yankee industrialism, they project all of their longing for the southern past onto the last Grierson. As Allen remarks, "If they are delighted by evidence that Emily is equal to them, this is because they do not wholly believe it." [13] Yet Faulkner does not allow the reader to sentimentalize that past as the townspeople do. The gracious Colonel Sartoris may seem more attractive than the introducers of more modern ideas, but it is he who "fathered the edict that no Negro woman would appear on the streets without an apron" (119–20). The verb *fathered* is significant; while aware of the virtues of aristocratic agrarian paternalism, Faulkner shows in stories like "Barn Burning" that he can also be critical of that system. Sentimentalizing their past and their landowning class, the modern townspeople are also "clinging to that which had robbed them, as people will." Faulkner suggests that embracing the present while sentimentalizing the past as a dead symbol falsifies and perverts both.

Miss Emily is also caught between a static view of her enduring "Griersonness" and her sense of herself as an aging woman. She in part accepts the town's definition of her symbolic status. That she at first only *accepts* this interpretation is suggested by the narrator's comment on her acceptance of another "story," Colonel Sartoris' dispensation freeing her from taxes: "Only a man of Colonel Sartoris' genera-

12. *Ibid.*, 692.
13. *Ibid.*, 693.

tion and thought could have invented it, and only a woman could have believed it" (120). She allows her father to drive away the young men who are not "good enough" to marry her and then denies his death. The insult of Homer's desertion after she has "lowered" herself from her status as southern lady leaves her with her "Griersonness"— "that quality of her father which had thwarted her woman's life so many times" and which "had been too virulent and too furious to die." The murder itself is, from Miss Emily's point of view, the supreme act which denies sequence at several levels: she brings together her earlier Oedipal attachment to her father and her later passion for Homer, she preserves Homer from death and change, and she negates her sexual "fall" and regains her status as icon through this "marriage." Only after she has killed Homer does she accept the town's repudiation of her life as a mortal woman who ages and "smells"; she grows fat and desexed, with hair a "vigorous iron-gray, like the hair of an active man," and sleeps with a corpse she can possess forever (128).

Miss Emily's affair with Homer Barron—a Yankee, a day laborer determined to escape the respectability of marriage—is her one attempt to assert her "woman's life." As many critics have pointed out, her choice of suitor is an active rejection of her status as an icon, the southern lady. She steps actively out of the frozen tableau in which her father blocks access to her with a horsewhip. Miss Emily, like the townspeople who first call in her relatives and then help her hoodwink them, does not fully accept the simultaneous, configurational reading of her life. Her involvement with Homer brings her into conflict with those who see her only as an eternal Grierson, the Alabama cousins. Even while she denies the passage of time and tells the town officials to consult Colonel Sartoris after he has been dead for years, a gold watch ticks at her side. And in contrast to the "immortal" rose, the tribute of art, is her rose room "decked and furnished as for a bridal," with curtains "of faded rose color" and with "rose-shaded lights," a room suggestive of her "woman's life" which exists in time and can decay (129). The appearance of this "rose" at the end of the story is the final reminder of Miss Emily's sequential reading of her own story.

Miss Emily's critics can be—and have been—classified in a number of different ways. The division explicitly raised in the text is between those who see the heroine's story as constituting a sequence and those, like the narrator and the townspeople, who subordinate chronology in favor of some "timeless" or otherwise symbolic reading. The latter are far more numerous. These readers, like the narrator, emphasize the timeless traits of Miss Emily's supposedly unchanging character, though some find her "noble" and others "terrible." Cleanth Brooks and Robert Penn Warren merge these two responses in a single reading of Miss Emily's "character": "Perhaps the horrible and the admirable aspects of Miss Emily's final deed arise from the same basic fact of her character: she insists on meeting the world on her own terms." A slight variation on the reading-for-character strategy is provided by those psychological critics, such as Edward Stone, who see Miss Emily's course set once and for all by her relationship with her father: "Her passionate, almost sexual relationship with her dead father forces her to distrust the living body of Homer and to kill him so that he will resemble the dead father she can never forget." [14] For other critics, Miss Emily is a timeless symbol, as she is for the narrator. Early critical responses to the story often portray the heroine as the embodiment of the Old South, in opposition to the new generation of townspeople, the New South, influenced by and in tune with the Yankees (represented by Homer). [15]

Critics generally supply a configurational interpretation of the text, but they often display a competing awareness of Miss Emily's story as that of an individual life unfolding in time. Allen portrays Miss Emily as a static sign: "Both grotesquely fat and excessively thin, living and dead, female and male, Miss Emily is, finally, 'undecidable,' the co-presence of opposites." Thus Allen eradicates sequence in Miss Emily's story in the same way that he claims she is trying to do. Not surprisingly, this interpretive strategy leads him to deny the historicity of the tale and to view it as the embodiment of a timeless, universal conflict: "The story explores aristocratic and democratic perspectives, seen less as local, historical entities than as conflicting ideologies. . . . At a more basic level, the story suggests, the conflict is between two human tendencies: the impulse to identify differences and to erect taxonomies and the contrary desire to deny distinctions." [16]

Although Allen finally opts for this interpretation—which suppresses narrative development and thus causality—as the "basic"

14. Cleanth Brooks and Robert Penn Warren, *Understanding Fiction* (New York, 1943), 413; Edward Stone, *A Certain Morbidness* (Carbondale, Ill., 1969), 96.

15. See George Dillon, "Styles of Reading," *Poetics Today*, III (Spring, 1982), 85, for a discussion of this critical view.

16. Allen, "Horror and Perverse Delight," 695.

one, he is aware of the story's narrative aspects. Indeed, he quotes Faulkner's own comments on the story only to dismiss them as "not particularly helpful." Far from being "diverse, faintly contradictory, and often vague," as Allen calls them, Faulkner's explanations as interpreted by Allen actually construct the story as a sequential cause-and-effect narrative in which a conflict is resolved in terms of action: "Emily murders Homer *because* he 'was about to quit her'; the story explores 'the *conflict* of conscience with glands,' the 'Old Adam,' and Emily's expiation for breaking 'the laws of her tradition'; Emily's actions *result from* her father's repression of her 'normal aspirations' for love."[17] The interesting questions here are why Allen foregrounds the configurational interpretation and why he finds Faulkner's explanations unsatisfying.

Robert Crosman, in "How Readers Make Meaning," records his own growing awareness of the sequential possibilities of Miss Emily's story. Like Allen, he originally organized the text as embodying contrasting signs and drew from this procedure a timeless "truth": "But I noticed the repeated differentiation at the story's beginning between men and women, and the put-downs of women. The story seemed to be setting me up for some attitude toward women, and even though I noticed this, I did take the attitude: women are mean, ill-willed, and therefore (though not men's equals) menacing." Challenged by a female student's admiration for Miss Emily, Crosman saw "how much there was in Faulkner's picture of Emily that *was* attractive, noble, tragic."[18]

Interestingly, in his reevaluation, Crosman emphasizes the gross sequence of events he reconstructed from the story: "Deprived of all normal suitors by a domineering father, she had clung to that father, even in death; deprived of her father, she had found a suitor outside the limits of respectability for a woman of her class and background; threatened with his loss as well she found a way to keep him, and then she remained true to him all the days of her life." Like the townspeople, Crosman is considerably more sympathetic to Miss Emily when he considers her story as a sequence of narrative events: "Poor Emily." This view of Miss Emily's character emphasizes development, not any "basic fact of her character" (Brooks and Warren) or static em-

17. *Ibid.*, 686–87, emphasis mine.
18. Robert Crosman, "How Readers Make Meaning," *College Literature*, IX (1982), 207–208, 209.

bodying of opposing traits (Allen): "A figure of pathos as a young girl under her father's thumb, she *develops* in later years into a formidable figure *herself*. Victimized *first* by her father and *then* by Homer Barron, she turns the tables and *becomes* a victimizer." Despite these readings that emphasize narrative sequence, Crosman returns to viewing the text as composed of "paired, antithetical elements," not mentioning that some of these elements follow others (either in the text or in an inferred event chain) and may be caused by them.[19]

Why do so many critics join the narrator in suppressing the sequential nature of Miss Emily's story? Why do they, like the townspeople, rush to reestablish her as a symbol or a sign? Those early critics who see her as a symbol of the Old South are very close to reading her story as the townspeople do, and even later critics who reject this view employ essentially the same way of organizing the text, processing it locally and sorting minimal units (details, even individual words) into polarized oppositions, emphasizing similarity and difference and ignoring sequence. This is especially odd because the text itself has emphasized the faulty or, at best, partial reading of the story which results from this interpretive process; we have seen that the narrator's preference for analogical rather than sequential associations prevents him from "putting things together" in order to understand what has happened. But is it true that the narrator and the townspeople *haven't* put the sequential, cause-and-effect story together? That the narrator always mentions the significant timing of a remembered event immediately after substituting an achronological link is more suggestive of repression than of stupidity. When I ask my students if the townspeople know about Homer's murder, they generally say something like, "Well, the people in the town know there's something really wrong, but they don't consciously admit to themselves what they know." Such comments bear an interesting resemblance to Crosman's more graceful description of his experience of reading the story: "As far as response goes, mine is a considerable fear of the discovery I know is waiting."[20]

The discovery of the story's "shock" is the discovery of the possibility of organizing the text as a narrative sequence; the repression of the one is the repression of the other. The narrator and the reader share in Miss Emily's denial of sequence and her recognition of sequence,

19. *Ibid.*, 209, 210, 212, emphasis mine.
20. *Ibid.*, 208.

and *may* participate in her rerepression of temporal process by converting it to a simultaneous sign. Allen has described Miss Emily's behavior well, though he is more interested in her repression of the body than in her repression of time:

> By disposing of Homer, she is able to repudiate her sexuality; by preserving his corpse, she can deny the reality of death. Yet, as murder, her crime admits the existence of death just as her necrophilia acknowledges her sexual drives. . . . If sexuality and death cannot be excluded successfully from the aristocratic world, if Emily is forced to recognize them, they can be rerepressed; Emily's recognition itself will be repudiated. Thus Homer is consigned to the closed room upstairs that, as a combined bridal chamber/tomb, contains and circumscribes not simply sexuality and death but the entire process of biological existence, from the nuptial relations, which are its origin, to the grave, which is its end.[21]

In short, Miss Emily's move from victim to victimizer is also her conversion from acceptance of a role as symbol to performance of a role as sign maker and manipulator. Her affair with Homer is her attempt to liberate her physical life from the configurational reading assigned to it by her neighbors and accepted by herself; when this attempt fails, she decides that she will at least design and control the configuration by which the sequential nature of her existence is denied.

Throughout "A Rose for Emily" Faulkner plays with the tension between sequential and configurational organization characteristic of the short story form. He does so on several different levels. Within the story, the sequence of gross narrative events threatens to break through the configurational reading imposed by the narrator. The story is also "about" Miss Emily's own attempts to break the reading of her story as eternal configuration, an attempt that fails. The final level on which this tension is resolved is generic. The reader's disposition to continue pairing minimal semantic units in terms of similarity and difference rather than in terms of a sequence of gross narrative events is in part controlled by the text's brevity. I have argued elsewhere that perceiving a work as a short story creates a strong drive to render all details "symbolic," that is, to interpret them symbolically.[22] Not only does the reader seek to avoid the "horror" of the sequential discovery, but the psychological tendencies engendered by brevity

21. Allen, "Horror and Perverse Delight," 695.

22. See Suzanne Hunter Brown, " 'Tess' and *Tess:* An Experiment in Genre," *Modern Fiction Studies,* XXVIII (1982), 40.

help Faulkner mislead the reader. Moreover, "A Rose for Emily," unlike most short stories, makes it clear to the reader that a tendency to process the work as a configurational structure obscures another important way of interpreting the text. The story thus becomes Faulkner's exploration of the limitations of the form.

JO ELLYN CLAREY

Appendix B: General Guide to Recent Short Story Theory

Essays in this volume serve as eloquent statement that short fiction theorists borrow whatever they like. Newcomers to the territory may find this habit necessary as well as delightful, but there are some standard materials they will find directly useful. *Studies in Short Fiction* is the venerable journal in the area, and general reference works are summarized by Douglas Tallack in a bibliographical essay cited below. Other listings in this guide range from studies carrying on well-established earlier work to others pointing in suggestive new directions.

In particular, we witness interdisciplinary groundbreaking by psychologists and anthropologists. They use short fiction because of the convenience of its brevity, of course. But there are other "short" forms of literature, and the assumptions these researchers make about specific subject matter and its management in short stories will be of interest to anyone studying the interpretation of social action in literature, the cultural contexts of genre.

Recently, two French journals joined the field of short fiction studies. Titles declaring their focus, *Journal of the Short Story in English* (*Les Cahiers de la nouvelle*) and *Visions critiques, revue sur la nouvelle de langue anglaise* have each cultivated the area by sponsoring conferences as well as by publishing articles. The conference proceedings published in a 1988 special issue of *Visions critiques* illustrate the various paths studies in short fiction take today. (At present, *Visions critiques* is not listed in serial directories. It may be ordered through Services des Publications de la Sorbonne Nouvelle, Paris.)

328

Although there is an increasing amount being published in other languages on the short story, this guide to recent theory accounts only for writings in English. It is offered as companion to, and eighties update of, Charles E. May's critical survey in *Short Story Theories* (1976). Perhaps it will also help provoke some long looks at short fiction.

Alderman, Timothy C. "The Integrated Short Story Collection as a Genre." Ph.D. dissertation, Purdue University, 1982.

Allen, Walter. *The Short Story in English*. New York, 1981.

Altic, Irene M. K. "The Short Story: The Order of Disorder in Lamb, Poe, and Melville." Ph.D. dissertation, University of Colorado, 1984.

"Authors' Statements" and "Editors' Statements." *Australian Literary Studies*, X (1981), 186–238, 239–74.

Aycock, Wendell M., ed. *The Teller and the Tale: Aspects of the Short Story*. Lubbock, Tex., 1982.

Balasubramanian, Radha. "The Craft of V. G. Korolenko's Fiction: Towards a Descriptive Poetics of His Short Stories." Ph.D. dissertation, Indiana University, 1987.

Bayley, John. *The Short Story: Henry James to Elizabeth Bowen*. Brighton, Sussex, 1988.

Beacham, Walton. "Short Fiction: Toward a Definition." In Vol. I of *Critical Survey of Short Fiction*, edited by Frank N. Magill. Englewood Cliffs, N.J., 1981.

Berces, Francis. "Poe and Imagination: An Aesthetic for the Short Story Form." *Journal of the Short Story in English*, No. 2 (1984), 105–13.

Berger, Roger A. "Telling Stories: Transformations of the Twentieth-Century American Short Story." Ph.D. dissertation, University of Wisconsin, 1984.

Besner, Neil. "The Language of 'Waiting': Voice, Idiom and Cliché in Keith Fraser's Short Fiction." *Visions critiques, revue sur la nouvelle de langue anglaise*, V (1988), 13–22.

Bhattacharya, Lokenath. "The Short Story and Social Change." *Indian Horizons*, XXXI (1982), 36–44.

Bhattacharya, Rimli. "Narrative Patterns in the Nineteenth Century Short Story." Ph.D. dissertation, Brown University, 1986.

Bliss, Corinne Demas. "The Short Story: Writer's Control/Reader's Response." Ph.D. dissertation, Columbia University, 1980.

Bonheim, Helmut. "How Stories Begin." *REAL: Yearbook of Research in English and American Literature*, I (1982), 191–226.

———. *The Narrative Modes: Techniques of the Short Story*. Cambridge, U.K., 1982.

Boulanger, Daniel. "On the Short-Story." *Michigan Quarterly Review*, XXVI (1987), 510–14.

Brewer, William F., and Keisuke Ohtsuka. "Story Structure, Characterization, Just World Organization, and Reader Affect in American and Hungarian Short Stories." *Poetics*, XVII (1988), 395–415.

Brombert, Victor. "Opening Signals in Narrative." *New Literary History*, XI (1980), 489–502.

Brown, Suzanne Hunter. "Dimension and Genre: Towards a Theory of the Short Story." Ph.D. dissertation, University of Pennsylvania, 1982.

———. "'Tess' and *Tess*: An Experiment in Genre." *Modern Fiction Studies*, XXVIII (1982), 25–44.

Burgess, Anthony. "On the Short Story." *Journal of the Short Story in English*, No. 2 (1984), 31–47.

Burns, Dan E. "*Bend Sinister* and 'Tyrants Destroyed': Short Story into Novel." *Modern Fiction Studies*, XXV (1979), 508–13.

Campbell, Ian. "The Kailyard School and Barrie's Short Stories." *Visions critiques, revue sur la nouvelle de langue anglaise*, V (1988), 243–51.

———. "The Scottish Short Story: Three Practitioners." *Journal of the Short Story in English*, No. 10 (1988), 17–44.

Case, Frederick. "Narrative Discourse in the Short Stories of Samuel Selvon." *Visions critiques, revue sur la nouvelle de langue anglaise*, V (1988), 185–95.

Chapman, Michael. "The Fiction Maker: The Short Story in Literary Education." *CRUX: A Journal of Teaching English*, XVIII (1984), 3–20.

Chénetier, Marc. "Why William S. Wilson Doesn't Write like Franz Kafka: The Story as Operation." *Visions critiques, revue sur la nouvelle de langue anglaise*, V (1988), 253–65.

Cochrane, Kirsty. "The Impressionistic Short Story in New Zealand." *Visions critiques, revue sur la nouvelle de langue anglaise*, V (1988), 197–210.

Collar, Mary L. "'Glossolalia': Genre, History, and What We Call Introduction to Literature." *Journal of General Education*, XXXIV (1982), 44–59.

Cortázar, Julio. "On the Short Story and Its Environs." Translated by Naomi Lindstrom. *Review of Contemporary Fiction*, III (1983), 34–37.

———. "Some Aspects of the Short Story." Translated by Aden W. Hayes. *Arizona Quarterly*, XXXVIII (1982), 5–18.

———. "Some Aspects of the Short Story." *Review of Contemporary Fiction*, III (1983), 24–33.

Current-Garcia, Eugene. *The American Short Story Before 1850*. Boston, 1985.

Dent, Charles Tilghman. "Irony in Hindi Short Stories: Translation and Structural Analysis." Ph.D. dissertation, University of Chicago, 1987.

Dhuicq, Bernard. "Aphra Behn's Contribution to the Rise of the 'Short Story.'" *Visions critiques, revue sur la nouvelle de langue anglaise*, V (1988), 35–42.

Diller, Hans-Jürgen, ed. "The Very Short Story, I." *Anglistik und Englischunterricht*, XVIII (1982). Special issue.

———. "The Very Short Story, II." *Anglistik und Englischunterricht*, XXIII (1984). Special issue.

Etter, Kathryn. "Genre of Return: The Short Story Volume." Ph.D. dissertation, University of Iowa, 1985.

Evans, Walter. "Nineteenth-Century American Theory of the Short Story: The Dual Tradition." *Orbis Litterarum*, XXXIV (1979), 314–30.

Ferguson, Suzanne. "Defining the Short Story: Impressionism and Form." *Modern Fiction Studies*, XXVIII (1982), 13–24.

———. "A Sherlook at *Dubliners*: Analogues Between the Detective Story and the Modern Short Story," *James Joyce Quarterly*, XVI (1979), 111–21.

———. "The Short Story as Parvenu in the Society of Genres." *Visions critiques, revue sur la nouvelle de langue anglaise*, V (1988), 267–74.

Firchow, Peter E. "The Americanness of the American Short Story." *Journal of the Short Story in English*, No. 10 (1988), 45–66.

Flora, Joseph M. "The Device of Conspicuous Silence in the Modern Short Story." In *The Teller and the Tale: Aspects of the Short Story*, edited by Wendell M. Aycock. Lubbock, Tex., 1982.

———, ed. *The English Short Story, 1880–1945*. Boston, 1985.

Foster, David William. *Studies in the Contemporary Spanish-American Short Story*. Columbia, Mo., 1979.

Fredman, Stephen. *Poet's Prose: The Crisis in American Verse*. New York, 1983.

Garrett, George. "Plain and/or Fancy: Where the Short Story Is and May Be Going." In *The Teller and the Tale: Aspects of the Short Story*, edited by Wendell M. Aycock. Lubbock, Tex., 1982.

Gereben, Agnes. "The Syntactics of Cycles of Short Stories." *Essays in Poetics*, XI (1986), 44–75.

———. "The Writer's 'Ego' in the Composition of Cycles of Short Stories." *Essays in Poetics*, IX (1984), 38–77.

Gerlach, John. "Closure in Modern Fiction: Cheever's 'The Enormous Radio' and 'Artemis, the Honest Well Digger.'" *Modern Fiction Studies*, XXVIII (1982), 145–52.

———. *Toward the End: Closure and Structure in the American Short Story*. University, Ala., 1985.

Green, John Charles. "The Modern Persian Short Story, 1921– 1981: A Bio-bibliographic Survey." Ph.D. dissertation, University of Michigan, 1987.

Gullason, Thomas A. "The Short Story: Revision and Renewal." *Studies in Short Fiction*, XIX (1982), 221–30.

Halász, László, János László, and Csaba Phlé. "The Short Story: Cross-Cultural Studies in Reading Short Stories." *Poetics*, XVII (1988), 287–303 (Introduction to special issue).

Hanson, Clare. *Short Stories and Short Fictions, 1880–1980*. London, 1985.

———. "The Short Story as a Late Twentieth Century Form." *Visions critiques, revue sur la nouvelle de langue anglaise*, V (1988), 287–96.

Harris, Wendell V. *British Short Fiction in the Nineteenth Century.* Detroit, 1979.

Hedberg, Johannes. "What Is a 'Short Story'? And What Is an 'Essay'?" *Moderna Sprak*, LXXIV (1980), 113–20.

Helprin, Mark. Interview by Anatole Broyard, "Mysterious Short Story." *New York Times Book Review*, March 1, 1981, p. 35.

Hemmerechts, Kristien. "The Modern Short Story, Continued." *Modern Fiction Studies*, XXIX (1983), 253–55.

Henning, Barbara Jeane. "Turn the Other Cheek: A Collection of Short Stories and an Essay on Minimalist Fiction." Ph.D. dissertation, Union for Experimenting Colleges and Universities, 1988.

Hesse, Douglas. "Defining the Short Story: A Demonstration Using William Carlos Williams' *Doctor Stories.*" *Visions critiques, revue sur la nouvelle de langue anglaise*, V (1988), 275–85.

———. "The Story in the Essay." Ph.D. dissertation, University of Iowa, 1986.

Imhof, Rüdiger. "Minimal Fiction, or the Question of Scale." *Anglistik und Englischunterricht*, XXIII (1984), 159–68.

Ingram, Forrest L. "The Dynamics of Short Story Cycles." *Northwest Ohio Quarterly*, II (1979), 7–12.

Kennedy, J. Gerald. "Toward a Poetics of the Short Story Cycle." *Journal of the Short Story in English*, No. 11 (1988), 9–25 (Introduction to special issue).

Kilroy, James F., ed. *The Irish Short Story.* Boston, 1984.

Klaus, H. Gustav. "The Other Short Story: Working-Class Tales of the 1920s." *Journal of the Short Story in English*, No. 7 (1986), 29–42.

Klooster, David J. "The Art of the Present Moment: Studies in the American Short Story." Ph.D. dissertation, Boston College, 1985.

László, János. "Readers' Historical-Social Knowledge and Their Interpretation and Evaluation of a Short Story." *Poetics*, XVII (1988), 461–81.

Lee, Robert A., ed. *The Nineteenth-Century American Short Story.* Totowa, N.J., 1985.

Leitch, Thomas M. "Action and Knowledge in the Short Story." In *What Stories Are: Narrative Theory and Interpretation.* University Park, Pa., 1986.

———. "Donald Barthelme and the End of the End." *Modern Fiction Studies*, XXVIII (1982), 129–44.

———. "From Detective Story to Detective Novel." *Modern Fiction Studies*, XXIX (1983), 475–84.

Liberman, M. M. "Stasis, Story, and Anti-Story." *Georgia Review*, XXXIX (1985), 527–33.

Lindauer, Martin S. "The Psychology of Literature and the Short Story: A Methodological Perspective." In *Literary Discourse: Aspects of Cognitive and Social Psychological Approaches*, edited by Lázló Halász. Berlin, 1987.

Litz, A. Walton. "The Modern Short Story." *Modern Fiction Studies*, XXVIII (1982), 3–4 (Preface to special issue).

Lohafer, Susan. *Coming to Terms with the Short Story*. 1983; rpr. Baton Rouge, 1985.

———. "Preclosure in the American Short Story." *Visions critiques, revue sur la nouvelle de langue anglaise*, V (1988), 297–304.

Luscher, Robert M. "American Regional Short Story Sequences." Ph.D. dissertation, Duke University, 1984.

McClave, Heather. Introduction to *Women Writers of the Short Story*, edited by Heather McClave. Englewood Cliffs, N.J., 1980.

Magill, Frank N., ed. *Critical Survey of Short Fiction*. Vols. I and II of 7 vols. Englewood Cliffs, N.J., 1981.

Mann, Susan Garland. "A Bibliographic and Generic Study of the Short Story Cycle." Ph.D. dissertation, Miami University, 1984.

———. *The Short Story Cycle: A Genre Companion and Reference Guide*. Westport, Conn., 1988.

Martindale, Colin, and Anne E. Martindale. "Historical Evolution of Content and Style in Nineteenth- and Twentieth-Century American Short Stories." *Poetics*, XVII (1988), 333–55.

May, Charles E. "From Small Beginnings: Why Did Detective Fiction Make Its Debut in the Short Story Format?" *Armchair Detective*, XX (1987), 77–81.

———. "The Nature of Knowledge in Short Fiction." *Studies in Short Fiction*, XXI (1984), 327–38.

———. "Short Fiction Criticism." In Vol. I of *Critical Survey of Short Fiction*, edited by Frank N. Magill. Englewood Cliffs, N.J., 1981.

Melville, Clyde B., Jr. "Short Fiction on Film: The 'Little Man' in Cinematic Adaptation." Ph.D. dissertation, University of Texas at Arlington, 1980.

Menikoff, Barry. "Class and Culture in the English Short Story: A Review of *The English Short Story*." *Journal of the Short Story in English*, No. 8 (1987), 125–39.

———. "Color and Culture in the Short Stories of Carlton Dawe." *Visions critiques, revue sur la nouvelle de langue anglaise*, V (1988), 91–100.

———. Introduction to *Journal of the Short Story in English*, No. 10 (1988), 9–14 (Special issue on cultural contexts and the short story).

———. "The Problematics of Form: History and the Short Story." *Journal of the Short Story in English*, No. 2 (1984), 129–46.

Moser, Charles A., ed. *The Russian Short Story*. Boston, 1986.

New, W. H. *Dreams of Speech and Violence: The Art of the Short Story in Canada and New Zealand*. Toronto, 1987.

Olson, Gary M., Robert L. Mack, and Susan A. Duffy. "Cognitive Aspects of Genre." *Poetics*, X (1981), 283–315.

Orel, Harold. *The Victorian Short Story: Development and Triumph of a Literary Genre*. New York, 1986.

O'Toole, L. Michael. *Structure, Style and Interpretation in the Russian Short Story*. New Haven, Conn., 1982.

Paulin, Tom. "Specks of Unhistorical Time." *Times Literary Supplement,* April 24, 1981, p. 455.

Peden, Margaret Sayers. "The Arduous Journey." In *The Teller and the Tale: Aspects of the Short Story,* edited by Wendell M. Aycock. Lubbock, Tex., 1982.

―――, ed. *The Latin American Short Story: A Critical History.* Boston, 1983.

Peden, William. "Realism and Anti-Realism in the Modern Short Story." In *The Teller and the Tale: Aspects of the Short Story,* edited by Wendell M. Aycock. Lubbock, Tex., 1982.

Penn, W. S. "The Tale as Genre in Short Fiction." *Southern Humanities Review,* XV (1981), 231–41.

Pickering, Samuel, Jr. "The Modern Short Story." *Review,* IV (1982), 89–95.

Portch, Stephen R. *Literature's Silent Language: Nonverbal Communication.* New York, 1985.

Pratt, Mary Louise. "The Short Story: The Long and the Short of It." *Poetics,* X (1981), 175–94.

Pritchett, V. S. "A Sense of Strangeness." *Book Choice,* IX (September, 1981), 20–21.

Quinn, Antoinette. "Angela Carter's Contemporary Fairy Tales." *Visions critiques, revue sur la nouvelle de langue anglaise,* V (1988), 101–10.

Reid, Ian. "'Always a Sacrifice': Executing Unities in Two Stories by Katherine Mansfield." *Journal of the Short Story in English,* No. 4 (1985), 77–94.

―――. "The Framing of Australian Short Stories." *Visions critiques, revue sur la nouvelle de langue anglaise,* V (1988), 307–13.

Roberts, Melinda Hilary. "Represented Perception and the Discovery Story." Ph.D. dissertation, University of California, Berkeley, 1986.

Rohrberger, Mary. "Fiction Writers on Writing Short Fiction: The State of the Definition." In Vol. II of *Critical Survey of Short Fiction,* edited by Frank N. Magill. Englewood Cliffs, N.J., 1981.

Rohrberger, Mary, and Dan E. Burns. "Short Fiction and the Numinous Realm: Another Attempt at Definition." *Modern Fiction Studies,* XXVIII (1982), 5–12.

Rueda, Ana M. "Spaceless Tales: A Critical Study of the Contemporary Hispanic Short Story." Ph.D. dissertation, Vanderbilt University, 1985.

Schleifer, Ronald. "Faulkner's Storied Novel: *Go Down, Moses* and the Translation of Time." *Modern Fiction Studies,* XXVIII (1982), 109–27.

Shaw, Valerie. *The Short Story: A Critical Introduction.* London, 1983.

Shourie, Usha. "The Legacy of Literary Images: Short Stories of the Harlem Renaissance and the Black Aesthetics Movement." *Visions critiques, revue sur la nouvelle de langue anglaise,* V (1988), 211–22.

Siebert, Hilary Goodfellow. "Represented Space in the Short Story: Reader Response to Environmental Experience." Ph.D. dissertation, University of Iowa, 1987.

Sillitoe, Alan. "The Short Story." *Visions critiques, revue sur la nouvelle de langue anglaise*, V (1988), 315–20.

Spove, Steen. "The Scholarly Journal and Short Fiction Criticism." In *The Teller and the Tale: Aspects of the Short Story*, edited by Wendell M. Aycock. Lubbock, Tex., 1982.

Stead, Christina. "Ocean of Story." *Australian Literary Studies*, X (1981), 181–84.

Stephens, Michael. *The Dramaturgy of Style: Voice in Short Fiction*. Carbondale, Ill., 1986.

Stevick, Philip, ed. *The American Short Story, 1900–1945*. Boston, 1984.

Stummer, Peter O., ed. *The Story Must Be Told: Short Narrative Prose in the New English Literatures*. Würzburg, 1986.

Szávai, János. "Towards a Theory of the Short Story." *Acta Litteraria Academiae Scientiarum Hungaricae*, XXIV (1982), 203–24.

Tallack, Douglas. "American Short Fiction: A Bibliographic Essay." *American Studies International*, XXIII (October, 1985), 3–59.

————. "Language and Form in Nineteenth Century American Short Fiction." Ph.D. dissertation, University of Sussex, 1982.

————. "'The Story of One's Story': A Technique of Authority in Benjamin, Sartre and the Tales of Henry James." *Journal of the Short Story in English*, No. 5 (1985), 33–54.

Tylutki, George Edward. "Short Fiction as Genre: An Analysis of Short Story Theory." Ph.D. dissertation, State University of New York at Binghamton, 1984.

Vannatta, Dennis, ed. *The English Short Story, 1945–1980*. Boston, 1985.

Vauthier, Simone. "The Interplay of Images in Murray Bail's *The Drover's Wife*." *Visions critiques, revue sur la nouvelle de langue anglaise*, V (1988), 137–45.

Venuti, Lawrence. "Dino Buzzati's Fantastic Journalism." *Modern Fiction Studies*, XXVIII (1982), 79–92.

Wain, John. "Remarks on the Short Story." *Journal of the Short Story in English*, No. 2 (1984), 49–66.

Walker, Warren S. "From Raconteur to Writer: Oral Roots and Printed Leaves of Short Fiction." In *The Teller and the Tale: Aspects of the Short Story*, edited by Wendell M. Aycock. Lubbock, Tex., 1982.

Weaver, Gordon, ed. *The American Short Story, 1945–1980*. Boston, 1983.

————. "One Writer's Perception of the Short Fiction Tradition: How Would Edgar Allan Poe Make a Duck?" In *The Teller and the Tale: Aspects of the Short Story*, edited by Wendell M. Aycock. Lubbock, Tex., 1982.

Weiss, Allan. "Magazines and the English-Canadian Short Story, 1950–1970." *Visions critiques, revue sur la nouvelle de langue anglaise*, V (1988), 223–30.

Weixlmann, Joe. *American Short-Fiction Criticism and Scholarship, 1959–1977: A Checklist*. Athens, Ohio, 1982.

Werner, Charles Dantzler. "Responses of College Readers with Different Cultural Backgrounds to a Short Story." Ph.D. dissertation, Georgia State University, 1987.

Willson, A. Leslie. "Constancy and Variation: The Short Story in Germany." In *The Teller and the Tale: Aspects of the Short Story*, edited by Wendell M. Aycock. Lubbock, Tex., 1982.

Yvard, Pierre. "V. S. Pritchett and the Short Narrative: A Fly in the Ointment." *Journal of the Short Story in English*, No. 6 (Spring, 1986), 111–21.

Zurlo, John A. "Literary Synthesis: With a Special Look at the Lyric Short Story." Ph.D. dissertation, East Texas State University, 1983.

Notes on Contributors

SUZANNE HUNTER BROWN teaches in the English department at Dartmouth College. In addition to writing criticism on short fiction, she publishes stories in such magazines as the *Southern Review* and *Carolina Quarterly*. She has had her work listed in *Best American Short Stories* (1984, 1985) and has been a fellow at artist colonies such as MacDowell and Yaddo.

JO ELLYN CLAREY, following Susan Lohafer's graduate seminar on short story theory at the University of Iowa, organized the discussions among critics from which *Short Story Theory at a Crossroads* grew. She has published an essay on D. H. Lawrence's understanding of *Moby-Dick* and is currently writing on issues of stasis and movement in the processing of short fiction.

SUZANNE FERGUSON is currently chair of the English department at Wayne State University. She has published on Randall Jarrell and on the relations between poetry and painting. Her work on short fiction includes "Defining the Short Story: Impressionism and Form" (1982), and she is now completing a book on English short fiction in the nineteenth and early twentieth centuries.

NORMAN FRIEDMAN, professor emeritus of English at Queens College, CUNY, and author of *Form and Meaning in Fiction* (1975), has a continuing interest in formal literary analysis and critical theory. In the past he has written on e. e. cummings and published poetry of his own. A practicing Gestalt psychotherapist, he is also working on a project involving relations among literature, psychology, and orientalism.

JOHN GERLACH teaches at Cleveland State University and has won fiction awards from *Ambergris* and *Fiction/Ohio*. His short fiction has been listed in *Best American Short Stories* (1983), and he has written numerous articles on short story writers. In 1985 he published *Toward the End: Closure and Structure in the American Short Story*.

DOUGLAS HESSE is on the faculty of Illinois State University, where he teaches English and directs the writing programs. His article "Persuading as Storying" is among several forthcoming articles on relations between the short story and essay genres. He is also at work on a study of William Carlos Williams' narrative rhetoric.

THOMAS M. LEITCH teaches English at the University of Delaware and directs its film studies program. In addition to his 1986 book *What Stories Are*, he has continued to publish essays on film and short fiction. A volume on the role of the short story in American literature is in the offing.

SUSAN LOHAFER, at the University of Iowa, teaches courses in American literature, the short story, and short fiction theory. She has published a book on nineteenth-century American fiction; short stories in the *Antioch Review*, the *Southern Review*, and other literary magazines; and a book on short story theory, *Coming to Terms with the Short Story* (1983). Her current work develops relationships between discourse analysis and narrative theory.

ROBERT M. LUSCHER is in the English department at Catawba College. He has been a member of the editorial staff of the *Henry James Review* and has published in the field of American literature. He continues to work with short story cycles and is writing a book on John Updike's short fiction.

CHARLES E. MAY, who teaches at California State University, Long Beach, has published over twenty pieces on short fiction in a variety of journals and books. He is also the editor of the 1976 collection *Short Story Theories*, and is currently writing on Edgar Allan Poe, as well as twentieth-century European short stories.

ARMINE KOTIN MORTIMER, a member of the French department at the University of Illinois, is also in the Unit for Criticism and Interpretive

Theory. Of her two books on narrative, one focuses on closure in French fiction (*La Clôture narrative*, 1985). Her most recent work includes an article on short fiction and intertextuality, and a book entitled *The Gentlest Law: Roland Barthes's "The Pleasure of the Text"* (forthcoming).

WILLIAM O'ROURKE teaches courses on creative writing and the short story at the University of Notre Dame. He is the author of three novels and editor of *On the Job: Fiction About Work by Contemporary American Writers* (1977). He has received a number of grants and was the first James Thurber Writer in Residence at the Thurber House in Columbus, Ohio.

IAN·REID teaches in the School of Humanities and directs the Centre for Studies in Literary Education at Deakin University, Geelong, Australia. He is the author of *The Short Story* (1977) and serves as editorial adviser for the new French periodical *Journal of the Short Story in English*. Currently, he is interested in genre and pedagogy, and is working on a study of narrative "exchanges."

MARY ROHRBERGER holds an administrative position at Oklahoma State University, where she also teaches English. She began her work on short fiction with *Hawthorne and the Modern Short Story* (1966), and since then has published numerous articles and several textbooks in the field. Recently, she organized an annual session on short story theory for the South Central Modern Language Association, and she is planning a journal which will focus on the short story.

AUSTIN M. WRIGHT, a member of the English department at the University of Cincinnati, received a Whiting Writers Award in 1985. In addition to his three novels, he has published *The American Short Story in the Twenties* (1961) and *The Formal Principle in the Novel* (1982). Currently, he is at work on another novel, and has just finished a new book on recalcitrance in literature.

Index